Communications in Computer and Information Science 2954

Rationale
The CCIS series is devoted to the publication of proceedings of computer science conferences. Its aim is to efficiently disseminate original research results in informatics in printed and electronic form. While the focus is on publication of peer-reviewed full papers presenting mature work, inclusion of reviewed short papers reporting on work in progress is welcome, too. Besides globally relevant meetings with internationally representative program committees guaranteeing a strict peer-reviewing and paper selection process, conferences run by societies or of high regional or national relevance are also considered for publication.

Topics
The topical scope of CCIS spans the entire spectrum of informatics ranging from foundational topics in the theory of computing to information and communications science and technology and a broad variety of interdisciplinary application fields.

Information for Volume Editors and Authors
Publication in CCIS is free of charge. No royalties are paid, however, we offer registered conference participants temporary free access to the online version of the conference proceedings on SpringerLink (http://link.springer.com) by means of an http referrer from the conference website and/or a number of complimentary printed copies, as specified in the official acceptance email of the event.

CCIS proceedings can be published in time for distribution at conferences or as post-proceedings, and delivered in the form of printed books and/or electronically as USBs and/or e-content licenses for accessing proceedings at SpringerLink. Furthermore, CCIS proceedings are included in the CCIS electronic book series hosted in the SpringerLink digital library at http://link.springer.com/bookseries/7899. Conferences publishing in CCIS are allowed to use our online conference service (Meteor) for managing the whole proceedings lifecycle (from submission and reviewing to preparing for publication) free of charge.

Publication process
The language of publication is exclusively English. Authors publishing in CCIS have to sign the Springer CCIS copyright transfer form, however, they are free to use their material published in CCIS for substantially changed, more elaborate subsequent publications elsewhere. For the preparation of the camera-ready papers/files, authors have to strictly adhere to the Springer CCIS Authors' Instructions and are strongly encouraged to use the CCIS LaTeX style files or templates.

Abstracting/Indexing
CCIS is abstracted/indexed in DBLP, Google Scholar, EI-Compendex, Mathematical Reviews, SCImago, Scopus. CCIS volumes are also submitted for the inclusion in ISI Proceedings.

How to start
To start the evaluation of your proposal for inclusion in the CCIS series, please send an e-mail to ccis@springer.com

Francesco Calise ·
Fontina Petrakopoulou-Robinson · Alexey Vinel ·
Jeroen Ploeg · Karsten Berns · Cornel Klein ·
Oleg Gusikhin
Editors

Smart Cities, Green Technologies, and Intelligent Transport Systems

13th International Conference, SMARTGREENS 2024
and 10th International Conference, VEHITS 2024
Angers, France, May 2–4, 2024
Revised Selected Papers

Editors
Francesco Calise
University of Naples Federico II
Naples, Italy

Alexey Vinel
Karlsruhe Institute of Technology
Karlsruhe, Germany

Karsten Berns
University of Kaiserslautern-Landau
Kaiserslautern, Germany

Oleg Gusikhin
Ford Motor Company
Dearborn, MI, USA

Fontina Petrakopoulou-Robinson
University Carlos III
Madrid, Spain

Jeroen Ploeg
Siemens Industry Software Netherlands B.V.
Eindhoven, The Netherlands

Cornel Klein
Siemens AG
Munich, Germany

ISSN 1865-0929 ISSN 1865-0937 (electronic)
Communications in Computer and Information Science
ISBN 978-3-032-23186-4 ISBN 978-3-032-23187-1 (eBook)
https://doi.org/10.1007/978-3-032-23187-1

This Springer imprint is published by the registered company Springer Nature Switzerland AG
The registered company address is: Gewerbestrasse 11, 6330 Cham, Switzerland

Preface

The present book includes extended and revised versions of selected papers from the 13th International Conference on Smart Cities and Green ICT Systems (SMARTGREENS 2024) and the 10th International Conference on Vehicle Technology and Intelligent Transport Systems (VEHITS 2024), held in Angers, France, from 2–4 May.

SMARTGREENS 2024 received 16 paper submissions from 10 countries, of which four (25%) are included in this book.

VEHITS 2024 received 70 paper submissions from 24 countries, of which 11 (16%) are included in this book.

The papers were selected by the event chairs and their selection was based on a number of criteria that included the classifications and comments provided by the program committee members, the session chairs' assessment and also the program chairs' global view of all papers included in the technical program. Reviews were double-blind, and each submission received three reviews on average. The authors of selected papers were invited to submit revised and extended versions of their papers with at least 30% innovative material.

The purpose of the International Conference on Smart Cities and Green ICT Systems (SMARTGREENS) is to bring together researchers, designers, developers and practitioners interested in advances and applications in the field of Smart Cities, Green Information and Communication Technologies, Sustainability, and Energy Aware Systems and Technologies.

The purpose of the International Conference on Vehicle Technology and Intelligent Transport Systems (VEHITS) is to bring together engineers, researchers and practitioners interested in advances and applications in the field of Vehicle Technology and Intelligent Transport Systems. This conference focuses on innovative applications, tools and platforms in all technology areas such as signal processing, wireless communications, informatics and electronics, related to different kinds of vehicles, including cars, off-road vehicles, trains, ships, underwater vehicles and aircraft, and the intelligent transportation systems that connect and manage large numbers of vehicles, not only in the context of smart cities but in many other application domains.

The papers selected to be included in this book contribute to the understanding of relevant trends of current research on Smart Cities and Green ICT Systems, and Vehicle Technology and Intelligent Transport Systems, including:

- Analysis of the interaction between the parameter settings and the solution quality in numerical calculations, evaluating the energy demand of different algorithms, also considering a Pareto optimization;
- The pivotal role of co-simulation in the development of complex dynamic simulation tools for smart grids;
- Development of a Framework for AI Trust enHancement (FAITH) to integrate personalized communication strategies with individual preferences, addressing the critical role of communication in human-machine interactions;

- Development of digital modeling for the calculation of the operating conditions of railway power supply systems (RPSS) based on renewable energy sources;
- Planning and control of autonomous and automated vehicles, V2V, V2I, V2X, vehicle environment perception, analytics for intelligent transportation systems, accident prevention, road safety and security-related topics.

We would like to thank the authors for their contributions and also the reviewers who helped to ensure the quality of this publication.

May 2024

Francesco Calise
Fontina Petrakopoulou-Robinson
Alexey Vinel
Jeroen Ploeg
Karsten Berns
Cornel Klein
Oleg Gusikhin

Organization

Conference Co-chairs

SMARTGREENS

Cornel Klein — Siemens AG, Germany

VEHITS

Oleg Gusikhin — Ford Motor Company, USA

Program Co-chairs

SMARTGREENS

Fontina Petrakopoulou-Robinson — University Carlos III of Madrid, Spain
Francesco Calise — University of Naples Federico II, Italy

VEHITS

Alexey Vinel — Karlsruhe Institute of Technology, Germany
Karsten Berns — University of Kaiserslautern-Landau, Germany
Jeroen Ploeg — Siemens Industry Software Netherlands B.V., Netherlands

Program Committee

SMARTGREENS

Javier M. Aguiar — Universidad de Valladolid, Spain
Nuri Azbar — Ege University, Turkey
Blanca Caminero — Universidad de Castilla-La Mancha, Spain
Juan Chen — Independent Researcher, China
Wanyang Dai — Nanjing University, China

Cléver Ricardo de Farias	University of São Paulo, Brazil
Venizelos Efthymiou	University of Cyprus, Cyprus
Adrian Florea	University "Lucian Blaga" of Sibiu, Romania
Yoshikazu Fukuyama	Meiji University, Japan
Andre Gradvohl	State University of Campinas, Brazil
Sachin Jain	Indian Institute of Information Technology, Design and Manufacturing, Jabalpur, India
Mani Krishna	University of Massachusetts Amherst, USA
Annapaola Marconi	Fondazione Bruno Kessler, Italy
Lucas Pereira	Interactive Technologies Institute, LARSyS, Técnico Lisboa, Portugal
Vitor Pires	Escola Superior de Tecnologia de Setúbal - Instituto Politécnico de Setúbal, Portugal
Marco Savino Piscitelli	Politecnico di Torino, Italy
Filipe Quintal	Independent Researcher, Portugal
Eva González Romera	University of Extremadura, Spain
Francesco Salamone	Construction Technologies Institute of the National Research Council, Italy
Javad Sardroud	Azad University Central Tehran Branch, Iran
Hussain Shareef	United Arab Emirates University, UAE
Nirmal Srivastava	Dr. B. R. Ambedkar National Institute of Technology Jalandhar, India
Thomas Strasser	AIT Austrian Institute of Technology, Austria
Afshin Tafazzoli	Siemens Gamesa Renewable Energy, Spain
Masoud Taghavi	Chung-Ang University, South Korea
Alexandr Vasenev	TNO-ESI, Netherlands
Ramin Yahyapour	University of Göttingen, Germany
Arda Yurdakul	Bogazici University, Turkey
Sotirios Ziavras	New Jersey Institute of Technology, USA

Program Committee

VEHITS

Khaled Al-Sahili	An-Najah National University, Palestine
Fabio Arena	Kore University of Enna, Italy
Antonio Artuñedo	Spanish National Research Council (CSIC), Spain
Ramachandran Balakrishna	Caliper Corporation, USA
Giulio Francesco Bianchi Piccinini	Aalborg University, Denmark
Francesco Biral	University of Trento, Italy

László Bokor	Budapest University of Technology and Economics, Hungary
Vinny Cahill	Trinity College Dublin, Ireland
Roberto Caldelli	National Inter-University Consortium for Telecommunications (CNIT), Italy
Fanta Camara	University of York, UK
Pedro Cardoso	Universidade do Algarve, Portugal
Rodrigo Carlson	Federal University of Santa Catarina, Brazil
Benjamin Coifman	Ohio State University, USA
Baldomero Coll-Perales	Universidad Miguel Hernández de Elche, Spain
Gonçalo Correia	TU Delft, Netherlands
Ángel Cuenca	Technical University of Valencia, Spain
Luis de la Cruz Llopis	Universitat Politècnica de Catalunya, Spain
Stefano de Luca	University of Salerno, Italy
Bart De Schutter	Delft University of Technology, Netherlands
Teresa Donateo	University of Salento, Italy
Oscar Esparza	Universitat Politècnica de Catalunya, Spain
Peppino Fazio	University of Venice, Italy
Evelio Fernandez	Federal University of Paraná, Brazil
Dieter Fiems	Ghent University, Belgium
Michel Gendreau	Polytechnique Montréal, Canada
Mehdi Ghatee	Amirkabir University of Technology, Iran
Paul Green	University of Michigan Transportation Research Institute, USA
Martin Greguric	University of Zagreb, Croatia
Nicolas Hautière	Gustave Eiffel University, France
Sonia Heemstra de Groot	Eindhoven Technical University, Netherlands
Sin C. Ho	Chinese University of Hong Kong, China
Tamás Holczer	Budapest University of Technology and Economics, Hungary
Mónica Aguilar Igartua	Universitat Politècnica de Catalunya, Spain
Edouard Ivanjko	University of Zagreb, Croatia
Govand Kadir	University of Kurdistan-Hewler, Iraq
Ahmed Khoumsi	University of Sherbrooke, Canada
Lisimachos Kondi	University of Ioannina, Greece
Zdzislaw Kowalczuk	Gdansk University of Technology, Poland
Hariharan Krishnan	General Motors LLC, USA
Yong-Hong Kuo	University of Hong Kong, China
Agnieszka Lazarowska	Gdynia Maritime University, Poland
Bernd Ludwig	University of Regensburg, Germany
Juraj Machaj	University of Zilina, Slovak Republic
Michael Mackay	Liverpool John Moores University, UK

Majid Majidi	Islamic Azad University, Iran
Martin Margreiter	Technical University of Munich, Germany
Barbara Masini	Italian National Research Council (CNR), Italy
Gabriella Mazzulla	University of Calabria, Italy
Wrya Monnet	University of Kurdistan-Hewler, Iraq
Jânio Monteiro	Universidade do Algarve, Portugal
Antonio Montieri	University of Naples Federico II, Italy
Pieter Mosterman	Raven Industries, Netherlands
Mirco Nanni	Italian National Research Council, Italy
Tomas Olovsson	Chalmers University of Technology, Sweden
Dario Pacciarelli	Roma Tre University, Italy
Brian Park	University of Virginia, USA
Cecilia Pasquale	Università degli studi di Genova, Italy
Christian Prehofer	DENSO Automotive Germany, Germany
Bo Qin	Independent Researcher, China
Hesham Rakha	Virginia Tech, USA
Prakash Ranjitkar	University of Auckland, New Zealand
Gianfranco Rizzo	University of Salerno, Italy
Enrique Romero-Cadaval	University of Extremadura, Spain
Oleg Saprykin	X5 Group, Samara State Aerospace University, Russian Federation
Michele Segata	University of Trento, Italy
Nirajan Shiwakoti	RMIT University, Australia
Jean-Claude Thill	University of North Carolina at Charlotte, USA
Junfang Tian	Tianjin University, China
Vicente Tomás	University Jaume I, Spain
Lourdes Trujillo	University of Las Palmas de Gran Canaria, Spain
Katarzyna Turon	Silesian University of Technology, Poland
Costin Untaroiu	Virginia Tech, USA
Ondrej Vaculin	Technische Hochschule Ingolstadt, Germany
Ottorino Veneri	Institute of Sciences and Technologies for Sustainable Energy and Mobility (STEMS), Italy
Shaw Voon Wong	University Putra Malaysia, Malaysia
George Yannis	National Technical University of Athens, Greece
Chung-Hsing Yeh	Monash University, Australia

Additional Reviewers

VEHITS

Oleg Gusikhin	Ford Motor Company, USA
William Lindskog	Technical University of Munich, Germany
Alexey Vinel	Karlsruhe Institute of Technology, Germany

Invited Speakers

SMARTGREENS

Henrik Lund	Aalborg University, Denmark
Stefania Santini	Università di Napoli Federico II, Italy
Vinny Cahill	Trinity College Dublin, Ireland
Fernando García	University Carlos III of Madrid, SAVIA Technologies, Spain

VEHITS

Fernando García	University Carlos III of Madrid, SAVIA Technologies, Spain
Arnaud de La Fortelle	Heex Technologies, France
Stefania Santini	Università di Napoli Federico II, Italy
Vinny Cahill	Trinity College Dublin, Ireland
Henrik Lund	Aalborg University, Denmark

Contents

Smart Cities and Green ICT Systems

Variant Selection of Parallel Applications to Achieve Pareto-Optimal Executions Concerning Time and Energy

Thomas Rauber[1] (✉) and Gudula Rünger[2]

[1] Department of Computer Science, University of Bayreuth, Bayreuth, Germany
rauber@uni-bayreuth.de

[2] Department of Computer Science, Chemnitz University of Technology, Chemnitz, Germany
ruenger@informatik.tu-chemnitz.de

Abstract. Parallel applications are often based on numerical algorithms which compute an approximation solution for a discretized scientific problem. Such an approximation solution has a specific accuracy, which denotes how well the approximation fits to the true solution. The accuracy can be controlled by parameters given to the solution process by the application programmer. Parameters include the tolerance value in time-stepping methods or the truncation of a series expansion of the unknown solution. However, the parameter selection does not only influence the numerical quality but also the time needed for computing the approximation solution. The associated energy consumption may also increase but may exhibit a different growth behavior. Each parameter setting leads to a different execution variant of the approximation algorithm with a different numerical accuracy property of the solution and different execution time and energy behavior of the computation process. This article considers the interaction between the parameter settings and the solution quality and examines the possibilities to select time- and energy-efficient execution variants with a desired accuracy. In particular, a selection process is proposed that determines a Pareto-optimal execution variant of the approximation algorithm.

Keywords: Numerical solution methods · Variant selection · Runtime performance · Energy consumption

1 Introduction

Parallel applications, especially in the area of scientific computing, have a high demand for computing power, since they are compute intensive and long running. Thus, the design and execution of software for solving discretized scientific problems not only concentrates on the quality of the approximation solution computed but also on the efficient implementation with respect to execution time and energy consumption. The quality of an approximation solution is indicated by its accuracy which is the property how well the approximation fits to

F. Calise et al. (Eds.): SMARTGREENS 2024/VEHITS 2024, CCIS 2954, pp. 3–25, 2026.
https://doi.org/10.1007/978-3-032-23187-1_1

the true solution. In general, a better accuracy comes with a more intensive computation, leading to higher execution time and energy consumption. For environmental reasons, it is an important concern to reduce this energy consumption [3]. Thus, finding a good execution variant with good properties of the approximation solution as well as suitable time and energy behavior is a problem including multiple criteria, which are to be chosen such that a good compromise results. Finding such a compromise is considered in this article.

A good energy behavior is especially important for compute-intensive applications executed on large parallel systems, since these applications often use large amounts of energy [25]. Compute-intensive applications often come from the numerical solution of differential equations modeling phenomena in science and engineering, including classical physics, economy, chemistry, and engineering. Since it is usually not possible to find the exact solution in closed form, the solution is approximated by a numerical method solving the discretized problem. The approximation method produces an approximation solution with an error due to the numerical calculations and it is an important concern to determine how good the approximation fits to the real solution at the approximation points [7]. The quality of an approximation can be studied by investigating the accuracy, which captures the global error of the approximation in comparison with the (unknown) exact solution. For many numerical methods, the accuracy can be influenced by algorithmic parameters, such as tolerance values and error bounds that are used to decide whether a computation step is accepted or needs be repeated. These algorithmic parameters can be set to indirectly influence the resulting requested accuracy. In this article, time and energy consumption is investigated for different tolerance values given to a selected scientific examples.

A specific execution run of a numerical method leads to a specific execution time and energy consumption which depends on the execution parameters and on the execution platform. Parallel numerical software can employ a varying number of execution units (processors or cores). Using a larger number of execution units can reduce the execution time until a certain saturation point that depends on the algorithmic structure and the parallel implementation. However, the energy consumption may exhibit a different characteristic of the growth behavior depending on the amount of parallelism. Different settings of execution parameters may lead to the smallest execution time or the smallest energy consumption, respectively. On recent multicore architectures, the computation time and the energy consumption of program executions can also be influenced by the setting the operational frequency of the execution units [34]. Smaller operational frequencies usually increase the execution time, but may lead to a smaller energy consumption due to a reduced power consumption. The interactions may be complex and they depend on the computational and memory access behavior of the software code executed.

Choosing an implementation version of a specific numerical algorithm is another aspect influencing time and energy. For each version the execution variants can be created and, thus, a large variety of different execution variants may result. It is usually not a priory obvious which of these execution variants provides the solution run with the best or optimal performance or energy consumption for a given accuracy requirement. It may even be possible that such a best or optimal parameter setting for both execution time and energy consumption does not exist and a compromise has to be chosen. This article studies these multi-dimensional requirements for parallel numerical computations.

As example application, solution methods for ordinary differential equations (ODEs) are considered [16]. Solution methods for ODEs are time-stepping methods which require a considerable amount of computation time and energy and, thus, it is desirable to optimize the performance of both. Embedded Runge-Kutta (RK) methods are popular ODE solver and, thus, these methods are adopted for the investigation in this article. Embedded RK methods, also called Runge-Kutta-Fehlberg methods, are one-step solution methods for ODEs with an error control and step size control mechanism that adapts the step-size to the growth behavior of the exact solution. The step-size control can be guided by a tolerance value used in the step-size control and leads to an approximation of a certain accuracy. A higher accuracy may increase the computation effort for the approximation calculation. The computation effort also depends on the specific RK method chosen and the computation mode of the architecture system used for the computation. For recent multi-cores with frequency scaling, the number of cores and the operational frequency chosen for acomputation run represent different architecture computation modes. This article studies the relationship of the execution time and the energy consumption of an execution run of an embedded RK method depending on the processor execution mode and the quality of the computed approximation.

The goal of this article is to find an execution variant for an RK method which provides an approximation of a certain accuracy and is optimal with respect to time and energy. The problem of finding such an execution variant is formulated as a **multi-criteria decision problem** considering execution time and energy consumption for executing the RK method. In this approach, the set of different execution variants of an ODE solver represents a decision space for which **Pareto-optimal solutions** are determined according to the positions of the performance values in the criterion space. First, a complete set of performance data for the criterion space is generated. Then, the criterion space is analyzed. The data analysis of the performance data exploits the elimination of execution variants which are dominated by other variants. The data analysis and a selection process for selecting an appropriate execution variant has been first presented in [31]. In this article, the data analysis process is extended by two demonstrators from the area of solving ODE problems. These problems are a reaction-diffusion ODE and a spectral ODE system.

The structure of the article is as follows: Sect. 2 introduces the generation of implementation versions and execution variants. Section 3 concentrates on the analysis of performance data. Section 4 presents the computational structure of ODE methods. Section 5 describes experiments and measurements. Section 6 discusses related work and Sect. 7 concludes.

2 Variant Generation for Numerical Algorithms

Numerical algorithms can be implemented in multiple ways with respect to method and programming decision, resulting in different implementation versions solving the same problem. Also, each such implementation version can be executed with different parameter settings leading to different execution variants each producing results with differences concerning accuracy of the solution as well as execution time and energy consumption needed for computing that solution. In this section, the generation of versions and variants is described.

2.1 Execution Platform and Parallel Programming Paradigm

The generation of implementation versions and execution variants for a specific numerical problem is based on several preliminaries, which are now summarized.

The implementation of a numerical method is given as a parallel program. The execution platform provides several execution units so that the parallel program can actually be performed in a parallel way. The coarse classification of parallel platforms distinguishes parallel environments with a distributed address space in contrast to environments with a shared address space. An example for distributed address space platforms are cluster systems and an appropriate programming environment is the message-passing paradigm, e.g. using MPI [12], which requires a special emphasis on the optimization of the communication operations exchanging data between the execution units. Popular platforms with shared address space are multicore systems providing several cores to be exploited for parallel executions by a multi-threaded program for which synchronization operations are crucial to avoid race conditions. In the work of this article, the shared memory paradigm with a multi-threaded programming paradigm is adopted. The programs discussed and used for the demonstrators are implemented in C with Pthreads and permit the setting of several execution parameters due to the parametric programming style. The techniques described in the following could also be transferred to distributed address spaces mentioned above

As parallel hardware platform, a multicore machine providing DVFS (Dynamic Voltage Frequency Scaling) is assumed. Frequency scaling for DVFS processors includes the implicit or explicit selection of the operational frequency from a discrete set of frequency values in the range $[f_{min}, f_{max}]$. The specific range of frequencies depends on the hardware system used.

2.2 Generation Process of Execution Variants

The possibilities for generating software versions and execution variants can be depicted as a decision tree, in which each level of nodes represents a specific decision for the specific level. Figure 1 illustrates the decision tree with levels for the coding, the compilation and for the execution with parameter selection. The starting point is a specific numerical solution method for which different implementation versions can be generated by using different computation schemes or applying different algorithmic optimizations and different program transformations, including standard transformations, such as loop tiling, loop interchange, loop fusion or loop unrolling. Each of the resulting different program versions can be compiled with different compiler options such as options to enable vectorization, loop optimizations or alignment. Standard compilers offer a large number of compiler options. For example the gcc compiler supports more than 200 options and the LLVM compiler has more than 150 compiler passes [2]. These compiler options leads to a large number of different executables, each with potentially different performance characteristics. Each of these executables can then be executed with different parameter settings concerning hardware and software parameters. The hardware parameters include different DVFS settings for the cores and uncores of the execution platform as well as the numbers of threads to be employed for the execution. The software parameters include parameters to control the global error of the approximation solution, e.g. different tolerance values to control the execution of the numerical method. Overall, a potentially large number of execution variants may result, each with different performance and energy behavior.

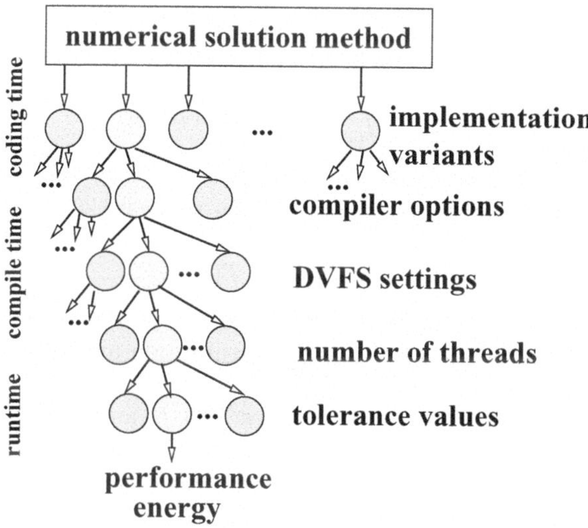

Fig. 1. Illustration of the **variant generation process** at different stages of software development and execution, i.e., coding time, compile time and runtime. In each level of the decision tree, a specific choice of a value for a parameter can be taken, such that a selection path (depicted as yellow circles) in the decision tree results. The leaf of a selected path corresponds to a specific variant with individual performance and energy data [31].

2.3 Performance Metrics For Assessing Execution Variants

The execution of variant V can be assessed with several performance metrics, such as the execution time or the energy consumption. Further performance and energy metrics are discussed in [30].

The energy E consumed for the execution of an execution variant V in the time interval $[0, t_{end}]$ depends on the given hardware platform and the power drawing P during the execution time of length $T = t_{end}$. The power drawing P may vary during the execution of the program code. Thus, E is expressed as $E = \int_{t=0}^{t_{end}} P(t)dt$, assuming that the program is executed from time $t = 0$ to time $t = t_{end}$ and that $P(t)$ denotes the power drawing at time t, $t \in [0, t_{end}]$.

Several execution variants can be generated for a single implementation version of the numerical method. For a multicore system with p_{max} cores, different execution variants result for any number p of cores between 1 and p_{max}. For DVFS systems with operational frequencies f ranging between a minimum frequency f_{min} and a maximum frequency f_{max}, different execution variants can be generated for each of the available operational frequencies. The power drawing P varies with the number of threads p used for the execution and the operational frequency f chosen, so that the power P can be expressed as a function of p and f, i.e.$P = P(p, f)$. Consequently, the energy consumption also depends on p and f, which is expressed by :

$$E(p, f) = \int_{t=0}^{t_{end}(p,f)} P(p, f)(t)dt. \tag{1}$$

For simplicity, it is often assumed that $P(p, f)$ is constant during the execution of an application program for fixed p and f. In this case, (1) can be expressed as:

$$E(p, f) = P(p, f) \cdot T(p, f). \tag{2}$$

Due to the influence of $P(p, f)$ on the energy consumption $E(p, f)$, there is no linear dependence between the energy consumption and the execution time, which has been investigated in detail in [26].

Besides the two non-functional properties $E(p, f)$ and $T(p, f)$, we also consider the accuracy $Acc(V)$ of an execution variant V, which is a functional property. The accuracy of the solution computed by an execution variant is indirectly guided by the tolerance value with which the solution method is executed. Although, at first glance a higher accuracy might require a higher execution time and energy consumption, this does not have to be the case and the dependencies between these performance metrics are more intricate. This is discussed in the next section.

3 Analysis of Performance Data and Solution Quality

Concerning the solution of a scientific problem with a numerical method a distinction can be made between the properties of the solution process and the quality of the solution resulting from the solution process. This section is concerned with the analysis of both.

3.1 Performance Optimization Problem

In this article, the solution process is represented by the execution of a certain execution variant of the numerical method. Properties of the solution process are the non-functional properties, which are the execution time T, the energy consumption E, and the power P in the case of this article. The solution resulting from the solution process, i.e. executing the numerical method, is the numerical approximation solution and the quality is given by its accuracy Acc, whch is a functional property All three types of data are dependent data resulting from executing the numerical algorithm. The independent variables are input to an execution run and influence the output properties. As input data, the operational frequency f, the number of threads p, and the chosen TOL values are used in this article.

Table 1 summarizes the variables used in the analysis of this article and gives their classification concerning solution process and resulting solution as well as dependent and independent variables. Table 2 concentrates on the functional relationship of these variables. For example, the execution time T is a function of the input parameters f, p, TOL and the accuracy ACC mainly depends on the input parameter TOL in the analysis of this article.

Table 1. Meaning of variables describing the properties of solution process (i.e. execution variant) and of the resulting solution.

Meaning of variables involved in the analysis			
Variable	meaning	type	solution/solution process
T	execution time	dependent	solution process
E	energy consumption	dependent	solution process
P	power	dependent	solution process
ACC	numerical accuracy	dependent	resulting solution
f	operational frequency	independent	solution process
p	number of threads	independent	solution process
TOL	tolerance value	independent	solution process and resulting solution

The main concern of this article is the analysis of the performance data T and E of the solution process with respect to the quality of the resulting solution. This includes the optimization of both values since it is usually desirable to have a low execution time and a low energy consumption. The specific focus is to analyse and optimize T and E with respect to the solution quality influenced the TOL parameter and to find an optimal or Pareto-optimal setting of the solution process, for choosing an execution variant. The following questions arise:

- Which relation can be observed between the execution time and the energy consumption when all independent variables f, p, TOL are each set to a fixed

Table 2. Functional dependence of the dependent variable on the independent variables introduced in Table 1

Functional dependence of variables		
	dependent variables	independent variables
Solution process	T, E, P	f, p, TOL
Resulting solution	ACC	TOL

Table 3. Optimization goals for execution time, energy consumption, and numerical accuracy [31]

Optimization goals with constraints			
	execution time	energy consumption	accuracy
1.	minimize	no constraint	no requirement
2.	minimize	constraint $< E_{max}$	no requirement
3.	minimize	no constraint	requirement < eps
4.	no constraint	minimize	no requirement
5.	constraint $< T_{max}$	minimize	no requirement
6.	no constraint	minimize	requirement < eps
7.	no constraint	no constraint	requirement < eps
8.	no constraint	constraint $< E_{max}$	requirement < eps
9.	constraint $< T_{max}$	no constraint	requirement < eps
10.	Pareto-optimization of time and energy		no requirement
11.	Pareto-optimization of time and energy		requirement < eps
12.	Pareto optimization of time and energy and accuracy		

value. More precisely: Is the relation a linear one or are there exceptions, e.g., caused by a varying power consumption?
- How can a best solution be identified in the two-dimensional space of execution time and energy consumption? Is there a unique best solution for optimizing both, execution time and energy consumption, in dependence of p, f and TOL? Or can a set of Pareto optimal solutions be identified?
- Given an upper bound of the energy consumption to be invested and a upper of the accuracy (a) Is it possible to find suitable values for p, f, and TOL so that the related approximation solution fulfills the constraint? (b) In case that several feasible solutions are available, which one is the best or which ones are in the set of Pareto-optimal solutions?

These questions lead to specific optimization problems summarized in Table 3: Optimization problems (1) - (3) minimize the execution time with different constraints for the energy consumption and the numerical accuracy. Problems (4) - (6) minimize the energy consumption with different constraints. Problems (7) - (9) address minimum requirements for the numerical accuracy. The three last optimization problems (10) - (12) address Pareto-optimal solutions, which is formalized in the next subsection.

3.2 Defining Pareto-Optimal Performance of Variants

The goal is to optimize execution time and energy consumption in the sense that an execution variant with specific f, p and TOL is identified so that its time and energy are optimal or Pareto-optimal. The problem of finding an optimal variant for a numerical solution method can be considered as a multi-criteria decision problem considering execution time, energy consumption and numerical accuracy together. For this problem, a decision space and a criterion space are defined as follows.

Definition 1. *The* **decision space** *represents all possible variants V to be executed on a certain number of cores with individual frequency scaling. The* **feasible set** $\mathcal{A}$ *is a subset of the decision space that contains the variants V that are available for the optimization problem.*

Definition 2. *The* **criterion (or objective) space** *is the image of the decision space under the objective function mapping, which are the execution time, the energy consumption, and the numerical accuracy. The* **criterion space for execution time and energy consumption** *can be represented by a diagram in which the x-axis denotes the execution time and the y-axis denotes the energy consumption.*

Each feasible variant $V \in \mathcal{A}$ is represented by a criterion value according to its execution time and its energy consumption. The image of the set $\mathcal{A}$ under the mappings execution time $T : \mathcal{A} \to \mathbb{R}$ and energy consumption $E : \mathcal{A} \to \mathbb{R}$ form the **feasible set in the criterion space** The set of feasible solutions $\mathcal{A}$ is built up according to the variant generation process given in Fig. 1. The image in the criterion space is determined by measuring the execution time and the energy consumption of the different variants available. The definition of an efficient implementation variant in the decision space and the related definition of non-dominated points in the criterion space is given as follows:

Definition 3. *An variant V is called* **efficient** *(also called* **Pareto optimal***), if there is no other implementation variant $\tilde{V}$ such that $T(\tilde{V}) < T(V)$ and $E(\tilde{V}) < E(V)$. If V is efficient, its entry $(T(V), E(V) \in \mathbb{R} \times \mathbb{R}$ in the criterion space is called* **non-dominated point***. The set of efficient implementation variants is denoted by $\mathcal{A}_{eff}$. The set of all non-dominated points is called the* **non-dominated set***. An implementation variant V_1* **dominates** *an implementation variant V_2, if $T(V_1) \leq T(V_2)$ and $E(V_1) \leq E(V_2)$.*

Thus, for the elements in $\mathcal{A}_{eff}$, there exists no alternative that has both a smaller execution time and a smaller energy consumption. The set of efficient solutions is sometimes also called a Pareto set [9]. In Fig. 2, the non-dominated points are depicted in red, whereas the black points are points that are dominated by other points and, therefore, do not need be considered further. All red points together represent the Pareto set. All execution variants that are not efficient can be excluded from the search for an optimal solution. For determining the non-dominated points, representing execution variants, different algorithms can be used, for example the algorithm from [27].

3.3 Summary of Variant Selection

The variant selection process for a parallel application algorithm based on performance data consists of several steps. In the first step (version determination), a suitable application algorithm is selected according to the required accuracy of the solution. The specific application problem to be solved and its characteristics are taken into consideration for this selection. Usually, several application algorithms are suitable for the combination of application problem and the required accuracy. These different choices lead to different basic implementation versions to be considered further in the selection process. and energy requirements. Moreover, different implementation versions can be generated by modifying the loop structure of the underlying implementation using loop transformations. For each of these versions, different execution variants can be generated by using different compiler options and by selecting different execution parameters such as the number of threads or using different operational frequencies based on DVFS. This may lead to a large number of execution variants that can be executed on the given hardware platform. During the execution of each of these execution variants, performance data are collected, including execution times, energy consumption and numerical accuracy. These data are then used to construct the time-energy criterion space according to Fig. 2 and to determine the Pareto set of the variants selected. The values in the Pareto set belong to execution variants, which are to be selected.

The variant selection can be supported by suitable optimization techniques, see [15] for a detailed treatment. The optimization goal would be to determine the parameters such that the resulting energy consumption is minimized. The energy consumption could be captured by a modeling equation according to Equ. (2), in which the expression for $T(p, f)$ and $P(p, f)$ are modelled in such a way that the essential parameters (in this case the number of threads p and the operational frequency f) occur in the expression. Suitable techniques include constrained methods, where the constraints define a maximum number of resources that are available for the execution or a frequency range in which the frequency value f determined by the optimization method has to fit.

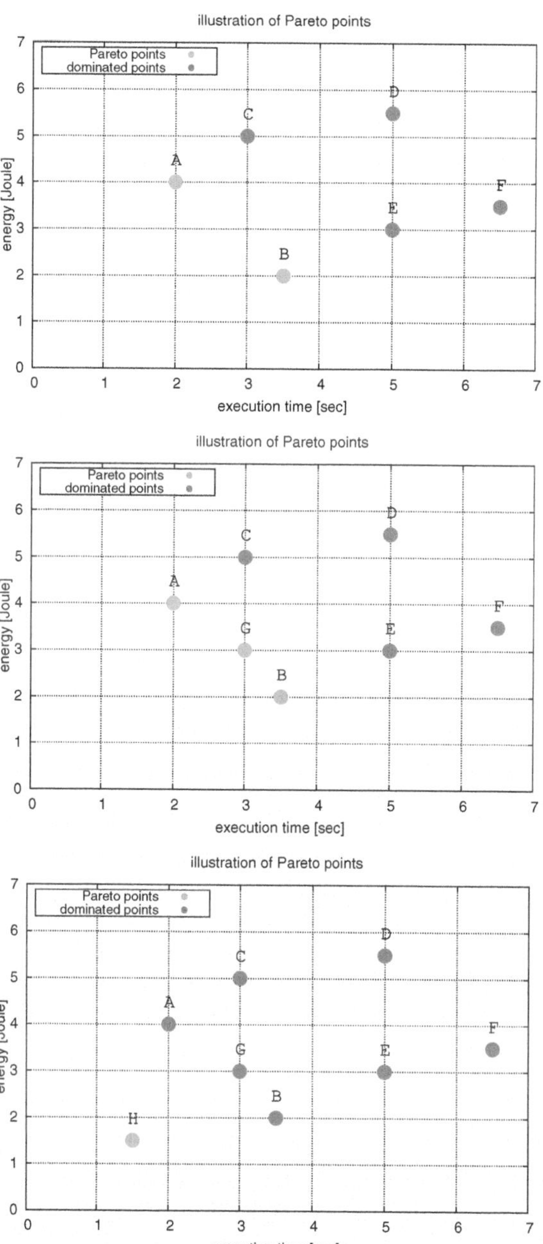

Fig. 2. Illustration of the two-dimensional criterion space with execution time and energy consumption. The red points are Pareto-optimal points. Top: A and B are Pareto points. Middle: the newly inserted point G is also a Pareto point. Bottom: the newly added point H dominates all other points and is therefore the only Pareto point. (Color figure online)

4 Variant Selection for ODE Solvers

In this section, the variant selection process is illustrated for solution methods for ODEs, which are available for different scenarios, such as initial value problems or boundary value problems. Explicit solution methods for non-stiff problems and implicit solution methods for stiff problems exist, see [16] for a detailed overview. Due to their wide-spread use, the popular Runge-Kutta (RK) methods are considered in the following to illustrate the variant selection process.

4.1 Selection of Runge-Kutta Method

RK methods are numerical approximation methods for the solution of initial value problems of systems of first order ODEs with system size $n \geq 1$ given as:

$$\mathbf{y}'(x) = \mathbf{f}(x, \mathbf{y}(x)) \text{ with } \mathbf{y}(x_0) = \mathbf{y}_0. \tag{3}$$

The unknown solution function $\mathbf{y}(\mathbf{x})$, the right hand side function $\mathbf{f}$ and the initial value $\mathbf{y}_0$ at point x_0 are vectors of size n. The family of RK methods includes explicit and implicit approximation methods, which are chosen according to the stiffness of the problem (3) to be solved. In the following, explicit RK methods are considered. Each explicit RK methods available provides a specific range of numerical accuracies. The numerical accuracy depends on the convergence order of the RK method, which can be determined by a mathematical analysis. Popular RK methods are the Dormand and Prince (DOPRI) methods of convergence order 5 (DOPRI5) or 8 (DOPRI8) and Verner's method (DVERK) with convergence order 6 [8,16].

The selection of a suitable RK method for the required accuracy is the first step in the selection process. If a high numerical accuracy is required, an RK method with a high convergence order is beneficial, whereas for a lower numerical accuracy, an RK method with a smaller convergence order might be sufficient and more energy-efficient, since less computations are performed.

Explicit RK methods compute a series of approximation vectors $\mathbf{y}_0, \mathbf{y}_1, \mathbf{y}_2 \cdots$ which approximate the exact solution at discrete x-values $x_0, x_1, x_2, \ldots$. One time step computing $\mathbf{y}_{\kappa+1}$ from $\mathbf{y}_\kappa$, $\kappa = 0, 1, 2, \ldots$ includes the following computation:

- Compute the stage vectors $\mathbf{k}_1, \ldots, \mathbf{k}_s$:

$$\mathbf{k}_l = \mathbf{f}(x_\kappa + c_l h_\kappa, \mathbf{y}_\kappa + h_\kappa \sum_{i=1}^{l-1} a_{li} \mathbf{k}_i) \text{ for } l = 1, \ldots, s. \tag{4}$$

  where value h_κ is the step-size used in the specific time step κ, i.e., $x_{\kappa+1} = x_\kappa + h_\kappa$, and $\mathbf{y}_\kappa$ is the previous approximation vector.
- Compute the next approximation vector $\mathbf{y}_{\kappa+1}$:

$$\mathbf{y}_{\kappa+1} = \mathbf{y}_\kappa + h_\kappa \cdot \sum_{l=1}^{s} b_l \mathbf{k}_l, \tag{5}$$

  using stage vectors $\mathbf{k}_1, ..\mathbf{k}_s$, computed in Equ.(4). The usage of a larger number of stage vectors leads to a higher convergence order.

Algorithm 1: Multithreaded implementation version of a generic RK method.

```
while (x < x_end) do
    data-parallel computation of vectors of length n on p cores:
    for (i = 0; i < s; i++) do
        computation of stage vector k_i according to Eq. (4);
        barrier synchronization;
    end
    computation of new approximation vector y_{κ+1} according to Eq. (5);
    computation of second approximation vector ŷ_{κ+1} according to Eq. (6);
    barrier synchronization;
    compute approximation error using y_{κ+1} and ŷ_{κ+1};
    compute new stepsize h_new for next iteration step;
    if (error > TOL) then
        repeat time step with h_new;
    end
    else
        accept time step;
        update x by x = x + h_new;
    end
end
```

- Compute an additional approximation vector $\hat{\mathbf{y}}_{\kappa+1}$:

$$\hat{\mathbf{y}}_{\kappa+1} = \mathbf{y}_{\kappa} + h_{\kappa} \cdot \sum_{l=1}^{s} \hat{b}_l \mathbf{k}_l. \tag{6}$$

for error control and step-size adaption in the case of embedded RK methods.

The computation schemes (4), (5) and (6) use the coefficients: s–dimensional vectors $b = (b_1, \ldots, b_s)$, $\hat{b} = (\hat{b}_1, \ldots, \hat{b}_s)$, and $c = (c_1, \ldots, c_s)$, as well as $s \times s$ matrix $A = (a_{il})$ which are specific for the particular RK method chosen and are usually depicted in the Butcher tableau [16]. For explicit RK methods, the matrix A is a strictly lower triangular matrix. The order r of the approximation vector $\mathbf{y}_{\kappa+1}$ and the order $\hat{r}$ of the second approximation vector $\hat{\mathbf{y}}_{\kappa+1}$ typically differ by 1 so that $r = \hat{r} + 1$ holds. An asymptotic estimate of the local error in the lower order approximation is computed by the difference between the two approximations $\mathbf{y}_{\kappa+1}$ and $\hat{\mathbf{y}}_{\kappa+1}$. This is used for stepsize control [10]. The approximation vector of the current step κ is accepted, if a suitable weighted norm of the local error estimate lies within the predefined tolerance level. Using different tolerance values leads to the generation of different variants of the ODE solver. Although the estimate of the local error is in the lower order approximation, the more accurate approximation is usually taken to advance the integration (local extrapolation). The investigations in this article are done for the explicit RK method DOPRI5, which uses 7 stages.

Algorithm 2: Workflow for building RK execution variants and gathering performance data.

select implementation version of an RK method according to Algorithm 1;
compile implementation version with selected compiler options;
measure data for several execution variants:
for *(each value of p, f and TOL* **do**
  execute specific execution variant;
  obtain performance data for T and E;
end
build decision and criterion space;
determine Pareto-optimal values and corresponding execution variants.

4.2 Parallel Implementation Variants

The implementation of the RK method is sequentially in the simulation time steps $\kappa = 0, 1, 2, \ldots$, since each new time step $\kappa{+}1$ needs the result of the previous time step κ, $\kappa \geq 0$. However, within each time step there is a possibility for a parallel computation. The multithreaded implementation given in Algorithm 1 is based on a parallel computation of the stage vectors and the approximation vectors. This kind of parallelism is called parallelism across the system [14]. Since we consider generic RK implementations, we cannot exploit parallelism across the method, which would need to be provided by the RK parameters. The parallelism across the system requires barrier synchronizations within a time step.

For the experimental evaluation, a multi-threaded implementation of a generic RK method is considered. Synchronization is achieved with the Pthreads library. The computations of the components of the argument vectors, the stage vectors, and the approximation vectors are distributed in a block-wise way over p threads. At the end of a time step, the error control and stepsize selection for the next time step is performed by a single thread. If the error control observes that the error is too large, the previous time step is repeated with a smaller step size. Synchronization operations are included to ensure numerical correctness. A first barrier synchronization is used after the computation of each stage vector so that the computation of the next stage vector uses the most recent values of the preceding stage vectors. A barrier synchronization is also used before and after the error control and stepsize selection, which ensures that the approximation vectors $\mathbf{y}_{\kappa+1}$ and $\hat{\mathbf{y}}_{\kappa+1}$ are completely computed before terror control and stepsize selection are performed and that all threads start the next time step not before the previous time step has been completed by all threads. This ensures that the numerical behavior of the parallel versions and the sequential versions are identical.

The workflow for building RK execution variants and gathering performance data is summarized in Algorithm 2.

5 Experimental Evaluation

The variant selection process is applied to performance data of measurements for solving two different ODE test problems which have been executed on a multicore system.

5.1 ODE Test Problems

The following two ODE test problems are used to explore different variants of the RK methods according to their performance and energy profile:

RD ODE: The RD ODE system results from a spatial discretization of a two-dimensional time-dependent partial differential equation describing a reaction-diffusion (RD) problem of two chemical substances [16]. Discretization with different grid sizes lead to different sizes of the resulting ODE system. More precisely, using N discretization points in both space dimension leads to an ODE system of size $n = 2N^2$. The resulting ODE system, called RD ODE in the following, has the property that each component f_i, $i \in \{1, ..., n\}$, of the right-hand side function $\mathbf{f}$ has a constant evaluation time that is independent of the size of the ODE system. The computational intensity of this ODE system is therefore small. The evaluation time of the entire function $\mathbf{f}$ including all components increases linearly with n.

SP ODE: The second ODE system results from applying a spectral (SP) method to a time-dependent one-dimensional partial differential equation describing the behavior of a collisionless electron plasma. The number of base functions N used for the spectral decomposition influences the accuracy of the solution and has an effect on the size n of the resulting ODE system according to $n = 4 \cdot N + 2$. The resulting ODE system, called SP ODE in the following, has the property that the evaluation time of each component of $\mathbf{f}$ increases linearly with the system size n. The computational intensity of this ODE system is therefore large. The evaluation time of the entire function $\mathbf{f}$ increases quadratically with n.

A first investigation of the power consumption and energy behavior of these ODE systems has been presented in [28]. However, this article does not take the Pareto aspect into consideration.

5.2 Hardware Platform

For the experimental evaluation, and an Intel Broadwell processor (i7-6950X) has been used. The processor has 10 cores on one socket, running at 3.0 GHz. The TDP is 140 W. Hyper-threading is supported. The memory hierarchy includes a 25 MB shared L3 cache, a 256 KB L2 cache and a 32 KB L1 cache per core. The main memory size is 32 GB. The frequency range supported lies between 1.2 GHz and 2.9 GHz. Only a discrete set of frequencies is available: the frequency has to be selected from the following set of frequencies: {1.2 GHz, 1.3 GHz, 1.4 GHz, 1.6 GHz, 1.7 GHz, 1.8 GHz, 1.9 GHz, 2.0 GHz, 2.2 GHz, 2.3 GHz, 2.4 GHz, 2.5 GHz, 2.6 GHz, 2.8 GHz, 2.9 GHz }.

The compilation has been performed with the gcc compiler (Version 7.3.1) using the highest optimization level -O3. The time and energy measurements have been performed using the Running Average Power Limit (RAPL) interface and sensors of the Intel architecture [18,32]. RAPL sensors can be accessed by control registers, known as Model Specific Registers (MSRs) [18]. In particular, the likwid tool-set, especially the likwid-perfctr tool in Version 4.3.2 [35] has been used for the experimental evaluation. The runtime and energy measurements have been performed with no other user on the system and no other process except the operating system running to keep disturbance effects as small as possible.

5.3 Selection of Pareto-Optimal Variants

There are many parameters that can be used to create different variants of a numerical method. This includes (i) algorithmic parameters, such as tolerance values for the error control, (ii) program parameters, such as different loop structures of the use of different compiler options, and (iii) execution parameters, such as the usage of different numbers of threads and different operational frequencies.

In the following, the variant selection process is illustrated for the operational frequency using DVFS as an example for an execution parameter. The variant selection process is applied to a parallel multi-threaded implementation version of the DOPRI5 RK method. Both the RD ODE using $N = 4096$ and the SP ODE using $N = 5000$ are considered.

Figure 3 shows the execution time (x-axis) and energy consumption (y-axis) of different implementation variants executed sequentially on one core of the Broadwell processor, using different operational frequencies and different tolerance values between 10^{-2} and 10^{-6}. Each dot in the decision space denotes the value $(T(V), E(V))$ for a specific variant V generated with a fixed frequency and a predefined tolerance value. The diagram shows five convex curves for the family of variants that are executed with the same tolerance value $TOL \in \{10^{-3}, 10^{-4}, 10^{-5}, 10^{-6}\}$. For each curve, the frequencies decrease from left to right.

The figure shows that smaller tolerance values such as 10^{-6} lead to larger execution times and larger energy consumptions that the usage of larger tolerance values. This is caused by a higher computational effort due to the execution of a larger number of time steps of the ODE method when using a smaller stepsize. The execution times and energy consumptions for the tolerance values 10^{-2} and 10^{-3} are quite close together due to a similar number of time steps.

Figure 3 also shows that the use of the highest operation frequencies leads to the largest energy consumption and the smallest execution time for each of the different tolerance values. Decreasing the operational frequency increases the execution time, and the largest execution time results when using the the smallest operational frequency. However, the use of the smallest operational frequency (1.2 GHz) does not lead to the smallest energy consumption. Instead, the smallest energy consumption results by using a slightly higher operational frequency. This frequency is 1.4 GHz for all tolerance values except 10^{-3}, for which the

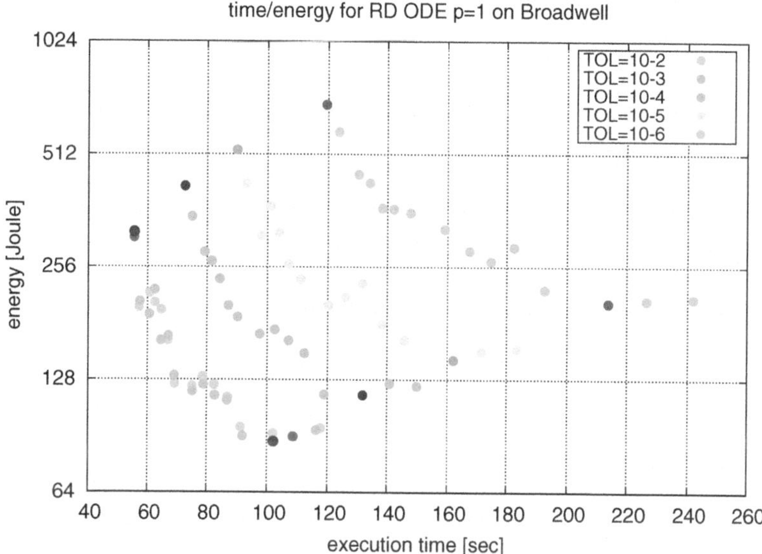

Fig. 3. RD-ODE: Execution time and energy for different frequencies and different tolerance values on Broadwell using a sequential execution [31].

smallest energy consumption results for 1.3 GHz. Since each of the five curves represents different tolerance values that lead to different numerical accuracies, the curves have to be considered in isolation. For each of the five curves, most of the points depicted are Pareto points. However, for each of the five curves, two important Pareto points can be identified that correspond to the smallest energy consumption and the smallest execution time compared to the other variants with the same tolerance value. These important Pareto points are shown as solid dots in the diagram to distinguish them from the other points, which are depicted in a lighter color.

Figure 4 shows the same information as Fig. 3 using a multithreaded execution with 10 threads. Again, for each curve the frequencies decrease from left to right. The important Pareto points are again shown as solid dots in the diagram. Similar to the sequential case, the use of smaller tolerance values leads to larger execution times and larger energy consumptions that the usage of larger tolerance values. Moreover, the use of the highest operation frequencies leads to the largest energy consumption and the smallest execution time for each of the different tolerance values.

However, there are also several differences between the diagrams in Figs. 3 and 4: For the parallel case, the use of the smallest operational frequency always leads to the smallest energy consumption. Moreover, the energy consumption for the parallel execution with 10 threads is much larger than the energy consumption for the sequential execution. This is caused by the significantly larger power consumption for 10 threads, which cannot be compensated by a corresponding reduction in the execution time.

Figures 5 and 6 show the same information for the SP ODE as Figs. 3 and 4 for the RD ODE. In principle, the corresponding figures exhibit a similar behavior for frequency scaling. However, there are also some differences. In particular for the SP ODE, the difference of the energy consumption for the best frequency and the highest frequency is larger than for the RD ODE. This can be observed both for a sequential execution (Fig. 5) and a parallel execution with 10 threads (Fig. 6). Moreover, especially for a sequential execution of the SP ODE, reducing the frequency has a larger impact on the energy consumption as for the RD ODE.

6 Related Work

Many different aspects of energy-aware and green computing are addressed in [1]. The handbook considers hardware aspects such as energy-efficient CPU architectures, energy-efficient storage systems, intelligent energy-aware networks, algorithmic aspects of energy-aware algorithms with an emphasis of energy-efficient scheduling methods. Other aspects include real-time systems, monitoring and evaluation methods, data centers and large-scale systems, as well as social and environmental issues. Similar topics with a focus on distributed systems, high-performance systems, and cloud systems are covered in [36]. The scheduling of parallel tasks with energy and time constraints on multiple manycore processors are addressed in [21,22]. Scheduling algorithms are proposed and worst-case asymptotic performance bounds and average-case asymptotic performance bounds are derived for the algorithms proposed. The analytical results are verified by extensive simulations.

The bi-objective optimization of data-parallel applications on homogeneous multicore clusters for performance and energy consumption has been addressed in [23]. In particular, it is shown by experiments on modern multicore CPUs that the relationship between execution time and energy consumption is complex. The paper formulates the bi-objective optimization problem for performance and energy is formulated as mathematical problem and a global optimization algorithm is proposed to determine globally Pareto-optimal solutions. As examples, matrix multiplication and fast Fourier transform are considered. For these applications, the only algorithmic parameter is the input size. In contrast, the RK methods considered in this article are more complex and the tolerance value for the error control is an additional algorithmic parameter that has a large influence on the numerical accuracy of the resulting approximative solution. The input size, which is related to the discretization, also plays an important role, since the size of the ODE system also influences the numerical accuracy. Moreover, matrix multiplication and fast Fourier transform can be more easily captured by an analytical modeling than the RK methods because the time-stepping nature of the RK methods. The number of time steps cannot be predicted in advance due to the error control and adaptive stepsize computation that both depend on characteristics of the ODE problem to be solved.

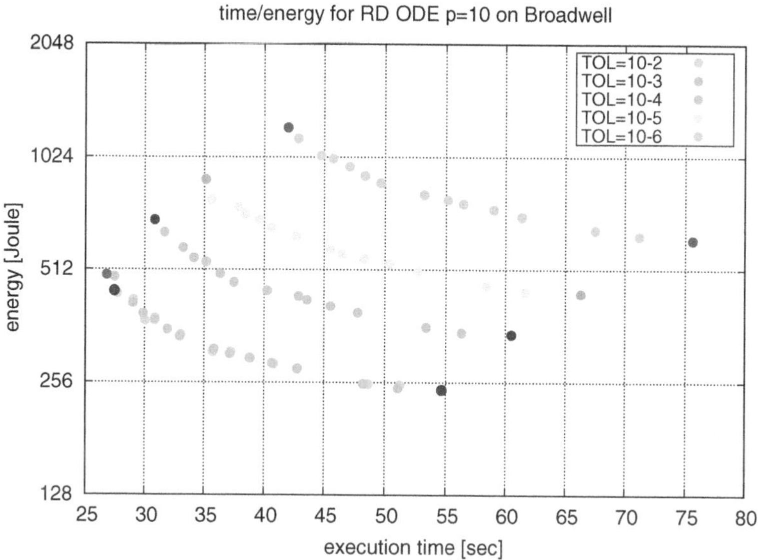

Fig. 4. RD-ODE: Execution time and energy for different frequencies and different tolerance values on Broadwell using a parallel execution with 10 threads [31].

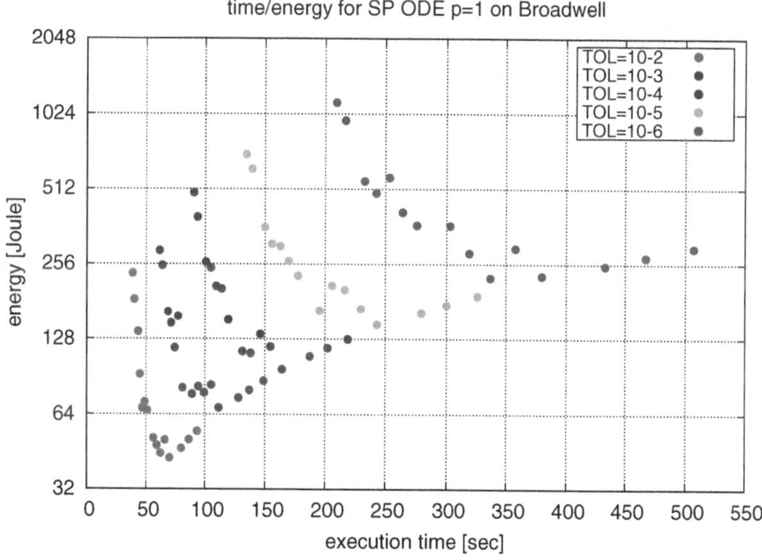

Fig. 5. SP-ODE: Execution time and energy for different frequencies and different tolerance values on Broadwell using a sequential execution [29].

The work in [23] has been extended in [20] to include heterogeneous platforms. There are other approaches in this direction, including [11] addressing

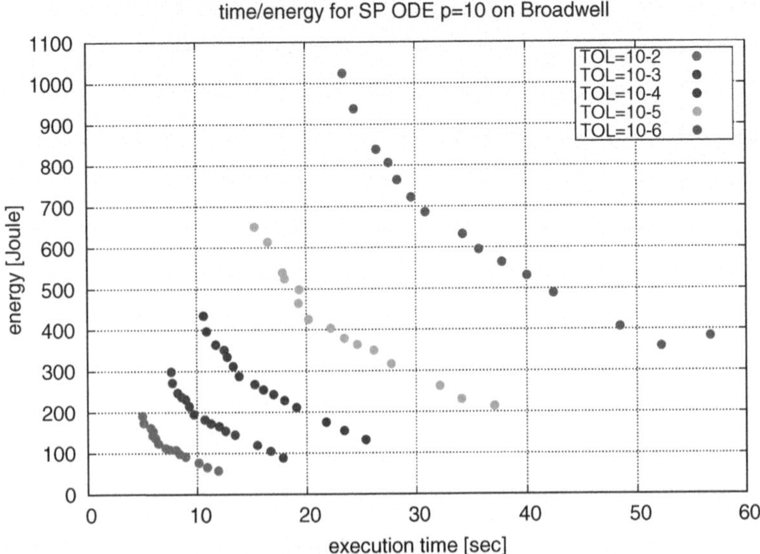

Fig. 6. SP-ODE: Execution time and energy for different frequencies and different tolerance values on Broadwell using a parallel execution with 10 threads [29].

heterogeneous environments, [24] considering cloud computing systems, and [13] investigating the occurrence of memory and communication bottlenecks in cluster systems.

The theoretical analysis of the error estimation and convergence for RK methods is covered in several textbooks [4,16] and research articles [5,17]. A theoretical analysis of the accuracy of Runge-Kutta methods is given in [6]. An accuracy analysis of explicit Runge-Kutta methods in the context of incompressible NavierâĂŞStokes equations is addressed in [33]. However, most of this research is a theoretical analysis and no practical test with parallel codes is included. A comparison of the efficiency of explicit RK methods, extrapolation methods and spectral deferred correction methods based on their accuracy and stability properties is given in [19]. The potential of parallelism across the method is covered for extrapolation methods and deferred correction methods. Embedded RK methods have no potential for parallelism across the method.

7 Conclusions

For compute-intensive, long-running applications, e.g., coming from the area of scientific simulations, the execution time and the energy consumption should be reduced as much as possible. Both are influenced by many different parameters, including the selection of a specific simulation algorithm, the selection of compiler options for the compilation, as well as the selection of execution parameters such as the number of threads used or the operational frequency.

Often, a complex interaction between the parameters can be observed and it is not a priori clear which combination of parameter values may lead to the best runtime performance and the smallest energy consumption. Since the number of potential parameter values and their combination is very large, it is usually not possible to test all combinations with an experimental evaluation to find the best combination.

In this article, the relationship between the execution time and the energy consumption has been considered for a complex example from the area of scientific computing, a solution method for solving ordinary differential equations that result from a spacial discretization of time-dependent partial differential equations. The investigation concentrates on the interaction between time and energy and uses the notion of Pareto efficiency for an exploration of the interaction and the detection of good compromises between execution time and energy consumption. In particular, two execution parameters, the number of threads and the operational frequency have been considered in more detail. A detailed experimental evaluation has been performed for two different execution platforms showing that the interactions are indeed complex and that there is no best combination that optimizes both the execution time and the energy consumption.

References

1. Ahmad, I., Ranka, S.: Handbook of Energy-Aware and Green Computing. Chapman & Hall/CRC (2012)
2. Ashouri, A.H., Killian, W., Cavazos, J., Palermo, G., Silvano, C.: A survey on compiler autotuning using machine learning. ACM Comput. Surv. **51**(5), 96:1–96:42 (2018)
3. Brown, D.J., Reams, C.: Toward energy-efficient computing. Commun. ACM **53**(3), 50–58 (2010)
4. Butcher, J.C.: The Numerical Analysis of Ordinary Differential Equations. Runge-Kutta and General Linear Methods. Wiley, New York (1987)
5. Calvo, M., Gonzalez-Pinto, S., Montijano, J.I.: Global error estimation based on the tolerance proportionality for some adaptive runge-kutta codes. J. Comput. Appl. Math. **218**(2), 329 – 341 (2008). Proc. of the 12th Int. Congress on Computational and Applied Mathematics
6. Carpenter, M., Gottlieb, D., Abarbanel, S., Don, W.: The Theoretical Accuracy of Runge-Kutta Time Discretizations for the Initial Boundary Value Problem: A Careful Study of the Boundary Error. Technical report, NASA Technical Report (1993)
7. Deuflhard, P., Hohmann, A.: Numerical Analysis in Modern Scientific Computing, volume 43. Springer (2003)
8. Dormand, J.R., Prince, P.J.: A family of embedded Runge-Kutta formulae. J. Comput. Appl. Math. **6**(1), 19–26 (1980)
9. Ehrgott, M.: Multicriteria Optimization. Springer-Verlag (2005)
10. Enright, W.H., Higham, D.J., Owren, B., Sharp, P.W.: A Survey of the Explicit Runge-Kutta Method. Technical Report 94-291, University of Toronto, Department of Computer Science (1995)

11. Fard, H.M., Prodan, R., Barrionuevo, J.J.D., Fahringer, T.: A multi-objective approach for workflow scheduling in heterogeneous environments. In: 2012 12th IEEE/ACM International Symposium on Cluster, Cloud and Grid Computing (ccgrid 2012), pp. 300–309 (2012)
12. Message Passing Interface Forum. MPI: A Message-Passing Interface Standard, Version 4.0. www.mpi-forum.org (2021)
13. Freeh, V.W., et al.: Analyzing the energy-time trade-off in high-performance computing applications. IEEE Trans. Parallel Distrib. Syst. **18**(6), 835–848 (2007)
14. Gear, C.W.: Massive Parallelism across Space in ODEs. Appl. Numer. Math. **11**, 27–43 (1993)
15. Gill, P.E., Murray, W., Wright, M.H.: Practical optimization. Academic Press Inc. [Harcourt Brace Jovanovich Publishers], London (1981)
16. Hairer, E., Nørsett, S.P., Wanner, G.: Solving Ordinary Differential Equations I: Nonstiff Problems. Springer-Verlag, Berlin (1993)
17. Higham, D.J.: Global error versus tolerance for explicit runge-kutta methods. IMA J. Numer. Anal. **11**(4), 457–480 (1991)
18. Intel. Intel 64 and IA-32 Architecture Software Developer's Manual, System Programming Guide (2011)
19. Ketcheson, D., Waheed, U.B.: A comparison of high-order explicit runge–kutta, extrapolation, and deferred correction methods in serial and parallel. Commun. Appl. Math. Comput. Sci.,**9**(2), 175–200 (2014)
20. Lastovetsky, A., Manumachu, R.R.: Energy-Efficient Parallel Computing: challenges to Scaling. Information, **14**(4) (2023)
21. Li. K.: Energy and time constrained task scheduling on multiprocessor computers with discrete speed levels. J. Parallel Distributed Comput. **95**, 15–28 (2016). Special Issue on Energy Efficient Multi-Core and Many-Core Systems, Part I
22. Li, K.: Scheduling parallel tasks with energy and time constraints on multiple manycore processors in a cloud computing environment. Futur. Gener. Comput. Syst. **82**, 591–605 (2018)
23. Manumachu, R.R., Lastovetsky, A.: Bi-objective optimization of data-parallel applications on homogeneous multicore clusters for performance and energy. IEEE Trans. Comput. **67**(2), 160–177 (2018)
24. Mezmaz, M., Melab, N., Kessaci, Y., Lee, Y.C., Talbi, E.-G., Zomaya, A.Y., Tuyttens, D.: A parallel bi-objective hybrid metaheuristic for energy-aware scheduling for cloud computing systems. J. Parallel Distributed Comput. **71**(11), 1497–1508 (2011)
25. Orgerie, A.-C., de Assuncao, M.D., Lefevre, L.: A survey on techniques for improving the energy efficiency of large-scale distributed systems. ACM Comput. Surv. **46**(4), 47:1–47:31 (2014)
26. Rauber, T., ünger, G.R.: Energy-aware execution of fork-join-based task parallelism. In: 20th IEEE International Symposium on Modeling, Analysis, and Simulation of Computer and Telecommunication Systems (MASCOTS'12), pp. 231–240. IEEE (2012)
27. Rauber, T., ünger, G.R.: A Scheduling Selection Process for Energy-efficient Task Execution on DVFS Processors. Concurrency and Computation: Practice and Experience, 31 (2019)
28. Rauber, T., ünger, G.R.: On the Energy Consumption and Accuracy of Multithreaded Embedded Runge-Kutta Methods. In: Proceedings of the The International Conference on High Performance Computing & Simulation (HPCS 2019), volume 15, pp. 382–389. IEEE (2019)

29. Rauber, T., ünger, G.R.: Performance and Energy Evaluation for Solving a Schrödinger-Poisson System on Multicore Processors. In: Computer Performance Engineering and Stochastic Modelling, pp. 18–33. Springer Nature Switzerland (2023)
30. Rauber, T., Rünger, G., Stachowski, M.: Performance and energy metrics for multi-threaded applications on DVFS processors. Sustain. Comput. Inform. Syst. **17**, 55–68 (2017)
31. Rauber, T., ünger, G.R.: Pareto-optimal execution of parallel applications with respect to time and energy. In: Proceedings of the 13th International Conference on Smart Cities and Green ICT Systems - Volume 1: SMARTGREENS, pp. 65–72. INSTICC, SciTePress (2024)
32. Rotem, E., Naveh, A., Ananthakrishnan, A., Rajwan, D., Weissmann, E.: Power-management architecture of the intel microarchitecture code-named sandy bridge. IEEE Micro **32**(2), 20–27 (2012)
33. Sanderse, B., Koren, B.: Accuracy analysis of explicit Runge-kutta methods applied to the incompressible Navier-Stokes equations. J. Comput. Phys. **231**(8), 3041–3063 (2012)
34. Schöne, R., Ilsche, T., Bielert, M., Gocht, A., Hackenberg, D.: Energy efficiency features of the intel Skylake-SP processor and their impact on performance. In: 2019 International Conference on High Performance Computing and Simulation (HPCS), pp. 399–406 (2019)
35. Treibig, J., Hager, G., Wellein, G.: LIKWID: a Lightweight Performance-Oriented Tool Suite for x86 Multicore Environments. In: 39th International Conference on Parallel Processing Workshops, ICPP '10, pp. 207–216. IEEE Comput. Soc. (2010)
36. Zomaya, A.Y., Lee, Y.C.: Energy Efficient Distributed Computing Systems. Wiley-IEEE Computer Society Pr, 1st edition (2012)

Leveraging Architectural Models for the Generation of Smart Grid Co-simulations

Markus Michael Peter(✉), Dominik Vereno, Jounes-Alexander Gross, and Christian Neureiter

Josef Ressel Centre for Dependable System-of-Systems Engineering, Salzburg University of Applied Sciences, Urstein Süd 1, 5412 Puch/Salzburg, Austria
{markusmichael.peter,dominik.vereno,jounes-alexander.gross, christian.neureiter}@fh-salzburg.ac.at

Abstract. Ensuring the reliability of critical infrastructure, such as smart grids, is paramount and must be addressed early in the systems engineering process. One effective method for verifying this reliability is through the simulation of smart grid models. Given the complexity of smart grids, which consist of diverse and interconnected subsystems, co-simulation has emerged as a leading approach. It enables the integration of various independently developed simulators, making it particularly suitable for complex systems. This paper examines the interoperability between architectural models and co-simulation, using a case study implemented as both a simulation and an architectural model to identify similarities and differences. While architectural models offer valuable insights into the high-level structure of System-of-Systems, such as smart grids, our findings indicate that the two tools do not achieve full interoperability for generating a comprehensive simulation directly from architectural models. This limitation arises because co-simulations require detailed, entity-level information, which type-based architectural models typically lack. To address this challenge, we propose using architectural models as a foundation for generating co-simulation code skeletons. This approach bridges the gap between the two tools, providing a practical framework for enhancing their integration. The research highlights the interoperability challenges and presents a feasible strategy for effectively combining architectural models and co-simulation.

Keywords: Model based systems engineering · SGAM · Cyber-physical energy system

1 Introduction

The rapid evolution of power grids has introduced significant challenges, primarily due to the decentralized nature of energy generation and the increasing heterogeneity of energy sources. In response, smart grids have emerged as a solution to overcome the limitations of traditional power grids, offering enhanced flexibility, efficiency, and

F. Calise et al. (Eds.): SMARTGREENS 2024/VEHITS 2024, CCIS 2954, pp. 26–43, 2026.
https://doi.org/10.1007/978-3-032-23187-1_2

resilience in power distribution. Smart grids, however, bring with them their own complexities, requiring sophisticated tools for design, simulation, and validation throughout the engineering process [35]. The decentralized and heterogeneous nature of smart grids makes system-level validation essential. This involves simulating different energy generation and consumption patterns, integrating renewable energy sources, and modeling the expansion of grid infrastructure. Simulation is a key tool in optimizing the performance of smart grid components, enabling decision-makers to explore various scenarios for feasibility, cost-effectiveness, and reliability [32]. However, due to the distributed and independent development of smart grid subsystems, constructing a single, monolithic simulation model becomes a challenging task. Smart grids function as a System of Systems (SoS) [22], with various subsystems developed by different organizations. This fragmented development process presents challenges in integrating the diverse components into a cohesive simulation. Co-simulation has emerged as a powerful approach to tackle this complexity. It enables different subsystems, each modeled and simulated in its native environment, to be interconnected and solved collectively. This method not only supports independent development but also facilitates collaboration across multiple organizations by allowing them to contribute their simulators without deep integration into a centralized system [20]. Despite the advantages of co-simulation, challenges remain, particularly in maintaining an overview of the complex interactions and interconnections between different simulators. As the number of subsystems and their interactions grow, it becomes increasingly difficult to track the dependencies and dynamics between the various components. Architectural models can serve as a solution to this challenge by providing a structured and comprehensive view of the entire system. These models offer an abstract representation of the smart grid's components and their relationships, acting as a unifying framework for understanding the interactions between subsystems. In the context of co-simulation, architectural models enable stakeholders to visualize how different simulators are integrated, facilitating better collaboration and coordination. Aligning with the European Guide for Power System Testing [35], architectural models are particularly useful in the design phase, where they provide a high-level abstraction of the system's structure. This helps in defining system-level requirements, use cases, and the overall architecture. Co-simulation, on the other hand, is more relevant in the implementation and validation phases, where it can be used to rigorously test the behavior of the smart grid under various conditions. By combining architectural modeling with co-simulation, it becomes possible to create a more robust and adaptable approach to smart grid engineering. This paper builds upon and elaborates the work presented in [23]. It investigates the feasibility of using architectural models to support the generation of co-simulations within the smart grid domain. The objective is to explore how architectural models can enhance system understanding, simplify collaboration, and streamline the development and validation processes. The insights gained are intended to not only advance smart grid simulations but also contribute to the broader field of cyber-physical systems development across various domains. This contribution is structured as follows: Sect. 2 provides an overview of related work in the field. Section 3 outlines the scientific approach used to validate the feasibility of integrating architectural models with co-simulation. Section 4 discusses the implementation of Mosaik for simulating industrial models. Section 4 demonstrates the feasibility of the proposed tool-chain through a use case. Finally, Sects. 5 and 6 summarize the results of the study and presents the concluding insights.

2 Background

This chapter aims to provide a brief introduction to the concepts of architectural models and co-simulation to establish a shared understanding of these crucial concepts for the research. It aims to ensure a common understanding of terminologies.

2.1 Model Based Systems Engineering

A smart grid involves a diverse range of stakeholders, each with unique interests and needs. Addressing these varied requirements necessitates a trans-disciplinary approach. Systems engineering is a key methodology for developing and managing complex technical systems [11], focusing on handling the inherent complexity of modern systems [17]. Given that a smart grid is composed of numerous subsystems, its complexity is inherently high and is further increased by the ongoing integration of innovative technologies such as 5G and artificial intelligence. To manage this complexity, modeling plays a crucial role through the application of two fundamental principles: abstraction and separation of concerns [18]. This approach leads to the integration of models throughout the engineering process, encapsulated by concepts like Model-Based Engineering (MBE) or Model-Driven Engineering (MDE) [17]. Another vital approach is "systems thinking," as articulated by Senge, which emphasizes understanding systems as wholes and recognizing their interrelationships rather than focusing on individual components [28]. The synergy of these concepts forms Model-Based Systems Engineering (MBSE) [17]. MBSE formalizes the use of modeling to support various system engineering activities, including requirements management, design, analysis, verification, and validation. Starting in the conceptual design phase, MBSE integrates system information into design models that serve as primary artifacts throughout the development process. These models are typically expressed using standardized modeling languages, such as the Systems Modeling Language (SysML) [11].

2.2 Architectural Models

In Model-Based Systems Engineering, architectural models are essential as they provide a structured and comprehensive view of system architecture. They serve as a bridge between abstract system requirements and concrete system implementations, ensuring that the overall design preserves conceptual integrity throughout the development process. Architectural models offer acomprehensive framework for understanding the system in its entirety, integrating various perspectives to address the concerns of different stakeholders. These models typically follow the ISO 42010 standard [13], which specifies the requirements for describing system, software, and enterprise architectures. This standard guarantees that different viewpoints are considered in system design, independent of specific technical concepts, modeling languages, or tools. In the context of smart grids, the Smart Grid Architecture Model (SGAM) [29] exemplifies the integration of architectural models within MBSE practices. SGAM provides a systematic approach to developing smart grid systems, aligning with MBSE principles by offering a standardized framework that emphasizes interoperability [6]. Originally designed to address gaps in smart grid standardization [36], SGAM has demonstrated its value in broader systems engineering contexts, showcasing the effective application of architectural models within the MBSE framework. The integration of MBSE with architectural models ensures that complex systems, such as smart grids, are designed with both structural coherence and functional integrity, leading to more reliable and interoperable systems.

2.3 Co-simulation

Loper provides a general definition of simulation as "the execution of a model over time" [15]. However, as noted by Gomez et al., a model itself is not inherently executable; it requires a runtime environment and specific input trajectories to function properly [10]. Co-simulation, as defined by Steinbrink et al., involves the coordinated execution of two or more models that differ in both their representation and their runtime environment [32]. A runtime environment is a software system that facilitates the execution of models or the solving of model equations. In this paper, a single pairing of a model with its runtime environment is referred to as a simulation unit. The core of co-simulation is the integration of multiple simulation units through a software interface [39]. This approach is particularly effective for simulating complex systems, such as system-of-systems scenarios found in smart grids [37]. A co-simulation framework generally comprises four main components: the *Scenario*, the *Orchestrator*, the *Simulator*, and the *Model Instance* [1]. Figure 1 illustrates the structure of a typical co-simulation framework, as well as the specific co-simulation framework Mosaik [33] used in this paper.

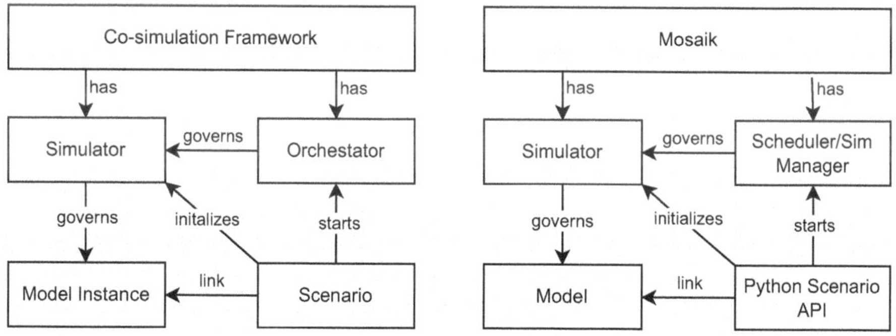

Fig. 1. Co-simulation frameworks structure [23].

Model Instances as represented in Fig. 1 represent various homogeneous physical entities, including models that may belong to different mathematical types, such as finite element methods or behavioral models. Simulators function as solvers, each associated with a specific Model Instance class. They serve as intermediaries between the Orchestrator and the Model Instances, by instantiating their models multiple times and managing the resulting collections. In practice, Simulators receive inputs from other models via the Orchestrator, execute commands on their Model Instance collections, and then send outputs back to the Orchestrator for further processing. The Orchestrator, in turn, oversees the data exchange between Simulators, regulating their timing and ensuring synchronization. Finally, the Scenario represents the simulated environment and encompasses the formal knowledge of the entire cyber-physical system. It manages the configuration provided by the co-simulation framework, including the startup of the Orchestrator, the initialization of the Simulators, and the definition of relationships among Model Instances [1].

2.4 Current State of Architecture-Based Co-simulation Generation

The idea of creating simulations based on architectural models is not a new concept. In the automotive field, Binder et al. proposed an approach to explore Industry 4.0 scenarios by implementing them as architectural models and simulating them [2]. Similar concepts can be found in the smart grid domain, where efforts were made to generate a certain part of a co-simulation out of an architectural model [4]. Another study [3] focused on developing a prototype interface within a modeling tool to customize simulation settings. However, achieving this required an expansion of the domain-specific language (DSL) used for modeling the architecture. The interface additionally facilitated the mapping of specific activity diagrams to co-simulation models. Despite the value in exploring this topic, the current state of the art reveals that none of the papers demonstrated complete interoperability between co-simulations and architectural models. The second approach even necessitated adjustments to the DSL itself, underscoring the need for a comprehensive understanding of the interoperability between architectural models and co-simulation. Which further emphasizes the importance of conducting a comprehensive evaluation of the interoperability between architectural models and co-simulation.

3 Approach

To address the research question formulated in Sect. 1, general insights can be gained through the development of a practical artifact connecting these concepts. For the development of such an artifact it is necessary to know which information a co-simulations requires and what information architectural models can provide. To gather this information a case study of a simple smart grid can be conducted and realized both as an architectural model as well as a co-simulation. By comparing the requirements and considerations for both approaches, valuable insights can be obtained concerning the generation of simulations from architectural models. Therefore in this chapter the used research methodology is explained as well as the case study used, and lastly the tool selection for the implementation is discussed.

3.1 Research Methodology

As research methodology the Design-Science Research Methodology (DSRM) [21] was used, since it places strong emphasis on developing a practical artifact as a central component of the research process. DSRM is characterized by iteration cycles, where each iteration contributes to the refinement of our practical artifact. With this paper being at the end of one iteration. Each iteration cycle unfolds through six iterative steps, [40] which can be mapped to different paragraphs of this paper as it can be seen in Fig. 2.

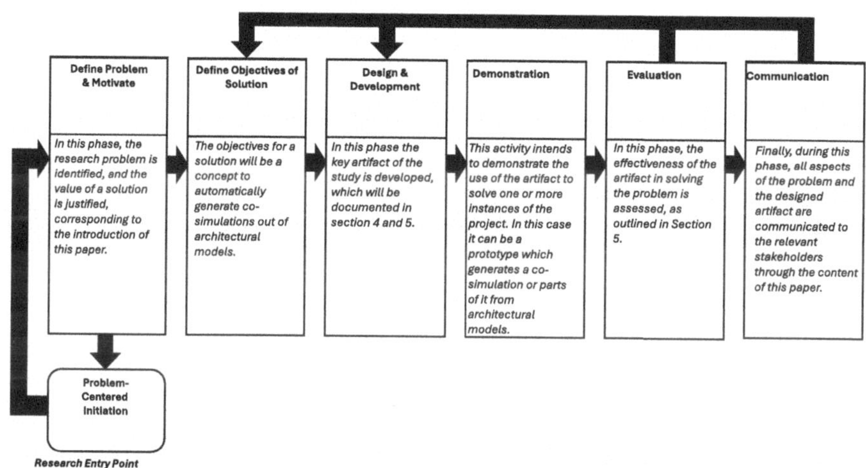

Fig. 2. Applied Design-Science Research Methodology based on [7, p. 172].

3.2 Case Study

To develop a simple case study of a smart grid, it is essential to establish a clear definition of what constitutes a smart grid. While different definitions exist, this work follows the definitions provided by [9] and [30] essentially defining a smart grid as an energy network combined with the bidirectional delivery of energy information to enable a more controllable energy delivery and transmission. Concluding this definition a most basic case study can be divided into the components of an electric grid one or more components using that grid and an component responsible for managing a bidirectional flow of data. One such case study could be the charging behaviour of an electric vehicle in combination with the energy generation of a wind turbine Where a Smart Meter connects these components in a partly bidirectional manner. The scenario entails the charging station purchasing energy from the wind turbine with lower cost than it obtains from the energy market. The basic structure of such can be seen in the Fig. 3.

Additionally the following specifications applied to this case study:

- The EV loading is based on a price threshold where the EV only loads below this specific threshold. This constraint is implemented in the charging station simulator. The threshold can be variable and handed over on initialisation.

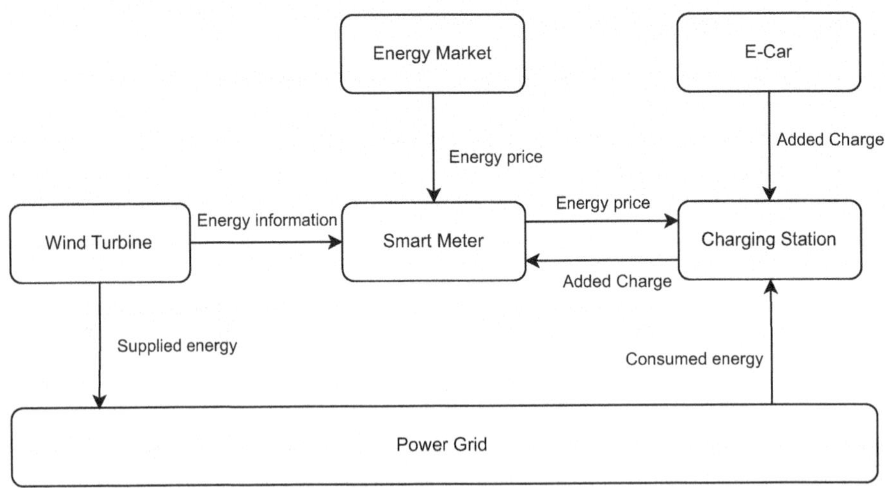

Fig. 3. Co-Simulation information flow [23].

- The power output of the wind turbine is calculated with the following formula:

$$P = \pi/2 * r^2 * v^3 * \varphi * n \tag{1}$$

[25]. With r being the rotor radius, v being the wind speed, φ being the wind density and n being the efficiency.
- The air density is assumed to be standard air density with 1,225 kg/m^3
- The wind turbine is assumed to have a rotor radius of five meter
- The EV's can charge freely for the energy generated by the wind turbine, anything above that consumption has to be bought from a market module with 0.32 cent per kWh

3.3 Tool Selection

To realize the case study and develop the artifact, two key tools will be utilized. First, for the creation of architectural models, the SGAM Toolbox [19] will be employed. This modeling tool is grounded in the concept of Model-Based Systems Engineering and closely aligns with the Smart Grid Architecture Model, a standardized architecture model for the smart grid domain. The SGAM Toolbox offers a robust foundation for creating architectural models tailored to the specific needs of this research. As for simulation, there are various different tools for simulating in the smart grid. The choice of a fitting tool was partly based on "A survey and statistical analysis of smart grid co-simulations" by Vogt et al. [39] reviewing 26 different smart grid simulation frameworks and their applications. Other factors where the availability in terms of being open source as well as the accessibility of an application programming interface. Considering this the choice fell on mosaik, a co-simulation framework specifically designed for smart grid research with a focus on the flexible creation of large-scale system configurations [34]. These attributes make it an ideal choice for integrating diverse simulation models within a unified co-simulation environment.

4 Implementation

In this chapter the realisation of the case study as architectural model in the SGAM Toolbox as well as a mosaik co-simulation will be done.

4.1 Realisation as Architectural Model

The SGAM Toolbox, in alignment with the SGAM framework, utilizes a range of models to create well-defined views across different abstraction levels. These viewpoints are crafted to address the diverse concerns of various stakeholders. This approach mirrors the SGAM cube, where each layer represents a fundamental viewpoint covering aspects such as business, functional, informational, communication, and physical domains. Each viewpoint is organized into a grid structure, with domains along the x-axis representing the electric conversion chain and the y-axis showcasing a hierarchical perspective of information management, as illustrated in Fig. 4.

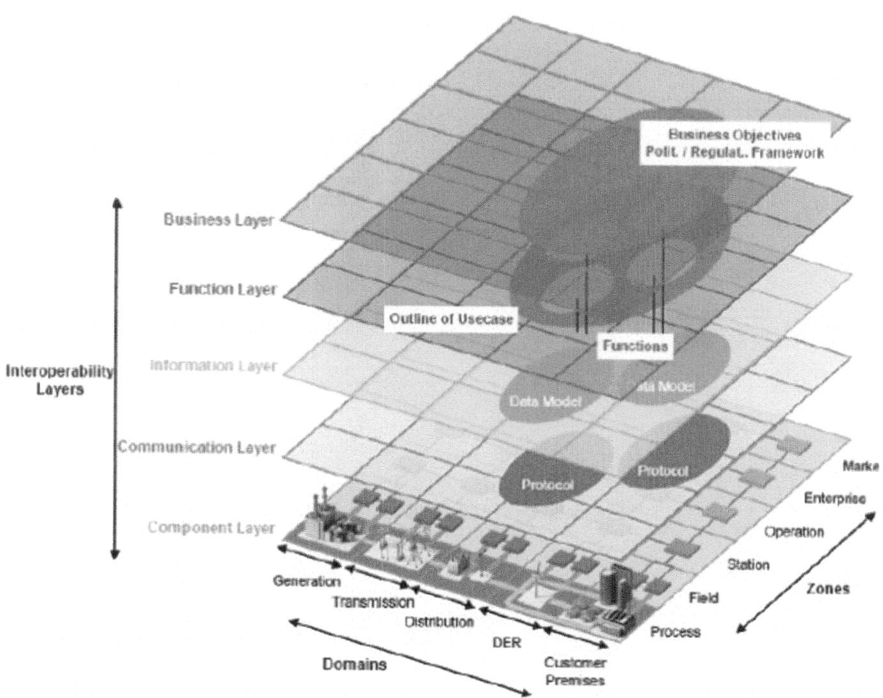

Fig. 4. SGAM Framework [6, p. 30].

The modeling within each layer is conducted using a domain-specific language (DSL) based on UML profiles, as implemented by the toolbox. UML serves as a visual modeling language for the architecture, design, and implementation of complex systems, while the DSL is tailored to address domain-specific considerations and to establish a common foundation for all stakeholders [17].

The implementation of the SGAM layers can be conceptually divided into two main phases: system analysis and system architecture.

1. *System Analysis Phase*: This phase provides a detailed description of the system's external perspective, encompassing the Business and Function layers. The Business Layer identifies all business actors and their respective goals, while the Function Layer outlines functions and their interrelationships.
2. *System Architecture Phase*: This phase covers the Information, Communication, and Component layers. The Information Layer focuses on facilitating information exchange, the Communication Layer defines communication protocols, and the Component Layer describes the ICT networks used for communication. Figure 5 illustrates the SGAM Information Layer, using SGAM-specific components to demonstrate the flow of information among the components in the case study.

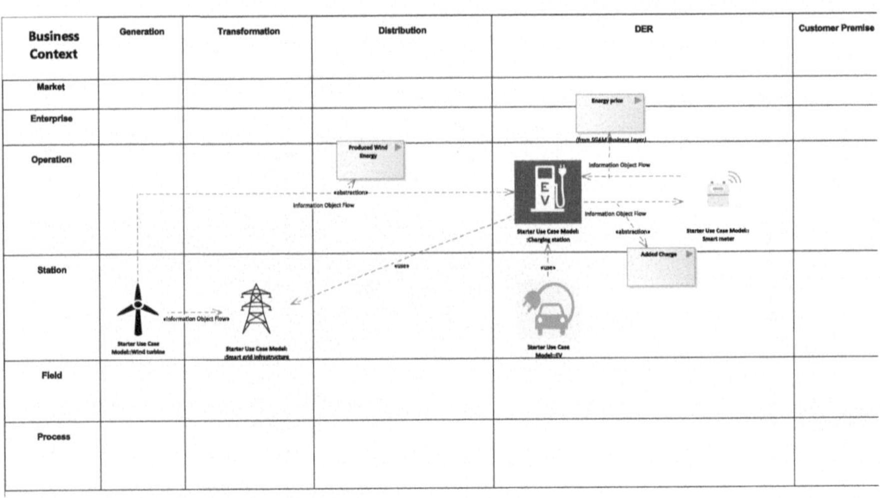

Fig. 5. SGAM Information Layer [23].

4.2 Realisation as Co-simulation

Implementing a co-simulation within the mosaik framework involves several key steps, as depicted in Fig. 1. The process begins by defining simulation units, each comprising a simulator and a model. Additionally, a Scenario must be outlined, which includes the instantiation of simulators and the specification of interconnections among model instances. For the power grid simulation, the pre-existing simulator PyPower [26] is utilized to model the power grid's structure and characteristics. The mosaik framework orchestrates the co-simulation, integrating and coordinating the various simulators. In summary, the implementation of the case study described in Sect. 3 within the mosaik framework involves developing the following components:

- A scenario file
- A simulator and a model respectively for the following components
  1. Electric Vehicle
  2. Charging station
  3. Smart meter
  4. Wind turbine

These components are developed using the API provided by mosaik, which allows developers to override inherited methods from mosaik's simulator, model, and scenario classes. For example, Listing 1.1 demonstrates the overridden step method for the ElectricVehicle class. This method defines the process for a single step of the model instance, where the electric vehicle model determines whether it can accept the provided charge based on its capacity and current charge level.

```
def step(self, loading_factor):
    if self.is_full():
        self.added_charge = 0
    else:
        self.added_charge = self.max_power * loading_factor
        self.current_charge = min(self.capacity, self.
            current_charge + self.added_charge)

def is_full(self):
    return self.current_charge >= self.capacity
```

Listing 1.1. Step method of the electric vehicle class [23].

A key aspect of using mosaik is leveraging existing simulators to enhance the usability of the co-simulation. This concept is known as the mosaik ecosystem. Examples of simulators within this ecosystem include ISAAC, an energy unit aggregation and planning software [33]; Odysseus, a framework for in-memory data stream management [33]; and PyPower, a power flow solver. PyPower, a Python port of MATPOWER—a collection of MATLAB files for solving steady-state power system simulation and optimization problems—uses a bus-branch model to represent power grids. The structure consists of buses (nodes) connected by branches (transmission lines), with transformers represented as a special type of branch. In this case study, PyPower is used alongside the IEEE-13 Test Feeder data to simulate the power grid. The IEEE-13 Test Feeder, published in 1992, provides a common dataset for validating different simulation tools. It includes many features of actual networks, such as overhead and underground lines and unbalanced loads. Specifically designed to test power flow convergence problems in highly unbalanced systems, the IEEE-13 Test Feeder is a 4.16 kV feeder with one substation voltage regulator comprising three single-phase units connected in wye [27]. The results of the co-simulation provide insights into the dynamics of a smart grid with bidirectional data flow. A key component in this scenario is the smart meter, which calculates an energy price based on the energy consumed by electric vehicles (EVs) and the wind power generated by the wind turbine. This calculated price, in turn, influences the amount of energy charged through the price threshold constraint on the charging stations. This bidirectional relationship can be observed by comparing the overall charging cost with the wind power generation and the total energy charged by all EVs combined. For instance, as shown in Fig. 6, a charging cost above the threshold of five euros resulted in a significant drop in the total amount of energy charged. This drop highlights how price sensitivity can impact charging behavior. Additionally, every peak in energy consumption is followed by a low point, suggesting the influence of other factors, such as wind power availability. Figure 7 illustrates that the generated wind power does not always correlate with charging costs, indicating that other attributes, such as charging station settings or grid conditions, may play a role.

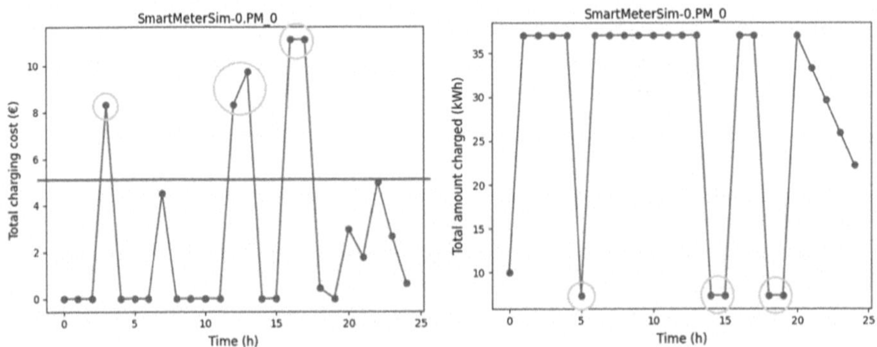

Fig. 6. Comparison of the generated energy generated with the total charging cost [23].

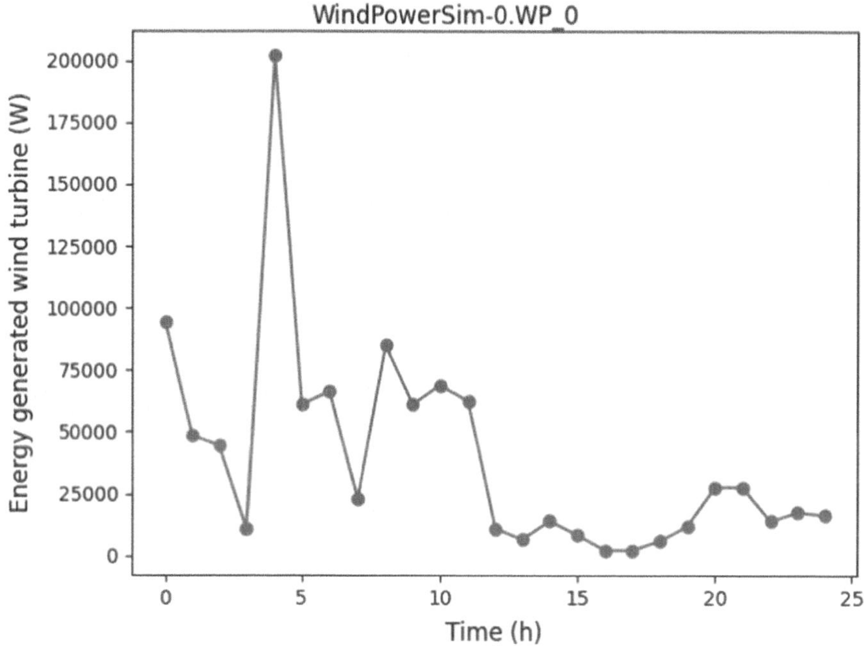

Fig. 7. Comparison of the generated energy generated with the total charging cost [23].

Moreover, the simulation revealed that low energy costs occur when EVs charge at only 20% capacity due to insufficient wind energy. This behavior underscores the importance of integrating renewable energy sources and optimizing charging strategies to maintain grid stability while accommodating fluctuating energy supplies.

4.3 Simulation Integration

Based on the implementation of the case study a differentiation between fixed syntactic and semantic parts and necessary information to implement different simulations can be made. A listing of the necessary information needed can be seen in Table 1.

Table 1. Necessary information needed for a mosaik co-simulation [23].

Mosaik component	Necessary information
Simulator	Time behavior Amount of instances Parameter Attributes Power Grid topology Voltage and cable information
Scenario	Simulation runtime Initial values
Model	Model behavior

The information modeled in the SGAM Toolbox can be extracted using the add-in functionality provided by Enterprise Architect [31]. Each element modeled in the toolbox is assigned a specific stereotype for identification, allowing its attributes and connections to be saved for further use. The integration of architectural model information into the mosaik simulation follows the approach proposed by Binder et al. [3], which involves using templates. However, in this iteration, only a code skeleton was generated. This decision was influenced by the limitation of the integrated solution for depicting model behavior, which relied on activity diagrams. These diagrams were considered unsuitable, as explained in more detail in the Evaluation section.

5 Evaluation and Discussion

This chapter examines the challenges encountered during implementation and discusses the suitability of architectural models for generating co-simulations.

5.1 Evaluation

As we proceeded through the necessary steps for generating co-simulations from smart grid architecture models, we encountered two main challenges.

1. The first challenge revolves around the modeling of specific behaviors within the architectural framework. While certain approaches tailored to modeling tools, such as using activity diagrams, may suffice for simpler examples, it's evident that this method isn't universally applicable for all behaviors. Additionally, different simulated entities are often modeled using a variety of tools. For instance, while automotive-specific modeling tools are most effective for modeling charging behavior, they may fall short in adequately capturing wind generation behavior. This needed diversity in modeling tools becomes more complex when considering various stakeholders, each potentially using different tools for their specialized functionality. Addressing this challenge could involve implementing simulators in a standardized format. One such example is the Functional Mockup Interface [5], supported by a plethora of tools. This standardization could facilitate seamless integration of diverse simulators, aligning with the overarching goal of uniting independently developed simulators within a single simulation framework.
2. The second challenge lies in reconciling the differing perspectives between architectural models and co-simulations. Architectural models provide a holistic view of a system through type-based models. In contrast, co-simulations necessitate detailed specification of each specific instances of the type based models and their interconnections within given scenarios. However, such specific instance information is frequently absent within architectural models.

While there may be targeted solutions to augment specific tools used for modeling architectural models, such as incorporating an additional instance viewpoint, the ultimate goal is not a one-size-fits-all tool solution. Instead, the emphasis is on leveraging architectural models as a means to integrate independently developed simulators into a broader context. Remarkably, tools like Powerworld [24], employed for power system simulations, possess the capability to export network topology data in auxiliary file formats. Therefore, akin to the aforementioned challenge, a potential solution could involve importing the missing information to bridge the interoperability gap.

Overall after taking a closer look at the interoperability between the architectural models and co-simulation has been taken, the conclusion can be drawn that a full interoperability and thus a complete simulation generation from architectural models as proposed by Binder et al. [3] is not deemed to be useful. Architectural models provide a holistic view on the general function of a smart grid in different layers and for different stakeholders. While co-simulations wants to simulate specific use cases of a smart grid and therefore needs specific information about the entity relation of the smart grid components. Therefore instead of forcing an interoperability of concepts with different purposes a combination of both strengths is proposed. Architectural models with their general view on a smart grid can offer a starting point from which simulations of different scenarios could be started. The idea is to generate skeleton co-simulation projects out of architectural models. By utilizing FMU's and integrating them in the models the skeleton code can provide anything but interconnections between the simulation units. The structure of such an approach can be seen in Fig. 8.

5.2 Architectural Models for Simulating System of Systems

While the challenges outlined in the evaluation section suggest that architectural models may not be inherently ideal for generating co-simulations, there are notable advantages to using architectural models, especially when describing Smart Grids. More broadly, from a System of Systems perspective, architectural models are particularly effective in illustrating the interdependencies between heterogeneous systems. Architectural modeling plays a crucial role in effective SoS engineering, By offering a comprehensive view of the entire SoS and its constituent systems, an architectural perspective helps in understanding the complex relationships and interactions within the system [8, 16]. Moreover, extensive research across various domains has focused on exploring architectural modeling of Systems of Systems, further highlighting their relevance and applicability in complex, interconnected environments [12, 14]. Based on our case study, we can infer certain assumptions about the general suitability of architectural models for co-simulations. SoS typically involves multiple independent systems that interact to achieve a higher-level objective. Architectural models effectively capture the relationships and dependencies between these systems, making them a solid foundation for co-simulation. In such a setup, each system can be simulated within its own domain and then integrated into a comprehensive simulation. One of the strengths of architectural models is their ability to provide different levels of abstraction. High-level architectural models can guide the overall structure and coordination of the simulation, while more detailed models can describe specific behaviors of individual systems. Moreover, architectural models can help identify critical interaction points, bottlenecks, or potential failure points within the SoS, which are important areas to focus on during co-simulation. By leveraging architectural models, co-simulations can be used to validate the overall SoS design and ensure that system interactions occur as intended. However, architectural models may have limitations. They often focus on structural aspects and

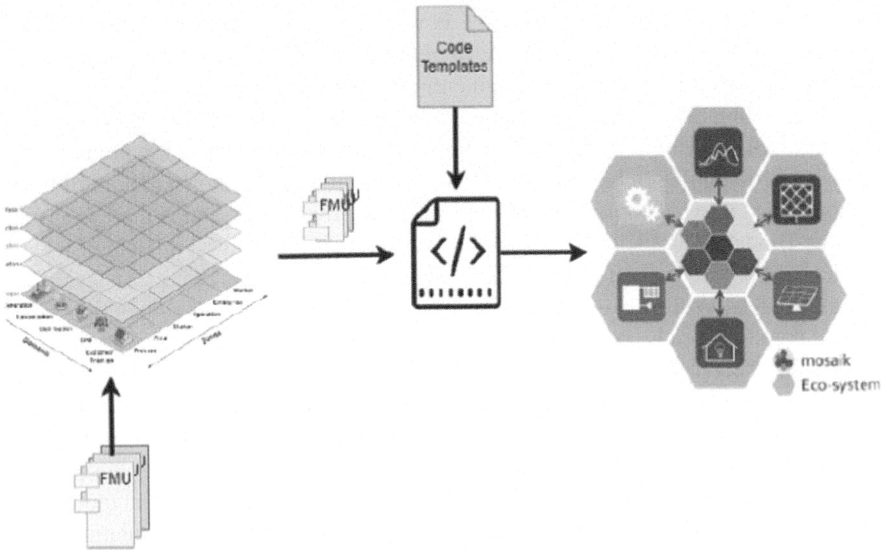

Fig. 8. Proposed artifact [23].

interaction protocols, but may lack the detailed dynamic behavior models necessary for realistic simulations. Additionally, architectural models might be developed using tools or frameworks that are not directly compatible with simulation tools, making integration into a co-simulation environment challenging. Architectural models also tend to be more static, focusing on structure and relationships rather than the dynamic behaviors of systems over time. Co-simulations, on the other hand, often need to capture dynamic interactions in real-time or near real-time, which might not be fully represented in the architectural model. In conclusion, architectural models of SoS can be a valuable foundation for developing co-simulations, particularly due to their ability to represent complex interactions and provide various levels of abstraction. However, they may require additional refinement or the integration of more detailed behavior models to ensure that the co-simulation accurately reflects the dynamic aspects of the systems involved. The ultimate suitability of architectural models for co-simulation depends on the specific goals of the simulation, the level of detail in the architectural model, and the compatibility with simulation tools.

6 Conclusion

In this paper, we explored the potential of architectural models as a foundation for generating co-simulations within the Smart Grid domain. Through a case study, we assessed the interoperability between architectural modeling and co-simulation. This involved both designing and implementing an architectural model and a corresponding co-simulation, while also developing a tool to generate co-simulation code skeletons from these models. However, our research identified two significant challenges that hinder the seamless generation of co-simulations. First, there is a lack of integration between tools, requiring different model behaviors to be specified in separate environments. Second, the architectural models, being more abstract, do not inherently contain the instance-level detail necessary for simulation. While these issues pose obstacles, they do not diminish the potential of architectural models in co-simulation. Despite the challenges highlighted in our evaluation, architectural models provide notable advantages, particularly in representing complex systems like Smart Grids. From a System of Systems perspective, architectural models are especially effective in illustrating interdependencies between heterogeneous systems. They offer a comprehensive view of the entire SoS, which aids in understanding the relationships and interactions within the system. Based on our case study, we observe that architectural models can be a strong foundation for co-simulations in SoS, as they capture system relationships and dependencies. High-level models offer guidance for the overall simulation structure, while detailed models describe specific system behaviors. Architectural models also help in identifying interaction points and potential failure areas within the SoS, which are critical for validating the system design through co-simulation. Nevertheless, there are limitations. Architectural models often focus on structural aspects and interaction protocols, lacking the dynamic behavior models required for realistic simulations. They also tend to be more static, making it challenging to capture the real-time dynamics that co-simulations often require. Additionally, the lack of compatibility between architectural and simulation tools further complicates integration.

In conclusion, architectural models hold significant promise as a foundation for co-simulations, particularly for systems with complex interactions like Smart Grids. However, to fully realize this potential, additional refinements—such as incorporating detailed behavior models and ensuring tool compatibility—are necessary. Functional Mockup Units provide a promising approach for abstracting model behaviors, and efforts like the taxonomy proposed by Vereno [38] offer solutions for entity-level modeling. By addressing these challenges, we can unlock the full potential of architectural models in enhancing the understanding, analysis, and development of complex systems, not just in Smart Grids, but across various domains.

References

1. Barbierato, L., Rando Mazzarino, P., Montarolo, M., Macii, A., Patti, E., Bottaccioli, L.: A comparison study of co-simulation frameworks for multi-energy systems: the scalability problem. Energy Inform. **5**(4), 1–26 (2022)
2. Binder, C., Agic, A., Neureiter, C., Lüder, A.: Applying model-based co-simulation on modular production units in complex automation systems. In: 2021 IEEE International Symposium on Systems Engineering (ISSE), pp. 1–6. IEEE (2021)
3. Binder, C., Fischinger, M., Altenhuber, L., Draxler, D., Lastro, G., Neureiter, C.: Enabling architecture based co-simulation of complex smart grid applications. Energy Inform. **2**(1), 1–19 (2019)
4. Binder, C., Fischinger, M., Neureiter, C., Lastro, G., Polanec, K., Gross, J.A.: Towards a tool-based approach for dynamically generating co-simulation scenarios based on complex smart grid system architectures. In: 2020 IEEE 15th International Conference of System of Systems Engineering (SoSE), pp. 199–204. IEEE (2020)

5. Blochwitz, T., et al.: The functional mockup interface for tool independent exchange of simulation models. In: Proceedings of the 8th International Modelica Conference, pp. 105–114. Linköping University Press (2011)
6. Bruinenberg, J., et al.: CEN-CENELEC-ETSI smart grid coordination group smart grid reference architecture. CEN, CENELEC, ETSI, Technical Report **23**, 24 (2012)
7. Conboy, K., Gleasure, R., Cullina, E.: Agile design science research. In: New Horizons in Design Science: Broadening the Research Agenda: 10th International Conference, DESRIST 2015, Dublin, Ireland, 20–22 May 2015, Proceedings 10, pp. 168–180. Springer (2015)
8. Dahmann, J., Baldwin, K.: Implications of systems of systems on system design and engineering. In: 2011 6th International Conference on System of Systems Engineering, pp. 131–136. IEEE (2011)
9. Falk, R., Fries, S.: Electric vehicle charging infrastructure security considerations and approaches. In: Proceedings of INTERNET, pp. 58–64 (2012)
10. Gomes, C., Thule, C., Broman, D., Larsen, P.G., Vangheluwe, H.: Co-simulation: state of the art. arXiv preprint arXiv:1702.00686 (2017)
11. Incose, T.: Systems engineering vision 2020. INCOSE, San Diego, CA, 2 (2007). Accessed 26 Jan 2019
12. Ingram, C., Payne, R., Fitzgerald, J.: Architectural modelling patterns for systems of systems. In: INCOSE International Symposium, vol. 25, pp. 1177–1192. Wiley Online Library (2015)
13. ISO: Software, systems and enterprise — Architecture description. Standard, International Organization for Standardization, Geneva, CH (2022)
14. Klein, J., Van Vliet, H.: A systematic review of system-of-systems architecture research. In: Proceedings of the 9th International ACM Sigsoft Conference on Quality of Software Architectures, pp. 13–22 (2013)
15. Loper, M.L.: Modeling and simulation in the systems engineering life cycle: core concepts and accompanying lectures. Springer (2015)
16. Maier, M.W.: Architecting principles for systems-of-systems. Syst. Eng. J. Int. Council Syst. Eng. **1**(4), 267–284 (1998)
17. Neureiter, C.: A domain-specific, model driven engineering approach for systems engineering in the smart grid. MBSE4U (2017)
18. Neureiter, C., Binder, C., Lastro, G.: Review on domain specific systems engineering. In: 2020 IEEE International Symposium on Systems Engineering (ISSE), pp. 1–8. IEEE (2020)
19. Neureiter, C., Uslar, M., Engel, D., Lastro, G.: A standards-based approach for domain specific modelling of smart grid system architectures. In: 2016 11th System of Systems Engineering Conference (SoSE), pp. 1–6. IEEE (2016)
20. Palensky, P., Van Der Meer, A.A., Lopez, C.D., Joseph, A., Pan, K.: Cosimulation of intelligent power systems: fundamentals, software architecture, numerics, and coupling. IEEE Ind. Electron. Mag. **11**(1), 34–50 (2017). https://doi.org/10.1109/MIE.2016.2639825
21. Peffers, K., Tuunanen, T., Rothenberger, M.A., Chatterjee, S.: A design science research methodology for information systems research. J. Manag. Inf. Syst. **24**(3), 45–77 (2007)
22. Pérez, J., Díaz, J., Garbajosa, J., Yagüe, A., Gonzalez, E., Lopez-Perea, M.: Large-scale smart grids as system of systems. In: Proceedings of the First International Workshop on Software Engineering for Systems-of-Systems, pp. 38–42 (2013)
23. Peter, M., Vereno, D., Gross, J.A., Neureiter, C.: Assessing the suitability of architectural models for generating smart grid co-simulations. In: Proceedings of the 13th International Conference on Smart Cities and Green ICT Systems - Volume 1: SMARTGREENS, pp. 38–45. INSTICC, SciTePress (2024). https://doi.org/10.5220/0012739800003714
24. PowerWorld: Powerworld (2024). https://www.powerworld.com/
25. Sarkar, A., Behera, D.K.: Wind turbine blade efficiency and power calculation with electrical analogy. Int. J. Sci. Res. Publ. **2**(2), 1–5 (2012)

26. Scherfke: mosaik-pypower: A mosaik extension for simulating power systems with pypower (2022). https://pypi.org/project/mosaik-pypower/. Accessed 10 Dec 2023
27. Schneider, K.P., et al.: Analytic considerations and design basis for the IEEE distribution test feeders. IEEE Trans. Power Syst. **33**(3), 3181–3188 (2017)
28. Senge, P.M.: The fifth discipline fieldbook: strategies and tools for building a learning organization. Crown Currency (2014)
29. Smart Grid Coordination Group: CEN-CENELEC-ETSI Smart Grid Coordination Group Smart Grid Reference Architecture (2012)
30. SmartGrids, E.: Vision and strategy for Europe's electricity networks of the future. European Commission (2006)
31. SparxSystems: Enterprise architect 15 im Überblick (2019). https://www.sparxsystems.de/fileadmin/user_upload/pdfs/EAReviewersGuide_EA-15-DE.pdf
32. Steinbrink, C., et al.: Simulation-based validation of smart grids - status quo and future research trends. In: Mařík, V., Wahlster, W., Strasser, T., Kadera, P. (eds.) Industrial Applications of Holonic and Multi-Agent Systems, pp. 171–185. Springer, Cham (2017)
33. Steinbrink, C., et al.: CPES testing with mosaik: co-simulation planning, execution and analysis. Appl. Sci. **9**(5) (2019). https://doi.org/10.3390/app9050923. https://mosaik.offis.de/. https://www.mdpi.com/2076-3417/9/5/923
34. Steinbrink, C., et al.: Smart grid co-simulation with MOSAIK and HLA: a comparison study. Comput. Sci. Res. Dev. **33**(1), 135–143 (2018)
35. Strasser, T.I., de Jong, E.C., Sosnina, M.: European guide to power system testing: the ERIGrid holistic approach for evaluating complex smart grid configurations. Springer Nature (2020)
36. Uslar, M., et al.: Applying the smart grid architecture model for designing and validating system-of-systems in the power and energy domain: a European perspective. Energies **12**(2), 258 (2019)
37. Vereno, D., Harb, J., Neureiter, C.: Paving the way for reinforcement learning in smart grid co-simulations. In: International Conference on Software Engineering and Formal Methods, pp. 242–257. Springer (2023)
38. Vereno, D., Polanec, K., Gross, J.A., Binder, C., Neureiter, C.: Introducing a three-layer model taxonomy to facilitate system-of-systems co-simulation. In: 34th Annual INCOSE International Symposium (2024)
39. Vogt, M., Marten, F., Braun, M.: A survey and statistical analysis of smart grid co-simulations. Appl. Energy **222C** (2018). https://doi.org/10.1016/j.apenergy.2018.03.123
40. Vom Brocke, J., Hevner, A., Maedche, A.: Introduction to design science research. Design Science Research. Cases, pp. 1–13 (2020)

FAITH: A Framework for Personalized Trust Management in Smart Cities

Nazek Fakhoury, Jessica Ohnesorg(✉), Noura Eltahawi, and Mouzhi Ge

Deggendorf Institute of Technology, Max-Breiherr-Street 32, Pfarrkirchen, Germany
{jessica.ohnesorg,mouzhi.ge}@th-deg.de

Abstract. As it is challenging to adapt trust management to accommodate different individual preferences due to the growing adoption of artificial intelligence (AI) in smart cities, this paper conducts a review of the internal and external factors that influence trust, such as personal values, personality traits, and cultural background. The paper focuses on the critical role of communication in human-machine interactions, particularly in the context of AI technologies. To strengthen trust in smart city systems, we propose a Framework for AI Trust enHancement (FAITH) to integrate personalized communication strategies with individual preferences. The proposed FAITH framework is validated through two case studies in healthcare and the results derived from case studies not only deepen the understanding of trust management systems in smart cities but also provide insights for how to cater different preferences in trust management systems.

Keywords: Trust · Individual preferences · Communication · Artificial Intelligence · Smart cities

1 Introduction

In modern urban environments, smart cities are using cutting-edge technologies to transform urban life. As these cities embrace digital transformation, they develop into intricate ecosystems, requiring a refined strategy for data governance and smooth integration of technologies [9]. One of the challenges in this area is the variation in individual preferences [19]. Each user brings unique perspectives and personalities, making it difficult to design a one-size-fits-all trust management system [2]. The concept of trust is interpreted differently by each person, further complicating the creation of a system that meets everyone's needs. This highlights the necessity for a flexible approach to trust management that takes into account the diverse human factors affecting trust perceptions. Crafting a system that aligns with the individual preferences of a varied population is a significant challenge in achieving effective trust management in smart cities [18].

The objective of this paper is to address the research question *How can trust management systems be tailored to accommodate diverse individual preferences in the evolving landscape of artificial intelligence adoption?*. We introduce a framework designed to capture individual preferences, emphasizing the importance of effective

F. Calise et al. (Eds.): SMARTGREENS 2024/VEHITS 2024, CCIS 2954, pp. 44–57, 2026.
https://doi.org/10.1007/978-3-032-23187-1_3

communication. This framework provides a practical approach to developing trustful applications in smart cities.

The remainder of the paper is structured as follows: Sect. 2 describes the related works and provides an overview of previous research on internal and external factors, offering insights into individual preferences regarding AI adoption. Section 3 proposes the framework, which is evaluated and discussed in Sect. 4 by two case studies in healthcare domain. Finally, Sect. 5 summarizes the research findings and suggests directions for future research.

2 Related Works

Given the difficulty in accurately capturing individual preferences, creating a dependable environment is crucial for sustaining trust among people in smart cities. However, this effort faces two significant challenges: First, while intelligent systems require trust in certain situations, the lack of human involvement raises concerns in real-world contexts, where people often prefer human interaction over smart systems. Second, there is the potential resistance from some users to adopting the proposed trust mechanism, highlighting that a one-size-fits-all approach to trust may not accommodate the varied preferences and viewpoints of individuals in smart cities [18].

[6] highlighted this concept in his Technology Acceptance Model, which evaluates the factors that influence technology adoption based on two key aspects: perceived usefulness and ease of use. A potential challenge of non-adoption arises when individuals perceive the technology as either not fulfilling their needs or being too difficult to use.

As illustrated in Fig. 1, trust levels in AI adoption are shaped by both internal and external factors, which also affect the future adoption of AI in smart cities. This section examines how specific factors influence trust. Personal values play a crucial role in the adoption of systems and services; users are more likely to embrace systems that resonate with their values. For instance, environmental concerns and time efficiency have been found to influence the adoption of e-governance services, with users who prioritize paper conservation and appreciate the convenience of accessing services without physical visits being more inclined to use these services [3].

Personality traits are another factor that can influence trust. Recent research indicates that individual differences in personality traits result in varying trust levels. The Big Five personality model, which categorizes personality into five dimensions – Extroversion, Agreeableness, Conscientiousness, Neuroticism, and Openness–is often used to analyze these differences. Some studies suggest that agreeableness and neuroticism have the most significant effects on trust. For instance, [24] found that individuals with high levels of agreeableness or conscientiousness tend to exhibit greater trust in automation. Additionally, [4] concluded that higher levels of extroversion and agreeableness are associated with greater trust, whereas openness tends to have a negative relationship with trust.

Moreover, personal experience plays a crucial role in shaping trust, with each success by the trusted party leading to increased trust, while each failure diminishes it. However, according to causal attribution theory, failure doesn't necessarily lead to a crisis of trust; the way the cause of failure is interpreted is key in this context. The same

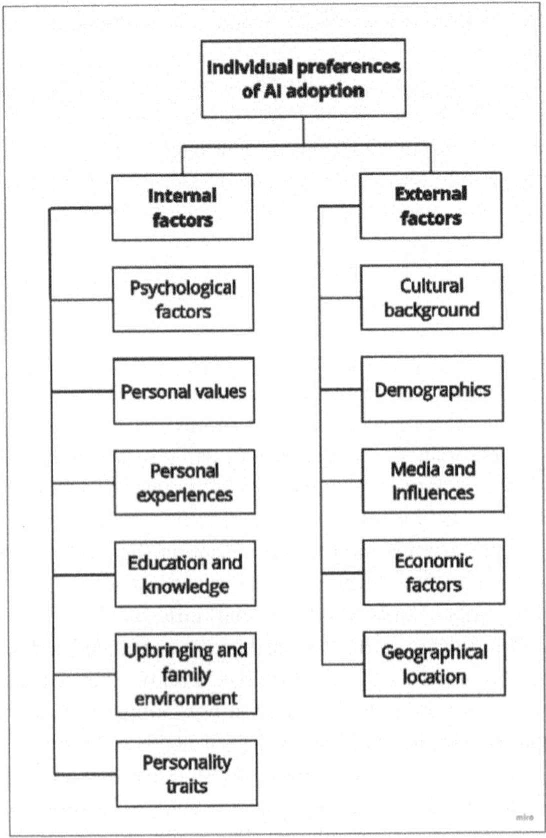

Fig. 1. A set of individual preference factors [17].

principle applies to success, where the perception of success can greatly strengthen trust levels [8].

Upbringing and family environment are thought to influence trust, with individuals from less urbanized areas potentially developing a protective mechanism that leads to a rapid increase in trust after positive social interactions [16]. Other research indicates that people raised in families where older generations exert dominance over younger ones tend to exhibit lower levels of trust. In contrast, households with more horizontal, egalitarian structures are generally more conducive to fostering trust [13].

Psychological factors are also crucial in shaping trust. Some research suggests that a natural tendency to trust may have genetic roots, with common genes exerting a greater influence than shared environmental upbringing. Trust from a psychological perspective can be categorized into two types: person-based trust (focused on the trustee as an individual) and depersonalized trust (viewing the trustee as a member of a group). Studies indicate that depersonalized trust significantly impacts overall trust levels, as individuals are more likely to trust someone they perceive as socially familiar or part of the same social group. This form of trust reflects an agreement among in-group members [7]. Another important internal factor is education and knowledge. Evidence suggests that individuals in countries with strong governments and higher levels of education tend to be more trusting, whereas those in less effective states show a negative correlation between education level and trust [10].

Regarding external factors, cultural background plays a significant role in shaping trust. According to literature based on Hofstede's six cultural dimensions–power distance (PDI), individualism (IDV), masculinity (MAS), uncertainty avoidance (UAI), long-term orientation (LTO), and indulgence (IND) – individuals from cultures with high levels of individualism and long-term orientation are more inclined to trust others. Conversely, those from cultures with high power distance and uncertainty avoidance are less likely to trust [23]. Another external factor is demographics. Research suggests that females tend to have lower levels of trust in automation compared to males. Additionally, as the workload required by the user increases, the likelihood of trusting an autonomous agent decreases. Moreover, users tend to place greater trust in agents that are perceived as more reliable [11].

Media and its influence represent another key external factor. Research has shown that information disseminated through both social and traditional media significantly impacts trust [15]. Additionally, geographical location plays a role in trust levels. Studies have found that higher absolute geographical latitude is associated with lower exposure to diseases, reduced linguistic and ethnic diversity, and decreased income inequality, all of which contribute to higher levels of trust [14].

Additionally, a crucial external factor is economic conditions. Previous research indicates that economic wealth influences institutional trust primarily among rural, less educated, and economically disadvantaged individuals, who tend to have higher levels of trust in institutions. Conversely, in environments characterized by significant diversity, advanced education, and greater wealth, personal wealth does not necessarily correlate with increased trust in government and institutional systems [20].

According to [1] in health care exist several crucial factors, which influence trust in AI. Based on the focus of this study, the following strategic improvement related to transparency has been extracted from the initial overview and brought together with the three main factors such as complex algorithm, lack of subject knowledge and role of artificial intelligence. In terms of complex algorithm it can be difficult for users to understand how decisions are made, which potentially reduces trust. Moreover, users without sufficient knowledge of AI or the subject matter may find it hard to trust AI systems. Thirdly, the perceived role of AI e.g., as a decision-maker versus an assistant can impact trust levels. Considering those three elements and improving the level of trust can be achieved by increasing transparency in AI for health care applications.

Furthermore, the same study identified two other factors that influence behavior in AI. These additional factors are data sensitivity and cognitive bias. In addition, the properties of machine learning algorithms carry the risk of amplifying existing biases in the data, which can lead to unfair treatment of people from protected groups defined by sensitive characteristics such as gender, ethnicity or sexual orientation. Bias, which arises from a discrepancy between the training data distribution and an ideal fair distribution, can lead to unequal outcomes in prediction or classification tasks. To ensure fairness in AI systems, it is essential to identify and mitigate biases arising from clinicians' subjective judgments during the processes of validation and verification. This study therefore argues for the concept of optimal trust, where both the human and the AI maintain a certain degree of skepticism about each other's decisions, recognizing that both can make mistakes. The level of skepticism required for the most accurate clinical outcomes depends on the capabilities of both the human user and the AI system. As a result, AI development must include mechanisms that promote and sustain a well-calibrated, balanced level of trust between the user and the system that is aligned with the capabilities of AI [1].

3 FAITH Framework

After reviewing both external and internal individual preference factors, it's time to leverage them effectively. The framework discussed in the following sections focuses on aligning communication strategies with individual preferences to create clear communication practices. These practices help individuals understand how systems work, thereby enhancing their trust in the system. As shown in Fig. 2, the FAITH framework functions as a cyclical process powered by AI. It starts with identifying personal traits and moves through several stages, including choosing an appropriate communication strategy based on individual factors, implementing feedback and evaluation mechanisms, and ensuring ongoing learning and adaptation.

The framework begins by identifying a range of individual preference factors, emphasizing the need to understand the diverse backgrounds and personal traits of users. This process involves developing detailed profiles for each individual and determining their preferences. These profiles are then input into a machine learning system, which analyzes them to determine the most appropriate communication strategy for each person. The objective is to ensure clear information delivery and a thorough understanding of the systems, ultimately aiming to enhance trust in the system.

The communication strategies are subsequently customized according to each individual profile. This adjustment ensures that the approach is aligned with the distinct characteristics and preferences of each user, thereby improving the effectiveness of the communication process. By tailoring these strategies, the framework seeks to enhance the reception and understanding of information, ultimately strengthening trust in the system.

Next, the framework conducts experimental trials, adhering to established standards. The results are then fed into an AI-driven machine learning system, which evaluates the success of the trials. If the outcomes are positive, the system is implemented as planned. If the results are unsatisfactory, the system adjusts its approach and uses the feedback to learn and improve from the outcomes.

Continuous learning and adaptation are central to the framework. No matter the results of a trial, the system consistently evolves and adjusts based on the feedback it receives. This iterative process enables ongoing refinement and enhancement, ensuring that communication strategies stay effective and responsive to users' needs.

The framework is based on recognizing individual preferences, customizing communication approaches to fit those preferences, running experimental tests, and making

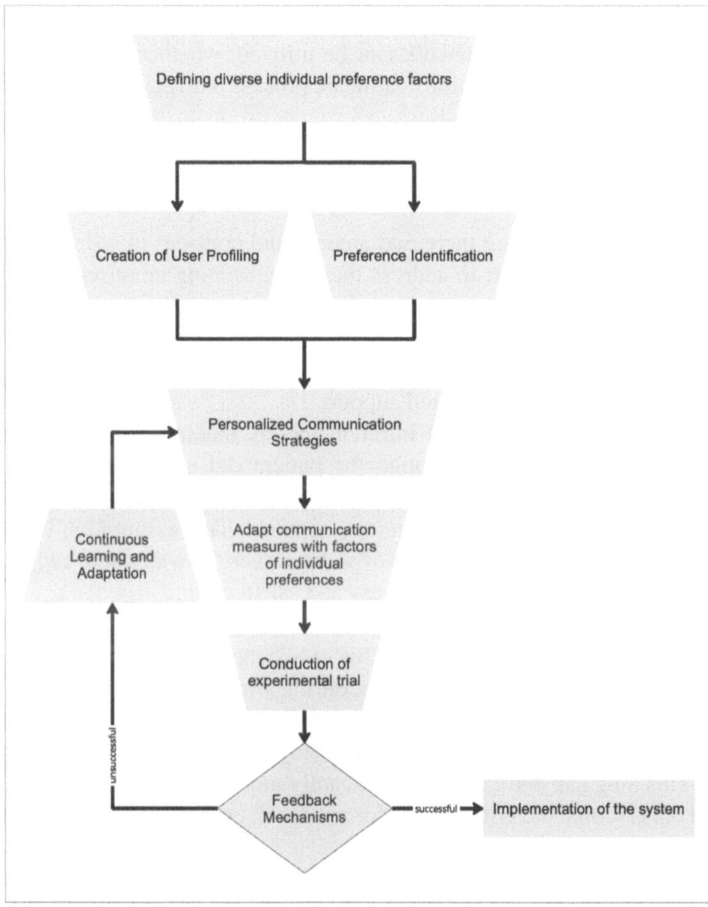

Fig. 2. Framework for AI Trust enHancement (FAITH) [17].

iterative adjustments based on feedback. By focusing on personalized communication and ongoing refinement, the framework can significantly improve trust management systems in smart cities.

4 Trust Management in Healthcare: Case Studies

After conducting research and developing the FAITH Framework, the authors present two real-life scenarios in this section to validate its application. The first scenario demonstrates how AI can be employed to eliminate misjudgments that may occur between patients and healthcare providers, thereby fostering trust in mental healthcare through enhanced communication and support.

The second scenario examines how healthcare professionals' trust in an AI-driven tool for managing Type 2 Diabetes Mellitus (T2DM) is influenced by their personal values, experiences, and the reliability of data sources. Both scenarios illustrate different aspects of how the FAITH Framework can be utilized, whether it is to deploy smart systems to build trust within a specific healthcare process or to ensure that smart systems themselves are trusted by individuals.

4.1 Deploying FAITH in Mental Healthcare

Consider a patient experiencing increased anxiety and episodes of sadness sought professional mental health support to address their deteriorating emotional state. Despite recognizing the need for therapy and securing an appointment with a highly regarded therapist, the patient's experience was far from satisfactory. During the therapy session, the patient made an effort to describe the symptoms and feelings in detail for a comprehensive assessment and tailored support.

However, the therapist displayed implicit bias by making assumptions about the patient's socioeconomic status. Although the patient did not disclose their financial background, the therapist presumed that the patient was from a wealthy background based solely on their ability to afford therapy sessions. This assumption led the therapist to believe that the patient's episodes of sadness were unwarranted, suggesting that financial comfort should equate to happiness and satisfaction.

As a result, the patient felt misunderstood and judged, leading to a profound loss of trust in the mental healthcare system. This experience discouraged the patient from seeking further therapy for nearly two years, during which they did not receive the necessary professional help. When the patient eventually decided to consult a new therapist, rebuilding trust was challenging due to the lingering fear of encountering similar biased judgments. This long gap in treatment significantly impacted the patient's mental health journey and underscored the critical need for unbiased, empathetic care in mental health services.

If the FAITH framework had been implemented in the real-life scenario described, the outcome could have been significantly different. Smart systems have the potential to enhance the effectiveness of therapy sessions by utilizing a smart grid that analyzes the appropriate communication methods on a case-by-case basis, thereby creating a safer and more supportive environment for the patient. The results of this analysis would depend on various external and internal factors.

To illustrate the potential of a structured approach to building trust in mental healthcare, we can apply this framework to the earlier case scenario. As shown in Fig. 3, the process would begin by defining diverse individual preference factors through a comprehensive intake process that gathers detailed information about the patient's background, symptoms, and mental health needs, without making any assumptions. In the previously mentioned case, the relevant preference factors would include cultural influences, such as societal views on wealth and mental health, and psychological influences, like the patient's current mental state, personal values, and past experiences with therapy.

The next step involves defining communication measures using smart systems. These systems analyze the patient's data and preferences to tailor communication strategies specifically for the individual, ensuring that the language used is empathetic, non-judgmental, and aligned with the patient's needs. For example, based on the patient's cultural background, the smart system could suggest avoiding assumptions about the patient's financial status or recommend focusing on areas of emotional distress that the patient has emphasized as particularly significant.

During the therapy session, the therapist would accommodate these communication measures by actively applying the smart system's suggestions, ensuring a personalized and supportive dialogue that resonates with the patient's unique preferences and emotional state. This approach fosters a more inclusive and understanding environment. Additionally, the session would serve as an experimental trial to test the effectiveness of these tailored communication strategies, allowing for real-time adjustments based on the patient's reactions and feedback. Following the session, an evaluation of the trial would be conducted by gathering feedback from the patient about their experience. This evaluation focuses on assessing how well the communication measures met the patient's needs and whether they felt understood and supported. Such feedback is crucial for identifying any gaps or areas for improvement to prevent misunderstandings or feelings of judgment.

If the trial is successful, this iterative process would inform the adaptation of the trust management system, ensuring continuous refinement and fostering a more empathetic and trustworthy mental healthcare environment. By incorporating smart systems to define and refine communication measures, this model enhances the ability to provide personalized, unbiased care, thereby helping to restore and maintain trust in a variety of fields, including healthcare services. Ultimately, ensuring that patients feel completely comfortable and that all their unique factors are taken into consideration will lead to better outcomes. As users observe improved trends and experiences, both personally and from others, the system will gradually earn increased trust and confidence.

4.2 Deploying FAITH in Medication Prescription

A case study was carried out on participants from medical backgrounds including Endocrinologists, Primary care providers, Nurse Practitioners, Pharmacists and Internal medicine doctors regarding their trust levels of an AI-informed clinical decision support (CDS) to manage the health of patients suffering from T2DM.

T2DM is a common chronic illness spread worldwide, it is detected by high blood glucose level resulting from a proportional or complete inadequacy of the pancreatic hormone insulin. In the absence or decreased responsiveness of insulin in the body, glucose remains in the blood causing high blood sugar levels which may eventually lead to complications such as blindness, limb amputations and heart attacks.

In this study the machine learning model underlying the T2DM AI-enhanced CDS was trained on a large dataset taken from health insurance claims. This dataset was optimized to train the CDS model on refining medication options for decreasing Hemoglobin A1c, which is a measure of diabetes severity. The tool was used to provide clinicians with AI insights regarding most efficient medications to lower a patient's Hemoglobin A1c, using information from past similar patients.

In this situation, the personal values and personal experiences of clinicians played a huge role in building trust in the AI-enhanced CDS tool. For example, when the clinicians were first introduced to the tool, participants wanted to know the source of data from which the AI tool supports its insights regarding a medication or selection of

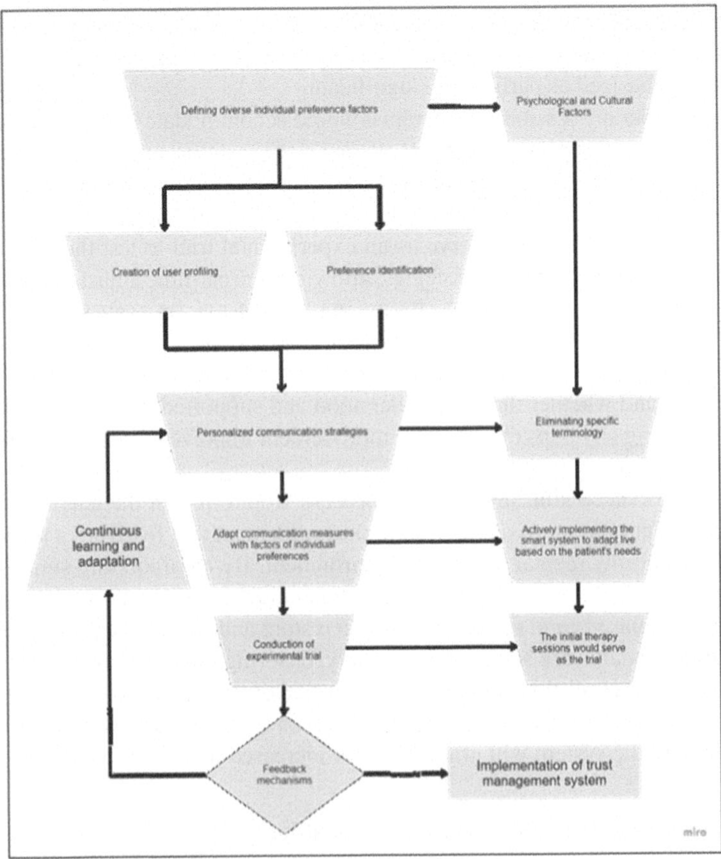

Fig. 3. First validation of FAITH framework.

medications. Once they get informed about the data source they build trust to utilize the insights within their workflow. With other clinicians, it was enough for them to know that CDS was powered by AI to obtain their trust. In other words, some participants described discomfort using a CDS tool supported by pharmaceutical companies. While other participants saw that if an insurance company was providing the tool, this would provide a canonical source of information as the medication supported by the tool would be covered by the insurance plan [5].

The diversity of the opinions of clinicians show the importance of taking into consideration the personal values and experiences when building trust in such a smart system. This case study could be used to prove the FAITH framework presented previously in this paper. Moreover, FAITH recommends to personalize the communication strategy to earn trust by keeping the participants informed about the source of the data. In some further case scenarios it is known that the solution is powered by AI might be sufficient. Therefore, this information should be included in the introduction of the CDS tool. Participants can then decide whether to seek more details about the resource of data or proceed with the information provided. If this approach proves to be successful, it can be simply adapted and transitioned into the trial phase. Success would be indicated by a significant percentage of clinicians trusting the system without raising follow-up concerns. If this level of trust is not achieved, a new communication strategy will be necessary. This could involve implementing training sessions and enhancing transparency regarding data processing within the CDS tool.

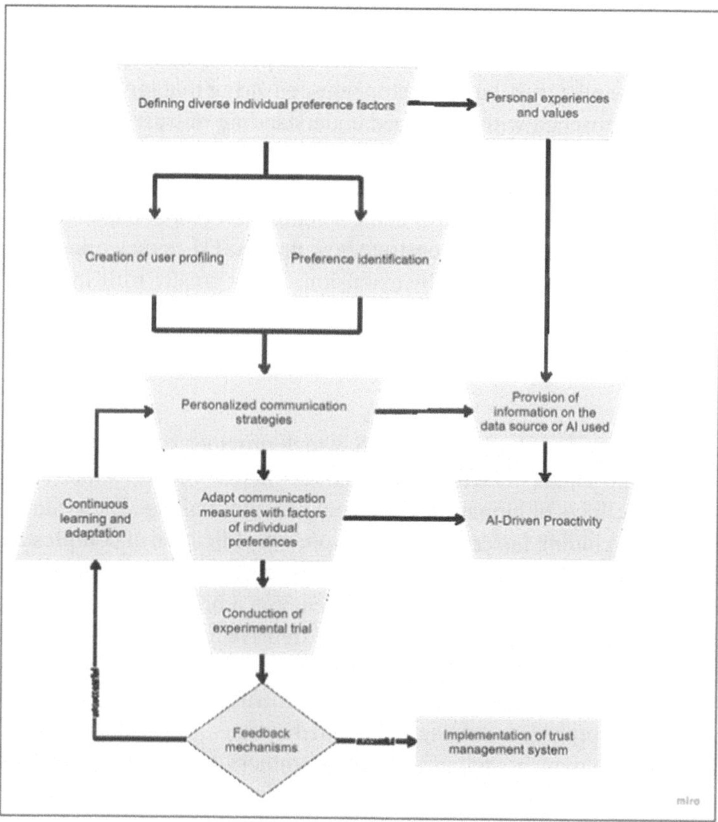

Fig. 4. Second validation of FAITH framework.

The Fig. 4 shows how the FAITH framework would be adapted to this case scenario. Each user contributes unique perspectives, values, and personality traits, which makes developing a universally applicable trust management system a challenging task. Individual interpretations of trust vary widely, necessitating an adaptive approach to trust management that accounts for these differences. To address this challenge, a detailed understanding of both internal and external factors shaping individual preferences is essential. Factors such as personal values, personality traits, cultural background, and personal experiences all significantly influence trust levels.

The proposed FAITH framework offers a practical solution to these challenges by integrating personalized communication strategies with individual preferences, aiming to build and sustain trust in smart city systems. By aligning communication measures with diverse user needs, FAITH promotes trust, collaboration, and innovation. The framework has shown considerable flexibility across various contexts and case scenarios, whether at an organizational level, as demonstrated in medication prescriptions for diabetes management, or on a more individualized basis, such as in mental healthcare. This adaptability underscores FAITH's potential to be customized for different fields, providing a robust tool for enhancing trust in both professional and personal settings. By accommodating specific requirements and preferences, FAITH can guide the development of effective trust-building strategies, ensuring that processes and personal interactions are approached with a nuanced understanding of trust dynamics.

The previous case scenarios were selected from the healthcare sector due to the critical role smart systems play in this field. With a long history of integration and continuous development, smart systems have made a significant global impact on healthcare. These scenarios were chosen to demonstrate how the FAITH framework can be applied to establish trust in smart grids and, by extension, foster greater trust in the healthcare system as a whole.

4.3 Discussions

AI is recognized as a technological approach, which provides substantial advantages by making decisions grounded in factual analysis rather than emotions, which can help mitigate the negative effects of human emotions on decision-making. The systems benefits are considerable, including faster task completion, simplification of complex and stressful work, achieving difficult objectives in shorter times, effective multitasking, high success rates with fewer errors, improved efficiency in a brief period, reduced physical space and size requirements, ability to perform extensive and complex calculations and support in the exploration of new areas such as space. However, AI also poses significant disadvantages in daily life, such as potential misuse leading to widespread harm, occasional errors in programs causing unintended actions, job displacement contributing to higher unemployment, reliance on programmers for creativity, lack of human interaction, encouraging laziness in younger generations, high time and financial costs, and increased technological dependency [12].

The integration of AI techniques into various fields has been a trans-formative phenomenon, particularly within medicine and healthcare. Since the 1950s, physicians have aimed to enhance their diagnostic processes through computer-aided programs leveraging vast amounts of data. These early efforts marked the inception of AI applications in healthcare, paving the way for its evolution into a cornerstone of modern medical practices. Nowadays, AI is ubiquitous across numerous medical domains, including diagnostic, surgical, and predictive practices. Its utilization of extensive datasets generated from medical procedures enables the derivation of new insights and continuous learning from past experiences, revolutionizing how healthcare is delivered and managed. The journey from computer-aided diagnostics to sophisticated AI-driven healthcare solutions underscores the power of technology in reshaping medical paradigms [21].

In a comprehensive review published in 2021, researchers undertook an exhaustive analysis of existing literature on AI and healthcare, spanning over three decades and covering approximately 288 peer-reviewed articles. This meta-analysis provided invaluable insights into the trajectory of AI applications in healthcare, shedding light on the trends and developments driving this rapidly evolving field [21].

One example of AI applications is patient data and diagnostics which present significant challenges and opportunities in healthcare. These technologies facilitate the management and analysis of enormous amounts of patient data, aiding in screening, diagnosis, and treatment assignment. AI techniques also enhance rehabilitation therapy and surgical procedures, with the development of robots to support motor therapy and perform semi-automated surgical tasks. Telemedicine has seen increased adoption for remote patient diagnostics, providing healthcare professionals with valuable support tools. Several authors have analyzed AI in healthcare research, examining both its positive applications and ethical implications. While some focus on future advancements in health service management and diagnostics, others explore concerns such as data protection and accountability. Transparency in technology for patients is seen as crucial for AI development. AI shows promise in improving patient care and addressing organizational challenges. Algorithms enable comprehensive data analysis, aiding decision-making and facilitating predictive analytics for better patient outcomes, and the accuracy of the data used to feed these algorithms is very crucial [22].

The healthcare industry is undergoing a profound shift driven by rising costs and a shortage of healthcare professionals, prompting a search for new technology-based solutions. Issues like limited access, high costs, and an aging population are exacerbated by events like the COVID-19 pandemic, highlighting the need for innovative approaches to healthcare delivery. AI emerges as a promising solution to simplify processes and enhance patient care across various domains, from drug discovery to clinical trials and patient treatment. AI applications in healthcare address a range of challenges, including drug discovery and clinical trial automation [22].

Pharmaceutical companies use AI to accelerate drug discovery processes and repurpose existing drugs, streamlining workflows and reducing redundancy. Collaboration between bio-pharmaceutical companies and AI platforms marks a significant shift towards faster, cheaper, and more effective drug development, albeit with some skepticism remaining in the industry. Clinical trials, essential for testing new treatments, have historically been time-consuming and costly. AI-driven automation in clinical trials streamlines data monitoring and enhances accuracy, paving the way for more efficient drug development processes. Intelligent clinical trial designs, enabled by AI, promise shorter cycle duration's and improved outcomes, particularly when combined with predictive models and advanced analytics. AI's impact extends to patient care, where it enhances clinical intelligence systems and aids in personalized treatment approaches. Technologies like healthcare robotics, genetics driven medicine, and AI-powered stethoscopes are transforming patient care delivery. From assisting paralyzed patients in walking to predicting high-risk pregnancies, AI enabled solutions are improving patient outcomes and increasing access to healthcare services [22].

5 Conclusion

In this paper, we have proposed the FAITH framework to build trust and facilitate collaboration within the rapidly evolving landscape of AI adoption in smart cities. By integrating personalized communication strategies with individual preferences, this framework addresses the challenge of tailoring trust management systems to accommodate the different individual needs in the digital era. The framework offers practical insights to manage user preferences and create inclusive and resilient smart city environments. To validate the framework, we have applied the proposed framework in two case studies. The results of the case studies have demonstrated how personalized communication strategies can effectively cater to the different user preferences.

Further research is planned to address the challenges associated with trust management in smart cities. This research will further explore solutions to ensure the trustworthy use of AI technologies in urban environments. Specifically, future studies will focus on developing and implementing standardized trust profiles to enhance trust assessment in both emerging and established business relationships.

References

1. Asan, O., Bayrak, A.E., Choudhury, A., et al.: Artificial intelligence and human trust in healthcare: focus on clinicians. J. Med. Internet Res. **22**(6), e15154 (2020)
2. Bangui, H., Buhnova, B., Ge, M.: Social internet of things: ethical AI principles in trust management. In: The 14th International Conference on Ambient Systems, Networks and Technologies (ANT 2023) 15–17 March 2023, Leuven, Belgium. Procedia Computer Science, vol. 220, pp. 553–560. Elsevier (2023)
3. Belanche, D., Casaló, L.V., Flavián, C.: Integrating trust and personal values into the technology acceptance model: the case of e-government services adoption. Cuadernos de Economía y Dirección de la Empresa **15**(4), 192–204 (2012)
4. Böckle, M., Yeboah-Antwi, K., Kouris, I.: Can you trust the black box? The effect of personality traits on trust in ai-enabled user interfaces. In: International Conference on Human-Computer Interaction, pp. 3–20. Springer (2021)
5. Burgess, E.R., et al.: Healthcare AI treatment decision support: design principles to enhance clinician adoption and trust. In: Proceedings of the 2023 CHI Conference on Human Factors in Computing Systems, pp. 1–19 (2023)
6. Davis, F.D., et al.: Technology acceptance model: Tam. Al-Suqri, MN, Al-Aufi, AS: Information Seeking Behavior and Technology Adoption, pp. 205–219 (1989)
7. Evans, A.M., Krueger, J.I.: The psychology (and economics) of trust. Soc. Pers. Psychol. Compass **3**(6), 1003–1017 (2009)
8. Falcone, R., Castelfranchi, C.: Trust dynamics: how trust is influenced by direct experiences and by trust itself. In: Proceedings of the Third International Joint Conference on Autonomous Agents and Multiagent Systems, 2004, pp. 740–747. IEEE (2004)
9. Ge, M., Buhnova, B.: DISDA: digital service design architecture for smart city ecosystems. In: Proceedings of the 12th International Conference on Cloud Computing and Services Science, CLOSER 2022, Online Streaming, 27–29 April 2022, pp. 207–214. SCITEPRESS (2022)
10. Güemes, C., Herreros, F.: Education and trust: a tale of three continents. Int. Polit. Sci. Rev. **40**(5), 676–693 (2019)

11. Hillesheim, A.J., Rusnock, C.F., Bindewald, J.M., Miller, M.E.: Relationships between user demographics and user trust in an autonomous agent. In: Proceedings of the Human Factors and Ergonomics Society Annual Meeting, vol. 61, pp. 314–318. SAGE Publications Sage CA: Los Angeles, CA (2017)
12. Khanzode, K.C.A., Sarode, R.D.: Advantages and disadvantages of artificial intelligence and machine learning: a literature review. Int. J. Libr. Inf. Sci. (IJLIS) **9**(1), 3 (2020)
13. Kravtsova, M., Oshchepkov, A.Y., Welzel, C.: The shadow of the family: historical roots of social capital in Europe (WP BRP 82/SOC/2018) (2018)
14. Le, S.H.: Societal trust and geography. Cross-Cult. Res. **47**(4), 388–414 (2013)
15. Lee, J., Baig, F., Li, X.: Media influence, trust, and the public adoption of automated vehicles. IEEE Intell. Transp. Syst. Mag. **14**(6), 174–187 (2021)
16. Lemmers-Jansen, I.L., Fett, A.K.J., van Os, J., Veltman, D.J., Krabbendam, L.: Trust and the city: linking urban upbringing to neural mechanisms of trust in psychosis. Australian New Zealand J. Psychiatry **54**(2), 138–149 (2020)
17. Ohnesorg, J., Fakhoury, N., Eltahawi, N., Ge, M.: Customizing trust systems: personalized communication to address AI adoption in smart cities. In: International Conference on Smart Cities and Green ICT Systems, pp. 73–79 (2024)
18. Ohnesorg, J., Fakhoury, N., Eltahawi, N., Ge, M.: A review of ai-based trust management in smart cities. In: ITM Web of Conferences, vol. 62, p. 01003. EDP Sciences (2024)
19. Persia, F., Pilato, G., Ge, M., Bolzoni, P., D'Auria, D., Helmer, S.: Improving orienteering-based tourist trip planning with social sensing. Future Gener. Comput. Syst. **110**, 931–945 (2020)
20. Sechi, G., Borri, D., De Lucia, C., Skilters, J.: How are personal wealth and trust correlated? A social capital–based cross-sectional study from latvia. Int. Soc. Sci. J. (2023)
21. Secinaro, S., Calandra, D., Secinaro, A., Muthurangu, V., Biancone, P.: The role of artificial intelligence in healthcare: a structured literature review. BMC Med. Inform. Decis. Mak. **21**(1), 1–15 (2021)
22. Shaheen, M.Y.: Applications of artificial intelligence (AI) in healthcare: a review. ScienceOpen Research (2021)
23. Thanetsunthorn, N., Wuthisatian, R.: Understanding trust across cultures: an empirical investigation. Rev. Int. Bus. Strategy **29**(4), 286–314 (2019)
24. Zhou, J., Luo, S., Chen, F.: Effects of personality traits on user trust in human-machine collaborations. J. Multimodal User Interfaces **14**, 387–400 (2020)

Simulation of Operating Modes of Traction Power Supply Systems Equipped with Renewable Energy Sources

Andrey Kryukov[1,2], Konstantin Suslov[1,3](✉), Aleksandr Cherepanov[2], Alexander Kryukov[1], and Nguyen Quoc Hieu[1]

[1] Department of Power Supply and Electrical Engineering, Irkutsk National Research Technical University, Irkutsk, Russia
dr.souslov@yandex.ru

[2] Department of Transport Electric Power, Irkutsk State Transport University, Irkutsk, Russia

[3] Department of Hydropower and Renewable Energy, National Research University, Moscow Power Engineering Institute, Moscow, Russia

Abstract. The results of research aimed at developing digital models for calculating the operating conditions of railway power supply systems (RPSS) using wind power plants (WPP) and solar power plants are presented. The implementation of the models relies on the methods of phase coordinates, which enable a systems, universal, and comprehensive approach. The systems dimension is achieved by considering all the significant properties of a complex RPSS and a supply network. The versatility is ensured by modeling traction networks, power lines, and transformers of various designs. The comprehensiveness lies in the possibility of calculating the normal, emergency, and special operating conditions in the RPSS. The study highlights a variety of applications of the wind turbines: to power the facilities located in regions with unstable energy supply; to enhance the reliability of power supply to the consumer whose disconnection could lead to serious consequences; to supply energy to relatively low-power facilities. The creation of the calculation model for the RPSS requires the implementation of an algorithm for the interaction of models of individual components and includes the following stages: modeling the rolling stock traffic schedule; developing instantaneous diagrams corresponding to specific time instants and calculating their operating parameters; determining integrated modeling indices. The results obtained using the Fazonord software indicate that the use of wind turbines and solar power plants can bring about the following benefits: cutting down energy supply costs; reducing unbalance on the busbars of traction substations, stabilizing voltage levels on the current collectors of electric locomotives. Digital models have been developed to determine the modes of power supply systems for railways equipped with inverter generation units. A solar power plant based on photovoltaic panels was considered as such an installation. To improve the power quality on 10 kV buses, a phase-controlled reactive power source and an active harmonic conditioner were used. The simulation results showed that by connecting a solar power plant, consumption from the electric power system is reduced and with the mass use of photovoltaic panels, a noticeable technical and economic effect can be obtained. In addition, additional energy sources will improve the reliability of power supply to train traction, as well as signaling and auto-locking facilities that ensure the

F. Calise et al. (Eds.): SMARTGREENS 2024/VEHITS 2024, CCIS 2954, pp. 58–78, 2026.
https://doi.org/10.1007/978-3-032-23187-1_4

safety of cargo and passenger transportation processes. The presence of an inverter leads to an increase in harmonic distortion, the values of which can be reduced to acceptable limits based on the use of an active harmonic conditioner. Deviations and asymmetry of voltages on 10 kV buses of traction substations can bc reduced on the basis of a phase-controlled reactive power source or a symmetrical device implemented according to the Steinmetz scheme.

Keywords: Traction power systems · Wind turbines · Modeling the operation · Renewable energy sources

1 Introduction

In order to enhance the reliability of power supply, improve the power quality, and reduce the cost of energy supply in railway transport, an emerging solution is the adoption of self-generation (SG) plants utilizing renewable energy sources (RES), for example, micro hydroelectric power stations, wind turbines [1, 2], solar power plants [3] geothermal and solar power plants [4–6].

The self-generation plants can be used to:

- power the facilities located in regions with unstable energy supply;
- boost the reliability of power supply to the consumer whose disconnection could lead to serious consequences;
- supply energy to individual facilities of relatively low power.

The significance of the use of renewable energy sources (RES) in transport is confirmed by numerous publications offering various approaches to solving this problem. For example, [7] provides an overview of fault-tolerant traction power supply systems (TPSS) and concludes that the integration of RES ensures a reduction in damage from disruptions and failures in the network. The use of renewable energy sources to improve the efficiency of solar power plants in India is discussed in (Bade, 2018). The findings of the study into short circuit processes in power plants with renewable energy sources are presented in [8, 9]. The efficiency of a traction network incorporating renewable energy sources is assessed in [10]. Methods for solving the problem of integrating renewable energy sources into traction power system to reduce carbon emissions and energy costs are discussed in [11]. An overview of the traction power systems equipped with RES is given in [12]. Important aspects related to the use of renewable energy sources to ensure train safety are considered in [13]. The problem of forming wind-solar traction power systems is solved in [14]. A comparative analysis of options for integrating photovoltaic sources into traction networks is carried out in [15]. The tasks of using solar power plants in transport energy systems are described in [16]. A method for generating a traffic schedule, considering a wind farm, is described in [17]. A traction power supply system with photovoltaic modules is presented in [18]. Hybrid DC traction power system with renewable energy sources is described in [19]. The photovoltaic system for traction power system and a strategy for its control are presented in [20]. The issues of integrating rail-based public transportation system and using regenerative energy are considered in

[21]. The issue of identifying optimal sites for installing solar-powered permafrost stabilization systems on railways is resolved in [22]. The efficiency of photovoltaic panels placed on locomotive roofs is the focus of [23].

In modern context, the integration of renewable energy sources must be addressed on the basis of digital models that take into account the specifics of RPSS, which are as follows:

- traction loads greatly worsen the power quality in electrical networks of non-traction consumers, where it is planned to use RES-based SG plants;
- the non-stationary nature of single-phase traction loads leads to significant voltage deviations on the busbars of substations to which SG plants are connected;
- single-phase traction load causes a marked unbalance on these busbars, which, sometimes, considerably exceeds permissible limits;
- electric locomotive converters generate harmonics into the network.

An analysis of the presented publications shows that modelling the RPSS with SG plants based on RES has not been fully examined. To study this issue comprehensively, one can use the methods presented in [24–27]. Based on the approaches proposed in these articles, it is possible to implement the modeling methodology that has the following distinctive features:

- possibility of modeling operating conditions taking into account the properties and characteristics of a complex traction energy system and power supply system (PSS);
- the versatility, providing modelling of traction networks (TN), power lines, and transformers of various designs;
- the comprehensiveness, which implies the possibility of determining normal, emergency, and special conditions in RPSS, for example, those arising when ice melts on the traction networks.

Below are the results of the research aimed at developing methods for modeling RPSS incorporating wind turbines.

2 Methodology

A formalized description of the RPSS can be provided by the following model [28]:

$$\frac{d\mathbf{X}}{dt} = \mathbf{\Phi}(\mathbf{X}, \mathbf{V}, \mathbf{S}, \mathbf{C}, t), \quad (1)$$

where $\mathbf{X}$ is *an* n- dimensional vector of parameters characterizing the operating condition, for which Cartesian or polar coordinates of nodal voltages are used; $\mathbf{\Phi}$ is an n-dimensional nonlinear vector function; $\mathbf{V}$ is an m-dimensional vector of disturbances, the components of which are active and reactive loads and generations; $\mathbf{C}$ is an ℓ-dimensional vector of control actions, generated based on the train schedule, and instructions coming from the control centre; $\mathbf{S}$ is a q -dimensional vector, including elements of the conductance matrix corresponding to the RPSS electrical network.

Due to insufficient information available, the practical use of model (1) is only possible in the future. Therefore, it is reduced to a set of static (instantaneous) diagrams. In doing so, the interval under study T_M is divided into small intervals Δt, within which the above parameters are considered to be constant. At each interval Δt, the following nonlinear system of equations describing the steady state of the corresponding instantaneous diagram is solved:

$$\mathbf{F}[\mathbf{X}_k, \mathbf{S}_k, \mathbf{C}_k, \mathbf{V}_k] = \mathbf{0}, \tag{2}$$

where $\mathbf{X}_{k,}\mathbf{S}_k, \mathbf{C}_k, \mathbf{V}_k$ are the vector values of $\mathbf{X}, \mathbf{S}, \mathbf{C}, \mathbf{V}$ for the *k-th* instantaneous diagram.

The simulation modelling methodology proposed in [27] and implemented in the Fazonord software enables calculations of operating parameters for the RPSS, including the supply network of EPS, the traction power system, and areas of power supply to non-traction consumers.

3 Results of Modeling

The results of modeling the modes of traction power supply systems equipped with self-generating units based on renewable energy sources are presented below. The simulation was carried out in two versions. In the first case, wind turbines were considered, and in the second, a solar power plant.

Model in the form of system (2) is used for modelling the operating conditions of the RPSS with SG plants based on wind turbines. The mathematical model, which can be used for wind turbines, is as follows [28]:

$$\left.\begin{array}{l}
P_{Gj}^{(A)} - P_{Hj}^{(A)} - P_{Cj}^{(A)}(\mathbf{X}) = 0; \\
P_{Gj}^{(B)} - P_{Hj}^{(B)} - P_{Cj}^{(B)}(\mathbf{X}) = 0; \\
P_{Gj}^{(C)} - P_{Hj}^{(C)} - P_{Cj}^{(C)}(\mathbf{X}) = 0; \\
Q_{Gj}^{(A)} - Q_{Hj}^{(A)} - Q_{Cj}^{(A)}(\mathbf{X}) = 0; \\
Q_{Gj}^{(B)} - Q_{Hj}^{(B)} - Q_{Cj}^{(B)}(\mathbf{X}) = 0; \\
Q_{Gj}^{(C)} - Q_{Hj}^{(C)} - Q_{Cj}^{(C)}(\mathbf{X}) = 0,
\end{array}\right\} \tag{3}$$

where $P_{Gj}^{(k)}, Q_{Gj}^{(k)}$ are active and reactive power of the wind turbine generator connected to phase k (k = A, B, C) of the j-th network node; $P_{Hj}^{(k)}, Q_{Hj}^{(k)}$ are active and reactive power of the load connected to phase k of the j-th network node; $P_{Cj}^{(k)}, Q_{Cj}^{(k)}$ are network active and reactive power of phase k of the j-th network node.

The effects of using wind turbines are quantified by modeling the traction power system, including three traction substations (TSs). The modeling is carried out using the Fazonord software version 5.3.4.1–2024 [29]. A fragment of the original RPSS diagram is shown in Fig. 1 [28]. Consideration is given to the movement of trains weighing 3200 tons in a down direction and 6000 tons in an up direction, with an interval of 30 min (Fig. 2 [28]). The modelling results are presented in Figs. 3, 4, 5 and 6 [28].

Modeling was performed for two options:

1. There are no wind turbines in the RPSS.
2. Wind farms (WFs) with the total capacity of wind turbines shown in Fig. 1 are connected to 6 kV busbars of traction substations.

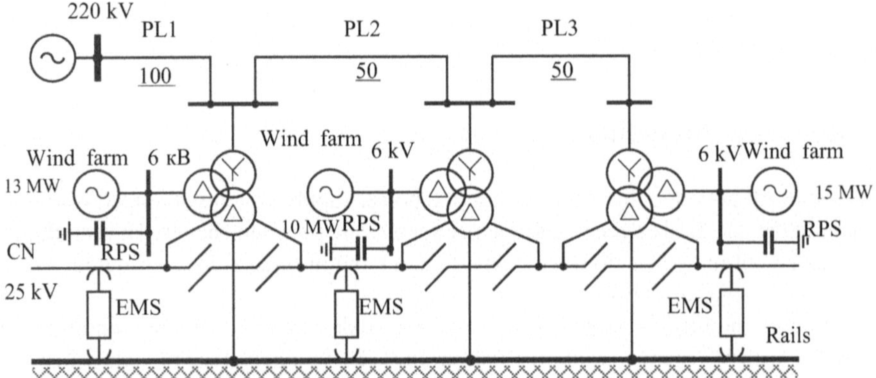

Fig. 1. RPSS diagram: CN – contact network; EMS – electromotive stock [28].

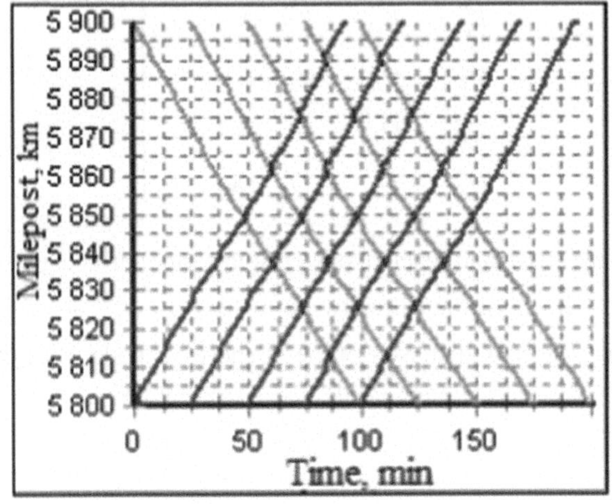

Fig. 2. Train schedule [28].

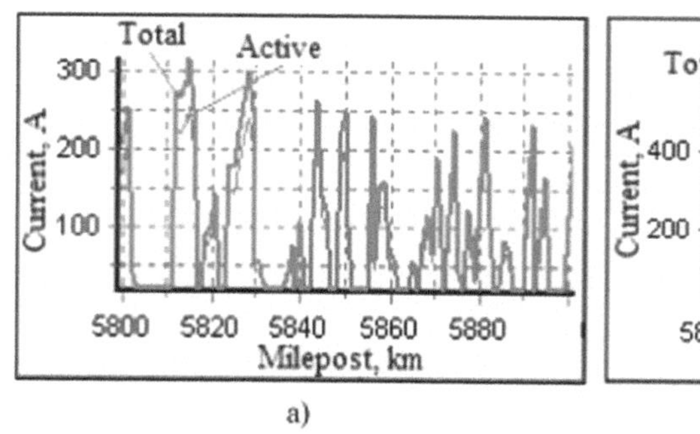

a)

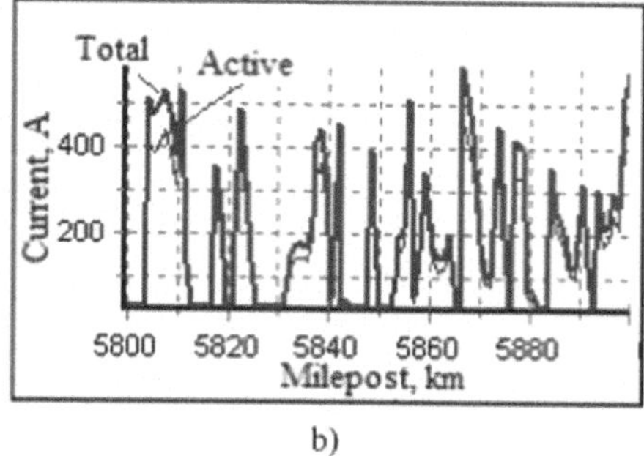

b)

Fig. 3. Current profiles of electric locomotives; a – down direction; b – up direction [28].

Graphs of changes in WF power are shown in Fig. 4.

Single-phase traction loads create significant unbalance on the busbars of 6 kV traction substations (TSs), which can have a negative impact on wind turbine equipment. This problem can be addressed by using phase-controlled sources of reactive power (SRP), (Fig. 5 [28]), which can reduce the unbalance to acceptable limits. The power equipment of SRP represents reactors and static capacitor banks, which can be connected in a "star" (Fig. 6 [28]) or "delta" (Fig. 7) configuration.

The SRP models are built by fixing the required levels of linear or phase voltages with the possible setting of constraints on generated reactive power:

$$\begin{aligned} Q_{j\min}^{(A)} \le Q_j^{(A)} \le Q_{j\max}^{(A)}; \\ Q_{j\min}^{(B)} \le Q_j^{(B)} \le Q_{j\max}^{(B)}; \\ Q_{j\min}^{(C)} \le Q_j^{(C)} \le Q_{j\max}^{(C)}, \end{aligned} \tag{4}$$

where $Q_{j\min}^{(k)}$, $Q_{j\max}^{(k)}$ are reactive power constraints.

The studies performed for a real-world railway power supply system show that the use of SRP with delta-connected power equipment provides better balancing. A "star" connection of the SRP phases with a grounded neutral causes a zero-sequence voltage. SRPs with delta-connected equipment do not have this disadvantage. Therefore, the models used below are based on SRP circuits with delta-connected power equipment.

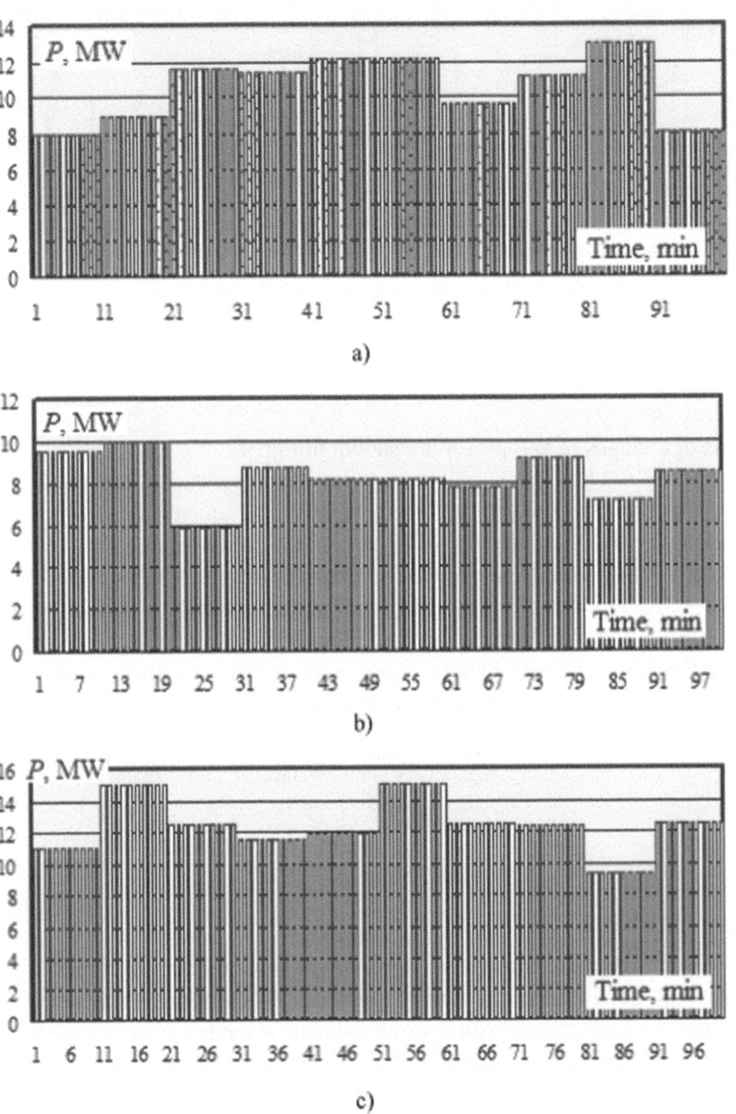

Fig. 4. Dynamics of changes in the total power of wind farms: a – WF connected to TS1; b – WF connected to TS 2; c – WF connected to TS 3 [28].

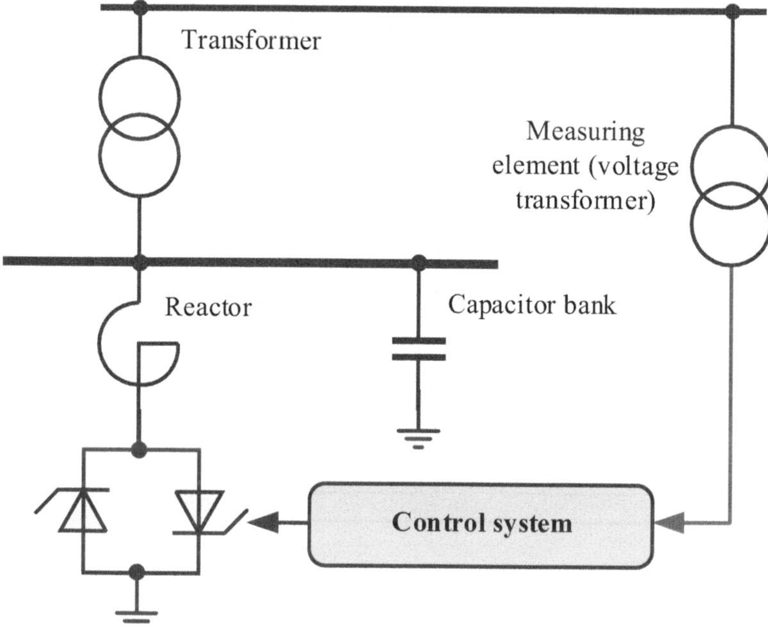

Fig. 5. SRP diagram.

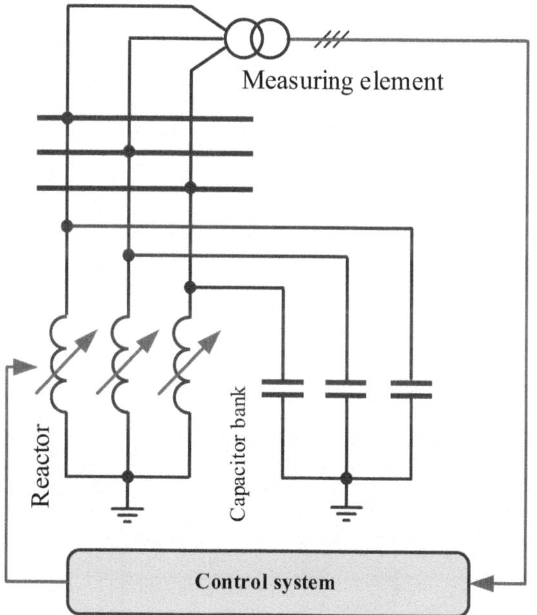

Fig. 6. SRP in the case of star connection [28].

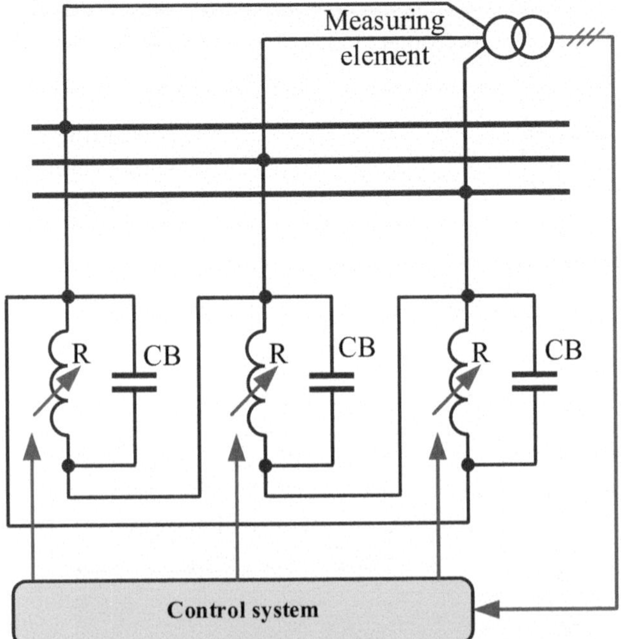

Fig. 7. SRP in the case of delta connection [28].

The modeling results are presented in Figs. 8, 9, 10, 11, 12, 13, 14, 15, 16 and 17 [28]. Figures 8, 9 and 10 [28] show the graphs characterizing voltage changes on the current collectors of electric locomotives. As seen in the Figures, when the wind farm is connected, the minimum levels of these voltages increase by 3.2% for a down train and by 5.3% for an up train.

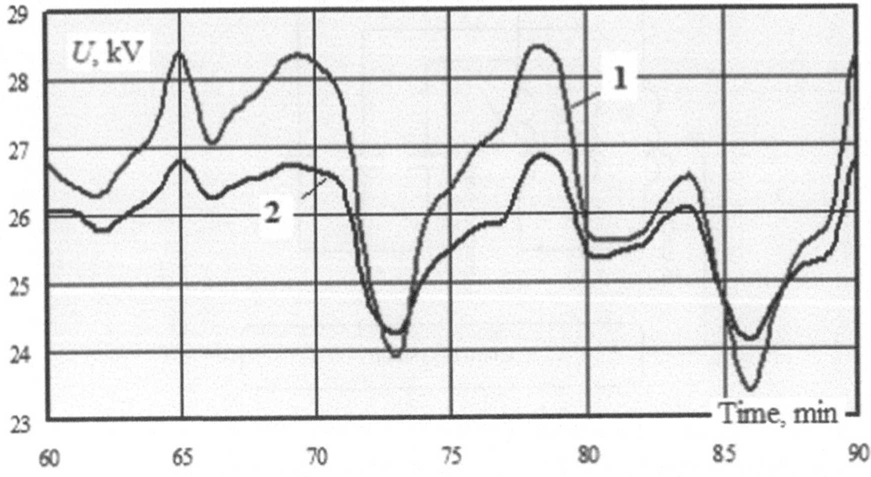

Fig. 8. Dynamics of voltage changes on the current collector of the first down train: 1 – WFs are on; 2 – WFs are turned off [28].

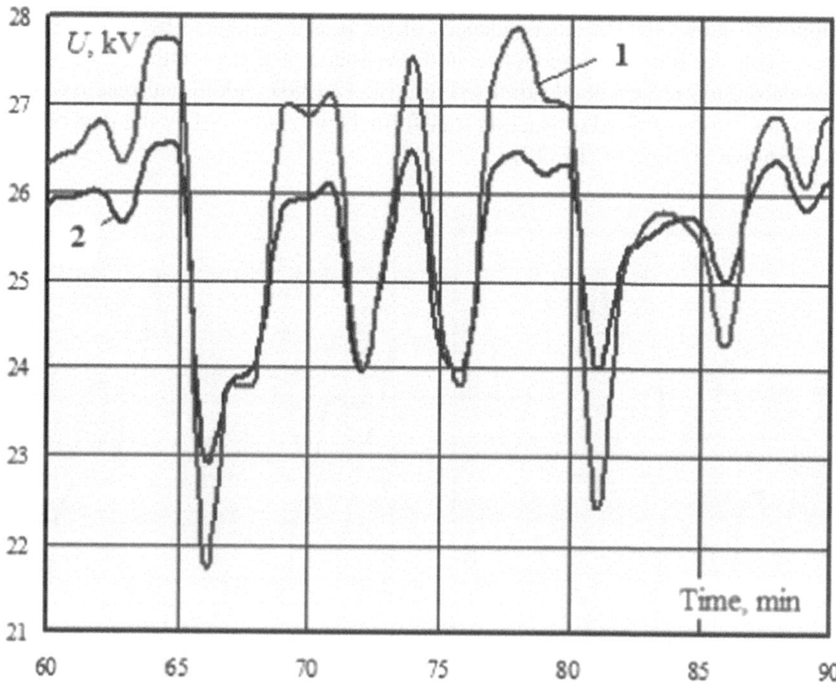

Fig. 9. Dynamics of voltage changes on the current collector of the first up train: 1 – WFs are on; 2 – WFs are turned off [28].

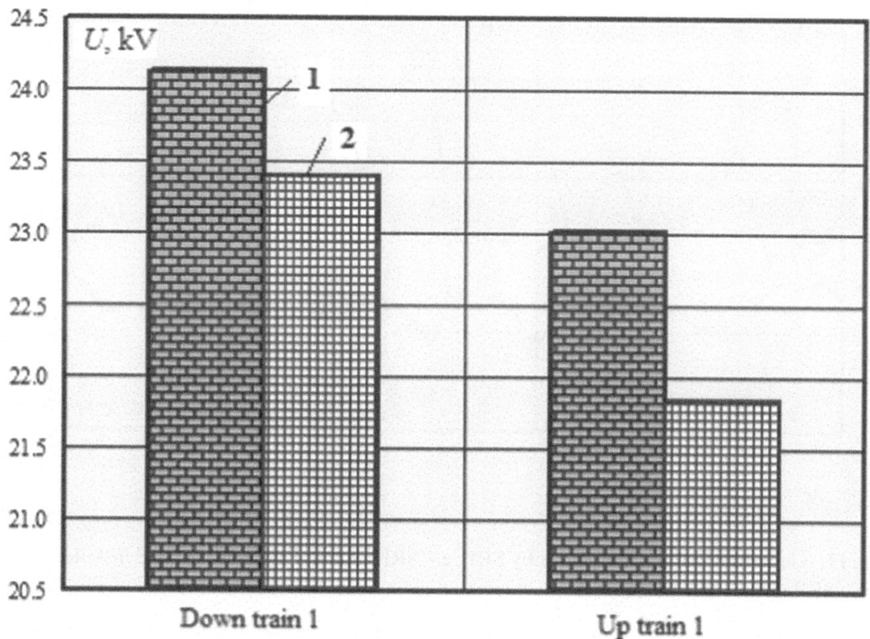

Fig. 10. Minimum voltage levels on current collectors of electric locomotives: 1 – WFs are on; 2 – WFs are turned off [28].

Figure 11 shows the time dependences of the power generated by reactive power sources. Their use provides a reduction in the voltage unbalance on the buses of 6 kV traction substation to acceptable limits (Figs. 12, 13 [28]). Additional reactive power flows do not cause overload of traction transformers, as evidenced by the dependences of losses shown in Figs. 14, 15 [28].

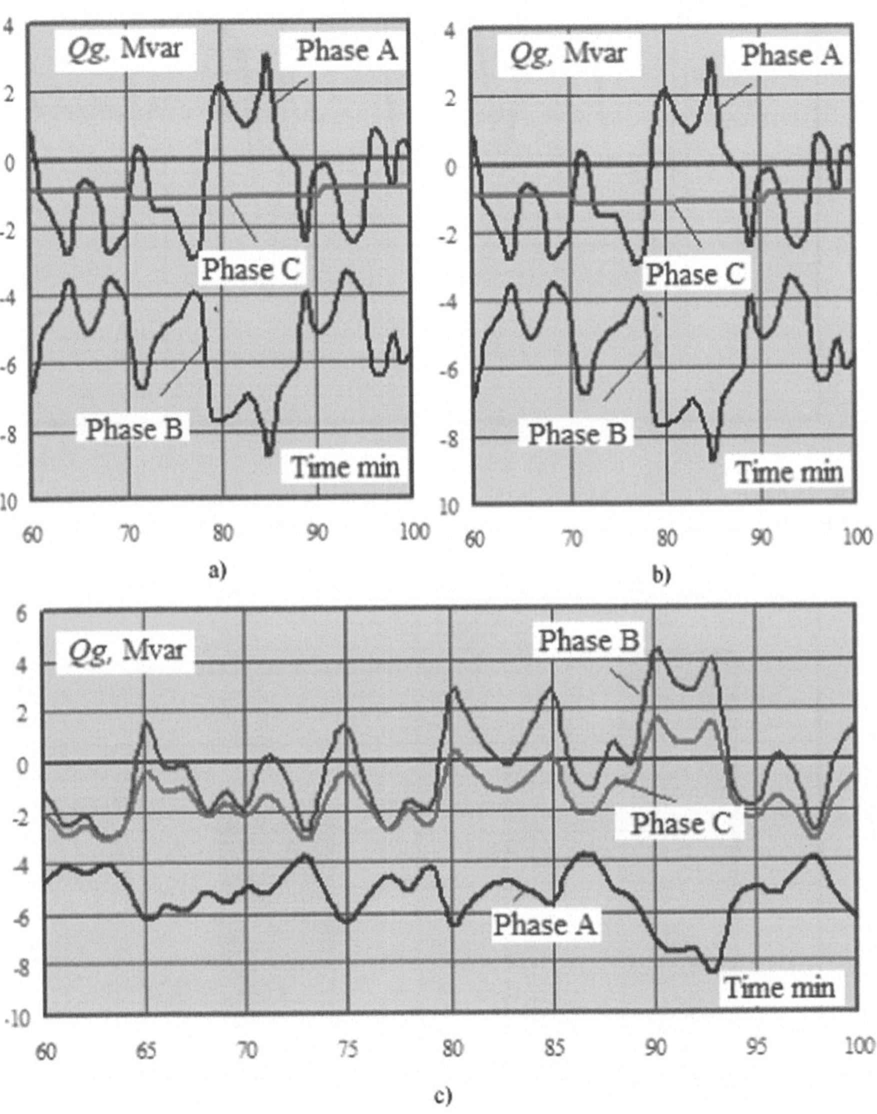

Fig. 11. Generation of reactive power by SRP: a – SRP installed at TS 1; b – SRP installed at TS 2; c – SRP installed at TS 3 [28].

When the wind farms are turned on, the power consumption from the EPS goes down, as evidenced by the graphs of changes in active power flows along power line 1 (Fig. 16 [28]); At the same time, at some points in time, the energy of the wind farm is transferred to thc EPS. The maximum power losses in power line 1, when the wind farm is turned on, are reduced by a factor of 2.5 (Fig. 17 [28]).

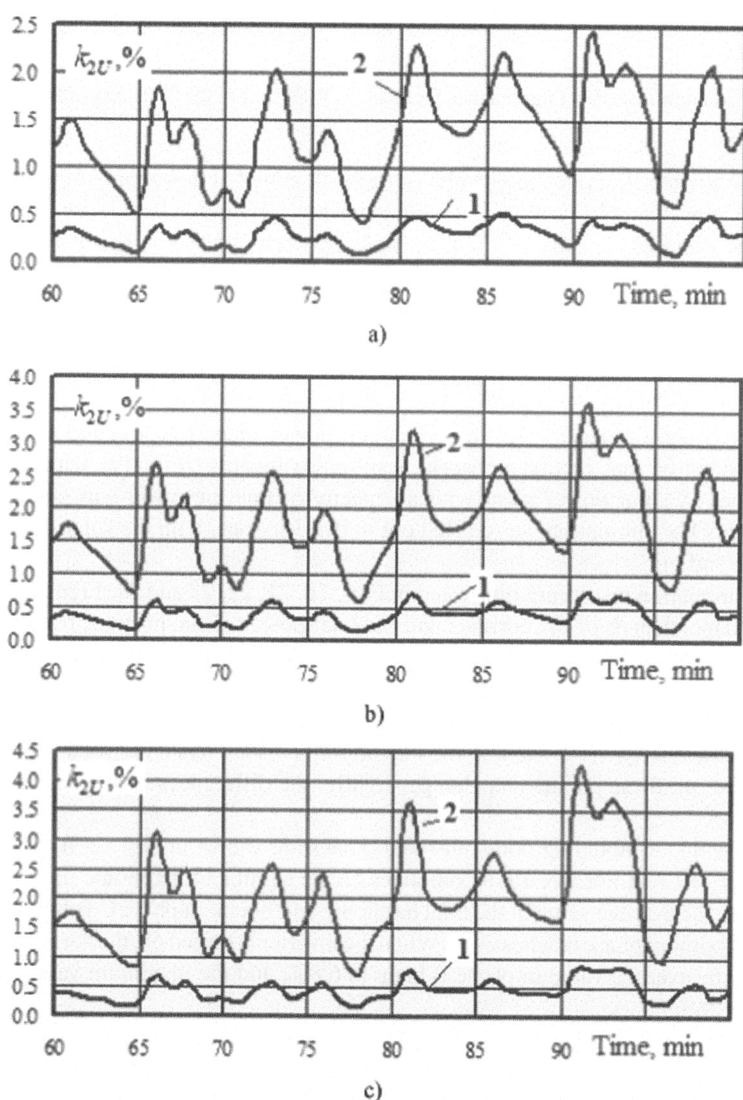

Fig. 12. Dynamics of changes in factors of negative-sequence unbalance on busbars of 220 kV traction substations: a –TS1; b –TS2; c –TS3; 1–WFs are on; 2–WFs are turned off [28].

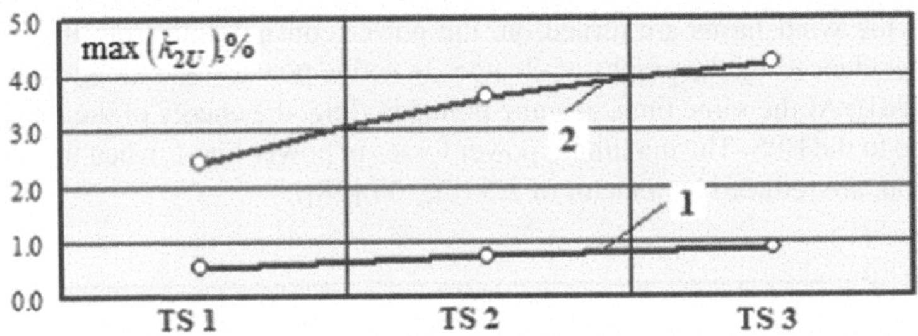

Fig. 13. Maximum values of unbalance factors: 1 – WFs are on; 2 – WFs are turned off [28].

The following describes the results of research aimed at developing digital models of railway power supply systems that include inverter generation based on a solar power plant. The scientific novelty of the proposed approach consists in the use of original methods and algorithms based on phase coordinates and allowing to determine the modes of electric networks with subsystems of direct and alternating currents.

To determine the effect of inverter power on the modes of the mainline railway power supply system, models of typical railway power supply systems were formed in the Fazonord software package (Fig. 18). Including the following segments: an external 220 kV network formed by five double-circuit power lines; four traction substations; three sections of the traction network; a six-pulse inverter (Fig. 19) with a step-up transformer. A solar power plant with a capacity of one megawatt was connected to the inverter. The simulation was carried out in two versions: with the solar power plant turned on and off.

The simulation results are illustrated in Figs. 20, 21, 22, 23 and 24. Figure 20 shows the time dependences of the currents and the total power of the inverter, from which it can be seen that it provides stable output of 998 kW of active power to the network. The traction load creates a noticeable asymmetry (Fig. 21) on the 10 kV of the TS 3 district winding, to which the inverter is connected; at the same time, the average value of the coefficient k_{2U} is 2.4%, and the maximum is 9.4%. When the solar power plant is switched off, these parameters change slightly: the differences in average values are 0.26%.

The results of modeling non-sinusoidal modes are shown in Fig. 22. It can be seen from them that rectifier electric locomotives create significant harmonic distortions on 10 kV TP): the average value of the total harmonic coefficient of phase C voltage is 6.2%, and the maximum phase reaches 24%. When the inverter is turned on, the harmonic levels increase; the average value in phase B is up to 6.8%, and the maximum value in phase C is up to 26%.

To improve the power quality [30, 31], active harmonic conditioners and phase-controlled reactive power sources can be used. The results of modeling non-sinusoidal modes in the presence of active harmonic conditioners are shown in Fig. 23, from which it can be seen that the harmonic coefficients do not exceed 0.2%.

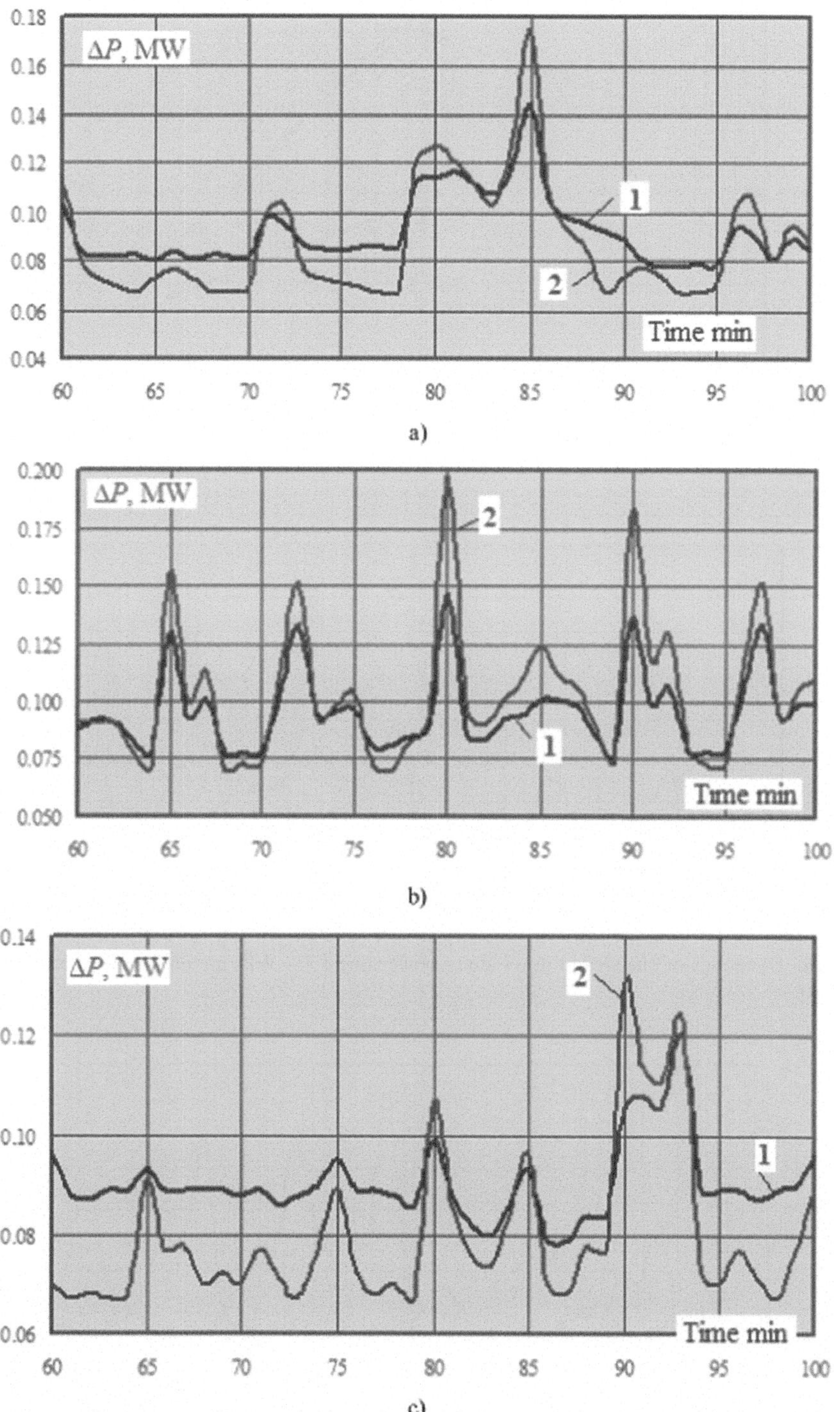

Fig. 14. Dynamics of changes in losses in traction transformers: a – TS 1; b – TS 2; c – TS 3; 1 – WFs are on; 2 – WFs are turned off [28].

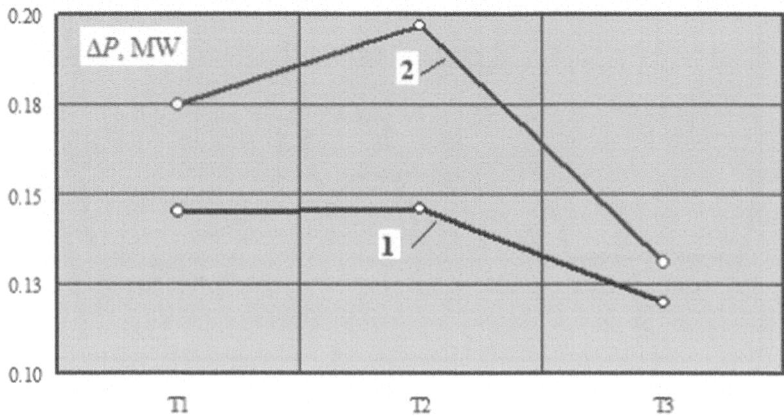

Fig. 15. Maximum loss levels in traction transformers: 1 – WFs are on; 2 – WFs are turned off [28].

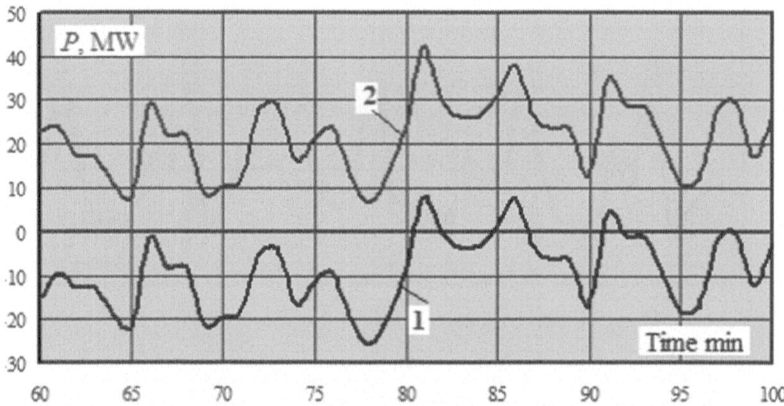

Fig. 16. Dynamics of changes in flows along power line 1:1 – WFs are on; 2 – WFs are turned off [28].

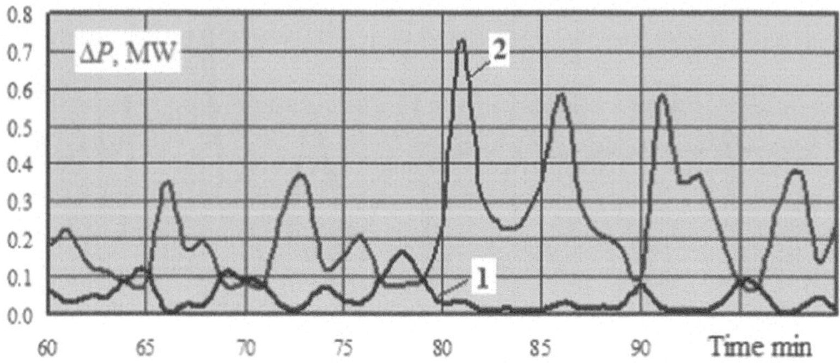

Fig. 17. Dynamics of changes in losses in power line 1: 1 – WFs are on; 2 – WFs are turned off [28].

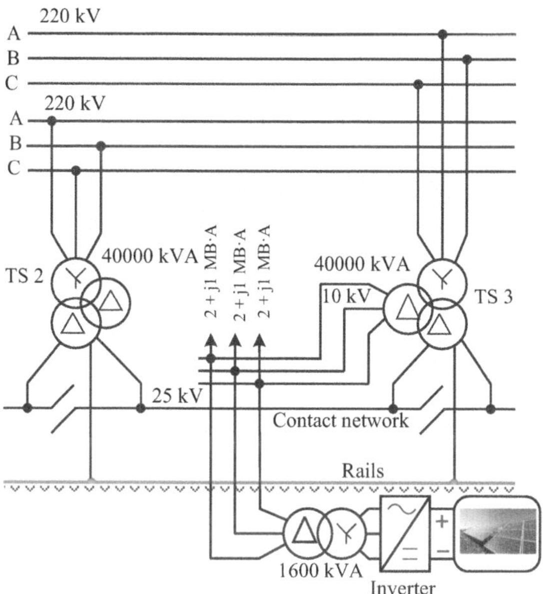

Fig. 18. The central part of the initial network diagram.

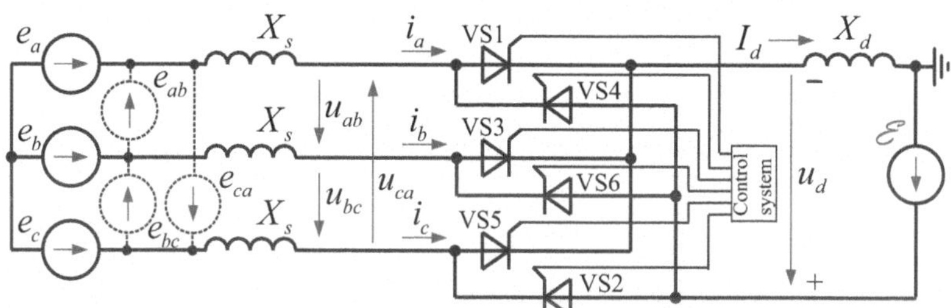

Fig. 19. Bridge diagram of a six-pulse inverter.

The simulation results for the installation of a phase-controlled reactive power source on 10 kV TS 3 buses are shown in Fig. 24; at the same time, a sufficiently high voltage stability is ensured: the coefficient of variation for phases A and C is 2%, and for phase B – 3%. The average value k_{2U} is 1.96%. The available capacities of reactive power sources are assumed to be equal to –5…5 Mvar.

To fully stabilize the voltages, it will be necessary to place reactive power sources at all TS sites. In addition to reactive power sources, a device based on the Steinmetz circuit, as well as symmetrical transformers, can be used to reduce deviations and reduce asymmetry.

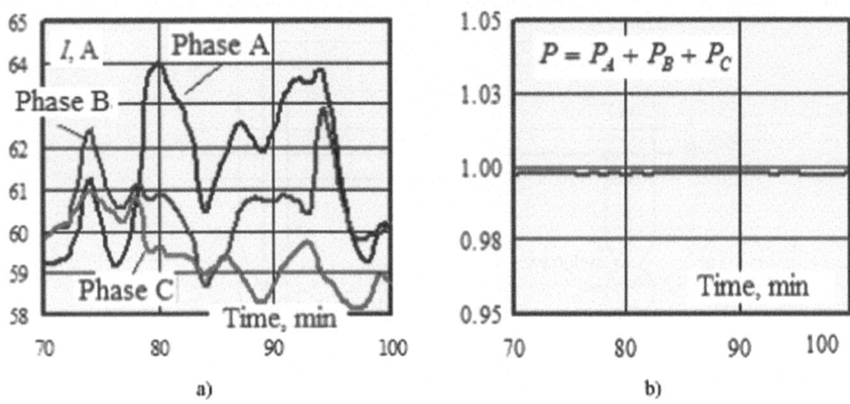

Fig. 20. Currents (a) and total power of the inverter (b).

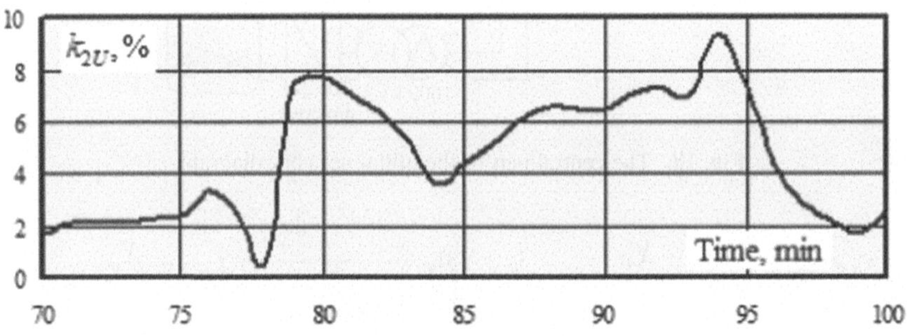

Fig. 21. Asymmetry coefficients on 10 kV TS 3.

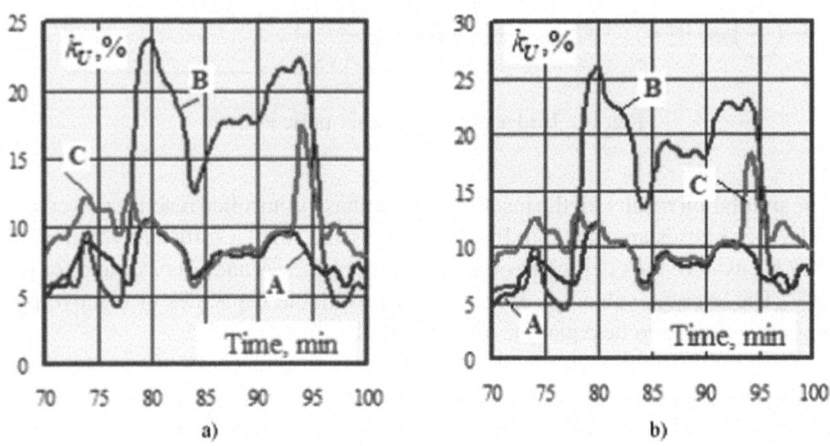

Fig. 22. Harmonic coefficients of voltage on 10 kV TP 3. a – the solar power plant is turned off; b – the solar power plant is turned on.

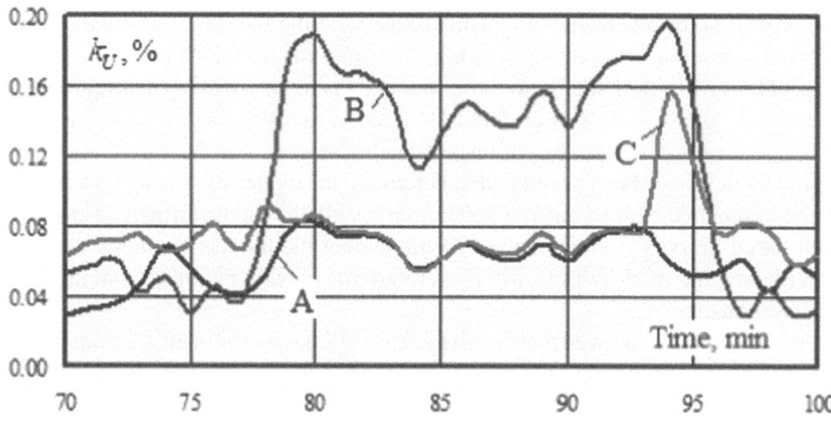

Fig. 23. The resulting harmonic coefficients when switching on active harmonic conditioners.

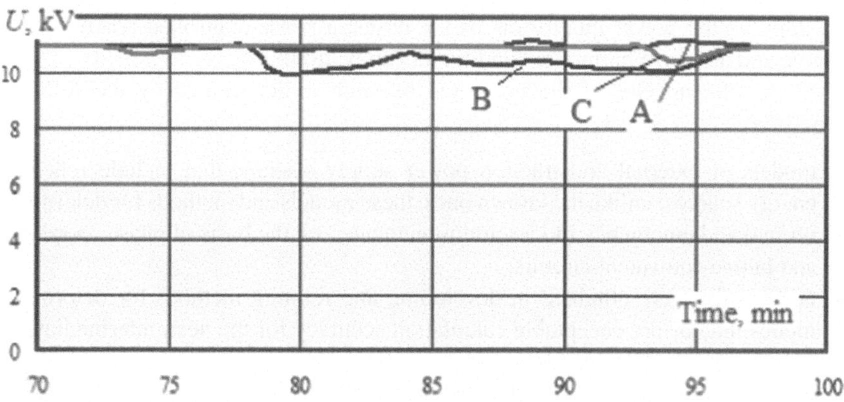

Fig. 24. Bus voltages of 10 kV traction substation.

4 Conclusions

1. The results of research aimed at developing digital models for calculating the operational parameters of railway power supply systems using wind farms are presented. The implementation of these models involved a methodology for modelling the operating parameters in phase coordinates. This methodology is distinguished by the following features: systems dimension, consisting in the ability to factor in all the important characteristics of traction and external power supply systems; versatility, providing modelling of traction networks and power lines of various designs; comprehensiveness, which implies the possibility of calculating normal, emergency, and special operating parameters.
2. Modeling of the operating conditions was carried out for two options. The first focused on a typical RPSS without self-generation plants. The second involved modelling the RPSS with wind generators connected to the 6 kV busbars of traction substations.

3. The modelling results have demonstrated that with the wind farms operating in the RPSS, it is possible to cut down electricity consumption from EPS networks; increase the reliability of power supply to the essential consumers by using wind turbines for backup; and improve the power quality in traction networks and 6–10 kV networks, which power stationary railway transport facilities.
4. Digital models have been developed to determine the modes of railway power supply systems equipped with an inverter generation installation in the form of a solar power plant based on photovoltaic panels. To implement the models, methods were used to determine the modes of electric power systems containing direct and alternating current segments.
5. The results obtained showed that due to the use of a solar power plant, the consumption of electricity from the electric power system is reduced and with the mass use of solar panels, a noticeable technical and economic effect can be obtained. In addition, additional energy sources will improve the reliability of power supply to train traction, as well as signaling and auto-blocking facilities that ensure the safety of cargo and passenger transportation processes.
6. To improve the power quality on 10 kV buses, a phase-controlled reactive power source and an active harmonic conditioner can be used.
7. The scientific novelty of the presented research is determined by the following provisions:

   - models of external and traction power supply systems that include renewable energy sources; unlike the known ones, these models and methods for determining normal and emergency modes are implemented on the basis of phase coordinates and lattice equivalent circuits;
   - new results were obtained in developing and refining methods for determining modes that ensure acceptable calculation accuracy for the near, intermediate and far zones of the Carson integral;
   - digital models that ensure determination of the modes of a power supply system equipped with an inverter generation unit in the form of a solar power plant based on photovoltaic panels;
   - the model of a six-pulse converter is made with three current sources for the AC subsystem and an EMF source for DC; this model plays the role of a separating element of the AC and DC subsystems; current sources are connected to the secondary winding of the converter transformer, and the EMF source is connected to the nodes of the DC subsystem; the methodology for modeling six-pulse converters allows for the simple creation of models of twelve-pulse devices by appropriately connecting six-pulse models;
   - along with the results presented above, the developed models allow for the solution of a number of additional problems relevant to the design and operation of power supply systems with renewable energy sources: calculation of heating temperatures of current-carrying parts, traction and converter transformers; determination of ice melting modes; calculation of electromagnetic field strengths, modeling of active elements of intelligent electrical networks.

Acknowledgements. The research was conducted within the framework of the State Assignment "Conducting applied scientific research" on the topic "Development of methods, algorithms, and software for modeling the operation of traction power systems for DC railways".

References

1. Shevlyugin, M.V., Zhumatova, A.A.: Possibility of using renewable energy sources in the railway traction power system. Sci. Technol. Transp. **4**, 25–28 (2008)
2. Petrushin, A.D., Chernyaev, S.S.: Rationale for the use of energy from renewable energy sources being part of traction power system. Proc. Rostov State Trans. Univ. **4**(57), 78–82 (2021)
3. Rylov, A., Ilyushin, P., Kulikov, A., Suslov, K.: Testing photovoltaic power plants for participation in general primary frequency control under various topology and operating conditions. Energies **14**(16), 5179 (2021)
4. Samarov, K.L., Strenaluk, Yu.V.: Analysis of technical and economic indices of self-generation sources on railways. World Transp. Transp. **15**(70), 142–146 (2017)
5. Karamov, D.N., Suslov, K.V.: Structural optimization of autonomous photovoltaic systems with storage battery replacements. Energy Rep. **7**, 349–358 (2021)
6. Monakov, Y., Tarasov, A., Ivannikov, A., Murzintsev, A., Shutenko, N.: Optimization of equipment operation in power systems based on the use in the design of frequency-dependent models. Energies **16**(18), 6756 (2023)
7. Cheng, P., Kong, H., Ma, J,, Jia, L.: Over-view of resilient traction power supply systems in railways with interconnected microgrid. CSEE J. Power Energy Syst. **7**(5) (2021)
8. Bade, S.K., Kulkarni, V.: Use of Renewable energy in performance enhancement of Indian traction power supply system. In: Proceedings of International Conference on Smart Electric Drives and Power Systems (ICSEDPS) (2018)
9. Andreev, M.V., Suslov, K.V., Bay, Y., Radko, P.P.: Technology for determining the operational settings of remote protection of electric transmission lines using mathematical models. Power Technol. Eng. **57**(4), 637–649 (2023)
10. Kuznetsov, V., Kuznetsov ,V., Bondar, O., Rojek, A., Hubskyi, P., Stypulkowski, P.: Study of short circuit currents in a distributed traction power supply system with renewable electric power sources. In: Proceedings of 2022 IEEE 3rd KhPI Week on Advanced Technology (KhPIWeek) (2022)
11. Singh, L., Vaishnav, C., Shrivastava, V.: Performance Analysis of hybrid network of indian traction power system using renewable energy sources. In: Proceedings of International Conference on Micro-Electronics and Telecommunication Engineering (ICMETE) (2016)
12. Tian, Z., Kano, N., Hillmansen, S.: Integration of energy storage and renewable energy sources into AC railway system to reduce carbon emission and energy Cost. renewable energy sources. In: Proceedings of 2020 IEEE Vehicle Power and Propulsion Conference (2020)
13. Bade, S.K., Kulkarni, V.A.: Analysis of Railway traction power system using renew-able energy: a review. In: Proceedings of International Conference on Computation of Power, Energy, Information and Communication (ICCPEIC) (2018)
14. Spunei, E., Protea, B., Piroi, I., Navrapescu, V., Piroi, F.: Use of renewable energy sources to power railroad traffic safety installations. In: Proceedings of 11th International Symposium on Advanced Topics in Electrical Engineering (2019)
15. Bakre, S., Gokhale, P.: Neural network based source selection scheme for wind-solar based auxiliary supply in railway traction systems. In: Proceedings of IEEE Pune Section International Conference (PuneCon) (2020)

16. D'Arco, S., Piegari, L., Tricoli, P.: Comparative analysis of topologies to integrate photovoltaic sources in the feeder stations of AC railways. IEEE Trans. Transp. Elect. **4**(4) (2018)
17. Di Noia, L.P., Rizzo, R.: Analysis of Integration of PV power plant in railway power systems. In: Proceedings of 8th International Conference on Modern Power Systems (MPS) (2019)
18. Wu, C., Han, B., Lu S., Xue, F., Zhong, F.: Carbon-reducing train rescheduling method for urban railway systems considering the grid with wind power supply. In: Proceedings of IEEE 25th International Conference on Intelligent Transportation Systems (ITSC) (2022)
19. Rageh, M., Ndtoungou, A., Hamadi, A., Al-Haddad, K.: Railway traction supply with PV integration for power quality issues. In: Proceedings of 44th Annual Conference of the IEEE Industrial Electronics Society (2018)
20. Yu, H., Wang, Y., Chen, Z.: A renewable electricity-hydrogen-integrated hybrid dc traction power system. In: Proceedings of IEEE Southern Power Electronics Conference (2021)
21. Mingliang, W., Weiying, W., Wenli, D., Huabo, C., Chaohua, D., Weirong, C.: Back-to-back PV generation system for electrified railway and its control strategy. In: Proceedings of IEEE Transportation Electrification Conference and Expo, Asia-Pacific (ITEC Asia-Pacific) (2017)
22. Çiçek A., et al.: Integrated rail system and EV parking lot operation with regenerative braking energy, energy storage system and PV availability. IEEE Trans. Smart Grid **13**(4) (2022)
23. Loktionov, E.Y., Sharaborova, E.S., Asanov, I.M.: Prospective sites for solar-powered permafrost stabilization systems integration in Russian railways. In: Proceedings of 8th International Conference on Renewable Energy Research and Applications (ICRERA) (2019)
24. Lencwe, M.J., Chowdhury, S.P., ElGohary, H.M.: Solar photovoltaic integration on locomotive roof top for South African railway industry. In: Proceedings of 51st International Universities Power Engineering Conference (UPEC) (2016)
25. Zakaryukin, V.P, Kryukov, A.V.: Complicated asymmetrical modes of electrical systems. Irkutsk, p. 273 (2005)
26. Bulatov, Y.N.,Cherepanov, A.V., Kryukov, A.V. Suslov, K.: Distributed generation in railroad power supply systems. In: Proceedings of 3rd International Colloquium on Intelligent Grid Metrology, SMAGRIMET (2020)
27. Zakaryukin, V.P., Kryukov, A.V.: Modeling the DC traction power systems based on phase coordinates, p. 198. Moscow: Direct-Media Publishers (2023)
28. Kryukov, A., Suslov, K., Cherepanov, A., Kryukov, A.: Modeling the operation of traction power systems incorporating wind turbines. In: Proc. of SMARTGREENS 2024 - 13th International Conference on Smart Cities and Green ICT Systems (2024)
29. Bulatov, Y.N., Kryukov, A.V., Suslov, K.V.: Group predictive voltage and frequency regulators for small hydro power plants in the context of low power quality. Renew. Energy **200**, 571–578 (2020)
30. Smirnov, A.S., Solonina, N.N., Suslov, K.V.: Separate measurement of fundamental and high harmonic energy at consumer inlet - A way to enhancement of electricity use efficiency. In: Proceedings of 2010 International Conference on Power System Technology: Technological Innovations Making Power Grid Smarter, POWERCON2010 (2010)
31. Suslov, K., Solonina, N., Gerasimov, D.: Assessment of an impact of power supply participants on power quality. In: Proceedings of Proceedings of International Conference on Harmonics and Quality of Power, ICHQP (2018)

Vehicle Technology and Intelligent Transport Systems

Autonomous Driving Low-Level Control System Validation Using Digital Twins

Heiko Pikner(✉), Mohsen Malayjerdi, and Raivo Sell

Department of Mechanical and Industrial Engineering,
Tallinn University of Technology, Tallinn 19086, Estonia
{heiko.pikner,mohsen.malayjerdi,raivo.sell}@taltech.ee

Abstract. Autonomous vehicles (AVs) rely not only on complex high-level decision-making systems but also on the safety and reliability of low-level control systems, including actuators and electronic control units (ECUs). This paper introduces a novel framework for validating these low-level systems using digital twin-based simulations, integrating an AI-driven monitoring system to observe and analyze control signals from the higher-level autonomous software. The AI system detects real-time anomalies, such as localization loss or erratic throttle commands, and automatically triggers corrective actions like reducing speed or initiating emergency stops to prevent accidents. By leveraging digital twins to simulate realistic failure conditions, the framework enhances both low-level and high-level validation, contributing to a more robust and reliable AV system. This approach demonstrates a significant advancement in the validation and verification (V&V) process, providing a powerful tool for improving safety in autonomous driving technologies through comprehensive testing and proactive failure management.

Keywords: Autonomous vehicle · Low-level · Digital twin

1 Introduction

Developing and validating the low-level control systems of AVs is a complex task due to the intricate nature of these systems, which include actuators, sensors, and electronic control units (ECUs). These low-level systems translate high-level decisions from the autonomous software into real-world vehicle actions such as steering, braking, and accelerating. Ensuring the correct functionality of these components is critical for overall vehicle safety. Model-based design (MBD) has emerged as an effective methodology for designing and validating complex systems [17]. MBD, based on the V-model testing approach in ISO 26262, allows engineers to create system models, automatically generate code, and perform validation through various X-In-the-Loop (XIL) tests, including Model-In-the-Loop (MIL), Software-In-the-Loop (SIL), Processor-In-the-Loop (PIL), and Hardware-In-the-Loop (HIL) tests.

F. Calise et al. (Eds.): SMARTGREENS 2024/VEHITS 2024, CCIS 2954, pp. 81–90, 2026.
https://doi.org/10.1007/978-3-032-23187-1_5

MBD enables the entire design cycle to be model-centric, from algorithm development to control system validation, significantly enhancing communication accuracy and design efficiency. These XIL tests progressively validate system models, software code, and hardware integration. For example, HIL testing provides a high-fidelity simulation environment where control systems can be tested in realistic scenarios without risking actual hardware. This process is essential for verifying AV systems' deterministic and stochastic elements. Deterministic components, such as ECUs, have predictable behavior with well-known inputs and outputs, while stochastic processes like object detection introduce probabilistic behavior, requiring extensive testing to ensure system reliability across varied scenarios.

This paper focuses on using high-fidelity simulations to validate low-level systems of an AV within a virtual environment. The concept of a digital twin (DT) is leveraged to replicate the AV system, allowing us to simulate different scenarios, test operational design domains, and observe vehicle responses in real-time [13,15]. Game-engine-based simulation platforms such as CARLA [3] and Autoware AWSIM [8] offer flexible environments for integrating the digital twin and conducting scenario-based validation. By doing so, we can comprehensively evaluate the system's performance and safety, especially in detecting high-level control anomalies, such as localization loss, and predicting risky maneuvers that could lead to accidents.

Moreover, this paper introduces an AI-driven monitoring system, integrated into the AV's master control unit, to enhance real-time supervision of control signals from the higher-level autonomous software stack. The AI system continuously monitors and evaluates these signals for potential anomalies, such as localization errors or abrupt commands, which could lead to unsafe vehicle behavior. When such anomalies are detected, the AI system triggers corrective actions, such as reducing speed or initiating emergency stops. By combining digital twins, high-fidelity simulations, and AI monitoring, this paper demonstrates a robust and scalable framework for testing and validating the entire AV system, ultimately contributing to the development of safer and more reliable autonomous driving technologies.

2 Related Work

The development and validation of low-level control systems in AVs presents significant challenges due to the complexity of these systems, which encompass actuators, sensors, and electronic control units (ECUs). One of the most widely adopted methodologies for managing this complexity is Model-Based Design (MBD). MBD is used extensively in the automotive and aerospace industries and follows the V-model testing framework outlined in ISO 26262. MBD facilitates the design, validation, and verification (V&V) of safety-critical systems by allowing engineers to create system models, automatically generate code, and use X-In-the-Loop (XIL) tests such as Model-In-the-Loop (MIL) [1], Software-In-the-Loop (SIL), and Hardware-In-the-Loop (HIL) [13]. XIL testing progressively evaluates the system's models, software, and hardware, ensuring the system performs as expected in real-world scenarios without requiring excessive field tests [5].

The V&V process is crucial in both deterministic and stochastic systems. Deterministic systems, like ECUs and hardware components, exhibit predictable behaviors with well-defined inputs and outputs. However, stochastic components, such as object detection systems that rely on artificial intelligence (AI), introduce probabilistic elements that require extensive testing across a wide range of scenarios [4]. As a result, high-fidelity simulations have become an essential tool for V&V. These simulations enable the testing of AV systems in diverse operational design domains (ODDs), such as varying weather conditions and traffic environments. Real-world testing alone would take decades to accumulate the billions of kilometers required for statistically significant results [7], so simulations provide a cost-effective and time-efficient alternative.

High-fidelity simulation platforms, such as CARLA and Autoware AWSIM, have emerged as critical tools in validating AV systems. These platforms leverage digital twin (DT) technology to create virtual replicas of vehicles and their environments, allowing researchers to evaluate both high- and low-level system components in complex, real-world-like conditions [9,15]. Simulators such as AWSIM, built upon game engines, offer highly detailed urban environments and assets to test AV performance in a controlled, repeatable manner. These environments enable the validation of AI-driven perception systems and low-level control units like actuators and ECUs. Autoware, an open-source AV software stack, is often used with these simulators for testing automated driving algorithms [13].

Recent research has also focused on integrating AI systems to improve fault detection in AV control architectures. AI-based monitoring systems have been developed to detect anomalies in perception systems, such as localization loss or risky maneuvers, which could lead to accidents [6]. These systems are trained using data generated from digital twin simulations and can monitor low-level control systems in real-time, enabling the detection of potential failures before they escalate into dangerous situations. For example, AI systems have been used to monitor the signals from higher-level decision-making software and detect anomalies in the vehicle's physical behavior, such as unexpected actuator responses or sensor failures. This real-time monitoring provides an additional layer of safety by initiating corrective actions, such as emergency stops or speed reductions, when necessary. These AI systems use machine learning algorithms trained on data collected from high-fidelity simulations to predict potential failures in real-time. By integrating AI with digital twin simulations, researchers can detect anomalies early and trigger preventive measures, such as reducing speed or executing emergency stops, to prevent hazardous outcomes. Studies have demonstrated the effectiveness of AI-driven monitoring systems in identifying and mitigating control system faults, further enhancing the reliability of AVs [2].

The concept of digital twins was first introduced by NASA in 2012, driven by the need to accurately model flight conditions for astronauts in space and other environments [16], and it later expanded into fields such as industrial engineering and robotics [12]. However, the true power of digital twins emerges when they begin receiving data from their physical counterparts, exploiting computational capabilities to predict potential failures and guide update strategies. In this way, a digital twin serves as a feedback loop, continuously gathering data and making adjustments to mitigate unexpected outcomes. This approach can also be applied to AVs, where their testing environments are connected to digital twins in simulated spaces, allowing for real-time monitoring and testing. Today, as commercial vehicles have an expected lifespan of 10–15 years, many AVs and traditional vehicles come equipped with software functionalities that can be updated over time without altering the hardware. Digital twinning allows manufacturers to simulate and analyze each vehicle's behavior continuously, gather data from the physical system, and detect faults in advance, enabling them to deploy software updates that address issues before they become critical.

In conclusion, validating AV systems through MBD, XIL testing, and digital twin simulations has become the foundation for modern V&V processes. AI-driven fault detection systems further enhance this process by providing real-time anomaly detection and corrective actions, ensuring both the high-level and low-level systems operate reliably. This paper builds on these methodologies by integrating an AI monitoring system into the AV's master control unit, demonstrating how high-fidelity simulations and digital twins can validate the entire AV system while fostering safer autonomous driving technologies.

3 Validation of AVs System Elements

A robust infrastructure ensures comprehensive validation and verification (V&V) of AVs systems. This methodology follows a structured approach similar to complex software development projects. The process involves several key validation methods for different elements of the AV stack. These components are modeled at various levels of fidelity to balance accuracy and simulation performance [11]. The core modules for validation include detection, control, localization, mission planning, and low-level control [13]. Open-source frameworks such as PolyVerif are provided for V&V purposes for researchers that can be expanded and customized for various use cases [14].

Detection Validation. This involves comparing ground truth data with the AV stack's detection logs to identify errors. The validation is conducted frame-by-frame, logging detailed object detection results and generating performance reports, particularly focusing on detection accuracy within different distance ranges.

Control Validation. This stage evaluates how detection influences the AV's control mechanisms, focusing on critical safety functions like automatic braking. The validation assesses parameters such as time-to-collision, the simulator and AV stack response times, and delays in perception or control initiation. This allows for analyzing the impact of detection on the AV's response to potential obstacles.

Localization Validation. This step tests the AV's ability to maintain accurate positioning using multiple sensors, including GPS, IMU, LIDAR, and RADAR. By introducing controlled noise into the GPS/IMU signals, the V&V framework evaluates the robustness of the localization algorithms under various conditions, including temporary GPS loss.

Mission Planning Validation. This phase validates the vehicle's ability to safely navigate to its destination based on the sensors' input and mission algorithms. The system tracks the global trajectory generated by the AV and monitors any errors, collisions, or deviations from the planned route.

Low-Level Control Validation. Low-level control systems, which consist of electronic control modules (ECUs) and actuators, are validated by simulating their operation within a digital twin environment. Tools like MATLAB and Simulink can be deployed to simulate the vehicle's low-level architecture connected to the higher-level layer, allowing the AV software's navigation signals to pass through the simulated control system (see Fig. 1). This configuration allows for testing individual ECUs or vehicle subsystems in a hardware-in-loop (HIL) environment, where the vehicle autonomously operates within a simulation and simultaneously generates all necessary network traffic.

Such a system enables fast and efficient validation of control modules and system operations. It allows for testing under a variety of predefined conditions and disturbances. Additionally, it offers the capability to simulate scenarios that would be too dangerous to recreate in real-world driving conditions. By running the tests over extended periods, the stability and durability of the system can be assessed. Moreover, by comparing the actual vehicle's performance against the digital twin's behavior under identical inputs, any differences can help identify potential faults.

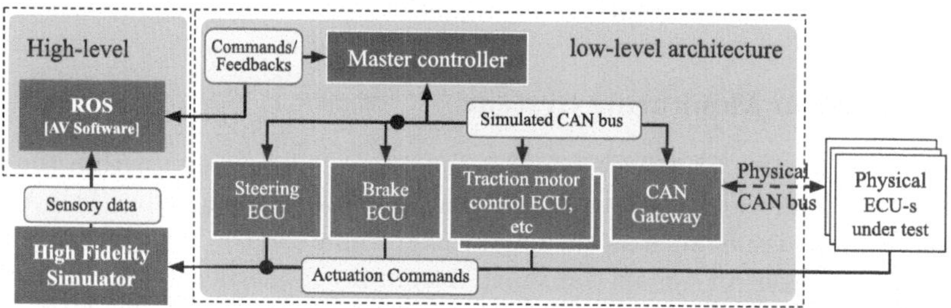

Fig. 1. Low-level control system HIL simulation experimental structure. All of the vehicle's controllers are simulated, and while the simulation is running, traffic is generated on a simulated data network that can be used to test and develop physical controllers [13].

4 Low-Level Control System Validation: Developing a Safety Layer

The Low-Level Control system validation framework can also be leveraged to develop safety add-on layers like an AI-driven monitoring system that actively observes the control signals from higher-level systems. By continuously monitoring control signals, the AI system can detect anomalies or failures that originate at the higher level, such as losing localization or sudden throttle inputs, which could result in hazardous situations like collisions. This approach enhances the safety and robustness of the AV system by allowing the low-level control to react appropriately to prevent accidents caused by errors at the higher level.

4.1 Case Study: IseAuto Shuttle with Digital Twin Integration

To illustrate the effectiveness of the validation framework and AI-driven monitoring system, we provide a case study focused on the iseAuto shuttle, an AV developed by the AV research group at Tallinn University of Technology (TalTech) [15]. The iseAuto shuttle operates on the TalTech campus for both experimental and research purposes, and its digital twin is used for V&V within a simulated environment [10]. This case study demonstrates how the AI-driven monitoring system, alongside the V&V platform, can be applied to improve both higher- and lower-level system validations.

The iseAuto shuttle and its real-world environment are connected to its digital twin, enabling all developments and tests to be run first in the virtual space. The digital twin has the same sensor configuration as the vehicle, with a highly detailed 3D graphical model. The virtual environment mirrors the campus, including urban details, vegetation, and obstacles. The Carla simulator, powered by the Unreal game engine, allows for creating any desired virtual environment, offering flexibility and compliance for performing various tests.

4.2 AI-Driven Monitoring System

In this use case, the AI-driven monitoring system is integrated within the low-level control validation framework to detect anomalies in real-time. The AI system can identify issues such as abrupt throttle commands or localization failures by tracking the control signals transmitted from the higher-level decision-making software. When the system detects abnormal behavior, such as losing GPS signal or receiving an inappropriate speed command, it triggers corrective actions, like adjusting speed or switching to a safe operational mode.

Figure 2 illustrates the high-level and low-level architecture of the iseAuto AV shuttle. The high-level architecture consists of decision-making components, including sensing, localization, detection, and mission and motion planning, which provide control commands (e.g., steering and throttle) to the lower-level system. In the lower-level architecture, the control system is responsible for executing these commands by interacting with the vehicle's actuators and sensors. The figure highlights the integration of an AI-driven monitoring system within the low-level control system. This AI system continuously monitors the incoming control signals from the high-level system, along with feedback from lower-level sensors. If any anomalies are detected, such as a sudden, sharp throttle increase or erratic steering input, the AI monitoring system generates corrective actions to maintain safety. For example, it may reduce the throttle to stabilize the vehicle and avoid abrupt movements. This layered architecture ensures that both high-level decisions and low-level execution are continuously supervised for safety and reliability, with the AI system adding an additional layer of protection against failures.

The Artificial Neural Network (ANN) model used in the AI-driven monitoring system of the iseAuto shuttle is shown in Fig. 3. The model takes several key inputs: the steering angle, the steering command, the throttle command, and the current velocity. The ANN processes these inputs to predict the likelihood of localization loss. The model's output is a probability value indicating whether a localization failure is likely. The ANN model was trained using data recorded from simulation testing of 400 overtaking scenarios conducted with the iseAuto shuttle, providing the model with a diverse range of inputs and conditions for learning. The system automatically initiates pre-programmed safety measures if the output is classified as "True" (i.e., a high probability of localization loss). This ANN-based monitoring system adds a predictive layer of safety, allowing the vehicle to respond proactively to potential issues.

5 Limitations and Future Directions

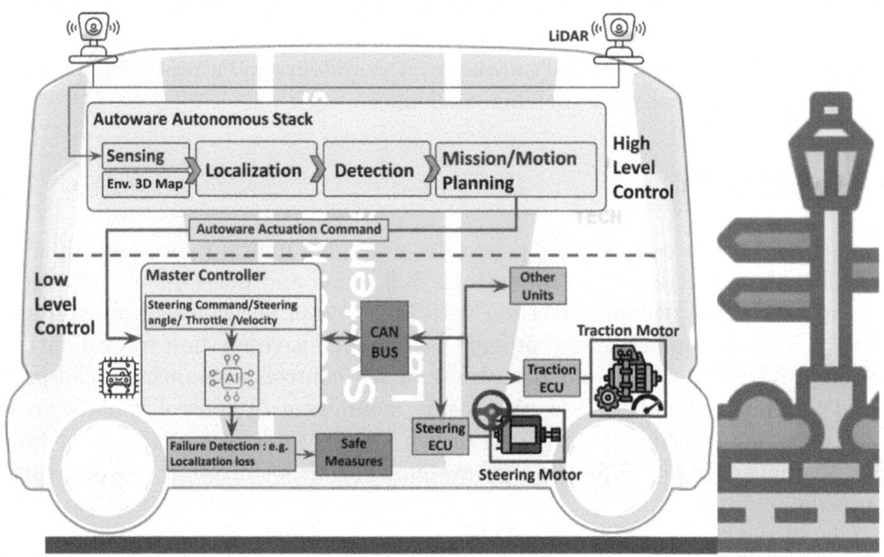

Fig. 2. Arcitecture for AI-driven monitoring for low-level system.

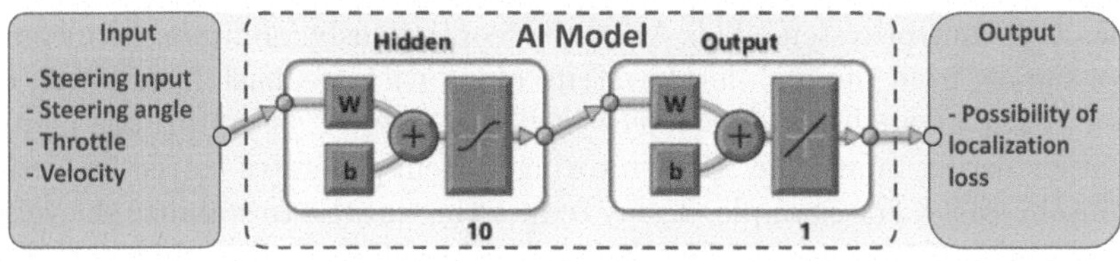

Fig. 3. ANN model, inputs and output used for the AI monitoring in the low-level system.

While the proposed approach appears promising, there are several limitations and potential areas for improvement. One of the primary challenges lies in the complexity of the ANN models used for anomaly detection. While more complex models, such as Long Short-Term Memory (LSTM) networks, could potentially improve the accuracy of predictions by capturing temporal dependencies in control signals like steering, throttle, and velocity, they also introduce additional computational overhead. This is particularly important to consider, as the low-level embedded system is responsible for real-time calculations, and excessive computational load could lead to performance bottlenecks. Thus, a balance must be struck between enhancing prediction accuracy and maintaining manageable computational requirements for the low-level control system.

Another critical area for future improvement is the testing of pre-programmed safety measures, such as reducing throttle to control vehicle movements during anomaly detection. These safety maneuvers must be rigorously tested in diverse scenarios to ensure their effectiveness under various conditions. Developing and validating the optimal pre-programmed responses for different situations is essential to improving the overall safety and robustness of the system. By continuously refining the AI models and safety measures, the system can become more reliable and responsive to real-world driving challenges.

6 Conclusion

This paper introduces a novel approach to leveraging digital twin-based simulations for AVs' lower-level control systems validation and development. By integrating lower-level system validation with higher-level decision-making systems under a unified framework, we provide a comprehensive method for validating and improving the safety and robustness of AV control mechanisms. The proposed approach allows for the continuous monitoring of control signals, such as throttle and steering, using an AI-driven system to detect anomalies or failures originating from the higher-level system, such as localization loss or erratic commands.

One of the key contributions of this work is implementing an AI monitoring system at the lower level, which can autonomously take corrective actions, like adjusting throttle or steering, in the event of system failures. This adds an extra layer of safety by allowing the low-level control system to respond in real time, reducing the likelihood of accidents caused by high-level errors. However, careful consideration must be given to the complexity of the AI model used, as it needs to remain lightweight and efficient enough to operate within the computational constraints of low-level embedded systems. Additionally, the pre-programmed safety measures should be rigorously tested across various scenarios to ensure their reliability under different conditions.

In conclusion, this paper demonstrates that integrating AI-driven monitoring systems with digital twin simulations provides a powerful framework for enhancing the safety and reliability of AV systems, particularly at the lower level. Future work will focus on refining the AI model and safety measures to ensure they can be deployed in real-world systems with optimal performance.

Acknowledgments. This work has been supported by the European Union through the H2020 project Finest Twins (grant No. 856602).

Disclosure of Interests. The authors have no competing interests to declare that are relevant to the content of this article.

References

1. Bruggner, D., Hegde, A., Acerbo, F.S., Gulati, D., Son, T.D.: Model in the loop testing and validation of embedded autonomous driving algorithms. In: 2021 IEEE Intelligent Vehicles Symposium (IV), pp. 136–141. IEEE (2021)
2. Chen, L., Wu, P., Chitta, K., Jaeger, B., Geiger, A., Li, H.: End-to-end autonomous driving: challenges and frontiers. IEEE Trans. Patt. Anal. Mach. Intell. (2024)
3. Dosovitskiy, A., Ros, G., Codevilla, F., Lopez, A., Koltun, V.: Carla: an open urban driving simulator. In: Conference on Robot Learning, pp. 1–16. PMLR (2017)
4. Gong, C.S.A., Su, C.H.S., Chen, Y.H., Guu, D.Y.: How to implement automotive fault diagnosis using artificial intelligence scheme. Micromachines **13**(9) (2022). https://doi.org/10.3390/mi13091380, https://www.mdpi.com/2072-666X/13/9/1380
5. Gupta, P., et al.: An x-in-the-loop (XIL) testing framework for validation of connected and autonomous vehicles. In: 2023 IEEE International Automated Vehicle Validation Conference (IAVVC), pp. 1–6. IEEE (2023)
6. Hou, W., Li, W., Li, P.: Fault diagnosis of the autonomous driving perception system based on information fusion. Sensors **23**(11), 5110 (2023)
7. Kalra, N., Paddock, S.M.: Driving to safety: how many miles of driving would it take to demonstrate autonomous vehicle reliability? Transp. Res. Part A Policy Practice **94**, 182–193 (2016)
8. Kato, S., et al.: Autoware on board: enabling autonomous vehicles with embedded systems. In: 2018 ACM/IEEE 9th International Conference on Cyber-Physical Systems (ICCPS), pp. 287–296. IEEE (2018)
9. Malayjerdi, M., Baykara, B.C., Sell, R., Malayjerdi, E.: Autonomous vehicle safety evaluation through a high-fidelity simulation approach. Proc. Est. Acad. Sci. **70**(4), 413–421 (2021)
10. Malayjerdi, M., Goss, Q.A., Akbaş, M.İ., Sell, R., Bellone, M.: A two-layered approach for the validation of an operational autonomous shuttle. IEEE Access (2023)

11. Malayjerdi, M., Kaljavesi, G., Diermeyer, F., Sell, R.: Scenario-based validation for autonomous vehicles with different fidelity levels. In: 2023 IEEE 26th International Conference on Intelligent Transportation Systems (ITSC), pp. 3411–3416. IEEE (2023)
12. Negri, E., Fumagalli, L., Macchi, M.: A review of the roles of digital twin in cps-based production systems. Procedia Manufact. **11**, 939–948 (2017)
13. Pikner, H., Malayjerdi, M., Bellone, M., Baykara, B., Sell, R.: Autonomous driving validation and verification using digital twins. In: Proceedings of the 10th International Conference on Vehicle Technology and Intelligent Transport Systems - VEHITS, pp. 204–211. INSTICC, SciTePress (2024).https://doi.org/10.5220/0012546400003702
14. Razdan, R., Akbaş, M.İ, Sell, R., Bellone, M., Menase, M., Malayjerdi, M.: Polyverif: an open-source environment for autonomous vehicle validation and verification research acceleration. IEEE Access **11**, 28343–28354 (2023)
15. Sell, R., Malayjerdi, E., Malayjerdi, M., Baykara, B.C.: Safety toolkit for automated vehicle shuttle-practical implementation of digital twin. In: 2022 International Conference on Connected Vehicle and Expo (ICCVE), pp. 1–6. IEEE (2022)
16. Shafto, M., Conroy, M., Doyle, R., Glaessgen, E., Kemp, C., LeMoigne, J., Wang, L.: Modeling, simulation, information technology & processing roadmap. National Aeronaut. Space Administr. **32**(2012), 1–38 (2012)
17. Wang, K., Gong, Z., Hou, Y., Zhang, M., Liu, C., Chen, R.: Model based design and procedure of flight control system for unmanned aerial vehicle. In: 2020 3rd International Conference on Unmanned Systems (ICUS), pp. 763–768. IEEE (2020)

A Hybrid Clustering Approach Using Accident Data for Prediction of Traffic Congestion by Bayesian Network

Kranthi Kumar Talluri(✉) and Galia Weidl

Connected Urban Mobility, University of Applied Sciences Aschaffenburg,
63743 Aschaffenburg, Germany
{KranthiKumar.Talluri,Galia.Weidl}@th-ab.de

Abstract. Traffic congestion is a crucial problem in urban environments with a significant impact on safety, social, and economic aspects. In this study, we discuss how accidents and traffic congestion are interconnected. For this purpose, we proposed a novel labeling approach to define congestion states based on accident variables. Three labeling techniques are introduced: formula-based, hotspot-based, and hybrid approaches. We focus on a hybrid approach, using the DBSCAN algorithm to identify the accident hotspots as clusters. Each cluster is assigned a congestion index score, which is categorized into congestion states (low, medium, and high). For deeper congestion analysis, we investigate two alternative models. Preliminary results show that the hybrid approach combined with the proposed Bayesian Network(BN) outperforms the other labeling approaches. Moreover, the results indicate the robustness of the Hybrid approach in traffic congestion analysis. The labels obtained from the hybrid approach are used to evaluate the BN model's performance in comparison to five popular Machine learning (ML) models. The BN model outperformed all five ML models in accuracy, precision, recall, and F1 Score. Furthermore, the BN model was used for root cause analysis of accidents, assessing their likelihood of causing congestion. Our study indicates that scenario variables like local authority (city) and road category (rural, urban, or highway) significantly impact the congestion probability, which is of value for improving traffic management.

Keywords: Traffic congestion · Prediction · Bayesian network · Data analysis · Clustering

1 Introduction

In the modern urban environment, road transportation is a fundamental source of mobility for all individuals. It serves as a foundation for economic advancement and social interactions. The exponential increase in population and development of metropolitan areas has imposed a critical array of challenges, especially regarding traffic congestion. These challenges have a crucial impact on life quality and regular economic activity [28]. Congestion is not just an inconvenience

F. Calise et al. (Eds.): SMARTGREENS 2024/VEHITS 2024, CCIS 2954, pp. 91–124, 2026.
https://doi.org/10.1007/978-3-032-23187-1_6

experienced by travelers. An increase in road transportation is causing a significant problem in daily life that influences public health, safety, the environment, and state economies [13]. Transportation infrastructures are being pressured due to increased motor vehicle usage, technical advancements, and urban population growth. Rapid urbanization and technological improvements have paved the way for various causes of congestion. High population density majorly contributes to the increasing congestion issue due to the increased requirement for road capacity. It mainly increases competition between vehicles, pedestrians, and public transport. This can be significantly observed in cities that maintain poor and old infrastructures, as the road networks fail to accommodate higher traffic volumes [6] (Fig. 1).

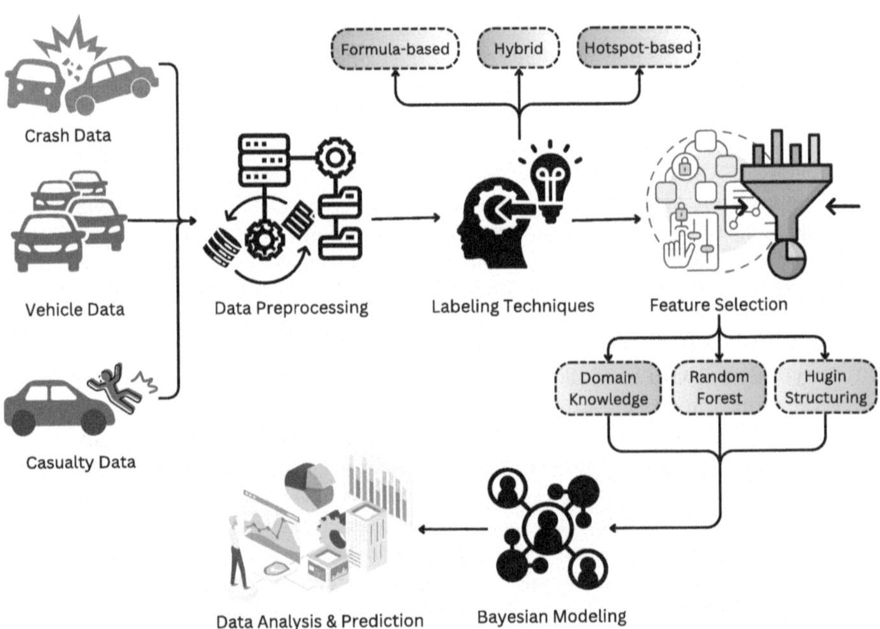

Fig. 1. Block diagram of the complete workflow of Traffic congestion Analysis and Prediction.

Moreover, technological improvements have made vehicles more affordable and accessible, causing a rapid surge in vehicle ownership and usage. However, inaccurate road expansions and lag in traffic management stall and delay daily travel. For instance, the rise in delivery services correlated with the e-commerce boom has added a new layer to the traffic problem. Frequent navigation of roadblocks or congestion is necessary for accurate and timely delivery [10]. Delivery vehicles are expected to travel on tight schedules and contribute to traffic stagnation or bottlenecks. Accidents are one of the main contributors to congestion. They cause a significant disruption in traffic flow, regardless of whether they are minor or major collisions. Accidents result in lane closures, distractions, diversions, and emergency response delays, ultimately resulting in traffic jams [1]. The impacts are particularly harsh in urban environments, as traffic volumes are already higher, especially during morning and evening peak hours. In urban areas, even a minor accident can prompt a series of delays and increased congestion. The situation intensifies with outdated traffic management strategies and static or improper coordination among traffic signals as they do not adapt to the dynamic traffic conditions.

The social and economic costs of congestion are significantly high, especially when combined with the impact of accidents. Some significant effects of congestion delay include productivity loss, increased fuel consumption, and higher transportation costs. Unpredictable congestion resulting from accidents is comparatively more stressful and frustrating for travelers due to unexpected delays and psychological pressure [2]. This, in turn, harms the environment as the pollutants and greenhouse gas emissions increase, affecting air quality, causing noise pollution, and fueling climate change. Consider the drastic increase in traffic levels in the United Kingdom over the past decades to justify the issue's importance. The UK Department of Transport (DfT) claims that vehicle travel has increased by approximately 450 billion over 58 years (from 1950 to 2008), causing a tenfold increase in traffic volume. This has imposed a significant economic burden and financial strain on the country's providence [26]. The annual cost of traffic congestion is estimated to range from 15 to 20 billion pounds. Furthermore, road accidents resulted in increased economic loss and casualties. 19 billion pounds is estimated to have been spent by the UK in 2007 on road accidents, and by the end of the first quarter of 2009, 2.2 million accident casualties were reported [26]. Traffic congestion is categorized into two types, namely recurring and non-recurring. Recurring congestion is predictable and occurs frequently at specific times of the day, like during morning or evening rush hours. Structural factors like increased traffic demand and limited road capacity drive this congestion. Effective and long-term traffic solutions like road expansions, traffic light optimization, and increasing public transport instead of private vehicles could help mitigate the recurring congestion [2]. On the contrary, non-recurring congestion is random and unpredictable. It results from unexpected scenarios like accidents, road construction, weather, or special events and temporarily disrupts traffic flow. Non-recurring congestion management is tricky and challenging due to the dynamic and immediate response requirement [2]. Traditional methods are inefficient in solving the complexity of non-recurring congestion, emphasizing the requirement for more sophisticated and flexible strategies.

Analysis of the relationship between accidents and traffic congestion has helped significantly improve understanding and optimization of traffic safety. Researchers have explored the impact of road types on the severity and probability of congestion related to accidents. For example, lower speed limits can decrease the severity of accidents but increase the possibility of minor incidents due to closer proximity to vehicles [8]. Moreover, the accident consequence worsens during congestion due to delays in emergency response services. Understanding these complexities and the effect of congestion highlights the need to develop effective traffic management and mitigation strategies. Traditional approaches focus mainly on infrastructure development, but this is insufficient to address the problem's complete scope, especially in the case of non-recurring congestion caused by accidents or other unforeseen events.

In response to these complications, this work introduces three novel labeling approaches to categorize congestion based on accident features. Furthermore, a Bayesian network is used to predict and analyze the congestion more accurately. The major objectives are as follows:

- Bayesian network development: A Bayesian network is built to predict the traffic congestion caused by accidents, and two alternative models, namely 3-class and 2-class models, are developed.
- Introduction of novel congestion labeling criteria: Three labeling techniques, namely formula-based, hotspot-based, and hybrid approaches, are developed for accurately categorizing congestion into low, medium, and high states.
- Root cause analysis: Eight scenarios are developed to highlight the influence of variables on congestion states.
- Evaluation of labeling approach: Compared the performance of the Bayesian network for three labeling approaches using metrics like error rate, average Euclidian distance, and average Kullback-Leibler divergence.
- Performance evaluation: The performance of proposed Bayesian network models is compared with different ML algorithms in terms of error metrics like accuracy, precision, recall, and F1 score.

The remaining work is organized as follows: Sect. 2 discusses related work in traffic congestion prediction. Sections 3 and 4 detail the labeling approach and data pre-processing, respectively. Regarding implementing the Bayesian network, scenarios driven for root cause analysis are discussed in Sect. 5. Furthermore, Sect. 6 consists of data analysis followed by results & discussion in Sect. 7. Finally, in the last section, we discuss the conclusion and future works.

2 Related Work

In recent years, researchers have contributed various solutions to optimize traffic congestion problems, including traffic congestion estimation, traffic demand analysis, accident prediction, and identification of accident hotspots. This section details some of the previous works.

In [11], the Kernal Density Estimator (KDE) helped to understand the severity of accidents in the danger zone by analyzing accident hotspots. The machine learning algorithms determine factors causing and influencing the severity of accidents. Sampling techniques like SMOTE and Random Forest achieved the best performance. Authors in [27], identified the abnormal hotspots through a designed congestion factor. GPS data from China helped analyze the relationship between traffic-related data and congestion factors. Based on the analysis, the traffic was effectively managed and re-routed during abnormal hotspots. Authors proposed BN in [2] to understand the variable's impact on congestion. They designed two BN models, one dedicated to recurring congestion and the other to non-recurring congestion. For the non-recurring case, information related to accidents and special events was used for BN modeling. Moreover, both models were used to perform qualitative and quantitative analyses to understand the congestion caused by speed and the number of vehicles. In work [12], the authors presented a unique model with a physical and digital road network. The authors used digital twins to simulate the physical road network to observe the information related to vehicles and traffic. Spatio-temporal features were extracted from the physical network using Conv-LSTM. Effective congestion prediction when an accident occurred was achieved by efficiently integrating both datasets. In paper [16], the author proposed a Gradient Boosting Decision Tree (GBDT) to estimate the time to clear the spots where accidents occurred. Congestion is directly influenced by the duration of clearance time; authors aimed to reduce this time by finding the complex correlation among variables using the proposed framework. Nine critical variables related to spatial, temporal, traffic, accidents, and environment were used in paper [28] to develop two multiple linear models. One model is considered to predict the accident clearance time, and the other estimates the accident duration. The findings showed that accident type, road, and traffic significantly influenced the duration of the accident, while emergency response duration and time of accident affected the clearance time. Results showed that the proposed linear models performed better than the baseline ANN model. Paper [19] shows the estimation of accident occurrence based on historical data using the proposed predictive model. Other supervised and unsupervised algorithms were also used to estimate the incident hotspots. Random forest was recorded to perform at its best among all the models. In [5], congestion and accident-prone regions were explored by authors primarily through a framework designed specifically to extract necessary information from the microblogs. The framework used NLP processing and deep learning algorithms to extract the information required from social media platforms. Then, the updated KDE was used to spot the accident-prone regions. Effective data analysis was performed to highlight the importance of mitigating accidents and congestion.

In [18], authors analyzed the accident-prone areas by categorizing them into low and high classes. For this purpose, the author extracted features like location, cause of the accident, and accident severity to create a Jakarta Bogor Highway dataset. Furthermore, the K-mean clustering algorithm performs cluster profiling to determine the cluster 3 with the most accidents. In paper [3], the author analyzed the spatial pattern of injuries caused by accidents by employing the Kernal Density Estimator and Geographical Information Systems (GIS) and identified accident hotspots to evaluate their application in strategies related to road safety. Author in [20] uses accident data obtained from the Nashville Fire Department to perform spatiotemporal estimation of incidents. A similarity-based agglomerative clustering categorizes accidents, and survival analysis forecasts the probability of accidents in every cluster. Finally, BN maps the clusters to spatial accident locations. The future scope of the author is to support the development of the allocation and dispatching of emergency vehicles to accident spots. Paper [9] uses unsupervised learning to analyze the injury patterns at the MAIS 3+ level. The authors used NASS-CDS data, which were classified based on serious injuries, belted occupants, crash severity, and biomechanical factors. Each cluster's injury pattern was analyzed and linked to the accident characteristics. The analysis provided valuable findings and a new roadmap for optimizing vehicle safety.

Hierarchical clustering and quasi-poisson regression models were used in [17] to analyze the factors contributing to congestion. Naturalistic driving experiments and self-reports were used to classify drivers into four risk groups. Miles driven, driver age and illegal parking history contributed the most to driving risk assessment. In paper [7], the authors developed a novel technique to predict the occurrence of road accidents using gamma updating, hierarchical multivariate Poisson-lognormal regression, and Bayesian inference. They find the correlation between risk factors and the outcome of accidents while mentioning the uncertainty. The method was demonstrated in Australian rural network case studies to predict accident probabilities and severities. The results showed impressive performance in prediction given optimal data.

In summary, previous works showcased a limited use of accident-related variables to estimate congestion occurrence. Although they used different clustering models and BN for congestion analysis, accidents were considered just as one of the other factors contributing to congestion. They failed to capture the nuances of accidents and their effects on congestion and traffic flow. On the contrary, our work highlights the significant role of accident-related variables in understanding traffic dynamics and defining congestion. By integrating the three proposed congestion classification approaches with BN analysis, we took advantage of a wide range of accident-related variables, namely severity, number of vehicles involved, speed limit, accident location, and many more, which supported in making efficient decisions on congestion states like low, medium or high. This makes our model more reliable and adaptable to the real-world scenarios.

3 Labelling Techniques for Congestion

Precise data labeling is essential during machine learning and statistical analysis, particularly in our case, where traffic congestion levels are predicted. This section introduces three crucial labeling approaches for categorizing congestion: clustering, formula-based, and hotspot-based. Each approach is further split into two labeling schemes: 3-class and 2-class, demonstrating their adaptability and applicability in different scenarios, depending on the number of categories allotted to the congestion variable. These congestion categorization techniques help effectively predict and analyze traffic conditions.

3.1 Formula Based Approach

The formula-based approach estimates the probability of traffic congestion, referred to in this work as congestion probability (CP), through a mathematical equation. Three key variables that majorly impact traffic flow are the number of cars involved in an accident, the severity of the traffic incident, and the speed limit. The mathematical formula is designed using these three variables from the dataset. Using these variables in formulating congestion probability is advantageous as they aid in precisely assessing traffic congestion. Moreover, the significant reasons for considering these variables over other variables in the data are as follows:

1. **Number of Cars Involved.** The scale and complexity of an incident are inferred significantly from the information about the number of vehicles involved in an accident. Accidents involving many vehicles can be more severe, causing a serious disruption in traffic flow. They could cause an increase in travel delays, congestion, and time required to clear the accident spot. For example, if a collision that occurs on a highway involves many vehicles, it could result in lane closure, towing service, efficient traffic management, and complex coordination among the emergency response teams as quickly as possible. The likelihood of severe congestion increases with the number of vehicles involved in accidents.
2. **Severity.** The next crucial factor in the formula is severity, which helps understand the extent of injuries, fatalities, and vehicle damage caused by an accident. Accidents with high severity involving significant injuries or deaths require an immediate emergency response, precise investigations, and increased road closure time. They could result in higher traffic congestion, immediate traffic diversion (escalating traffic in surrounding areas), and delays.
3. **Speed Limit.** The speed limit on the road where the accident occurred provides a crucial understanding of the accident's impact on congestion. Vehicles move at higher speeds on roads with high-speed limits, like highways. The severity and impact are significantly higher when these high-speed vehicles are involved in an accident. The disruption caused by such incidents can extend to larger areas, majorly affecting the traffic flow. This could cause delays for authorities to reach the spot, investigate the incident, clear the area, and divert the traffic.

The Congestion Probability (CP) is formulated using a heuristic approach. As shown in Eq. 1, the three variables briefed above are primarily used to define the CP. The formulation of this equation is majorly influenced by the Speed Performance Index (SPI) metric. SPI is a widely accepted metric for assessing traffic flow. It calculates the ratio of actual vehicle speed and maximum permissible speed on the given road, which in turn helps to classify and evaluate traffic states [25]. On the contrary, this work uses the speed limit variable to calculate the CP with some modifications customized to the concept of predicting congestion based on accidents. Equation 1 significantly articulates the disruption in traffic flow due to accidents. Parameters like severity and number of vehicles involved in accidents are used along with speed limit in Eq. 1 to capture the dynamic nature of traffic congestion effectively. A more detailed explanation of the formulated CP is as follows.

$$CP = 5 + 95 \cdot \tanh\left(\frac{2(N + S^2)}{\sqrt{V} + 1} \cdot \log_{10}(N + 1)\right) \tag{1}$$

Here, **S** represents the accident severity, **N** defines the number of cars involved in an accident, and **V** denotes the road's maximum allowed speed limit. The dataset's variable severity consists of 3 states: slight, serious, and fatal. For the calculation purpose, the states are given numeric values 'Slight': 1, 'Serious': 2, 'Fatal': 3. Where higher value indicates more severe the accident severity. The **S** and **N** are summed in the numerator of Eq. 1. More weightage is added to **S** by squaring as the severity variable reflects the spot clearance time along with casualties and seriousness of the accident. In the denominator, the square root of **V** is included due to its higher order of magnitude when compared with **S** and **N**. This also makes sure that the impact of the speed limit (**V**) is proportionate to **S** and **N**.

Moreover, a logarithmic function of **N** is introduced in the formula to compensate for the increase in complexity factor based on the number of vehicles involved in the incident. This ensures that the CP grows exponentially and non-linearly when more vehicles are involved. Finally, the tangent function (tanh(x)) is used in the equation to constrain the range of CP between [-1,1]. Additional shifting and scaling of the equation bring the final output of CP between 0 and 1. The equation, as a whole, smoothens the output by keeping the outliers under logical bounds, which indeed avoids unrealistic estimates. Congestion states are defined after computing the congestion probability from the above equation. These states are used as a target label for our designed Bayesian model. In this subsection, different models are developed based on congestion states, namely 3-class and 2-class models. This differentiation is performed to observe the performance of the Bayesian network. Furthermore, each classification type is illustrated in detail using the flow chart and logarithms in the below subsections.

3-Class Model. Variables like road type (e.g., rural, urban, highway), accident severity, and the number of vehicles involved are used with specific criteria to classify the congestion as low, medium, or high. The flow chart in Fig. 2 provides the criteria with a clear description of the decision-making process involved in classifying congestion states.

- Initialization: $Low_{\mathrm{TH}} = 50$, $High_{\mathrm{TH}} = 80$
- Condition-1: $N >= 3$ **OR** $CP = High_{\mathrm{TH}}$
- Condition-2: $Road_{\mathrm{Cat}} = (Urban$ **OR** $Rural)$ **AND** $S = (Fatal$ **OR** $Serious)$
- Condition-3: $CP > Low_{\mathrm{Th}}$ **AND** $Road_{\mathrm{Cat}} = Urban$ **AND** $S = Slight$

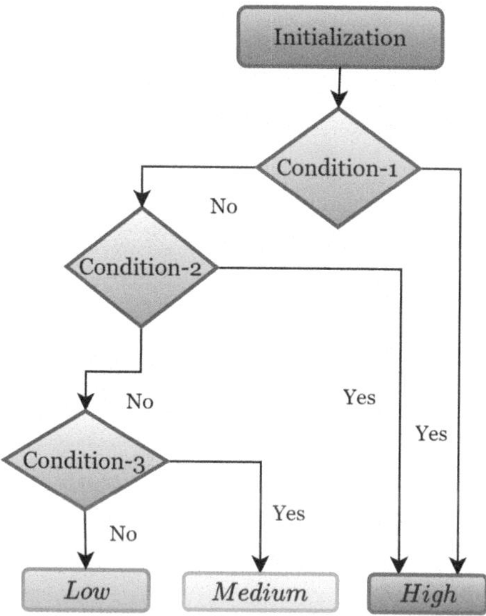

Fig. 2. Flow chart illustrating the Formula-Based 3-class classification process [25].

Here, $Road_{\text{Cat}}$ indicates the road category. Low_{TH} and $High_{\text{TH}}$ pointing to lower and higher thresholds, respectively, are selected precisely in such a way that the level of congestion is classified more accurately. Traffic conditions are analyzed more efficiently in detail using this 3-class model.

2-Class Model. In the 2-class model, congestion state classification is simplified by dividing the target labels into only two categories: low and high. Such binary classification is beneficial in cases requiring a more simple and efficient decision-making process. The 2-class approach is similar to the 3-class model but with reduced complexity. Road type, severity, and the number of vehicles involved are used as key variables here. The values of lower and higher thresholds are modified to fit the 2-class categorization model.

3.2 Hotspot Based Approach

The hotspot-based approach is a different method for congestion classification. It primarily focuses on the spatial distribution of incidents, unlike the formula-based approach, which highlights the use of characteristics of specific incidents. As a start, this method finds and creates a geographical hotspot based on the frequent occurrence of accidents in particular areas, as shown in Fig. 3. The accident coordinates, such as latitude and longitude, are available in the dataset, which helps map and visualize their location based on the occurrence frequency. Such analyses are crucial for analyzing the congestion patterns with regard to particular geographic locations rather than individual incidents [25].

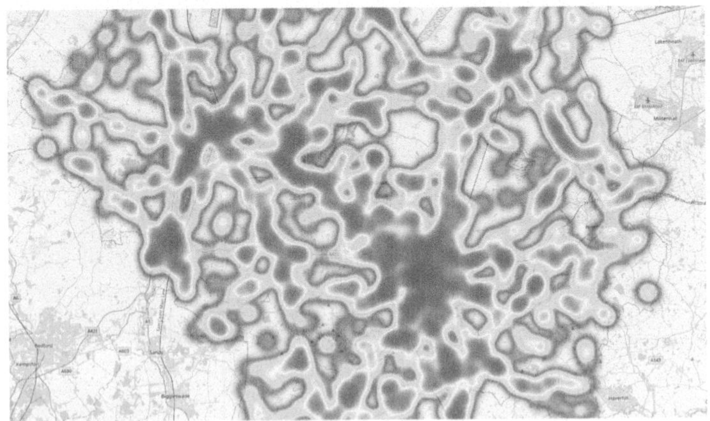

Fig. 3. Spatial Distribution of Road Accidents in Cambridgeshire [25].

Hotspot-based accident analysis is also labeled into two types: 3-class and 2-class models. Depending on the accident density within a particular region, these models classify the congestion into 3/2 states based on appropriate models. This provides a geographical aspect of congestion based on the density of accidents.

3-Class Model. Initially, a heat map based on accident density is generated for the Cambridgeshire area. Geospatial analysis techniques help create heat maps based on accident's latitude and longitude information. The number of accidents that occurred within a specific radius of each incident point is calculated to find areas based on varying accident densities. Depending on this accident frequency, these areas are classified into low, medium, and high congestion states, as shown in Fig. 4.

The designed congestion classification algorithm consists of 2 essential functions: NearbyAccident and CongestionLevel. The NearbyAccident function calculates the number of accidents within a 100-meter radius for each incident. Moreover, the congestion states are assigned based on accident count using the CongestionLevel function. For instance, if more accidents occurred within the specified radius, it would cause high congestion. The process is formulated and shown in Algorithm 1. It outlines the process of categorizing the hotspots into three congestion categories. The 3-class model precisely explains critical areas needing immediate traffic management attention.

2-Class Model. In the 2-class model, the congestion classification is simplified into low and high states. This categorization approach is similar to 3-class models except that the congestion states are reduced to only two categories. The congestion is classified based on the number of accidents that occurred within

```
Data: Road accident data with lat, lon
Result: Congestion levels: low, medium, or high
Function NearbyAccident(dataframe, Radius):
    for rows in dataframe do
        Get lat, lon of accident;
        Calculate distance to all points in dataframe using Haversine formula;
    end
    return NearbyCount;
return
Function CongestionLevel(NearbyCount):
    for rows in NearbyCount do
        if NearbyCount < 3 then
            return low;
        else
            if NearbyCount < 6 then
                return medium;
            else
                return high;
            end
        end
    end
return
Initialization: Radius;
CALL NearbyAccident(dataframe, Radius) ;
CALL CongestionLevel(NearbyCount) ;
```

Algorithm 1. Algorithm for 3 class congestion [25].

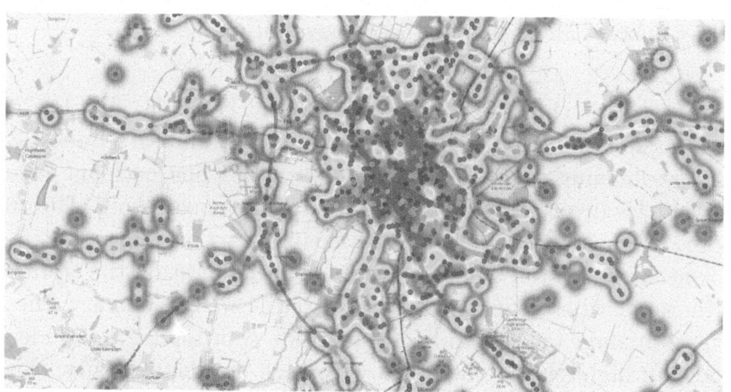

Fig. 4. Visualization of Congestion Intensity Using Color Mapping [25].

the given radius. Here, the threshold for classification as high congestion is modified to four accidents. The congestion is considered low if the accident count is less than four; otherwise, congestion is considered to be high.

```
Data: NearbyCount - a count of nearby elements
Result: Congestion level: low or high
Function CongestionLevel(NearbyCount):
    for rows in NearbyCount do
        if NearbyCount < 4 then
            return low;
        else
            return high;
        end
    end
return
```

Algorithm 2. Algorithm for 2 class congestion [25].

The binary approach helped maintain a balanced dataset, which is essential for better ML model performance. A higher threshold value of accident count results in an imbalance, with one category dominating the other. This leads to biased predictions of congestion occurrence. With the 2-class model, such risks are reduced due to its simple and efficient categorization of congestion. The Algorithm 2 provides a detailed explanation of congestion classification.

3.3 Hybrid Approach

This section briefly illustrates the third labeling technique, the hybrid approach. It is developed to highlight the strengths of the previously introduced labeling technique and mitigate its weaknesses. The hybrid approach showcases robust and better analytics of traffic congestion due to the integration of spatial clustering and extensive calculation of the congestion index.

Rationale Behind the Hybrid Approach. Formula and hotspot-based congestion classification falls short because of the limited scope of variables. Formula-based labeling depends solely on variables like accident severity, the number of vehicles involved in the incident, and the speed limit. Although these variables are significant for understanding their impact on congestion, they fail to account for accident spatial dispersion, which sheds light on the traffic patterns based on the area where the accident occurred. On the contrary, the hotspot-based focus is mainly on geographical accident coordinates (latitude and longitude). Despite highlighting the areas with high accident density, this method neglects the accident-related crucial parameters. The hybrid approach combines the strengths of these two methods and offers a thorough analysis with the help of spatial and contextual information.

Spatial Clustering with DBSCAN. In the hybrid-based approach, the DBSCAN (Density-Based Spatial Clustering of Application with Noise) algorithm is applied primarily to perform clustering using the accident's geographical coordinates (longitude and latitude). This algorithm helps to group accidents based on geographical proximity, as seen in Fig. 6. One primary concern with DBSCAN is fine-tuning its parameters. This algorithm consists of two key parameters: epsilon (esp) and the minimum number of samples(min_samples). For this purpose, we plotted the K-distance graph, which gives the optimal eps values, typically identified at the elbow of the curve that is indicated with a red dotted line as seen in Fig. 5.

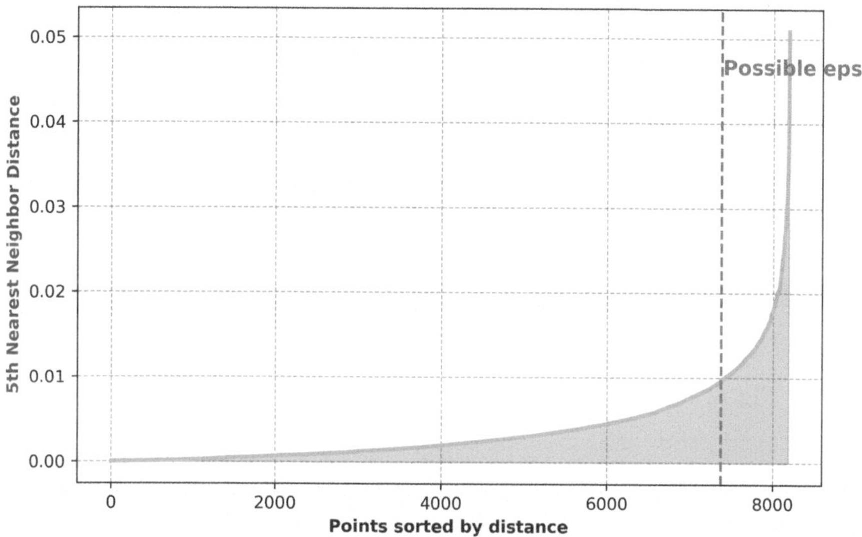

Fig. 5. K-Distance Graph for Determining Optimal epsilon value in DBSCAN.

Congestion Index Calculation. The next step is to identify the clusters containing high accident density while filtering out the outliers. Areas with severe and frequent accident occurrences are highlighted, as DBSCAN plays a significant role in understanding the spatial dynamic of congestion. Each cluster is formed in this process, representing a unique geographical location with a different accident density profile. This step forms a foundation for more detailed congestion analysis within these geographically detached areas.

We defined a parameter named the congestion index for the obtained clusters and assigned a value to them. The index quantifies the congestion level within each cluster using several accident-related variables, such as the total number of accidents (accident count), severity, and number of vehicles involved. The congestion index is calculated using the equation below.

$$\begin{aligned} \text{Congestion Index} = {} & 0.3\,(\text{Accident Count}) \\ & + 0.4\,(\text{Avg\_Severity}) \\ & + 0.3\,(\text{Avg\_Vehicles}) \end{aligned} \tag{2}$$

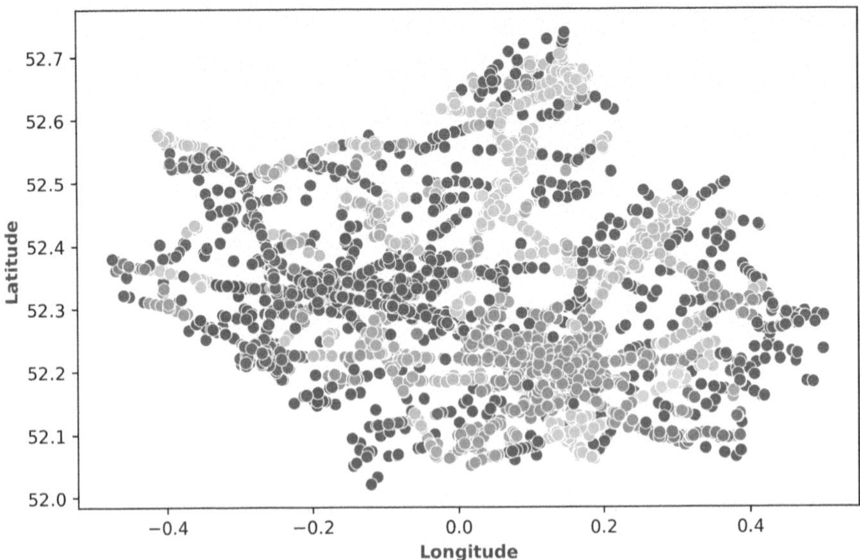

Fig. 6. Formation of accident cluster using DBSCAN algorithm.

In our work to simplify the calculation of the congestion index, the average values of severity and the number of vehicles involved in the accidents are computed for each cluster separately. The weightage assigned to each variable is selected through a trial and error process. The highest weightage is given to average severity as it significantly impacts congestion occurrence in terms of significant disruption due to the immediate need for emergency services. Accident count and average vehicle involved are given a medium weightage of 0.3 as frequent accident occurrence areas may require an efficient traffic management strategy, and situations involving many vehicles in an incident can have a cascading effect on road traffic. This Eq. 2 is advantageous as it helps capture the nuanced information about congestion within each cluster.

3-Class Model. 3-class Model: The final step involves the classification of clusters depending on the congestion index. In the 3-class classification, the clusters are categorized as low, medium, and high depending on the given thresholds. Congestion index distribution is analyzed thoroughly to determine these thresholds appropriately. As we discussed the condition in 3.1, similarly, we defined conditions for the hybrid 3-class model, and the process of classification is shown briefly in Fig. 7. The conditions for categorizing the congestion states are given below.

- Initialization: $Low_{\mathrm{TH}} = 200$, $High_{\mathrm{TH}} = 400$
- Condition-4: $congestion\_index < Low_{\mathrm{TH}}$
- Condition-5: $Low_{\mathrm{TH}} <= congestion\_index < High_{\mathrm{TH}}$

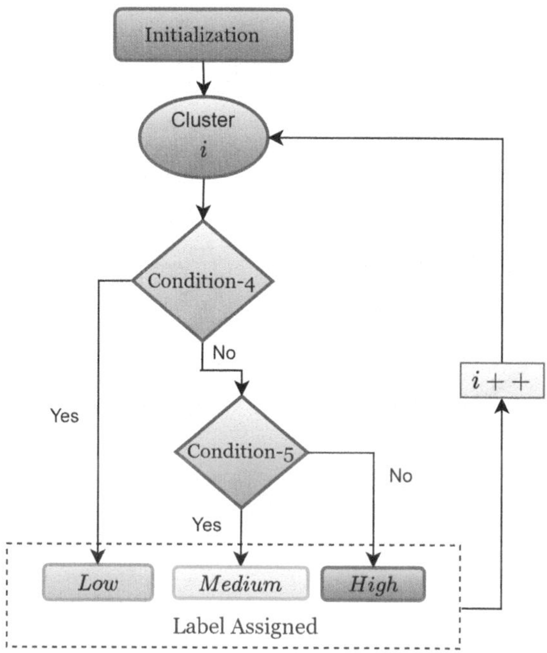

Fig. 7. Flow chart illustrating the Hybrid 3-class classification process.

These thresholds ensure that the categorization is meaningful. Each cluster classification is then applied to all its accident records to maintain consistent labeling across the dataset's accident records.

2-Class Model. For the 2-class classification, the categorization is considered to be only two states: low and high. The classification process is similar to the 3-class model but has reduced states. The threshold of the congestion index is also modified by setting the congestion index as less than 250 as low or high after thorough analysis to ensure the distribution is balanced.

4 Data Pre-processing

4.1 Dataset

The dataset used in this work provides detailed information about traffic accidents in the Cambridgeshire region [4]. It covers a considerable period from January 1, 2017, to July 31, 2023. The dataset is precisely chosen based on several criteria to ensure accuracy and admissibility. An accident is considered to be included in the dataset only if it is reported to the police and at least one person is injured. Also, for the incident to qualify as a collision, at least one vehicle should be involved. The dataset consists of 3 distinct components: Crashes,

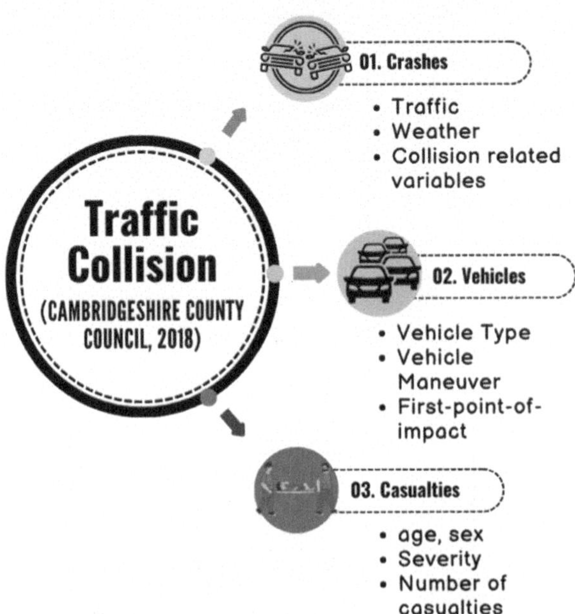

Fig. 8. Dataset Composition: Crashes, Vehicles, and Casualties with relevant variables.

Vehicles, and Casualties, as shown in Fig. 8. Each component provides detailed information on the collision's respective features.

- **1.Crashes.** Crash data consists of all the critical information regarding the accident. It consists of variables related to the condition at the time of the incident. These variables provide information about traffic conditions, weather, and other environmental or situational details influencing the collision.
- **2.Vehicles.** This dataset stores vehicle-related information. It provides detailed information about the vehicle involved in the accident, such as the vehicle type, maneuver when the accident occurred, and initial point of impact.
- **3.Casualties.** This dataset contains information about the people injured during the collision. It stores essential information like age, gender, the severity of the accident, and other details related to the crash's impact on human life.

The key feature of this dataset is the unique identifier variable 'Collision Reference No.' This variable is available across all three data components and helps cross-reference the data between crash, vehicle, and casualty datasets. Using this unique reference, the data across all the components can be correlated. The correlated data helps in the precise analysis of congestion patterns and gain insights about their relationship with accidents that occurred in the Cambridgeshire region. They also facilitate the detailed investigation of factors causing the collisions, the conditions under which they occur, and their consequences.

The dataset's granularity and diversity and the provision to correlate make it perfectly suitable for in-depth traffic safety analysis and congestion mitigation strategies design.

4.2 Variables Discretization

The dataset consists of many variables, but from each dataset, only certain variables are considered based on the assumption that these variables could contribute more to the congestion analysis.

Many variables are available in the dataset related to crashes, vehicles, and casualties. Only certain variables are considered based on the assumption that they significantly contribute to congestion analysis. we are considering only 15 variables from the obtained dataset for the BN modeling. All the continuous variables are converted into discrete states, as shown in Table 1. To have a balanced distribution, if the variable states are very few, then those are categorized into states named Others.

5 Implementation of a Bayesian Network

5.1 Bayesian Network

Bayesian network (BN) is a powerful and sophisticated graphical model based on probabilities. The conditional dependencies between the set of variables are modeled by Directed Acyclic Graph (DAG). The variables are represented as nodes within the graph, and the conditional relationship between them is shown through directed edges. Bayesian network is considered a robust tool due to its ability to capture complex hidden relationships between the variables and offer reasoning during uncertainty [14]. Its versatility and efficiency make it suitable for a broad range of applications in various domains like traffic management, healthcare, diagnosis, and decision-making. BNs are known by multiple names, such as Bayes networks or Belief networks, and the Bayes theorem is a foundation for building a Bayesian network.

Essential Components of Bayesian Networks. The features of BNs are critical for their practical functionality and efficient modeling of complex systems. The significant features of BNs include:

- **Nodes.** The BN model features, or variables, are represented as nodes. These variables can be discrete or continuous depending on the modeled data characteristics. The nodes are denoted as $X_1, X_2, \ldots, X_n$.
- **Edges.** The arrows connecting the variables indicate the edges. They exhibit the firmness and direction of conditional dependencies between the nodes. These edges more clearly showcase the relation among multiple variables and the flow of information within the BN. i.e., Directed edge between node X_i and X_j shows that X_j is conditionally dependent on X_i.

Table 1. Variables used in BN, their descriptions, and discrete states.

Variables	Description	Discrete States
Day	Day of the week	Sunday, Monday, Tuesday, Wednesday, Thursday, Friday, Saturday
Time period	Time of the accident	AM Peak, PM Peak, OFF Peak
Road Condition	Condition of the road	Dry, Wet
Lighting Condition	Light condition	Daylight, Darkness
Quater	Quater of the accident	Q1, Q2, Q3, Q4
Local Authority	District authority	Huntingdonshire, South Cam--bridgeshire, Cambridge City, Fenland, East Cambridgeshire
Road Category on Speed	Type of the road	Urban Roads, Rural Roads, Highways
Vehicle First Point of Impact	Point of impact	Front, Offside, Nearside, Back, Did not impact, Unknown
Vehicle near Junction	Location at junction	Not Junction, At Junction, Approaching Junction, Leaving Junction, Other Actions
Vehicle Manoeuvre	Type of manoeuvre	Going Ahead, Turning, Other Actions, Overtaking, Waiting, Changing lane
Alcohl Breath Test	Driver breath test result	Negative, Positive, Unknown
Casualty Sex	Sex of the Casualty	Male, Female
Casualty Age	Age of the Casualty	Young age, Middle age, Old age
Number of Casualties	Count of Casualty	Low, Medium, High
Seat Belt Used	Seatbelt worn	Not applicable, Unknown, Worn Unconfirmed, Worn Confirmed, Not Worn

- **Conditional Independence.** The representation of conditional independence
  among variables is considered one of Bayesian's core and essential features. This enables the network to facilitate uncomplicated complex relations among the variables. It breaks down the intricate relationships into feasible and interpretable components [21]. For instance, let us consider that nodes X_1 and X_2 are conditionally independent, and there is node X_3 whose information is known. Knowing the state of node X_1 does not help in understanding node X_2 as no additional knowledge has been gained about X_2. This can be expressed mathematically as shown in Eq. 3. This feature is significant for computation complexity reduction and network interpretation enhancement.

$$P(X_1, X_2 \mid X_3) = P(X_1 \mid X_3) \cdot P(X_2 \mid X_3) \tag{3}$$

- **Joint Probability Distribution.** In the context of Bayesian network modeling and probability theory, the joint probability distribution is the fundamental concept for representing the distribution of a set of variables and providing an extensive overview of complex relationships between those variables [24]. Let us consider the variables $X_1, X_2, \ldots, X_n$. The joint probability distribution can be formulated as the product of conditional probability between each node while considering that information regarding their parent nodes is available, as shown in the Eq. 4. The formula highlights the decomposition of a complete probability distribution into a simpler local distribution, which facilitates analysis and computation.

$$P(X_1, X_2, \ldots, X_n) = \prod_{i=1}^{n} P(X_i \mid \text{Parents}(X_i)) \tag{4}$$

Bayesian Theorem and Learning. This subsection briefly explains the mathematical principles used in constructing a Bayesian network to analyze traffic congestion based on accident information [23]. The precise application of these principles helps the BNs in complex modeling and effective uncertainty management.

- **Bayes' Theorem.**
  The fundamental process of the BN involves Bayesian inference, which enables the probabilities to be dynamically updated depending on the incoming new evidence [14]. This principle effectively models and predicts congestion irrespective of rapidly changing conditions. Bayes theorem is mathematically represented as:

$$P(H \mid E) = \frac{P(E \mid H) \cdot P(H)}{P(E)} \tag{5}$$

  Where, $P(H|E)$ is the posterior probability of hypothesis H, given that there is some evidence that E and $P(E|H)$ is the probability of the evidence E with H assumed to be true. $P(H)$ represents the probability of initial hypothesis belief before the evidence is considered. Finally, $P(E)$ helps normalize the result to ensure a valid probability. It is called marginal likelihood.

- **Marginalization in Bayesian Networks.**
  Marginalization calculates the probability of a subset of variables. This is crucial for the effective operation of the Bayesian network, especially when the interest is on a specific outcome like cumulative congestion level [22]. Marginalization makes the analysis easier as it does not depend on underlying factors. Given a joint distribution $P(X_1, X_2, X_3)$, the marginal probability of X_1 is formulated as follows:

$$P(X_1) = \sum_{X_2} \sum_{X_3} P(X_1, X_2, X_3) \tag{6}$$

- **Posterior Probability and Evidence.**
  Related variable probabilities should be updated regularly based on new evidence observed in the Bayesian network. This process is called posterior probability computation. Let us consider evidence E related to variable X_1 is given. The posterior probability of another variable X_2 is formulated as:

$$P(X_2 \mid E) = \frac{P(X_2, E)}{P(E)} \tag{7}$$

  Where, $P(X_2, E)$ is the joint probability and $P(E)$ is the total probability of evidence observation integrated over all the possible outputs.

5.2 Bayesian Networks: Design and Learning Frameworks

Effectively designing a Bayesian network structure is crucial for ensuring the precise modeling of variable relationships in the traffic congestion use case. This section briefly explains the methods involved in designing a Bayesian network. It focuses mainly on variable selection and learning of the network structure (Fig. 9).

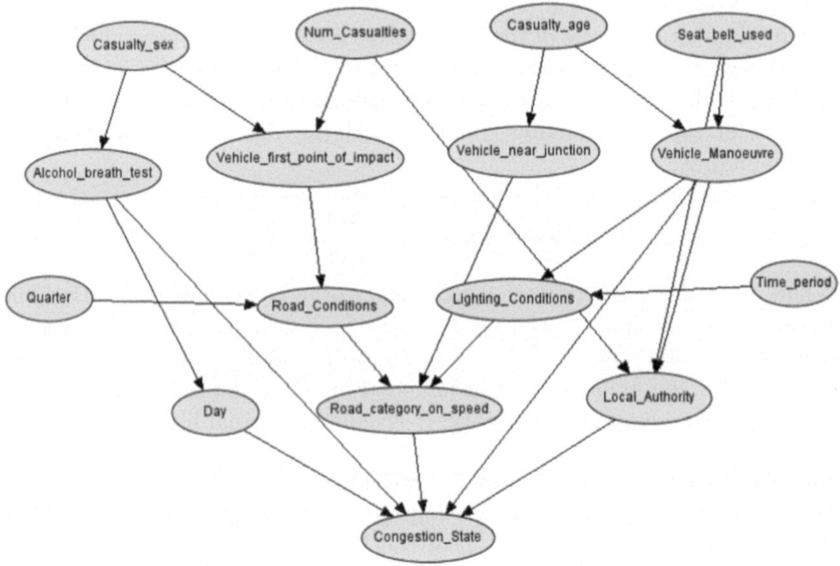

Fig. 9. Architecture of proposed Bayesian Network.

Structure Learning and Feature Selection. The Bayesian network structure is characterized by using nodes and directed edges to showcase the relationship between the different variables. This work uses a combination of domain knowledge and data-driven approaches to structure the Bayesian network. The random forest model significantly guided the selection of the crucial features contributing to congestion, as shown in Fig. 10. Primarily, each variable's feature importance is calculated based on its contribution to reducing information gain for splitting in a random forest model. Then, these values are used to prioritize the variables in the Bayesian network.

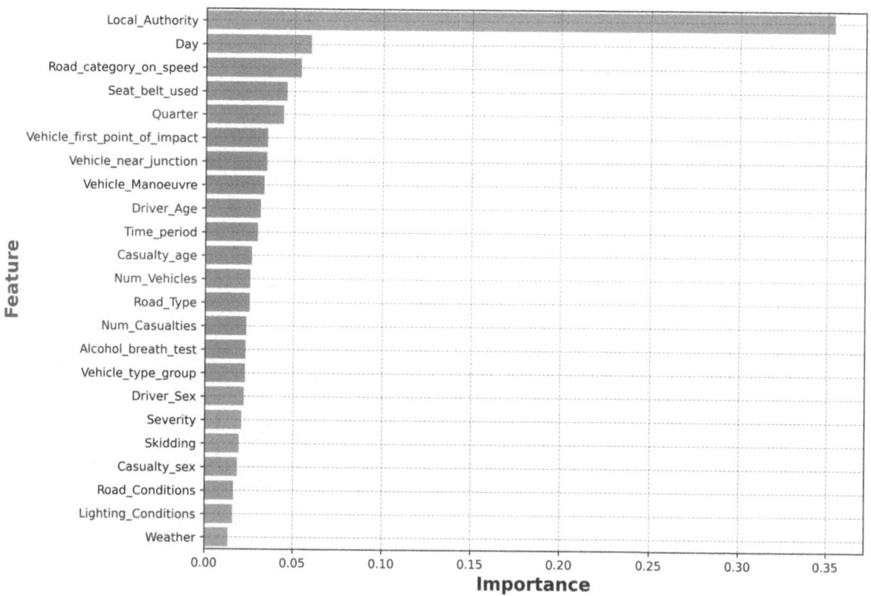

Fig. 10. Feature importance for variable selection of BN using Random Forest.

Parameter Learning: Estimating Conditional Probabilities. After the establishment of the Bayesian network structure, parameter learning is regulated. Conditional Probability Tables (CBTs) are estimated here to quantify the variable's dependencies. Let θ be the parameters of CPTs and D be the combined dataset. Maximization of the following likelihood function helps in precisely estimating the parameters. It guarantees that the observed data is explained better through the learned parameters for accurate forecasting and inference within the network.

$$\hat{\theta} = \arg\max_{\theta} P(D \mid \theta) \tag{8}$$

5.3 Scenario-Driven Root Cause Analysis

This section demonstrates the root data analysis for causing congestion using the Bayesian network model. For this purpose, eight different scenarios are created. Four scenarios of each classification model, i.e., scenarios 1 to 4, explain the influence on the 3-class model with low, medium, and high congestion states as shown in Table 2. On the other hand, scenarios 5 to 8 illustrate the impact on the 2-class model (congestion states are low and high) as shown in Table 3.

Scenario 1, 2. These scenarios are created to observe the impact of variables, namely Day and Seat belts, on traffic congestion. Two evidence are considered in scenario 1, where the first evidence is the person wearing the seat belt while driving, and the other evidence is it happens to be a weekend; the probabilities of congestion states being low, medium, and high are 43.72%, 23.86%, and 32.43% respectively. In scenario 2, one of the two pieces of evidence is changed; that is, now the congestion is observed for the weekday, that is, Friday, and a person is driving wearing a seat belt, then the likelihood of high congestion is increased by around 4%. From these two scenarios, it can be illustrated that the probability of congestion on weekdays is higher than on weekends.

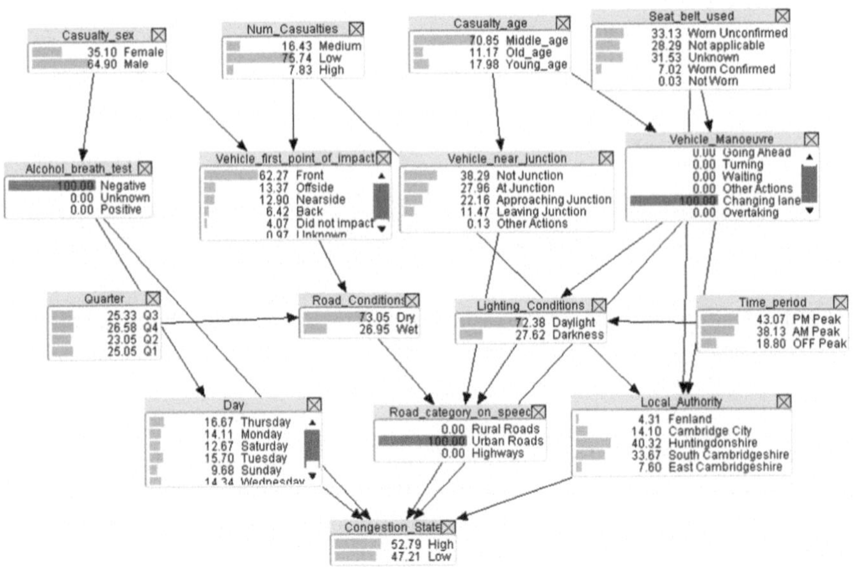

Fig. 11. Diagram of proposed BN with three evidence for 2-class model.

Table 2. Scenarios to demonstrate the variable's influence on 3-class classification.

Scenarios	Variable (state)	Congestion
1	Day (Saturday) & Seat_belt_used (Worn confirmed)	Low (43.72%), Medium (23.86%), High (32.43%)
2	Day (Friday) & Seat_belt_used (Worn confirmed)	Low (41.35%), Medium (22.78%), High (35.87%)
3	Road_category_on_speed (Rural Roads) & Local_Authority(Huntingdonshire)	Low (65.29%), Medium (24.89%), High (9.83%)
3	Road_category_on_speed (Rural Roads) & Local_Authority(Cambridge City)	Low (10.86%), Medium (3.95%), High (85.19%)

Scenario 3, 4. In these scenarios, the Road category and local authority of the city to whom the accident was reported are considered. Here also, two pieces of evidence are given that when the accident happened on a rural road and in the city of Huntingdonshire, the chances of being congested is low, with a probability of 65.29%. In contrast, in scenario 4, the evidence is given as the accident happened in Cambridge city, then the percentage of occurring congestion is very high at 85.19%. It can be understood from these scenarios that, depending upon the accident region, the congestion probability is drastically changed.

Scenario 5, 6. The influence of road conditions and vehicles near junctions on congestion is discussed in these scenarios. In scenario 5, the road condition is set as dry, and there is no junction near the vehicle when the accident happened; in those cases, the possibility of low and high congestion is 57.18% and 42.82%, respectively. In scenario 6, the vehicle is considered to be present at the junction, and the road condition is unchanged; then, there is a slight increase in the probability of high congestion from 42.82% to 43.65%. This indicates that the junction at the accident spot has a lesser impact on the congestion state.

Table 3. Scenarios to demonstrate the variable's influence on 2-class classification.

Scenarios	Variable (state)	Congestion
5	Road_Conditions (Dry) & Vehicle_near_junction (Not Junction)	Low (57.18%), High (42.82%)
6	Road_Conditions (Dry) & Vehicle_near_junction (At Junction)	Low (56.35%), High (43.65%)
7	Alcohol_breath_test (Negative) & Road_category_on_speed (Urban Roads) & Vehicle_Manoeuvre (Changing lane)	Low (47.21%), High (52.79%)
8	Alcohol_breath_test (Negative) & Road_category_on_speed (Highways) & Vehicle_Manoeuvre (Changing lane)	Low (64.67%), High (35.33%)

Scenario 7, 8. These two scenarios are created using three variables: alcohol breath test, road category, and vehicle manoeuvres. So, three pieces of evidence are given to observe the influence of these variables on congestion. In scenario 7, at the time of the accident, when the alcohol bread test is negative, and an accident happens on an urban road while a vehicle changes lanes, there is more likely to happen high congestion, with 52.79% as shown in Fig. 11. In contrast, in this scenario, the road category is changed to the highway while the evidence of alcohol bread test and vehicle manoeurve remain the same as in scenario 7, then there is a drastic drop in the possibility of high congestion state to 35.33%. In these two scenarios, it is evident that the road category has a strong influence on traffic congestion because when an accident happens on highways, other vehicle users can escape by using other lanes, whereas in urban roads, the escape lanes will be restricted.

Using all the above scenarios, we can analyze the impact of various variables or factors that are key in causing congestion and bottleneck situations. Such analysis can help traffic management people take precautions regarding these specific factors and prioritize dealing with the features causing a greater impact on traffic disturbance and mitigating congestion as soon as possible.

5.4 Performance Evaluation Metrics

Performance evaluation plays a significant role in defining Bayesian network prediction quality. This section explains the metrics, such as accuracy, precision, recall, F1-score, Error Rate, Average Euclidean Distance, and Average Kullback-Leibler Divergence, calculated for each model to assess the network's efficiency and reliability.

$$\text{Accuracy} = \frac{\text{True Positives} + \text{True Negatives}}{\text{Total Number of Predictions}} \tag{9}$$

$$\text{Precision} = \frac{\text{True Positives}}{\text{True Positives} + \text{False Positives}} \tag{10}$$

$$\text{Recall} = \frac{\text{True Positives}}{\text{True Positives} + \text{False Negatives}} \tag{11}$$

$$\text{F1-Score} = 2 \times \frac{\text{Precision} \times \text{Recall}}{\text{Precision} + \text{Recall}} \tag{12}$$

Error Rate. This metric represents the percentage of incorrect predictions made by the BN model among the total predictions. A lower error rate indicates good model performance.

$$\text{Error Rate} = \frac{\text{Number of Incorrect Predictions}}{\text{Total Number of Predictions}} \tag{13}$$

Average Euclidean Distance. This metric calculates the average distance between the predictions and true values in multi-dimensional space [29]. This metric provides insight into the average closeness of predictions to actual values. Less value indicates more accurate prediction due to less difference of estimates from actual values.

$$\text{Average Euclidean Distance} = \frac{1}{N}\sum_{i=1}^{N}\sqrt{\sum_{k=1}^{n}(p_{ik} - q_{ik})^2} \tag{14}$$

Average Kullback-Leibler Divergence. The divergence between the probability distribution of prediction and actual values is measured using this metric [15]. The low value of kullback-leibler divergence showcases that the predictions are closely aligned with actual distribution, which ensures the better performance of the BN model.

$$\text{Average KL Divergence} = \frac{1}{N}\sum_{i=1}^{N}\sum_{k=1}^{n} q_{ik}\log\left(\frac{q_{ik}}{p_{ik}}\right) \tag{15}$$

6 Data Analysis

This section discusses data distribution using visualization plots and the methods used to categorize accident records into congestion states. Furthermore, we will dive deeper into the challenges posed by the data skewness and the techniques adapted to determine congestion states.

Initial Data Examination. Understanding basic data characteristics is essential before analyzing congestion and its root causes. The dataset consists of variables related to accident records, such as incident occurrence time, severity, location, and many others.

In the dataset, the number of accidents that occurred every hour in the Cambridgeshire region is illustrated using a count plot as shown in Fig. 12. The graph shows that accident occurrence peaks in the early morning and late afternoon hours, with a maximum of around 701 cases. The highest number of accidents is recorded around 8:00 AM, 4:00 PM, and 5:00 PM. These time stamps correspond to rush hours when people travel for work or school and return home. This graph shows a clear correlation between traffic volume and the probability of accident occurrence. So, a dynamic and intelligent traffic management system is required to address congestion and reduce accidents.

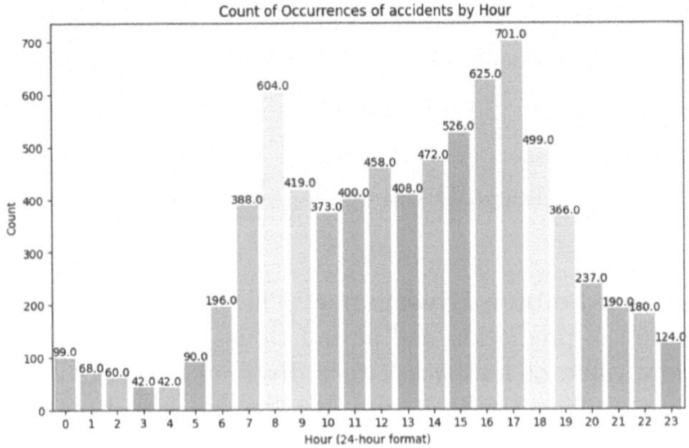

Fig. 12. Number of road accidents happened on an Hourly basis [25].

Figure 13 shows the impact of accident severity on congestion probability using a violin plot. It shows the distribution of congestion across various severity levels: slight, serious, and fatal. The shape becomes wider with increased congestion probability. It can be observed that congestion increases during the occurrence of severe accidents. In contrast, slightly severe accidents do not significantly impact congestion compared to serious and fatal cases.

These primary analyses help us gain more knowledge and provide valuable insights into the dataset. Furthermore, the data highlights the accident's temporal patterns and their relationship with severity and congestion occurrence. Indeed, this sets the stage for a deeper examination of the data distribution and the appropriate methodology needed based on the data, which can be explored in the coming subsections.

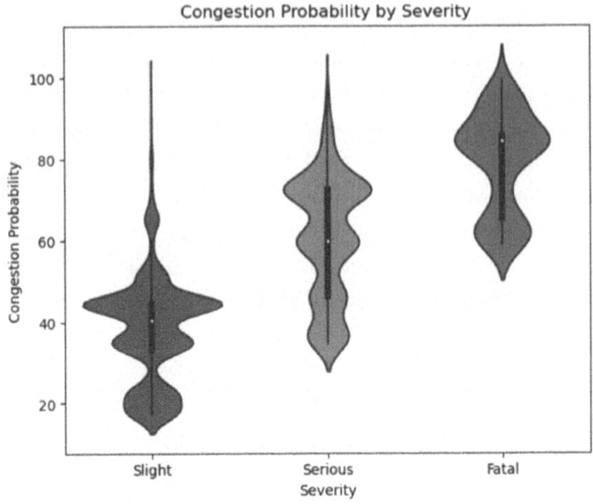

Fig. 13. A plot of level of severity impacting the congestion probability [25].

Data Skewness and Distribution Analysis. The working process of a hybrid approach consists of two main steps: clustering the accident record using the DBSCAN algorithm and computing the congestion index for each cluster. Calculating the congestion index is crucial for congestion classification in a hybrid approach. The next step involves deciding what threshold should be used for categorizing congestion states. Understanding the congestion index obtained before deciding the threshold values is essential.

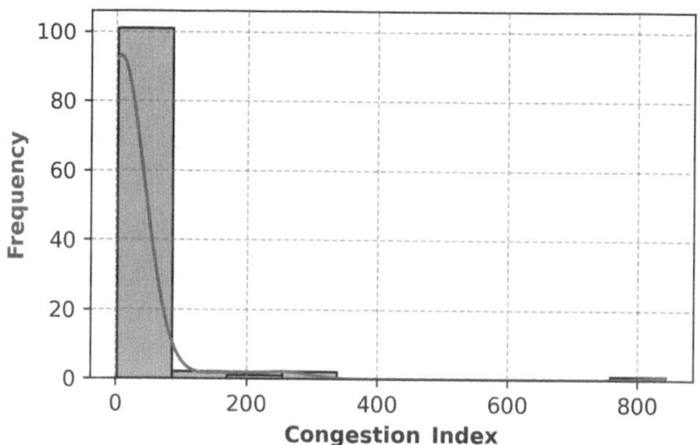

Fig. 14. Plot to demonstrate the skewed distribution of Congestion Index for the clusters.

For this purpose, a histogram is plotted between the congestion index value and frequency (representing the number of accident clusters), as shown in Fig. 14. This figure indicates that the data is highly right-skewed. Most clusters have low congestion index values, and only some exhibit extremely high values due to such a skewed distribution. The skewness suggests that in this dataset, most areas experience low congestion probability, and few specific hotspots have high congestion probability. This poses a significant challenge in deciding the appropriate threshold technique to effectively classify the clusters into congestion states (low, medium, and high). To handle this problem, we will use some data normalization methods like log transforms.

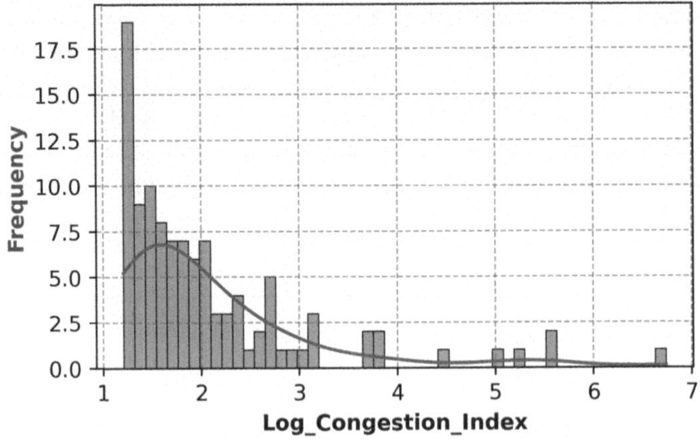

Fig. 15. Plot for indicating the Log-transformed Congestion Index.

Log-Transformation and Its Limitations. Log-transform is applied to the index values to reduce the heavy skewness in the congestion index distribution. The Histogram of log-transformed values is shown in Fig. 15. Normalization of distribution through log transform makes threshold selection for congestion states easier. Although the log transform helped reduce the skewness by normalizing the distribution, it had a limited impact on the congestion state classification. The majority of clusters still follow the low congestion index. This indicates the presence of solid skewness in our dataset.

Threshold Method for Cluster Classification. Due to the skewness and log transformation challenges, original index values were used for cluster classification. The clustered congestion index is shown in Fig. 16. The bar plot shows the congestion index values across all 107 clusters formed using the DBSCAN algorithm.

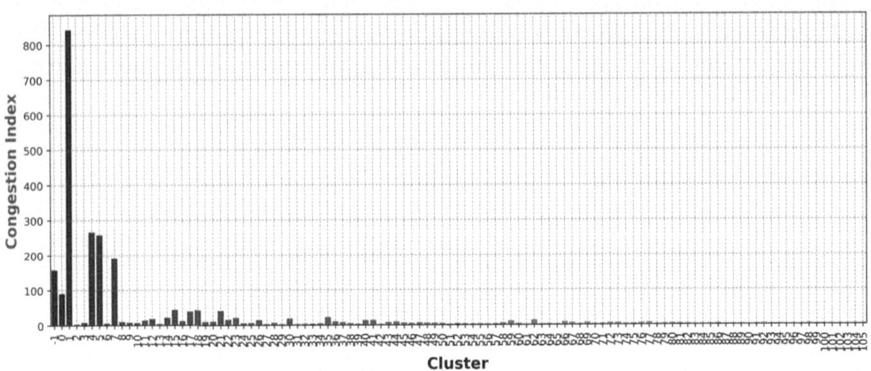

Fig. 16. The distribution of Congestion index value for each cluster.

This figure clearly highlights the variation in congestion indexes between clusters. Clusters with higher accident counts and severity show high congestion indices. In these cases of highly imbalanced data distribution, we cannot opt for data-driven techniques to categorize the clusters into congestion states. So, finally, we decided to go with the manual threshold criteria technique.

To set the manual threshold, we did some rigorous trial and error by categorizing the cluster into the congestion states and observing the performance of the proposed model. Hence, for this dataset, we set low and high thresholds of 200 and 400 to classify congestion into 3 classes: low, medium, and high. For the 2-class, the threshold is set to 250 to classify the congestion states into low and high classes, which is illustrated in Sect. 3.3. This allowed more balanced categorization and reflected better variation in congestion levels across various geographical areas.

There are other alternatives for manual threshold techniques, such as (1.) quantile-based thresholding: when the data is in the normal distribution or bell curve distribution, then quantile can be applied by setting different percentiles; we can split the data into necessary groups; in our case, congestion states. Due to the skewness in data, this technique will form all the clusters into a single group. Similarly, (2.) Z-score normalization is another technique that operates similarly, considering the data for normal distribution. Lastly, (3.) A decision tree-based thresholding method can also be employed automatically to maximize the separation between the congestion states. However, due to highly imbalanced data, the Decision tree may overfit our data, which does not align with real-world traffic situations. Hence, it is crucial to decide the appropriate approach based on the dataset in order to reflect the real traffic situation. Furthermore, manual thresholds can be proven advantageous for traffic management as they can set thresholds that align best with specific regional or city-level traffic patterns.

7 Results and Discussion

In this section, results & discussion are illustrated in three tables. Table 4 discusses the performance of the proposed BN model using different labeling approaches for both 3-class and 2-class classification. In Table 5, additional metrics obtained from the HUGIN tool for the proposed BN model are discussed. Lastly, the proposed model performance is compared with five popular ML models.

Table 4 shows the performance of the proposed BN model for congestion state classification using the Formula, Hotspot, and Hybrid labeling approaches. Both 3-class- and 2-class classification models are evaluated based on accuracy, precision, recall, and F1-score metrics. Firstly, in the case of 3-class classification, the hybrid approach outperforms the other two labeling approaches. The hybrid model achieves an accuracy of 0.74, precision of 0.73, recall of 0.74, and F1-score of 0.74 for 3-class. On the contrary, formula-based approaches show the least performance across all metrics. The hotspot approach performs moderately better than the formula-based approach, with an accuracy of 0.49 and an F1-score of 0.47.

For 2-class classification, the hybrid approach again shows superior performance across all metrics with accuracy, precision, recall, and F1-score of 0.73, 0.75, 0.73, and 0.74, respectively. The hotspot and formula-based approaches perform better, with an accuracy of 0.67 and 0.55, respectively, compared to their 3-class counterparts. However, they still lag behind the hybrid approach, irrespective of classification type.

Table 4. Comparison of performance of proposed BN model w.r.t different labelling approaches for 3 class and 2 class.

Model Classification	Labelling Appraochs	Accuracy	Precision	Recall	F1-Score
3 Class	**Formula Based**	0.46	0.45	0.46	0.45
	Hotspot Based	0.49	0.50	0.49	0.47
	Hybrid Based	**0.74**	**0.73**	**0.74**	**0.74**
2 Class	**Formula Based**	0.55	0.58	0.55	0.52
	Hotspot Based	0.67	0.66	0.65	0.66
	Hybrid Based	**0.73**	**0.75**	**0.73**	**0.74**

The hybrid approach's effectiveness in terms of performance metric values highlights its performance. It exhibits the importance of integrating spatial and contextual data in a hybrid classification model. Furthermore, the proposed BN model using a hybrid-based approach signifies its reliability and balance of performance concerning 3-class and 2-class compared to other congestion labeling techniques.

Table 5 provides more explicit insight into the performance of three labeling approaches applied along with BN modeling. The error rate, average Euclidian distance, and average Kullback-Leibler divergence offer a deeper understanding of the BN prediction accuracy and alignment of distribution across 3-class and 2-class classifications. All these three metrics are computed in the HUGIN tool.

The 3-class classification achieves the lowest error rate of 26.5% using the hybrid approach. Formula and hotspot-based approaches have higher error rates, 54.1%, and 51.83%, respectively. The lower error indicates the effective performance of the hybrid approach in correctly predicting the congestion states. Moreover, in evaluating the performance of BN, the Euclidean distance and Kullback-Leibler divergence are used, and these metrics showcase that predictions and their distributions are closer to the actual values. The low value indicates better model performance, as discussed in Sect. 5.4. Hence, the hybrid approach achieves a smaller Euclidean distance of 0.33 and a Kullback-Leibler divergence of 0.55. In contrast, formula-based and hotspots have achieved Euclidean distances of 0.77 and 0.67, whereas the divergence values of 1.27 and 1.18, respectively. These metric values are more than double, displaying the poor performance of these two labeling techniques.

Similarly, for 2-class classification, the hybrid approach shows superior performance with the lowest error rate and Euclidean distance of 27.17% and 0.35,

Table 5. Deeper evaluation of three approaches and comparing its performance.

Appraochs	Error rate	Avg. Euclidian distance	Avg. Kulbach-Leibler divergence
3 Class Classification			
Formula Based	54.4	0.77	1.27
Hotspot Based	51.83	0.67	1.18
Hybrid Based	**26.5**	**0.33**	**0.55**
2 Class Classification			
Formula Based	45.60	0.52	0.81
Hotspot Based	32.84	0.44	0.68
Hybrid Based	**27.17**	**0.35**	**0.69**

respectively, and moderate Kullback-Leibler Divergence of 0.69. The formula-based approach performs the worst, irrespective of the classification type.

The Hybrid approach effectively labels the congestion states among all the labeling techniques and classifications. It provides accurate prediction with a lower error rate and smaller divergence and distance between predictions and actual test instances. These metrics ensure the reliability and effectiveness of the hybrid approach for use with BN.

Table 6 compares the performance of the proposed BN model with five widely used ML models: logistic Regression, Decision Tree, Random Forest, Support Vector Machine, and K-nearest neighbor. The data with target congestion labels classified based on a hybrid labeling approach is used across all the models for a fair comparison. The performance of all the models is evaluated for both 3-class and 2-class classifications.

Table 6. Performance evaluation of proposed BN model against five different ML models.

3 Class Classification				
Models	Accuracy	Precision	Recall	F1-Score
Logistic Regression	0.60	0.68	0.60	0.53
Decision Tree	0.69	0.68	0.69	0.69
Random Forest	0.72	0.71	0.72	0.71
SVM	0.72	**0.75**	0.72	0.70
K-NN	0.65	0.64	0.65	0.65
Bayesian Network	**0.74**	0.73	**0.74**	**0.74**
2 Class Classification				
Logistic Regression	0.63	0.59	0.56	0.57
Decision Tree	0.70	0.66	0.70	0.67
Random Forest	0.73	0.68	0.74	0.71
SVM	0.67	0.60	**0.75**	0.67
K-NN	0.65	0.60	0.61	0.61
Bayesian Network	**0.73**	**0.76**	0.73	**0.75**

Bayesian network shows superior performance in comparison to other ML models and achieves the highest accuracy(0.74), recall (0.74), and F1-score(0.74) in 3-class classification. Except for SVM, BN's precision(0.73) is comparatively better than other ML models. SVM performs better for a precision of 0.75 but falls behind the BN model in maintaining balance across all metrics. Logistic regression and K-NN models show the lowest performance with an F1-score of 0.53 and 0.65, respectively. Furthermore, a strong performance can also be seen in Random forest, but BN outperforms it due to better handling of uncertainty and efficient capturing of data complexity.

Similarly, BN performs the best in the case of 2-class classifications, too, with accuracy, precision, recall, and Fi-score of 0.73, 0.76, 0.73, and 0.75, respectively. SVM again shows the superior performance of all the ML models with a high recall of 0.75. Still, compared to other metrics, it falls short of balancing true positives and false negatives. Random forest and decision tree models showcase a strong performance but are still not up to the mark as the effective BN.

This performance comparison analysis highlights that the hybrid approach proves to be a robust congestion labeling strategy when used along with BN. BN displays superior performance when compared with other ML models. BN's ability to maintain high performance in all metrics across both classification models emphasizes its capability to handle complex and imbalanced data. Furthermore, BN's ability to understand the influencing variables on the congestion states could help develop early mitigation strategies and prioritize the issues that are more likely to lead to road blockage. Moreover, it is advantageous to predict the likelihood or probability of the outcomes, showcasing the explainability nature of the BN model.

8 Conclusion

This paper analyzes the relationship between road accidents and traffic congestion. For this purpose, we proposed a Bayesian network, which is used to analyze accident variables and predict congestion. In the analysis part of the work, we created scenarios to understand the variable's influence and likelihood of causing congestion. Eight such scenarios were developed to observe some variables that impact the congestion state. The proposed BN model identified that local authority (city) and road category (rural, urban, or highway) significantly affect the congestion probability.

In the prediction part of the work, first, we assigned the accident data with target congestion labels using three proposed labeling approaches: Formula-based, Hotspot, and Hybrid. The working of formula-based considers variables like severity, speed limit, and number of vehicles involved, whereas the Hotspot approach uses only the coordinates of accidents. The shortcomings of these two labeling approaches are combined by leveraging geospatial and contextual accident data to form a hybrid approach. After computing the target label (congestion), the performance of the proposed BN model is evaluated using the target label obtained from these three labeling approaches. Out of the three labeling approaches, the hybrid approach is superior to formula and hotspot based on both 3-class and 2-class model classification. Furthermore, to evaluate the proposed BN model's performance, it is compared against five ML models (Logistic Regression, Decision Tree, Random Forest, Support Vector Machine, and K-nearest neighbor). The proposed BN model performs best with labels derived from the hybrid approach. Therefore, the target label obtained from the hybrid approach compares the BN performance to that of five ML models. Results show that the BN model has outperformed all the ML models in the evaluation metrics: accuracy, precision, recall, and F1-score in the 3-class and 2-class models.

The hybrid approach's current limitation is the manual threshold strategy, which is only suitable for this dataset due to its skewness. Future work will improve the hybrid approach by incorporating more real-time data and exploring generic or data-driven techniques for automating the threshold strategy to adjust dynamically according to the dataset's nature.

References

1. Adeniyi, A.O.: Traffic mitigation and congestion in IBADAN, OYO state nigeria: causes and solutions. The University of North Dakota (2021)
2. Afrin, T., Yodo, N.: A probabilistic estimation of traffic congestion using bayesian network. Measurement **174**, 109051 (2021)
3. Anderson, T.K.: Kernel density estimation and k-means clustering to profile road accident hotspots. Acc. Anal. Prevention **41**(3), 359–364 (2009)
4. Cambridgeshire County Council: Cambridgeshire road traffic collision data. https://data.cambridgeshireinsight.org.uk/dataset/cambridgeshire-road-traffic-collision-data (2018), Accessed 10 Oct 2023
5. Chang, H., Li, L., Huang, J., Zhang, Q., Chin, K.S.: Tracking traffic congestion and accidents using social media data: a case study of shanghai. Acc. Anal. Prevention **169**, 106618 (2022)
6. Davidović, J., Pešić, D., Antić, B.: Professional drivers' fatigue as a problem of the modern era. Transport. Res. F: Traffic Psychol. Behav. **55**, 199–209 (2018)
7. Deublein, M., Schubert, M., Adey, B.T., Köhler, J., Faber, M.H.: Prediction of road accidents: a bayesian hierarchical approach. Acc. Anal. Prevention **51**, 274–291 (2013)
8. Dias, C., Miska, M., Kuwahara, M., Warita, H.: Relationship between congestion and traffic accidents on expressways: an investigation with bayesian belief networks. In: Proceedings of 40th Annual Meeting of Infrastructure Planning (JSCE), Japan (2009)
9. Suarez-del Fueyo, R., Junge, M., Lopez-Valdes, F., Gabler, H.C., Woerner, L., Hiermaier, S.: Cluster analysis of seriously injured occupants in motor vehicle crashes. Acc. Anal. Prevention **151**, 105787 (2021)
10. Gomides, T.S., Robson, E., Meneguette, R.I., de Souza, F.S., Guidoni, D.L.: Predictive congestion control based on collaborative information sharing for vehicular ad hoc networks. Comput. Netw. **211**, 108955 (2022)
11. Gupta, U., Varun, M., Srinivasa, G.: A comprehensive study of road traffic accidents: hotspot analysis and severity prediction using machine learning. In: 2022 IEEE Bombay Section Signature Conference (IBSSC), pp. 1–6. IEEE (2022)

12. Ji, X., Yue, W., Li, C., Chen, Y., Xue, N., Sha, Z.: Digital twin empowered model free prediction of accident-induced congestion in urban road networks. In: 2022 IEEE 95th Vehicular Technology Conference:(VTC2022-Spring), pp. 1–6. IEEE (2022)
13. Jian, T., Zhi-Qiang, L., Jian-feng, X., Hong-yu, G.: Cause analysis and countermeasures of fatal traffic accidents on road passenger transportation based on typical cases. In: 2019 5th International Conference on Transportation Information and Safety (ICTIS), pp. 951–955. IEEE (2019)
14. Kjaerulff, U.B., Madsen, A.L.: Bayesian networks and influence diagrams. Springer Sci. Bus. Media **200**, 114 (2008)
15. Kullback, S.: Information theory and statistics. Courier Corporation (1997)
16. Ma, X., Ding, C., Luan, S., Wang, Y., Wang, Y.: Prioritizing influential factors for freeway incident clearance time prediction using the gradient boosting decision trees method. IEEE Trans. Intell. Transp. Syst. **18**(9), 2303–2310 (2017)
17. Naji, H.A., Xue, Q., Zheng, K., Lyu, N.: Investigating the significant individual historical factors of driving risk using hierarchical clustering analysis and quasi-poisson regression model. Sensors **20**(8), 2331 (2020)
18. Puspitasari, D., Wahyudi, M., Rizaldi, M., Nurhadi, A., Ramanda, K., et al.: K-means algorithm for clustering the location of accident-prone on the highway. In: Journal of Physics: Conference Series. vol. 1641, p. 012086. IOP Publishing (2020)
19. Santos, D., Saias, J., Quaresma, P., Nogueira, V.B.: Machine learning approaches to traffic accident analysis and hotspot prediction. Computers **10**(12), 157 (2021)
20. Singh, S., Tripathy, A.: Incident analysis and prediction using clustering and bayesian network. In: Proceedings of the 2019 International Conference on Communication and Signal Processing (ICCSP), pp. 0405–0409, Chennai (2019)
21. Studeny, M.: Probabilistic conditional independence structures. Springer Science & Business Media (2006)
22. Studer, L., Paulevé, L., Zechner, C., Reumann, M., Martinez, M.R., Koeppl, H.: Marginalized continuous time bayesian networks for network reconstruction from incomplete observations. In: Proceedings of the AAAI Conference on Artificial Intelligence. vol. 30 (2016)
23. Sun, J., Sun, J.: A dynamic bayesian network model for real-time crash prediction using traffic speed conditions data. Transp. Res. Part C Emerging Technol. **54**, 176–186 (2015)
24. Sun, L., Erath, A.: A bayesian network approach for population synthesis. Transp. Res. Part C Emerging Technol. **61**, 49–62 (2015)
25. Talluri, K.K., Weidl, G.: Bayesian network for analysis and prediction of traffic congestion using the accident data. In: VEHITS, pp. 19–30 (2024)
26. Wang, C.: The relationship between traffic congestion and road accidents: an econometric approach using GIS. Ph.D. thesis, Chao Wang (2010)
27. Zeng, L., et al.: Abnormal hotspots detection method based on region real-time congestion factor. In: 2016 IEEE 19th International Conference on Intelligent Transportation Systems (ITSC). pp. 749–753. IEEE (2016)
28. Zhang, J., Junhua, W., Shou'en, F.: Prediction of urban expressway total traffic accident duration based on multiple linear regression and artificial neural network. In: 2019 5th International Conference on Transportation Information and Safety (ICTIS), pp. 503–510. IEEE (2019)
29. Zhu, M., Liu, S., Jiang, J.: A novel divergence for sensitivity analysis in gaussian bayesian networks. Int. J. Approximate Reason. **90**, 37–55 (2017)

OpTC: Automatic Compression and Performance Estimation for Deployment of Neural Networks on AURIX TC3xx Microcontrollers

Christian Heidorn[1(✉)], Frank Hannig[1], Dominik Riedelbauch[2], Christoph Strohmeyer[2], and Jürgen Teich[1]

[1] Department of Computer Science, Friedrich-Alexander-Universität Erlangen-Nürnberg (FAU), Erlangen, Germany
christian.heidorn@fau.de

[2] Schaeffler Technologies AG & Co. KG, Herzogenaurach, Germany

Abstract. Compression and quantization techniques are key for deploying neural network (NN) models on highly resource-constrained microcontroller architectures. Particularly for AURIX TriCore microcontrollers, widely used in automotive applications, there is a lack of support for automatic compression, conversion, and deployment of pre-trained NN models. Therefore, in this paper, we present OpTC, a toolchain designed to bring neural networks to TriCore microcontrollers. OpTC achieves this by employing automatic sensitivity-based NN pruning and quantization. Testing whether a given neural network fits on a microcontroller, by compiling, deploying, and then evaluating memory and performance constraints can be quite time-consuming, particularly when applying our automatic compression scheme that iterates multiple pruned variants of an NN. To speed up the deployment process in our design flow, we contribute a cost modeling approach for TriCore microcontrollers that estimates the required ROM, RAM, and execution time for given neural networks without requiring compilation or explicit measurements on the target. We evaluate our approach for selected applications, including an autoencoder and a convolutional neural network for keyword spotting from the MLPerf Tiny benchmark. Our experiments show that OpTC can find compressed NN variants, that significantly reduce the memory requirements and execution time without increasing the error over the baseline model.

Keywords: Neural network compression · AURIX TriCore · TinyML

1 Introduction

The demand for deploying neural networks (NNs) on resource-constrained devices such as microcontrollers continues to grow. For example, neural networks can be used in electric vehicles to predict battery charge [22] or implement thermal management of electric motors [18]. In recent years, several mature end-to-end ML frameworks (e.g., TensorFlow [1], PyTorch [21], and Keras [4]) have emerged centered around GPUs as

F. Calise et al. (Eds.): SMARTGREENS 2024/VEHITS 2024, CCIS 2954, pp. 125–145, 2026.
https://doi.org/10.1007/978-3-032-23187-1_7

the workhorse. As a consequence, many neural network models come with high memory requirements and high computational complexity. This hampers NN deployment on microcontrollers.

For deploying NNs on microcontrollers, inference libraries are typically designed to efficiently manage the few available resources and fit the tight memory budget [20]. Typically, those lightweight inference libraries are implemented in C or C++ in combination with a conversion workflow [5,6,20] that generates library function calls for an NN. These workflows are often realized directly within machine learning (ML) frameworks or rely on an exchange format description, such as ONNX (Open Neural Network Exchange, [2]).

When it comes to developing a new NN model, most of the existing workflows do not provide any information about how the model will perform on the target microcontroller, especially considering the execution time. Hence, during the development, a programmer or data scientist is typically unaware of whether the neural network model can deliver predictions within specified time constraints. This leads to time-consuming trial-and-error cycles, as the model has to be adapted, trained, and deployed on the target device several times until it meets the time and memory constraints of the target hardware while still achieving acceptable accuracy.

As a remedy, Heidorn et al. [12] introduced OpTC, a *microcontroller-in-the-loop* approach for highly resource-constrained microcontroller targets, specifically the AURIX TriCore 3xx family [12]. OpTC mitigates this manual trial-and-error process by automatically exploring differently pruned neural networks and assessing their performance (e.g., execution time, memory utilization) by on-device measurement. As a result, the toolchain produces compressed neural network models and corresponding C code that strike a balance between memory footprint, execution time, and prediction quality. Although the toolchain is automated, compiling and measuring each individual design point on the target microcontroller can take a significant amount of time (e.g., 18 s for an autoencoder model). This has so far hindered the approach to scale towards larger design space explorations of different optimization and compression techniques. The main contributions of this paper can be summarized as follows:

- A modular toolchain for automatic optimization and deployment of various neural network types on AURIX TriCore microcontrollers, including compression techniques.
- Performance and cost models for estimating the execution time and memory usage (RAM and ROM) for a given neural network and a targeted microcontroller to enable a rapid analysis of trade-offs between execution time, memory requirements, and prediction quality without explicit compilation and deployment.
- Introduction of full and weight-only quantization support to OpTC [12] that currently supports only operator fusion and pruning for network compression to further reduce execution time and memory footprint on the target microcontroller.
- Evaluation of the resulting full toolchain for applications from the MLPerf Tiny benchmark [3] and a dataset for predicting the temperature in an electric motor [17] and showcasing OpTC when exploring these applications in terms of memory footprint (RAM and ROM), execution time, and prediction quality on an AURIX TriCore 387 microcontroller.

2 Fundamentals

Neural networks (NNs) consist of multiple layers of neurons of different types and can be represented as data flow graphs. NNs have trainable layers with weight tensors, such as fully connected and convolutional layers. For efficient deployment of neural networks on microcontrollers, pruning [9] and quantization [15] have emerged as the most common compression techniques.

2.1 Pruning

Pruning reduces the number of neurons and their connections, thereby also reducing the number of weights and the number of floating point operations (FLOPs). *Structural pruning* is a technique where entire structures, e.g., output neurons, are set to zero and can be removed from computation [6]. For example, entire filters can be removed from convolutional layers, or rows and columns of the weight matrix can be eliminated in fully connected layers. This approach can effectively decrease execution time by reducing the number of loop iterations required to process the layers. Let a neural network be given that consists amongst other layers (e.g., activation and pooling layers) of a set V of layers with trainable weights. Further, let M_i denote the number of output neurons (or filters) of each corresponding layer $v_i \in V$. In the case of *layer-wise pruning*, each layer v_i is assigned a pruning rate p_i where $0 \leq p_i < 1, \; p_i \in \mathbb{R}$. Here, the resulting number m_i of output neurons after pruning layer $v_i \in V$ is

$$m_i = \lceil M_i \cdot (1 - p_i) \rceil . \tag{1}$$

The higher the pruning rate (p_i), the fewer weights have to be stored, and the fewer FLOPs are required. There exist several heuristics to determine which weights or weight structures should be removed. The most commonly used techniques are the ℓ^1 or ℓ^2 norm of the weights [13]. Here, the filters (or rows and columns) with the lowest ℓ^1 norm values are set to zero and removed. However, for many neural networks, this design space is excessively large, so it would take a prohibitively long time to explore and evaluate all design points. For example, the autoencoder model for anomaly detection from the MLPerf Tiny benchmark [3] contains ten fully connected layers ($|V| = 10$), where the number of output neurons ranges from $M_i = 8$ to 128; then, the number of possible pruned configurations is nearly $|\Omega_{\text{layer\_wise}}| = 10^{20}$. In our previous work [12], we presented techniques to reduce the design space based on *sensitivity analysis* and introduced a parameter to control the number of pruned configurations to be explored.

2.2 Quantization

Quantization reduces the numerical resolution of parameters and computations. In addition to reducing memory requirements, it can also reduce the computational complexity of a neural network [6].

Let r denote a real-valued input (activation or weight), S a real-valued scaling factor, and Z an integer zero point. The quantized value $Q(r)$ of r is given by

$$Q(r) = \text{round}(r/S) - Z, \tag{2}$$

where the round function maps a real value to an integer value by a rounding operation (e.g., "round to nearest"). The scaling factor S is determined by the maximum of data values β (e.g., the maximum value in a weight matrix) and the respective minimum α, and by the range[1] of the considered datatype A, i.e., its minimal and maximal value $q_{\min}(A)$ and $q_{\max}(A)$, respectively:

$$S = \frac{\beta - \alpha}{q_{\max}(A) - q_{\min}(A)}. \tag{3}$$

In the case of symmetric quantization, the zero point is set to $Z = 0$. This convention is used throughout this paper. The computation of a fully connected layer $v_i \in V$, consisting of N_i input neurons and M_i output neurons, can be described by a matrix-vector multiplication of weights $W \in \mathbb{R}^{M_i \times N_i}$ and the input vector $x \in \mathbb{R}^{N_i}$, resulting in vector $y \in \mathbb{R}^{M_i}$ as follows:

$$y_m = \sum_{n=0}^{N_i - 1} W_{m,n} \cdot x_n, \text{ with } 0 \leq m < M_i. \tag{4}$$

Such layers can be quantized as follows:

Weight-Only Quantization. In the case of only quantizing the weights ($W^q_{m,n} = \text{round}(W_{m,n}/S_W) - Z$) according to Eq. 2 and with $Z = 0$, we obtain

$$y_m = \sum_{n=0}^{N-1} S^W \cdot W^q_{m,n} \cdot x_n = S^W \sum_{n=0}^{N-1} W^q_{m,n} \cdot x_n, \tag{5}$$

with $W^q \in \mathbb{Z}^{M \times N}$ and a scaling parameter $S^W \in \mathbb{R}$.

Full Quantization. In the case of full quantization, the inputs x_n and outputs y_m are also quantized according to Eq. 2 to be represented by integer numbers, i.e.,

$$y^q_m = \text{clamp}\left(\text{round}\left(\frac{S^W \cdot S^x}{S^y} \sum_{n=0}^{N-1} W^q_{m,n} \cdot x^q_n\right)\right), \tag{6}$$

with quantized input $x^q \in \mathbb{Z}^N$, quantized output $y^q \in \mathbb{Z}^M$, and scaling parameters S^x, S^W,
$S^y \in \mathbb{R}$. Usually, the clamp function has to be applied on the output to avoid any numeric overflow, e.g., for a wordlength of 8 bits:

$$\text{clamp}(x) = \begin{cases} -127 & \text{if } x < -127 \\ 127 & \text{if } x > 127 \\ x & \text{otherwise} \end{cases}$$

[1] E.g., for symmetric quantization of 8-bit integers, $q_{\max}(\text{int8}) = 127$ and $q_{\min}(\text{int8}) = -127$.

Here, the scaling parameters are real-valued ($S^W, S^x, S^y \in \mathbb{R}$), whereas quantized weights $W^q_{m,n}$, quantized inputs x^q_n, and quantized outputs y^q_m are integers ($\in \mathbb{Z}$). Contrasting to Eq. 4, where $N_i \cdot M_i$ real-valued multiplications need to be computed, the fully quantized representation in Eq. 6 only requires one real-valued multiplication per element y^q_m, thus M_i in total for layer $v_i \in V$.

3 Related Work

Conventional techniques for neural network deployment often ignore tight computational and memory constraints, which hinders their application to highly resource-constrained microcontrollers. Therefore, a dedicated approach is required when developing and compiling neural networks for resource-constrained microcontroller targets. It has to ensure that the computational and latency budget is within the device limits while still achieving a desired performance [25].

3.1 Workflows for Compressing and Deploying Neural Networks on Microcontrollers

MCUNet [20] uses neural architecture search (NAS) to find networks that meet target platform constraints. Each identified network candidate is guaranteed to be deployable on the platform. However, the models have to be trained from scratch, which is time-consuming, especially when considering that more models have to be trained in parallel or one huge so-called "supernet" has to be trained to identify subnets afterward. Typically, there exist expert-designed pre-trained neural network models that already perform well on given datasets [3]. In this case, such a compute- and time-expensive search strategy should be avoided.

TFLite Micro [5] and DNNruntime [6] have the advantage of starting to explore networks obtained by applying weight sharing or pruning and full quantization to a given pre-trained neural network. The advantage here is that existing trained neural networks can be used for deployment on the target microcontroller. However, after compression, the model's prediction quality might be impaired. Therefore, pruning rates may have to be readjusted, and training has to be performed iteratively. Especially in the case of *iterative pruning*, when retraining is applied after each pruning step, this process becomes time-consuming. If the model's prediction or the compression is not sufficient, this process has to be repeated several times. This is a major shortcoming, as the developer will only find out if the developed neural network meets the constraints of the target hardware after deployment.

Our proposed toolchain OpTC introduced in [12] automatically determines pruning rates based on sensitivity analysis and is able to reduce the vast design space to typically just a few evaluations (which can be decided by the user).

All the above workflows have in common that they do not provide any estimates of the resulting execution time of the compiled and deployed network implementation on the platform. The satisfaction of either soft or hard real-time constraints is often a must in safety-critical application areas as frequently encountered in automotive systems. Thus, many solutions proposed by the above workflows might turn out to be infeasible with respect to to timing constraints. In this paper, we investigate models for estimating execution time and memory footprints to reduce the exploration time and propose to only compile and deploy promising solutions.

3.2 Execution Time Estimation for Neural Networks on AURIX TriCores

For estimating the execution time of uninterrupted instruction sequences on AURIX microcontrollers, Fricke et al. [7] have proposed the use of artificial neural networks. In their work, the authors train different artificial neural networks (e.g., recurrent neural networks) with instruction traces extracted from a real system. A disadvantage of this approach is the effort to record and pre-process instruction traces to obtain the training data since this requires the integration of a trace module into the AURIX microcontroller (i.e., a Lauterbach serial trace device). In our specific case, where we estimate the execution time based on the different layers appearing in a neural network, this approach becomes cumbersome as each neural network would need to be compiled to obtain the instruction traces.

By contrast, Groth et al. [8] describe an approach to measure the execution time of building blocks of a neural network only once and estimate the total execution time of a neural network by summing up the individual execution time estimates of the layers for the case of GPUs. Only when so far uncharacterized layers in terms of one or more hyperparameters changing (e.g., the number of input and output neurons in a fully connected layer) are encountered, a new measurement has to be taken.

Taking inspiration from this idea, we present a novel approach to estimate the execution time as well as required memory (ROM and RAM) for neural networks when deployed on AURIX TriCores in Sect. 5. To our knowledge, this is the first work on performance estimation of neural networks for these types of microcontrollers.

4 The OpTC Toolchain

Figure 1 shows the OpTC workflow. Given a neural network model X and a dataset, a sensitivity analysis of the pruning rate on the prediction error E is performed first for each layer v_i (Sect. 4.1). Based on the pruning sensitivities s_i of each layer v_i, initial pruning rates p_i^{init} are determined. Subsequently, a linear design space of networks X_j with proportionally increasing pruning rate p_i of each layer v_i is traversed. In addition to pruning, we incorporate two quantization modes, weight-only and full quantization (see Sect. 2.2), to further compress the neural network model.

The resulting pruned and quantized neural network configurations are evaluated regarding execution time T_j, memory requirements M_j^{ROM}, M_j^{RAM}, respectively, and prediction error E_j using our model-based estimation methods (Sect. 5). The output is a set of *non-dominated* solutions [27] according to the four objectives T_j, M_j^{ROM}, M_j^{RAM}, and E_j of each sampled solution. It is thus no longer necessary for developers to perform this cycle manually and search for the optimal trade-off between pruning rates and NN prediction quality in a trial-and-error fashion. The final step consists of code generation and compilation: OpTC encompasses a template-based code generator (Sect. 4.2) that translates a pruned neural network given in ONNX format to C code exploiting the static

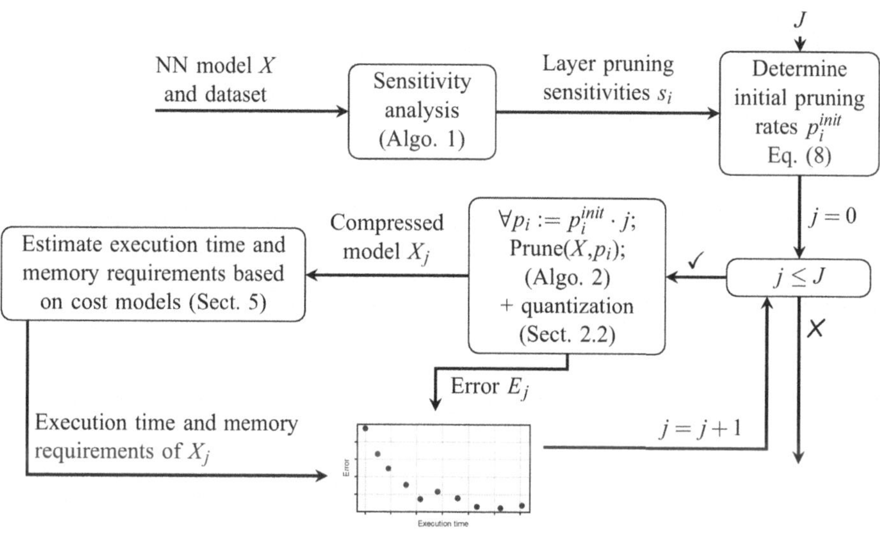

Fig. 1. Overview of our OpTC approach to automatic compression by exploration of network configurations by iteratively increasing the degree of pruning of a neural network X for deployment on the target microcontroller (μC).

properties of trained neural networks (i.e., fixed layer configurations and parameters), such that no dependence on an inference library is required. The steps and algorithms shown in Fig. 1 are described in detail next.

4.1 Automatic Compression

Typically, the workflow starts as follows: a user provides the neural network model and the dataset as well as the granularity the search space of feasible pruning rates/configurations is explored. The neural network model is assumed to be pre-trained by an ML expert. For achieving high flexibility, different Python libraries, such as Microsoft Neural Network Intelligence (NNI)[2], can be integrated to compress the neural network. This provides different options for pruning a neural network X, resulting in a set of J pruned and quantized neural network configurations, with different trade-offs between prediction quality and execution time.

Sensitivity Analysis. Previous works [10, 14, 24] have shown that a layer can be differently important for the prediction quality of the overall neural network. We introduce pruning sensitivity to describe how pruning of a single layer $v_i \in V$ affects the overall prediction quality, and use this knowledge of sensitivity to adaptively control the design space exploration. Algorithm 1 determines the maximal pruning rates $p_i^{\max}$ for each layer $v_i \in V$ in a given neural network model X.

[2] Microsoft, "Neural Network Intelligence (NNI)", https://github.com/microsoft/nni.

For analysis of sensitivity, we define a sequence of pruning rates, e.g., $P = \{0.1, 0.2, \ldots, 0.9\}$. For each layer v_i, the pruning rate p_i is increased while the other layers stay unpruned, and the prediction quality of the overall neural network is measured on the test dataset without re-training.

Algorithm 1. Sensitivity analysis.

Input: NN model X with set V of trained layers, test dataset, ascending sequence of pruning rates $P = \{p^{\min}, \ldots, p^{\max}\}$, threshold $E_{\max}$
Output: Layer sensitivities S, i.e., $s_i \in S$ for each layer v_i

```
for v_i ∈ V do
    for p ← p^min to p^max do
        Y ← prune layer v_i of model X with pruning rate p
        E ← obtain prediction error of pruned model Y by evaluating it with given test dataset
        if E > E_max then
            s_i = 1 − p                    ▷ maximal pruning rate p_i^max of layer v_i found
            break
        end if
    end for
end for
```

If the prediction error E of the partially pruned neural network model is above a given threshold $E_{\max}$ (e.g., the error rate of the unpruned model), the pruning rate applied at this point defines the maximum pruning rate $p_i^{\max}$ for layer v_i. The layer sensitivity s_i is then defined as

$$s_i = 1 - p_i^{\max}. \tag{7}$$

Global Weighted Compression (GWC). For a given layer v_i, the initial pruning rate p_i^{init} is determined based on the layer sensitivity s_i and by introducing a positive integer number J called steps, which defines how many differently pruned network configurations should be evaluated:

$$p_i^{\text{init}} = \frac{1 - s_i}{J} = \frac{p_i^{\max}}{J} \qquad \forall i \,:\, v_i \in V. \tag{8}$$

Note that if $s_i = 1$, p_i^{init} turns to zero, i.e., the respective layer v_i will stay unpruned. We call this technique *global weighted compression*, short GWC, where each layer $v_i \in V$ gets assigned the initial pruning rate p_i^{init}, which is incremented in each iteration $j, 0 \leq j \leq J$ that is input to Algorithm 2.

Algorithm 2. Global Weighted Compression.

Input: NN model X with set V of trained layers, initial pruning rate p_i^{init} per layer v_i, quantization mode $Q_{\text{mode}} \in \{\text{none, weight-only, full quantization}\}$, iteration j with $0 \leq j \leq J$
Output: pruned model X_j

for $i \leftarrow 0$ **to** $|V|-1$ **do**
  $p_i = p_i^{\text{init}} \cdot j$ ▷ Determine pruning rate p_i of layer v_i
end for
$X_j \leftarrow$ compressed model of X by pruning each layer v_i with pruning rate p_i and

quantization mode Q_{mode}

By definition, $j = 0$ denotes the initial (unpruned) neural network model X. Compared to [13], where a global step size for each layer was defined, p_i^{init} can also be interpreted as a layer-specific step size, which is kept constant, and the pruning rate p_i is increased in each step j by p_i^{init}. The number of remaining filters m_i after pruning for each iteration j is obtained as

$$m_i = \lceil M_i \cdot (1 - p_i^{\text{init}} \cdot j) \rceil . \tag{9}$$

The design space is therefore of size $|\Omega_{\text{GWC}}| = J$, where J can be freely chosen. For further compression, users can optionally choose between two different quantization modes (weight-only or full quantization, see Sect. 2.2).

4.2 Template-Based C Code Generation and Operator Fusion

One way to compile an ONNX graph into an executable is to translate each layer directly into C code. However, it is beneficial to optimize the graph itself, e.g., by fusing the operation nodes of the graph, as C or C++ compilers typically do not perform these optimizations [23]. By contrast, our code generator [11] includes optimization techniques for merging activation functions into preceding convolutional or matrix multiplication operations. Operator or layer fusion can reduce the number of memory transfers. Moreover, it can reduce the execution time (number of loop iterations), as it merges subsequent loop nests. To this end, during code generation, patterns (e.g., convolution followed by ReLU) are recognized and operators are fused into functionally equivalent C loops. In the case of quantization, we support the fusion of quantization and dequantization of input and output data, as well as the fusion of the clamping function with the subsequent activation function.

5 Performance Estimation Models for Neural Networks on AURIX TriCores

So far, three steps are needed to measure the required memory (RAM and ROM), as well as the execution time: (1) compiling the generated C program, (2) flashing (and executing) the binary on the microcontroller, and (3) measuring the execution time of neural network inference. The latter usually depends not only on the compiled program but also on chosen compilation parameters. With standard tools and settings (see Sect. 6 for details), this process takes several seconds for each pruning configuration considered. Since our automatic compression approach (Fig. 1) possibly needs to explore large numbers of configurations, we present mathematical models to estimate the execution time and the memory requirements for ROM and RAM to avoid time-intensive compilation and measurements for each explored design point.

5.1 Estimation of Execution Time T_{est}

To estimate the execution time T_{est}, our approach is based on measuring the execution times of the neural network building blocks (layers or fused layers). We assume that a neural network consists of a chain of layers, which are executed sequentially on a single core. Then, the total execution time T_{est} is the sum of the individual execution times $f_{L_i}(h_i)$ for each layer of a neural network consisting of $|V|$ layers.

$$T_{\text{est}} = \sum_{\forall i\,:\, v_i \in V} f_{L_i}(h_i), \tag{10}$$

where $f_{L_i}(h_i)$ is the function for estimating the execution time for a layer $v_i \in V$ of type $L_i \in \{CONV, FC, POOL, \ldots\}$ with respect to its hyperparameters h_i.
Example. Consider a multilayer perceptron (MLP) that consists of a chain of fully connected layers $v_i \in V$ (i.e., $L_i = FC$), each having $N_i \in \mathbb{Z}^+$ and $M_i \in \mathbb{Z}^+$ input neurons and output neurons, respectively. Then, the total execution time T_{est} from Eq. (10) can be concretized to

$$T_{\text{est}} = \sum_{\forall i\,:\, v_i \in V} f_{FC}(M_i, N_i), \tag{11}$$

with hyperparameters $h_i = (M_i, N_i)$.
To obtain $f_{L_i}(h_i)$, we create a small dataset containing the execution times for different settings of the layer hyperparameters for each layer type. For this purpose, the template-based code generator [11] can be used to instantiate each C code template of a layer with different hyperparameters and use the automatic deployment pipeline (consisting of compilation and flashing) to obtain the resulting execution time[3]. Given these datasets, we then train small machine learning models for each layer type to predict the layer execution time given a set of hyperparameters. This approach has the advantage that the time measurements can be reused to evaluate different networks. Moreover, it can be scaled to various TriCore controller variants by collecting respective datasets. To motivate our proposed model to train f_{L_i}, consider the following experiment regarding $f_{FC}(M_i, N_i)$. We measured the execution time for different combinations of M_i and N_i, where $M_i, N_i \in \{1, 2, 4, 8, 16, 32, 64, 128\}$, resulting in 64 samples. Figure 2 shows the execution times on a TC387 for two samples with $M_i = 128$ and $N_i = 16$, $M_i = 16$ and

[3] The number of clock ticks (cycles) was measured using `Ifx_TickTime` functions as part of the IFX low-level driver library (iLLD), which accesses the TriCore performance counter. To determine the execution time of a single layer, we divide the number of cycles by the respective operating frequency of the core f (in case of the AURIX TC387 $f = 300$ MHz).

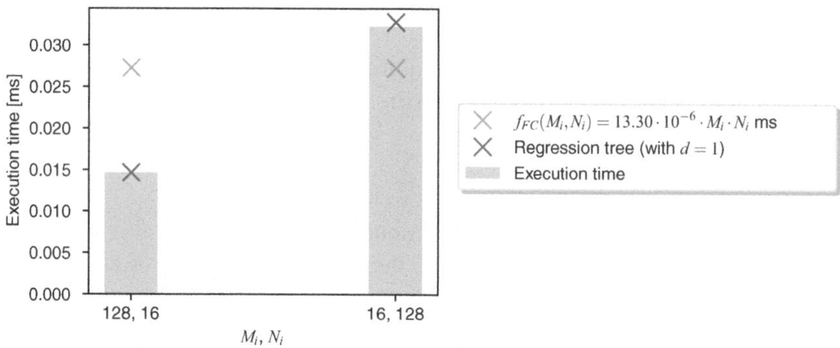

Fig. 2. Measured execution time for a fully connected layer, with $M_i = 128$ and $N_i = 16$, $M_i = 16$ and $N_i = 128$, respectively.

$N_i = 128$. The red markers indicate the estimated execution times using linear regression on the multiplied hyperparameters ($M_i \cdot N_i$). However, the estimated execution time is far off because there are cases (e.g., $N_i \leq 16$) where the execution time is significantly lower due to compiler optimizations such as loop unrolling. Hence, we propose to use a model that combines regression and decision trees, hereafter referred to as regression trees.

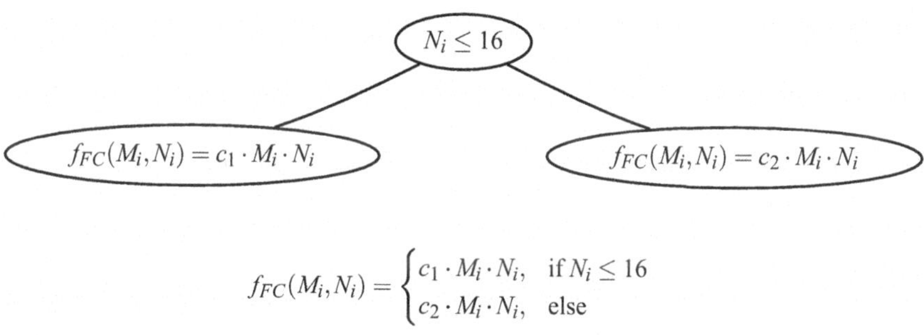

$$f_{FC}(M_i, N_i) = \begin{cases} c_1 \cdot M_i \cdot N_i, & \text{if } N_i \leq 16 \\ c_2 \cdot M_i \cdot N_i, & \text{else} \end{cases}$$

Fig. 3. Example of a regression tree to estimate the execution time $f^{FC}(M_i, N_i)$ of a fully connected layer v_i with the hyperparameters N_i (input neurons) and M_i (output neurons), and depth $d = 1$.

With regression trees (see example in Fig. 3), the piece-wise linear behavior introduced by loop optimizations, as in the example for the execution time for different M_i and N_i, can be modeled. In Fig. 3, the constants in the regression leaves are $c_1 = 6.96 \cdot 10^{-6}$ and $c_2 = 16.09 \cdot 10^{-6}$, respectively, so that for $N_i \leq 16$, the hyperparameters are multiplied by a smaller factor, resulting in more accurate execution time estimates. To trade off model complexity for prediction error, we can increase the tree depth d, for example, in the case of more complex layers, such as convolutional layers, which have more hyperparameters.

5.2 Estimation of Required ROM $M_{\text{est}}^{\text{ROM}}$

Similar to the execution time, the overall required ROM can be obtained by summing up the required ROM of the individual layers $\rho_{L_i,i}$:

$$M_{\text{est}}^{\text{ROM}} = \sum_{\forall i\,:\,v_i \in V} \rho_{L_i,i}. \tag{12}$$

For a neural network layer $v_i \in V$, additionally to the weights, also the program itself needs to be stored in the ROM. Hence, the required ROM $\rho_{L_i,i}$ of each layer can be computed as

$$\rho_{L_i,i} = w_{L_i,i} \cdot D_i(A) + cs_{L_i}, \tag{13}$$

where cs_{L_i} denotes the resulting code size for the respective layer of type L_i (in bytes), $w_{L_i,i}$ denotes the number of weights of layer v_i, with datatype A (e.g., $A \in \{\text{float, int8}\}$) of size $D_i(A)$ bytes. The code size cs_{L_i} (in bytes) is determined by compiling each layer type L_i once for the respective microcontroller platform. The number of weights of a fully connected layer is given by $w_{FC,i} = M_i \cdot N_i$. For a convolutional layer with N_i input feature maps, M_i filters (or output channels), and the filter dimensions $K1_i \times K2_i$, the number of weights of a convolutional layer is given by $w_{CONV,i} = M_i \cdot N_i \cdot K1_i \cdot K2_i$. For all other layers (e.g., activation and pooling layers), the number of weights is assumed to be zero.

5.3 Estimation of Required RAM $M_{\text{est}}^{\text{RAM}}$

For the intermediate tensors, tensor unionization is performed to wrap the tensors into unions to allow the compiler to reuse heap memory [11]. For each layer $v_i \in V$, u_i denotes the number of intermediate results. As example, for a fully connected layer $v_i \in V$, the number of intermediate results equals the number of output neurons $u_i = M_i$. Similarly, for a convolutional layer $v_i \in V$, the number of intermediate results equals the number of output neurons $u_i = R_i \cdot C_i \cdot M_i$, where R_i is the number of rows and C_i denotes the number of columns of the output feature map, and M_i denotes the number of output feature maps. The RAM allocated for the previous inputs of layer v_i can be reused to store the results of layer v_{i+1}, with $0 \leq i < |V|$. This results in two unions, consisting of the number of intermediate results u_i, with $\forall i \,:\, v_i \in V$ (one if i is odd and one with i is even).

$$U_{even} = \max_{\forall i\,:\,v_i \in V} \{u_i \mid i \text{ even}\}$$

$$U_{odd} = \max\{\max_{\forall i\,:\,v_i \in V} \{u_i \mid i \text{ odd}\},\, 0\}$$

Note that in case $|V| = 1$, $U_{odd} = 0$, as only one union is required to store the results. Analogous to the cost of ROM, we have to consider the number of bytes for the datatype required to store the intermediate tensors, again assuming that the same datatype is used for each intermediate tensor and input tensor. In addition, the input (tensor) must be stored, i.e., the number q_0 of input values or neurons of the first layer v_0 must be included. The overall required RAM is obtained as

$$M_{\text{est}}^{\text{RAM}} = D(A) \cdot (U_{even} + U_{odd} + q_0). \tag{14}$$

6 Experiments

In our experiments, we use three different benchmarks: an autoencoder (AE) for anomaly detection [19], a convolutional neural network (CNN) for keyword spotting [26] from the open-source MLPerf Tiny benchmark [3], and a temporal convolutional neural network (TCN) for predicting the temperature of an electric motor [11]. The three benchmarks are described in detail in [12].
Each model has been implemented and trained in PyTorch on the respective dataset for 100 epochs using the Adam optimizer [16] to minimize the Mean Squared Error (MSE) (anomaly detection and electric motor temperature) or the cross entropy (keyword spotting). A subset of the total dataset not used for training was used for testing. An Nvidia RTX 2080 Ti GPU was used to train and test each explored neural network.

Execution times were measured on the AURIX TC387_3.3 V_TFT evaluation board with a TriCore 387. For the AURIX TC387 microcontroller, the HighTec GCC compiler[4] with `-O3` optimization was employed consistently in the following analysis and experiments. For flashing and execution, the AURIX Flasher Software Tool[5] was utilized. The TriCore 387 supports floating-point computations running at a frequency of 300 MHz. It consists of 4 cores (CPU0, CPU1, CPU2, CPU3), which differ in the size of the scratchpad RAM, i.e., the size of scratchpad RAM of CPU0 and CPU1 is 240 kilobytes, whereas CPU2 and CPU3 are 96 kilobytes[6]. The TC387 has a ROM of size 10 megabytes, where the weights of the model and the program are stored. For a fair comparison, all models were run on a single core, with 240 kilobytes of scratchpad RAM.

6.1 Evaluation of Global Weighted Compression

Temporal Convolutional Neural Network (TCN) on Electric Motor Temperature. In the first experiment, we compare the two approaches of global pruning [11] with the introduced global weighted compression based on layer sensitivities (see Sect. 4.1). For this experiment, we pruned the TCN iteratively using the ℓ^1 norm, starting with a pruning rate of 50% in the case of global pruning. The pruning rate indicates how many filters are removed from each convolutional layer (the higher the pruning rate, the more filters are removed). After pruning the filters, we applied retraining for 50 epochs to allow the remaining filter weights to adjust properly. Similarly, the automatic compression toolchain was applied using global weighted compression, with $Q_{\text{mode}} =$ none, and $J = 10$.

The results are shown in Fig. 4. Here, the purple dots represent solutions obtained by global pruning, i.e., setting a fixed pruning rate (e.g., 50% to 90% annotated to the points). Solutions obtained by the global weighted compression approach are visualized as red dots with the corresponding iteration j annotated below each point. The red

[4] HighTec, "Tricore Development Platform v4.9.3.0-infineon-1.0", https://hightec-rt.com/en/products/development-platform, Date accessed: 03/19/2024.

[5] Infineon, "Tricore Development Platform v4.9.3.0-infineon-1.0", https://softwaretools.infineon.com/tools/com.ifx.tb.tool.aurixflashersoftwaretool, Date accessed: 08/07/2024.

[6] Infineon, "AURIX TC38x User Manual", https://www.infineon.com, Date accessed: 03/19/2024.

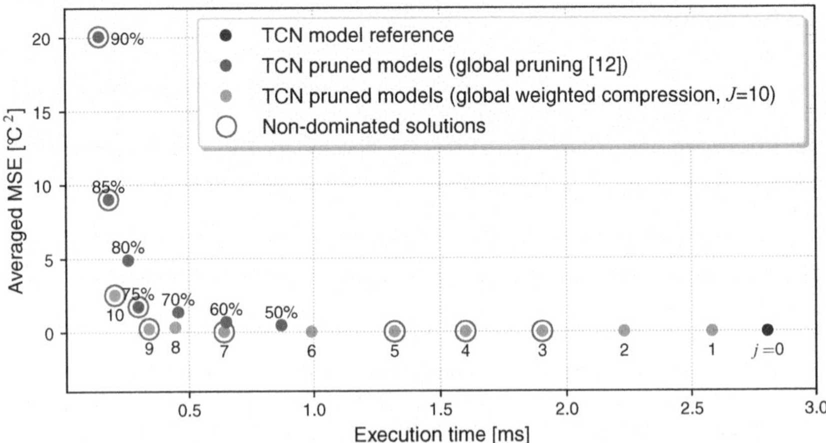

Fig. 4. Visualized is the trade-off between execution time and average MSE for different pruning rates of the temporal convolutional neural network (TCN) on the electric motor temperature dataset. In the case of global pruning (purple dots), the pruning rate was set manually in the range from 50 to 90%. In the case of global weighted compression (red dots), each dot is numbered with the corresponding iteration j ($0 \leq j \leq J = 10$) [12], and iteration $j = 0$ corresponds to the reference model (Color figure online).

circles around the dots denote the found *non-dominated* design points [27], in terms of the two objectives of minimizing the mean averaged MSE and execution time. It can be seen that our proposed concept of global weighted compression preserves the mean squared error (MSE) of the reference model (shown in blue) better than the global pruning concept. The two non-dominated solutions having the shortest execution time were obtained by manually setting the global pruning rate to high percentages of 85% and 90%. Note that the global weighted compression approach implicitly excludes these values, as the defined maximum pruning rate $p_i^{\max}$ is derived from the given MSE threshold $E_{\max}$ (in this case, the threshold of the unpruned TCN model $j = 0$).

6.2 Performance Estimation Model Errors

As we apply optimizations during C code generation (e.g., fusing fully connected layers with ReLU), we also generated cost models for these optimized templates. We used the dataset defined in Sect. 5 to train the regression trees for execution time, as the autoencoder model consists of fully connected layers with up to $M_i = 128$ output neurons. The depth of the trees was set to $d = 3$ for all layer types.

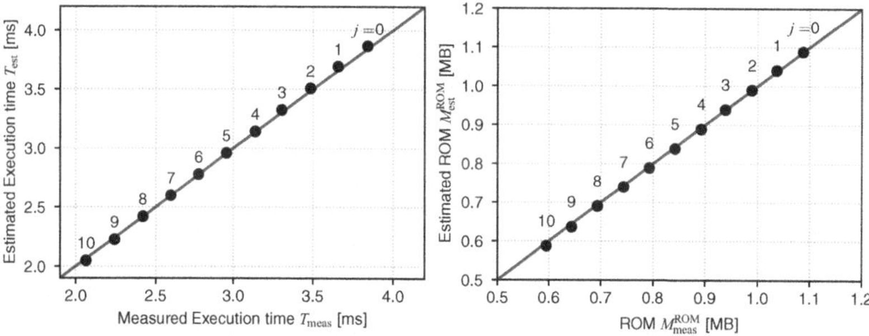

Fig. 5. Estimated execution time T_{est} and ROM M_{est}^{ROM} vs. the measured execution time T_{meas} and ROM M_{meas}^{ROM} required after the compilation for the configurations for the autoencoder for anomaly detection from [12].

We applied the toolchain for automatic compression by means of global weighted compression (see Sect. 4.1), with $J = 10$. The measured execution times T_{meas} and required ROM M_{meas}^{ROM} for the autoencoder, with the depicted 10 increasingly pruned model configurations from [12] are compared with the estimated execution time T_{est} and ROM M_{est}^{ROM} in Fig. 5. The estimation errors are evaluated by calculating the Root Mean Square Percentage Error *RMSPE* as follows:

$$RMSPE = 100\% \cdot \sqrt{\frac{1}{J+1} \sum_{j=0}^{J} \left(\frac{\text{measured}_j - \text{estimated}_j}{\text{measured}_j} \right)^2}.$$

For both execution time and ROM, our proposed performance model achieves an *RMSPE* of 0.56% and 0.59%, respectively. The estimated RAM (scratchpad) M_{est}^{RAM} based on the size to store the intermediate tensors can be calculated exactly ($RMSPE =$ 0%), as the size of all intermediate tensors is fixed for a given neural network. The small error in the ROM prediction may be due to compiler optimizations leading to slight variances in code size for the particular neural network model, e.g., when loop unrolling is applied, it typically leads to a slight increase in code size, which is also visible in Fig. 5 where the code size is slightly underestimated for $j \geq 9$. On a Windows notebook with an Intel Core i7-1165G7 @ 2.80 GHz, it took a total of about 18 s to compile (12 s), flash, and run the binary (6 s) of the autoencoder model from the MLPerf Tiny benchmark [3]. In comparison, on average, the time to estimate T_{est}, where we traverse the operators of the neural network and compute $f_{L_i}(h_i)$ (see Sect. 5.1), M_{est}^{ROM} (see Sect. 5.2), and M_{est}^{RAM} (see Sect. 5.3) for an autoencoder configuration j takes only 97 ms.

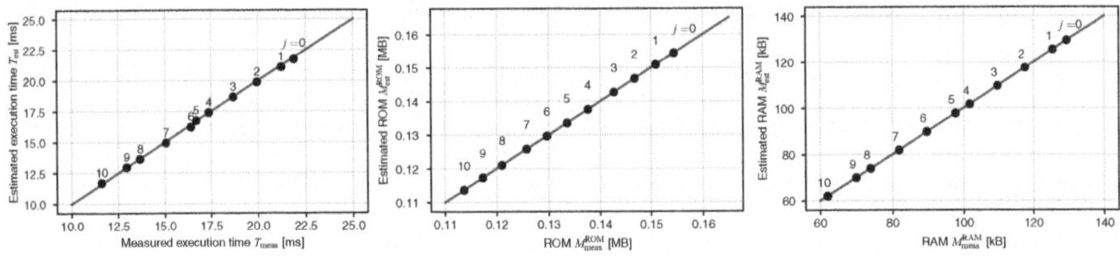

Fig. 6. Estimated execution time T_{est}, ROM $M_{\text{est}}^{\text{ROM}}$, and RAM $M_{\text{est}}^{\text{RAM}}$ vs. the measured execution time T_{meas}, ROM $M_{\text{meas}}^{\text{ROM}}$, and RAM $M_{\text{meas}}^{\text{ROM}}$ required after the compilation for the pruned configurations for the CNN for keyword spotting shown in Fig. 10 (red dots).

For the evaluation of the CNN for keyword spotting (see Fig. 6), our performance model achieved an RMSPE of 0.54% for the execution time. The memory usage could be accurately estimated for the CNN with a tiny RMSPE of only 0.004% (ROM) and 0.002% (RAM).

6.3 Evaluation of Combined Pruning and Quantization

Autoencoder for Anomaly Detection. As mentioned in Sect. 2, OpTC supports two types of quantization: (1) weight-only quantization and (2) full quantization. Present frameworks usually support full quantization, but this can increase the execution time compared to the single-precision floating-point reference model, because full quantization adds additional computational overhead due to the scaling, rounding, and clamping operations.

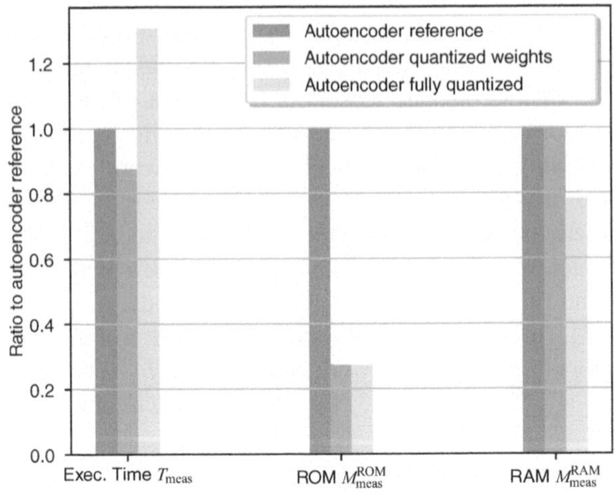

Fig. 7. Execution times T_{meas}, required ROM $M_{\text{meas}}^{\text{ROM}}$, and RAM $M_{\text{meas}}^{\text{RAM}}$ for the autoencoder reference with single-precision floating-point format (blue bars), weight-only quantization (green bars), and full quantization (cyan bars) to 8-bit integer, normalized to the reference.

This can also be seen in Fig. 7, where we applied weight-only quantization to 8-bit integer (green bars) and full quantization, where all weights and intermediate tensors are quantized to 8-bit integer (cyan bars). The TC387 has a floating-point unit, so the time for multiplication and addition cannot be reduced if they are performed as 8-bit integers, as there is no support for packed 8-bit data computations. If the weights are quantized to 8-bit integer, we can see a slight reduction in execution time compared to the reference model due to decreased loading times required to transfer the weights from the ROM. Obviously, the ROM (required to store the weights, biases, and program) is reduced by almost a factor of 4× by quantization to 8-bit integer[7]. In terms of RAM consumption, the reference and weight-only quantized model requires approximately 3.5 kB to store the input data (2,560 bytes) and the intermediate tensors (972 bytes). In the case of full quantization, we can reduce the size of the intermediate tensor by a factor of four (243 bytes), but the input data is still in floating-point format. Based on these findings, we applied weight-only quantization to the pruned configurations from [12] and finetuned the model with *quantization-aware training* [15] using 10 epochs.

In Fig. 8, the configurations with quantized weights (green dots) of found non-dominated design points after pruning (red dots) are visualized, as well as the reference autoencoder model (blue dot). Note that the respective y-axis denotes the error E, which for the autoencoder benchmark is the *area under the curve* (AUC) subtracted from 1 (E=1-AUC). Even though quantization-aware training was performed, one can see that the error increases slightly with quantization. The quantized and pruned autoencoder configuration $j = 7$ dominates the pruned autoencoder model $j = 10$ and has approximately the same error as the reference autoencoder model (blue dot, $j = 0$). This con-

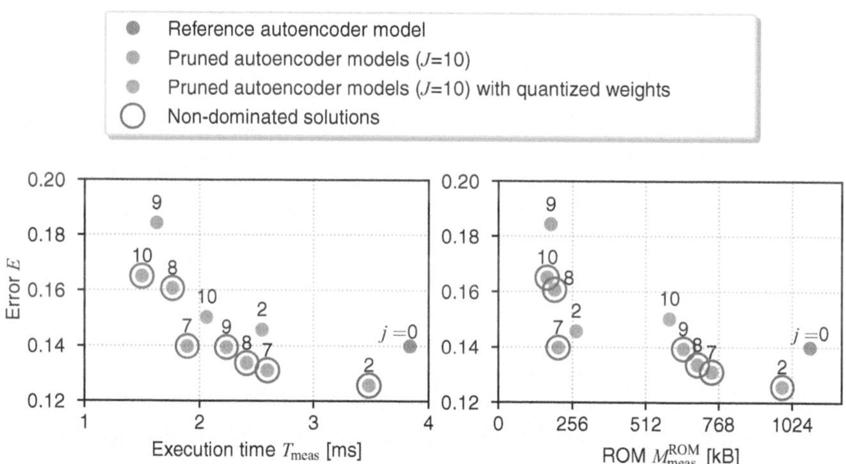

Fig. 8. Error E, execution times T_{meas}, and required ROM $M_{\text{meas}}^{\text{ROM}}$ for the non-dominated pruned-only configurations (red, from [12]) compared to the pruned and weight-only quantized configurations (green) of the autoencoder model (reference in blue).

[7] Note that the biases are not reduced in the case of weight-only quantization (32-bit float) as well as full quantization (32-bit integer), nor is the program size.

figuration achieves a speedup of about 2×, and the ROM can be significantly reduced to 207 kB (compared to 1.1 MB).

Convolutional Neural Network on Keyword Spotting. Quantizing the convolutional neural network (CNN) for keyword spotting also increases the execution time compared to the single-precision floating-point CNN reference, both for weight-only and full quantization (see Fig. 9).

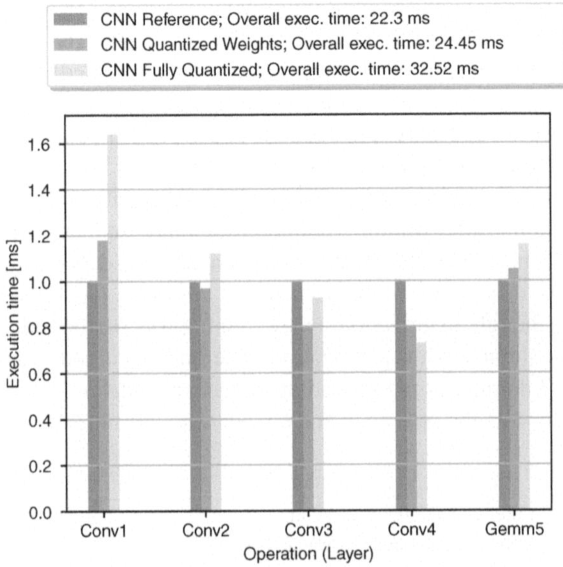

Fig. 9. Execution time per layer, required for the convolutional neural network (CNN) reference (blue bars), weight-only quantization (green bars) and full quantization (cyan bars), normalized to the reference. (Color figure online)

In particular, for full quantization, when looking at the execution time per layer, the first layer requires considerably more processing time because each element of the input vector (here the input consists of 8,000 values) has to be quantized according to Eq. 2. Therefore, we decided to omit the first layer (Conv1) from the quantization and fully quantized the remaining convolutional and fully connected layers (see Eq. 6). We applied quantization-aware training for 10 epochs to maintain a low error rate ("1-classification accuracy").

In Fig. 10, we compare the pruned only configurations from [12] with the pruned and fully quantized CNN configurations. As already seen in Fig. 9, there is a slight overhead due to the additional operations required. In principle, it might be possible to reduce the execution time with a dedicated DSP library, e.g., supporting 8-bit integer SIMD packing, which was not available for this work. However, ROM and RAM can

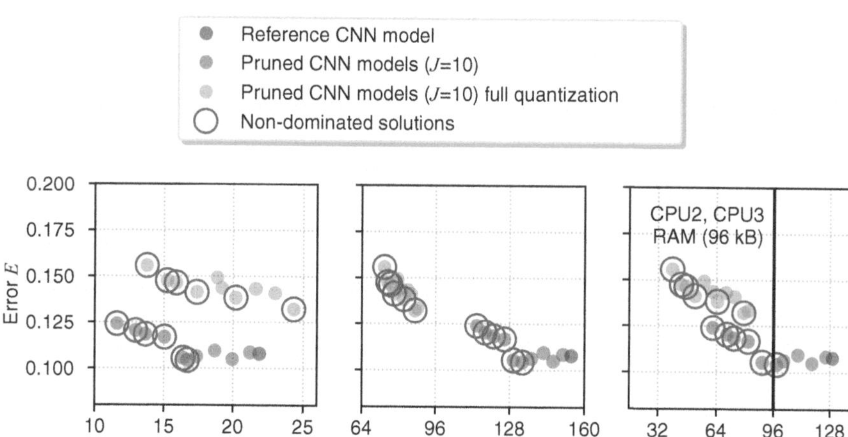

Fig. 10. Error E, execution times T_{meas}, required ROM $M^{\text{ROM}}_{\text{meas}}$ and RAM $M^{\text{ROM}}_{\text{meas}}$ for the pruned only configurations (red) compared to the pruned and fully quantized configurations (cyan) of the convolutional neural network (CNN) for keyword spotting (reference in blue).

also be significantly reduced. Considering RAM usage, the baseline model requires 130 kB of RAM, which is 54% of the available RAM for CPU0 and CPU1. The baseline CNN for keyword spotting exceeds the available RAM of CPU2 and CPU3 of TC387 (96 kB, marked by the black vertical line in Fig. 4). Each of the determined pruned and fully quantized configurations requires less than 94 kB, which fits into the RAM of CPU2 and CPU3, while the prediction error increases only marginally. Based on the results of OpTC, the users can decide on which CPU of the TC387 the model should be deployed and if the resulting trade-off in error still meets their constraints.

7 Conclusion

In this work, we presented OpTC [12], a toolchain for automated neural network model compression and C code generation for AURIX TriCore microcontrollers. In order to fit the limited memory available on microcontroller platforms, we first introduced a technique to reduce the vast design space of pruning configurations by performing a layer-based sensitivity analysis. We proposed and validated mathematical cost models to significantly expedite the time needed to evaluate the execution time and memory requirements of each explored network candidate. In our experiments, we applied the toolchain OpTC and analyzed the execution time, memory requirements, and accuracy of found non-dominated solutions for three different applications, two from the MLPerf Tiny benchmark and one real-world automotive case study. For the example of the autoencoder for anomaly detection, OpTC finds solutions that are twice as fast in execution time and at the same time 5× smaller in the memory footprint related to the implementation of a given unpruned and unquantized implementation without increasing the error over its baseline model. This design point would even be deployable on microcontroller targets with smaller amounts of available memory, e.g., the

TC32x with a ROM size of just 1 MB. For the CNN for keyword spotting from the MLPerf Tiny benchmark, we demonstrated the efficiency of OpTC in not only providing speedups but also reducing the memory footprint to make models deployable on targets with low scratchpad (RAM) capacity. By combining pruning and full quantization, non-dominated solutions are found that require less than 50 kB (baseline requires 130 kB) of scratchpad memory, with only a marginal increase in error compared to the baseline.

Acknowledgments. This work was supported by the Schaeffler Hub for Advanced Research at Friedrich-Alexander-Universität Erlangen-Nürnberg (SHARE at FAU).

References

1. Abadi, M., Agarwal, A., Barham, P., et al.: TensorFlow: large-scale machine learning on heterogeneous systems (2015). https://www.tensorflow.org
2. Bai, J., Lu, F., Zhang, K., et al.: ONNX: open neural network exchange (2019). https://github.com/onnx/onnx
3. Banbury, C.R., et al.: MLPerf tiny benchmark. In: Vanschoren, J., Yeung, S. (eds.) Proceedings of the Neural Information Processing Systems Track on Datasets and Benchmarks 1, NeurIPS Datasets and Benchmarks 2021, December 2021, virtual (2021). https://datasets-benchmarks-proceedings.neurips.cc/paper/2021/hash/da4fb5c6e93e74d3df8527599fa62642-Abstract-round1.html
4. Chollet, F., et al.: Keras. https://keras.io (2015)
5. David, R., et al.: TensorFlow lite micro: embedded machine learning on TinyML systems. Comput. Res. Repository (CoRR) (2020)
6. Deutel, M., Woller, P., Mutschler, C., Teich, J.: Energy-efficient deployment of deep learning applications on cortex-M based microcontrollers using deep compression. Comput. Res. Repository (CoRR) (2022)
7. Fricke, F., et al.: Application runtime estimation for AURIX embedded MCU using deep learning. In: Proceedings of the International Conference on Embedded Computer Systems: Architectures, Modeling and Simulation (SAMOS). Lecture Notes in Computer Science (LNCS), vol. 13511, pp. 235–249. Springer. https://doi.org/10.1007/978-3-031-15074-6_15
8. Groth, S., Schmid, M., Teich, J., Hannig, F.: Estimating the execution time of CNN inference on GPUs. In: Proceedings of the 27th Workshop on Methods and Description Languages for Modelling and Verification of Circuits and Systems (MBMV), pp. 53–62. VDE
9. Han, S., Mao, H., Dally, W.J.: Deep compression: compressing deep neural network with pruning, trained quantization and Huffman coding. In: Proceedings of 4th International Conference on Learning Representations (ICLR) (2016). https://doi.org/10.48550/arXiv.1510.00149
10. Han, S., Pool, J., Tran, J., Dally, W.J.: Learning both weights and connections for efficient neural networks. In: Proceedings of the Annual Conference on Neural Information Processing Systems (NIPS), pp. 1135–1143 (2015)
11. Heidorn, C., Hannig, F., Riedelbauch, D., Strohmeyer, C., Teich, J.: Efficient deployment of neural networks for thermal monitoring on AURIX TC3xx microcontrollers. In: Proceedings of the 10th International Conference on Vehicle Technology and Intelligent Transport Systems (VEHITS), pp. 64–75. SciTePress. https://doi.org/10.5220/0000186800003702

12. Heidorn, C., Hannig, F., Riedelbauch, D., Strohmeyer, C., Teich, J.: OpTC - a toolchain for deployment of neural networks on AURIX TC3xx microcontrollers. In: Kulzer, A., Reuss, H., Wagner, A. (eds.) Proceedings of the Stuttgart International Symposium on Automotive and Engine Technology, pp. 65–81. Springer. https://doi.org/10.1007/978-3-658-45018-2_4
13. Heidorn, C., Meyerhöfer, N., Schinabeck, C., Hannig, F., Teich, J.: Hardware-aware evolutionary filter pruning. In: Proceedings of the International Conference on Embedded Computer Systems: Architectures, Modeling and Simulation (SAMOS). Lecture Notes in Computer Science (LNCS), vol. 13511, pp. 283–299. Springer. https://doi.org/10.1007/978-3-031-15074-6_18
14. Heidorn, C., Sabih, M., Meyerhöfer, N., Schinabeck, C., Teich, J., Hannig, F.: Hardware-aware evolutionary explainable filter pruning for convolutional neural networks. Int. J. Parallel Program. **52**, 40–48. https://doi.org/10.1007/s10766-024-00760-5
15. Jacob, B., et al.: Quantization and training of neural networks for efficient integer-arithmetic-only inference. In: Proceedings of the IEEE Conference on Computer Vision and Pattern Recognition (CVPR), pp. 2704–2713. Computer Vision Foundation / IEEE Computer Society. https://doi.org/10.1109/CVPR.2018.00286
16. Kingma, D.P., Ba, J.: Adam: a method for stochastic optimization. In: Bengio, Y., LeCun, Y. (eds.) Proceedings of the 3rd International Conference on Learning Representations (ICLR). https://doi.org/10.48550/arXiv.1412.6980
17. Kirchgässner, W., Wallscheid, O., Böcker, J.: Electric motor temperature (2021). https://doi.org/10.34740/KAGGLE/DSV/2161054, https://www.kaggle.com/dsv/2161054
18. Kirchgässner, W., Wallscheid, O., Böcker, J.: Thermal neural networks: lumped-parameter thermal modeling with state-space machine learning. Eng. Appl. Artif. Intell. **117**, 105537 (2023). https://doi.org/10.1016/J.ENGAPPAI.2022.105537
19. Koizumi, Y., Saito, S., Uematsu, H., Harada, N., Imoto, K.: ToyADMOS: a dataset of miniature-machine operating sounds for anomalous sound detection. In: Proceedings of the IEEE Workshop on Applications of Signal Processing to Audio and Acoustics (WASPAA), pp. 313–317. IEEE. https://doi.org/10.1109/WASPAA.2019.8937164
20. Lin, J., Chen, W., Lin, Y., Cohn, J., Gan, C., Han, S.: MCUNet: tiny deep learning on IoT devices. In: Proceedings of the Annual Conference on Neural Information Processing Systems (NeurIPS) (2020)
21. Paszke, A., et al.: Automatic differentiation in PyTorch. In: Proceedings of NIPS Autodiff Workshop. OpenReview.net (2017). https://openreview.net/forum?id=BJJsrmfCZ
22. Petersen, P., Rudolf, T., Sax, E.: A data-driven energy estimation based on the mixture of experts method for battery electric vehicles. In: Proceedings of the 8th International Conference on Vehicle Technology and Intelligent Transport Systems (VEHITS), pp. 384–390. SCITEPRESS (2022). https://doi.org/10.5220/0011081000003191
23. Rotem, N., Fix, et al.: Glow: graph lowering compiler techniques for neural networks. Comput. Res. Repository (CoRR) (2018)
24. Sabih, M., Mishra, A., Hannig, F., Teich, J.: MOSP: multi-objective sensitivity pruning of deep neural networks. In: Proceedings of the IEEE 13th International Green and Sustainable Computing Conference (IGSC), pp. 1–8. IEEE. https://doi.org/10.1109/IGSC55832.2022.9969374
25. Saha, S.S., Sandha, S.S., Srivastava, M.B.: Machine learning for microcontroller-class hardware: a review. Comput. Res. Repository (CoRR) (2022)
26. Warden, P.: Speech commands: a dataset for limited-vocabulary speech recognition. Comput. Res. Repository (CoRR) (2018)
27. Zitzler, E., Laumanns, M., Bleuler, S.: A tutorial on evolutionary multiobjective optimization. In: Gandibleux, X., Sevaux, M., Sörensen, K., T'kindt, V. (eds.) Metaheuristics for Multiobjective Optimisation, pp. 3–37. Springer (2004). https://doi.org/10.1007/978-3-642-17144-4_1

Multi-pedestrian Tracking and Map-Based Intention Estimation in Autonomous Driving: Evaluating Algorithmic Reliability

Ali Dehghani(✉) and Lucila Patino Studencki

Faculty of Mechanical and Automotive Engineering, Coburg University of Applied Sciences and Arts, Coburg, Germany
{ali.dehghani,lucila.patino-studencki}@hs-coburg.de

Abstract. Multi-pedestrian tracking and intention estimation are critical for enhancing the safety and reliability of autonomous vehicles (AVs) in complex driving environments, as these technologies enable AVs to predict and respond to pedestrian behavior more effectively, thereby reducing the likelihood of accidents. This paper proposes an algorithm to model how multiple pedestrians behave and move depending on their environment map. A method that integrates a Gaussian Mixture Probability Hypothesis Density Filter (GMPHD) with the Generalized Potential Field Approach (GPFA) to concurrently track and predict the movements of multiple pedestrians within a short time frame is presented. The algorithm's reliability was validated through a comprehensive statistical analysis conducted over a substantial dataset of pedestrian movements, demonstrating the model's reliability and accuracy for tracking and predicting multiple pedestrians in an environment where multiple goals are possible. We aim to determine whether the algorithm can consistently predict pedestrian behavior in dynamic and complex environments, ensuring its applicability in real-world autonomous driving situations.

Keywords: Pedestrian intention estimation · Multiple pedestrian tracking · Situational awareness · Autonomous driving · Autonomous shuttle

1 Introduction

Intention estimation and tracking of pedestrians are critical for enabling intelligent vehicles to safely maneuver through complex environments, including those where vulnerable road users (VRUs), such as pedestrians, are present. The ability to protect vulnerable road users (VRUs) is crucial and plays a key role in improving the safety and comfort of passengers. By accurately predicting and understanding pedestrian behavior, autonomous vehicles can smoothly navigate through urban environments and adapt their driving strategies as needed.

F. Calise et al. (Eds.): SMARTGREENS 2024/VEHITS 2024, CCIS 2954, pp. 146–159, 2026.
https://doi.org/10.1007/978-3-032-23187-1_8

This enhances safety and ensures that these vehicles can fit seamlessly into busy traffic. Inspired by insights from the Shuttle Modellregion Oberfranken (SMO) project in Kronach, Germany [1], this study focuses on the urgent need for advanced techniques in reliable estimating pedestrian intentions within autonomous shuttle operations. As highlighted by [2], the challenges faced—especially those involving unexpected pedestrian behaviors that frequently result in sudden shuttle stops—underscore the importance of accurately predicting pedestrian intentions. The Fig. 1 illustrates a complex autonomous driving scenario under challenging conditions in Kronach, Germany. In this situation, the autonomous shuttle must evaluate its surroundings to navigate safely while anticipating the unpredictable intentions of pedestrians, who might cross the street at any moment. According to the taxonomy presented by [3], pedestrian motion prediction models can be categorized into physics-based, pattern-based, and planning-based approaches. An example is illustrated in Fig. 2; while physics-based models [5] follow Newton's laws (e.g. constant velocity), they are effective for short-term predictions, but they often overlook crucial environmental contexts like maps and pedestrian interactions. Pattern-based models (e.g., [6–8]), on the other hand, improve accuracy by leveraging observed data but struggle with the quality and quantity of data required, in this example, the most often observed trajectories in the training data are considered. These approaches often neglect interactions among multiple pedestrians. Planning-based models (e.g., [9,10]) are effective at understanding intentions (goals), but they struggle in dynamic environments characterized by frequent changes or a large number of objects.

Fig. 1. Autonomous shuttle navigating a complex urban intersection in Kronach, Germany, under challenging conditions, where it must anticipate and respond to the uncertain intentions of multiple pedestrians [4].

To achieve accurate pedestrian behavior prediction, [4] proposed a hybrid approach that combines physics-based and planning-based techniques to offer a

Fig. 2. From left to right, the images illustrate three different pedestrian intention prediction methods: 1) Physics-based prediction, 2) Pattern-based prediction, and 3) Planning-based prediction.

comprehensive solution for predicting pedestrian motion in complex automotive scenarios. This approach utilizes the precision of physics-based models, which follow Newton's laws to capture movement dynamics, and the strategic insights of planning-based models that interpret intentions and objectives to predict future pedestrian trajectories. By integrating these methods, the approach models immediate physical interactions and incorporates understanding of pedestrian behavior, resulting in more reliable predictions in environments where forecasting movements is critical. By integrating elements from both physics-based and planning-based approaches, our method addresses their individual limitations, offering a more adaptable solution for predicting pedestrian behavior in real-world scenarios. Given the critical need for reliable pedestrian intention prediction in autonomous vehicle systems, it is essential to rigorously evaluate the reliability of proposed algorithm. While our previous study [4], including the proposed hybrid approach (enhanced Gaussian Mixture Probability Hypothesis Density (GMPHD) Filter [11] with the Generalized Potential Field Approach (GPFA) [12]), have demonstrated promising results by testing the algorithm on a limited set of trajectories, these evaluations may not fully capture the algorithm's performance in real-world conditions. In this paper, we extend this investigation by systematically evaluating the reliability incorporating a data set of various pedestrian trajectories with multiple possible intentions. We aim to determine whether the algorithm can consistently predict pedestrian behavior in dynamic and complex environments, ensuring its applicability in real-world autonomous driving situations. The remainder of this paper is organized as follows: Sect. 4 introduces the proposed approach, detailing the environmental data modeling as a potential field, the dynamic pedestrian model, and the application of the Probability Hypothesis Density (PHD) Filter. Section 3 presents experimental results that validate the algorithm's effectiveness, and reliability. Finally, Sect. 4 offers conclusions and discusses potential directions for future research.

2 Multi-pedestrian Tracking

2.1 Tracking Algorithm

Tracking multiple pedestrians begins with detecting individuals through sensory input, followed by advanced algorithmic processing to interpret the data, differentiate pedestrians from other objects, and predict their intentions (c.f. Fig. 3). This study assumes that pedestrian detection has already been conducted, providing noisy positional data in a 3D coordinate system. Our primary focus lies on the consideration of environmental data as a potential field, the application of a tracking algorithm, and the prediction of pedestrian trajectories. The concept of potential fields has been widely applied across various domains, such as collective motion, trajectory planning, and pedestrian movement analysis. However, traditional methods like the social force model face significant limitations when applied to scenarios involving individual pedestrians or small groups, as these models are often optimized for crowd dynamics and require complex parameter settings. To address these challenges, we utilize the Generalized Potential Field Approach (GPFA), which integrates potential field theory with a kinematic motion model to effectively handle individual and small-group pedestrian scenarios, while also simplifying the necessary parameterization [14].

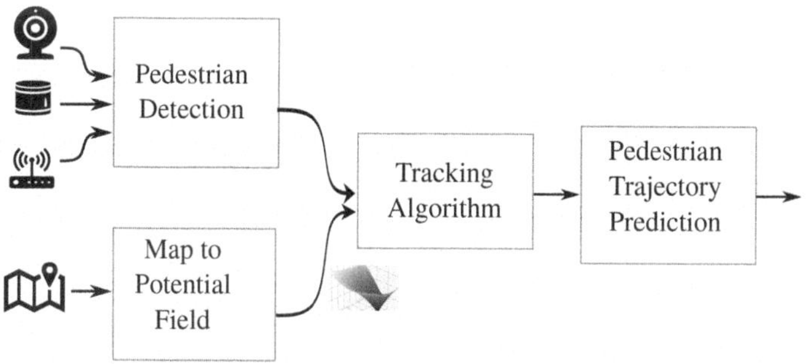

Fig. 3. General Architecture of the Multi-Pedestrian Tracking System [4].

In the GPFA, each pedestrian is modeled as a test particle within a set of potential fields, each representing a different source of information, such as environmental features. The potential field at the pedestrian's location is calculated as:

$$\phi_N^k = \sum_{i=1}^{n^k} p^k\left(d_{iN}^k\right)\phi_i^k \tag{1}$$

where $p^k(d_{iN}^k)$ denotes the weight associated with each potential source $i = 1...N$, determined by the Euclidean distance d_{iN}^k between the pedestrian and the source, independent of time.

This potential field influences pedestrian dynamics through an acceleration vector, $\boldsymbol{a}_N^k$, at position P_N, which incorporates both the gradient of the potential field $\boldsymbol{\nabla}\phi_N^k$ and the flow resistance:

$$\boldsymbol{a}_N^k = \frac{-\boldsymbol{\nabla}\phi_N^k - c_w v_N^2 \boldsymbol{e}_{vN}}{m_p} \tag{2}$$

where m_p and c_w are parameters representing the pedestrian's pseudo mass and drag coefficient, respectively.

Similar to previous work [12], a constant velocity model is employed within the Kalman Filter for predicting pedestrian movements. The Gaussian Mixture Probability Hypothesis Density (GMPHD) filter, a refinement of the original PHD filter developed by Mahler and Ronald [13] and later enhanced by Clark et al. [11], is particularly effective in scenarios involving a varying number of targets. This makes it well-suited for tracking multiple pedestrians with different intentions, as each target's state is independently modeled using a linear Gaussian framework. The GMPHD filter updates its predictions using a state transition matrix F_k and control input model B_k:

$$\mathbf{x}_k = F_k \mathbf{x}_{k-1} + B_k \mathbf{u}_k \tag{3}$$

$$\begin{pmatrix} x_k \\ y_k \\ v_{x,k} \\ v_{y,k} \end{pmatrix} = \begin{pmatrix} 1 & 0 & \Delta t & 0 \\ 0 & 1 & 0 & \Delta t \\ 0 & 0 & 1 & 0 \\ 0 & 0 & 0 & 1 \end{pmatrix} \begin{pmatrix} x_{k-1} \\ y_{k-1} \\ v_{x,k-1} \\ v_{y,k-1} \end{pmatrix} + \begin{pmatrix} \frac{\Delta t^2}{2} & 0 \\ 0 & \frac{\Delta t^2}{2} \\ \Delta t & 0 \\ 0 & \Delta t \end{pmatrix} \begin{pmatrix} a_{x,k-1} \\ a_{y,k-1} \end{pmatrix} \tag{4}$$

Here, $\mathbf{x}_k$ represents the state vector at time k, including position (x_k, y_k) and velocity ($v_{x,k}$ and $v_{y,k}$), while $\mathbf{u}_k$ incorporates the acceleration derived from the potential field.

The likelihood of a state $\mathbf{x}_k$ generating a detection $\mathbf{z}_k$ is given by the likelihood function:

$$g_k\left(\mathbf{z}_k \mid \mathbf{x}_k\right) \tag{5}$$

The posterior density is updated using Bayes' theorem:

$$p_k\left(\mathbf{x}_k \mid \mathbf{z}_{1:k}\right) = \frac{g_k\left(\mathbf{z}_k \mid \mathbf{x}_k\right) p_{k|k-1}\left(\mathbf{x}_k \mid \mathbf{z}_{1:k-1}\right)}{\int g_k\left(\mathbf{z}_k \mid \mathbf{x}\right) p_{k|k-1}\left(\mathbf{x} \mid \mathbf{z}_{1:k-1}\right) d\mathbf{x}} \tag{6}$$

This formulation allows the GMPHD filter to efficiently handle the complexities of multi-target tracking without the computational burden typically associated with such tasks.

Our proposed GMPHD-based GPFA (c.f. Fig. 4) initiates tracking by setting up system parameters and creating an 'Intention Map' based on the environment's topology. This map outlines the likely destinations of pedestrians. The GPFA then determines the acceleration towards these destinations, which becomes the input for the GMPHD prediction process. As the system collects real-time measurements of pedestrian movements, it generates multiple hypotheses that are iteratively refined to improve prediction accuracy. Only significant tracks are retained.

The GPFA's potential field, a crucial part of the algorithm, is designed to consider both attractive components (intended destinations) and repulsive components (obstacles). It is modeled based on a topological description of the environment and influences pedestrian behavior by depicting assumptions such as the preference for sidewalks, crossing at designated points, and collision avoidance. Sidewalks and pedestrian zebras are attracting components and show, therefore, lower Potential Field values (c.f. Fig. 5, Fig. 6). These potential fields allow the model to predict pedestrian trajectories more accurately by considering the dynamic interplay of environmental factors.

Using these defined potential fields, the tracking and posterior prediction of pedestrian trajectories are performed. The potential field is computed by evaluating the influence of various environmental components across a grid that spans the area of interest. While the influence of repulsive components typically decreases exponentially with distance, the influence of attractive components (e.g., intended destinations) is modeled to decrease linearly, as illustrated in Fig. 7.

3 Experimental Results

To assess the effectiveness of the proposed algorithm, we conducted three foundational experiments that build on the methodology developed in our previous study [4].

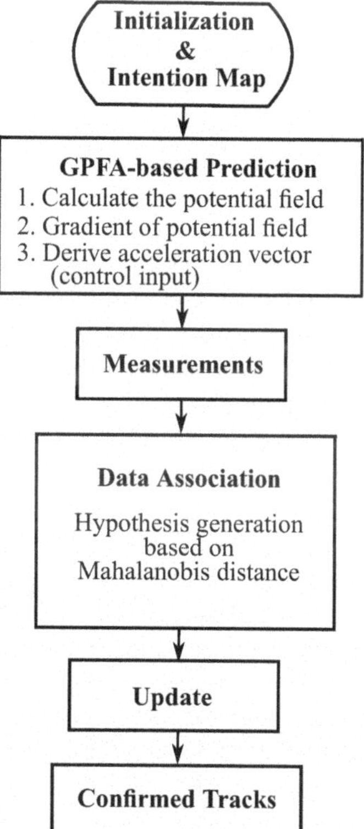

Fig. 4. PHD-GPFA Flow diagram [4].

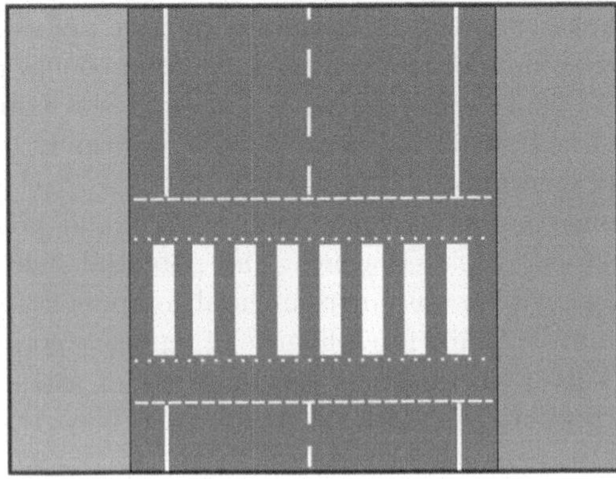

Fig. 5. Street scenario [4].

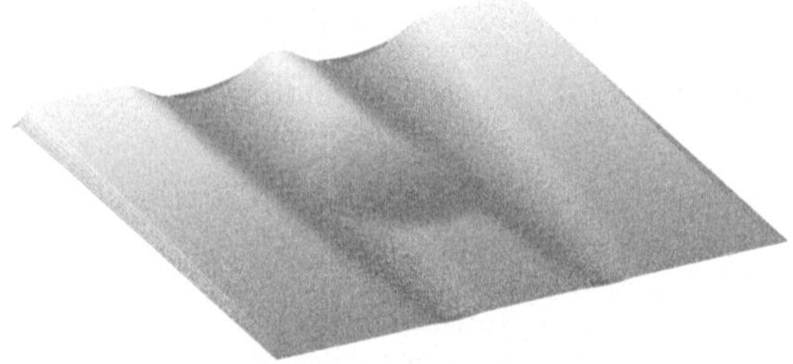

Fig. 6. Potential field example for a street scenario [4].

The first experiment focused on tracking a single pedestrian with a known destination. This setup provided a controlled environment to evaluate the potential improvements offered by integrating the Generalized Potential Field Approach (KF-GPFA) compared to the Kalman Filter (KF) baseline accuracy. As demonstrated in our prior research, the KF-GPFA method enhances prediction accuracy by incorporating environmental context and pedestrian intention modeling. The results of this experiment confirmed that the KF-GPFA outperforms the standard KF, particularly in scenarios requiring longer-term predictions, which are critical for autonomous vehicle applications [4].

The second experiment introduced uncertainty by assuming the pedestrian's destination was unknown, necessitating the algorithm to infer the pedestrian's intention from multiple potential options. This scenario closely mimics real-world conditions where pedestrian intentions are not always clear. Using the GMPHD-GPFA, we generated and evaluated several hypotheses about the pedestrian's possible destinations. Consistent with findings from our previous study, the algorithm successfully estimated the most probable trajectory, demonstrating its ability in handling dynamic and uncertain environments [4].

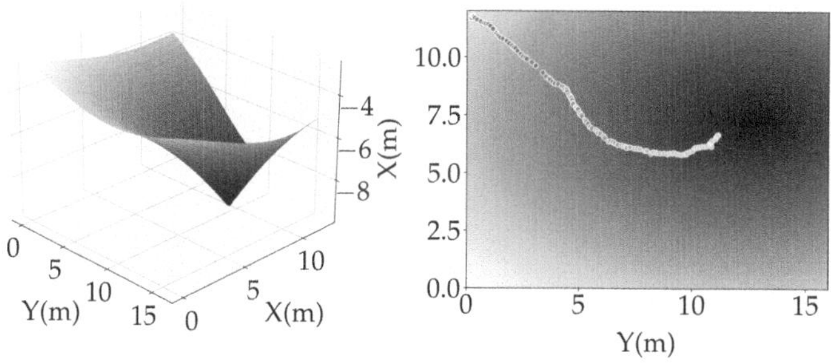

Fig. 7. Pedestrian in potential field map [4].

Building upon the previous experiments that concentrated on tracking a single pedestrian, we expanded our evaluation to address scenarios involving multiple pedestrians with varying potential intentions, which is one of the strengths of the PHD algorithm. In real-world autonomous driving, it is crucial to track and predict the intentions of several pedestrians simultaneously. This experiment aimed to validate the algorithm's capability to manage such complexity effectively. Specifically, three pedestrians were analyzed, each associated with two possible intentions, referred to as Intention 1 and Intention 2.

To assess the algorithm's performance, these pedestrians were observed within the same environment, each having two possible hypotheses for their intentions. The tracking results are presented in Fig. 8, showcasing the pedestrian trajectories on a 2D plot.

Since three pedestrians are tracked and each has two possible goals, six hypotheses are evaluated; from them, only three are correct. Figure 9 illustrates the root mean square error (RMSE) for each of the six hypotheses.

The analysis revealed that the hypotheses matching the actual intentions—*Pedestrian 1* with *Intention 1*, *Pedestrian 2* with *Intention 2*, and *Pedestrian 3* with *Intention 1*—exhibit lower RMSE values, consistent with our expectations. This result indicates that the algorithm contributes effectively to improve the accuracy of the correct hypotheses.

Moreover, the evolution of hypothesis weights over time, as shown in Fig. 10, supports the algorithm's ability to identify the correct intention after approximately 40 to 60 time steps, equivalent to 4 to 6 s in real time. Although this marks a significant improvement over existing methods, the time required for intention identification may still be challenging in fast-paced urban environments. The algorithm's reliance on position data means that clear differentiation of intentions only occurs when pedestrian trajectories significantly diverge.

In the preliminary experiments presented in [4], the algorithm was tested on three trajectories, where the estimated paths showed close alignment with the ground truths. To further assess reliability, we now expand the evaluation to 100 pedestrian trajectories as shown in Fig. 11, comparing estimations against ground truth data and evaluating the results statistically. We aim to evaluate

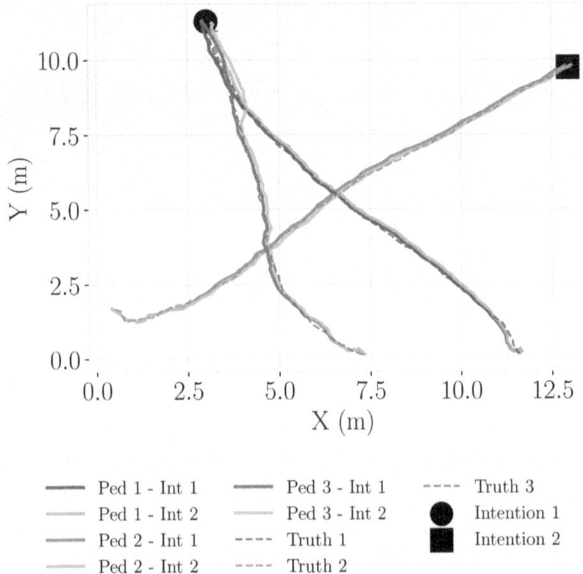

Fig. 8. Tracking performance for a multi-pedestrian scenario using GMPHD-GPFA. The plot includes three pedestrians, each with two potential intentions, resulting in six hypotheses [4].

how consistently our approach improves both tracking and pedestrian behavior prediction. The pedestrian trajectories were obtained from a publicly available dataset from the University of Edinburgh's School of Informatics [15], chosen for its overhead camera system that captures clear, minimally noisy pedestrian paths in a public space, we modeled measurement noise by combining inherent measurement noise with additional sensor noise (additive white Gaussian noise) to reflect real-world conditions accurately.

The skewed distribution of the RMSE (Fig. 12) of all 100 trajectories demonstrates that lower errors are more frequent. The median of 0.188 m for the successful hypothesis reveals that 50% of the errors of all trajectories are lower than this value, demonstrating the reliability of the algorithm for tracking pedestrians.

The RMSE for the GMPHD-GPFA, based on 100 trajectory trials, provides a clear statement of the prediction errors across different time horizons. Table 1 presents a comparison of the RMSE for estimation accuracy between successful (Hypothesis 1) and unsuccessful (Hypothesis 2) cases. The results show that successful estimations (Hypothesis 1) achieved a lower mean RMSE over the 100 trajectories; this demonstrates the contribution of the Potential Field approach.

The RMSE analysis for 100 pedestrian trajectories reveals key insights into the performance of the GMPHD-GPFA and PHD algorithms across different prediction horizons (c.f. Table 2). In short-term predictions (1-second), GMPHD-GPFA outperforms PHD, with a lower mean and median RMSE and a narrower error distribution (see Fig. 13).

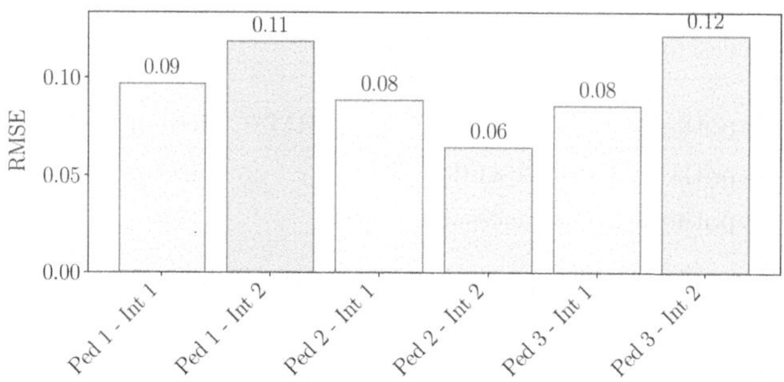

Fig. 9. Root Mean Square Error (RMSE) for each pedestrian's trajectory. Lower RMSE values indicate more accurate predictions [4].

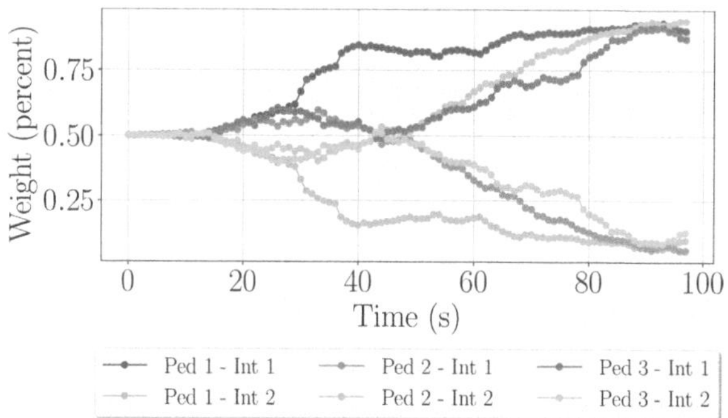

Fig. 10. Analysis of hypothesis weights over time, showing the algorithm's capacity to identify the correct pedestrian intention [4].

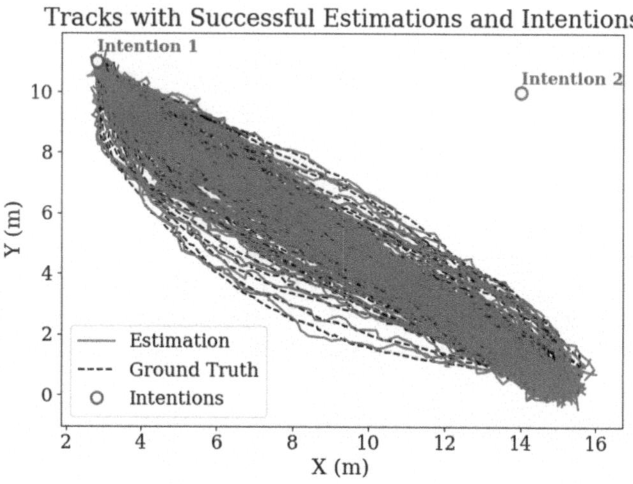

Fig. 11. Comparison of estimated and ground truth pedestrian trajectories over 100 trials.

Table 1. RMSE in meters, Comparison for Estimation Results of Successful (Hypothesis 1) and Unsuccessful (Hypothesis 2) Cases.

Hypothesis	Mean RMSE	Median RMSE
Hypothesis 1 (Successful)	0.188	0.163
Hypothesis 2 (Unsuccessful)	0.194	0.172

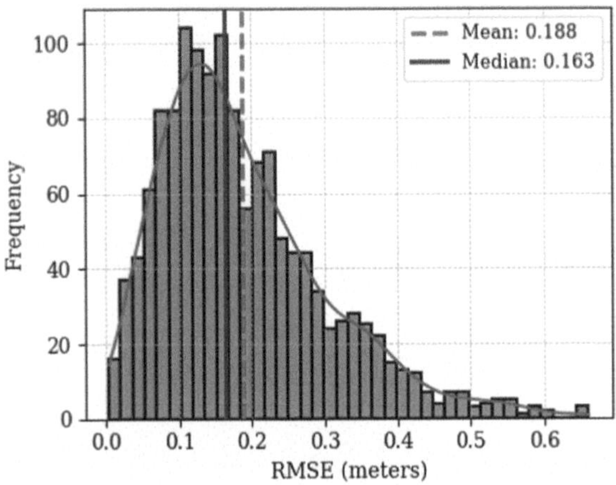

Fig. 12. RMSE Distribution for successful hypothesis estimations over 100 trials.

Table 2. RMSE in meters, Comparison of GMPHD-GPFA and PHD Algorithms Across Different Prediction Horizons.

Prediction Horizon	1 s		2 s		3 s	
	Mean	Median	Mean	Median	Mean	Median
GMPHD-GPFA	0.61	0.45	1.12	0.78	1.72	1.13
PHD	0.67	0.49	1.24	0.86	1.91	1.27

Most RMSE values for both algorithms cluster below 1 m, indicating high accuracy, but GMPHD-GPFA shows greater consistency. As the prediction horizon extends to 2 and 3 s, both algorithms experience increased RMSE values, reflecting the challenge of long-term trajectory forecasting (see Fig. 14). Overall, GMPHD-GPFA demonstrates more reliable and consistent performance, with tighter RMSE distributions and less variability, especially in short-term predictions.

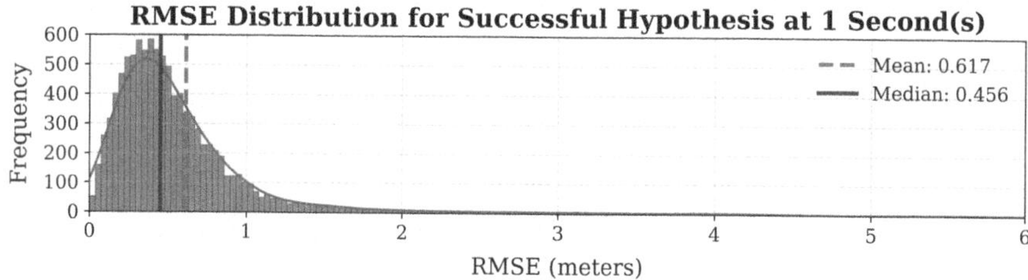

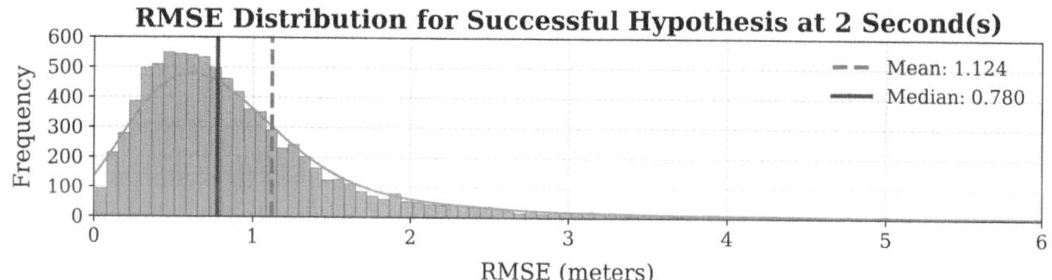

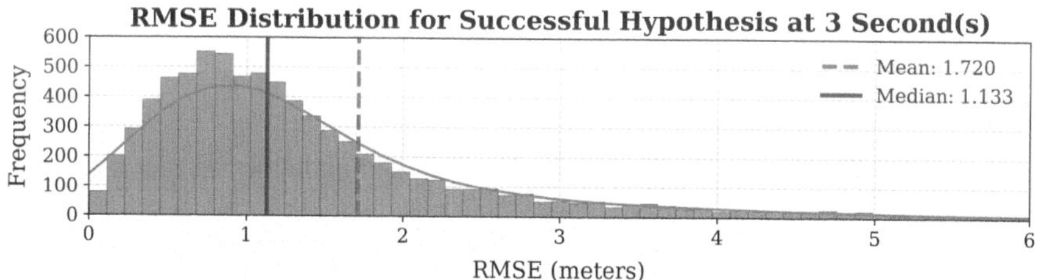

Fig. 13. GMPHD-GPFA predictions successful hypothesis.

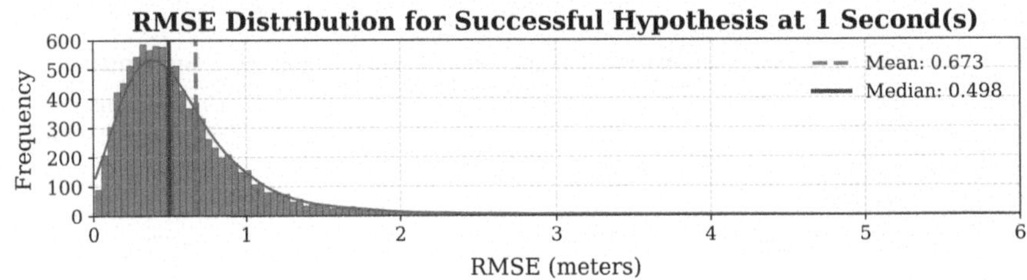

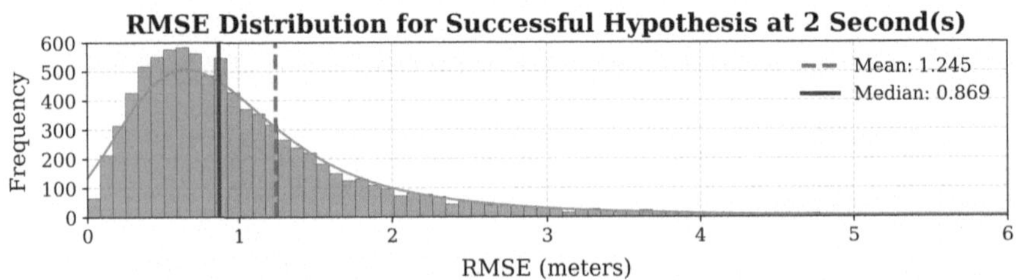

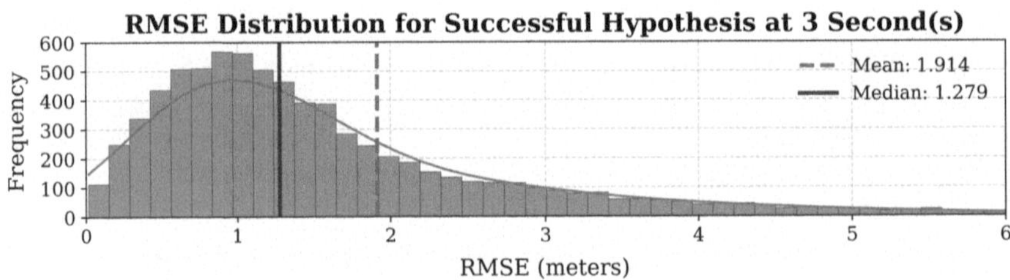

Fig. 14. PHD predictions successful hypothesis.

4 Conclusion

This paper introduces a hybrid approach that integrates physical-based and planning-based models for tracking and predicting the positions and intentions of multiple pedestrians around autonomous vehicles. By leveraging a Gaussian Mixture Probability Hypothesis Density Filter (GMPHD) combined with the Generalized Potential Field Approach (GPFA), the algorithm effectively generates and updates multiple hypotheses, accurately identifying pedestrians' actual intentions. This enables autonomous vehicles to forecast pedestrian movements and adjust maneuvers accordingly, significantly enhancing safety in complex environments. While the model demonstrates reliable performance confirmed through an evaluation using 100 pedestrian trajectories, future work will focus on evaluating the algorithm with real-world data from autonomous driving scenarios, and efforts will continue to accelerate intention detection to improve real-time applicability.

Acknowledgments. The SMO project is supported by the Federal Ministry of Transport and Digital Infrastructure of Germany. For more information about the project, please see: www.shuttle-modellregion-oberfranken.de.

References

1. SMO: Shuttle Modellregion Oberfranken (SMO) Project. https://www.shuttle-modellregion-oberfranken.de/. Accessed 2022
2. Dehghani, A., Salaar, H., Srinivasan, S., Zhou, L., et al.: Enhancing availability of Autonomous Shuttle Services: a conceptual approach toward challenges and opportunities. SAE Int. J. CAV **8**(3), 337–354 (2025). https://doi.org/10.4271/12-08-03-0023
3. Rudenko, A., Palmieri, L., Herman, M., Kitani, K.M., Gavrila, D.M., Arras, K.O.: Human motion trajectory prediction: a survey. Int. J. Robot. Res. **39**(8), 895–935 (2020)
4. Dehghani, A., Patino-Studencki, L.: Multi-pedestrian tracking and map-based intention estimation for autonomous driving scenario. In: VEHITS, pp. 386–393 (2024)
5. Elnagar, A.: Prediction of moving objects in dynamic environments using kalman filters. In: Proceedings 2001 IEEE International Symposium on Computational Intelligence in Robotics and Automation (Cat. No. 01EX515), pp. 414–419. IEEE (2001)
6. Chen, Y., Liu, M., Liu, S.-Y., Miller, J., How, J.P.: Predictive modeling of pedestrian motion patterns with bayesian nonparametrics. In: AIAA Guidance, Navigation, and Control Conference, p. 1861 (2016)
7. Razali, H., Mordan, T., Alahi, A.: Pedestrian intention prediction: a convolutional bottom-up multi-task approach. Transp. Res. Part C Emerg. Technol. **130**, 103259 (2021)
8. Keller, C.G., Gavrila, D.M.: Will the pedestrian cross? A study on pedestrian path prediction. IEEE Trans. Intell. Transp. Syst. **15**(2), 494–506 (2014). https://doi.org/10.1109/TITS.2013.2280766
9. Best, G., Fitch, R.: Bayesian intention inference for trajectory prediction with an unknown goal destination. In: 2015 IEEE/RSJ International Conference on Intelligent Robots and Systems (IROS), pp. 5817–5823. IEEE (2015)
10. Vasquez, D.: Novel planning-based algorithms for human motion prediction. In: 2016 IEEE International Conference on Robotics and Automation (ICRA), pp. 3317–3322. IEEE (2016)
11. Clark, D.E., Panta, K., Vo, B.-N.: The GM-PHD filter multiple target tracker. In: 2006 9th International Conference on Information Fusion, pp. 1–8. IEEE (2006)
12. Particke, F., Patino-Studencki, L., Thielecke, J., Feist, C.: Pedestrian tracking using a generalized potential field approach. In: VISIGRAPP (6: VISAPP), pp. 509–514 (2017)
13. Mahler, R.P.: Multitarget bayes filtering via first-order multitarget moments. IEEE Trans. Aerosp. Electron. Syst. **39**(4), 1152–1178 (2003)
14. Particke, F.: Predictive pedestrian awareness with intention uncertainties for autonomous driving. Ph.D. thesis, Friedrich-Alexander-Universität Erlangen-Nürnberg (FAU) (2020)
15. Majecka, B.: Statistical models of pedestrian behaviour in the forum. Master's thesis, School of Informatics, University of Edinburgh (2009)

Striving Towards a Comprehensive Generation of Test Scenarios for Highly Automated On-Sight Train Operations

Lucas Greiner-Fuchs[1,2] and Martin Cichon[1(✉)]

[1] Karlsruhe Institute of Technology, Rintheimer Querallee 2, 76131 Karlsruhe, Germany
{lucas.greiner-fuchs,martin.cichon}@kit.edu

[2] Nuremberg Institute of Technology, Keßlerplatz 12, 90489 Nürnberg, Germany

Abstract. Scenario-based testing is increasingly common for evaluating highly automated driving systems. The methodology is also used in the development and evaluation of highly automated rail vehicles. A scenario set can be derived using either a data-based or knowledge-based approach. As real measurement data is limited in the railway sector, our focus is on scenarios derived from knowledge-based methods. In addition to possessing a suitable knowledge base, it is crucial to follow a methodical approach to scenario definition and establish appropriate rules for creating scenarios. The objective is to achieve a convergence of scenario outcomes to enable a comprehensive evaluation of the automated system through testing. This paper is based on our scenario generation method for highly automated on-sight train operation, using an automated shunting system as an example, and highlights the challenges that arise when combining scenario elements. The paper demonstrates the logical combination process and describes the transfer of knowledge data into a scenario. It also outlines the rules and conditions for linking individual objects in the given scenario. The final section of the paper presents the methodological procedure for achieving convergence of the generated scenario set.

Keywords: Scenario-based testing · Scenario generation · Automatic train operation

1 Introduction

Rail transport is currently a high priority in politics and society due to its global and social benefits. While road transport offers personal independence and comfort, rail transport is more convincing in terms of global and social aspects. The system is environmentally friendly due to its low greenhouse gas emissions and high energy efficiency through the use of electromobility. Additionally, it provides a high level of traffic safety and requires less land consumption for passenger and freight transport. Despite its social and global benefits, rail passenger transport performance has stagnated in recent years and rail freight transport in Europe has declined. The rail system's low economic efficiency is primarily responsible for this issue. However, it is expected that the rail sector in Europe

F. Calise et al. (Eds.): SMARTGREENS 2024/VEHITS 2024, CCIS 2954, pp. 160–177, 2026.
https://doi.org/10.1007/978-3-032-23187-1_9

will experience significant growth. To cope with this expansion, the rail sector must increasingly focus on automation and digitalization [1].

In addition to the targeted development of Automatic Train Operation (ATO) systems, a comprehensive testing of these functions is necessary. In the railway sector, there is a lack of established test methods and strategies to demonstrate the safe operation of highly automated systems, especially for unrestricted and not intersection-free rail traffic. Approaches from the automotive industry [2] can provide inspiration, but they need to be reviewed as well as revised, and new methods for the testing process have to be derived. In the consecutive development of automated driving systems, distance-based testing is no longer applicable. Due to the high complexity, it would require too many driving kilometers in the field to check all possible situations. Therefore, scenario-based test methods are becoming increasingly popular. [3] In scenario-based testing, a complex system, such as a highly automated driving system, is tested in as many different situations as possible. To achieve this, scenarios are generated to cover the operational design domain (ODD) of the automated driving system as completely as possible. The system's reaction is then primarily tested in a virtual environment. Critical and purely functional scenarios are also tested in the field. In addition to its application in the automotive sector, this approach is also employed on an ongoing basis in the testing of highly automated rail vehicles.

During mainline operation, trains are controlled and monitored using a train control system. Automation through sensor monitoring of the environment is not safely implemented at the current state of the art. This is because trains have long braking distances that require a corresponding field of view, which is often not possible due to infrastructure limitations. Therefore, automation can only be achieved through a combination with the system, such as ATO over ETCS (European Train Control System). However, in the case of on-sight train operations, the train driver is responsible for safe driving operations and must be able to react to any environmental situation. An ATO-System for on-sight train operation may resemble automated road traffic, but it requires a test methodology tailored to the railway-specific ODD. One example of on-sight train operation is shunting. This use case is well-suited to automation due to its repetitive similar processes, a defined area of application, and maximum speeds of 40 km/h. Automation can also improve efficiency at the shunting yard, and thus in freight transport, and mitigate the increasing shortage of personnel. Therefore, automated shunting operations (ASO) are an adequate example for developing a scenario-based test methodology for testing ATO-Systems.

2 State of Research

The present study builds upon our existing body of research in the domain of scenario-based testing of railway vehicles, which has already yielded a large number of publications. The current state of research is initially delineated concerning the methodological approach to the knowledge-based generation of scenarios for the testing of highly automated railway vehicles. This is followed by a proposal for a railway-specific taxonomy to facilitate the definition of an ODD.

2.1 Knowledge-Based Scenario Generation for Testing Highly Automated On-Sight Train Operation

One of the primary challenges associated with scenario-based testing is the process of identifying appropriate scenarios. These scenarios should comprehensively represent the operational tasks and potential circumstances that may be encountered during the operation of the ATO-System. Various methods can be used to generate scenarios. A comprehensive overview of scenario generation and different methods of scenario derivation is presented as a survey in [4]. In order to generate effective scenarios, the data, and knowledge-based processes are particularly reliable.

When using measurement data for generation, it is necessary to have an adequate dataset of real driving situations available. Comprehensive endurance projects and data management are executed to record the necessary information. The utilization of actual driving data guarantees the realism and applicability of all derived scenarios. It is crucial to note, however, that the scenario set is limited to the data set's contents, and some critical situations may be absent. Various approaches can be used to generate scenarios from real measurement data. The overview in [5] demonstrates several possibilities, including feature dimension reduction, rule-based derivation, as well as unsupervised and supervised machine learning. Predefined programs and toolboxes are already available for use [6].

Having a strong knowledge foundation is essential when using the knowledge-based approach. To generate scenarios, it is important to appropriately link information collected from various sources. The use of an ontology is a commonly employed method for achieving this [7]. Alternatively, combination languages that are equivalent or specially developed, as mentioned in [8], can also be used. Based on the work of [7], an elaborate example of a knowledge-based scenario generation is mentioned in [9]. The process based on ontology generates descriptions of semantic scenarios. The functional scenarios are specified using the 6-Layer Model presented in [10]. The semantic variables are parameterized to create concrete test scenarios for use in OpenSCENARIO [11]. This provides a proprietary interface to a range of simulation tools used in the automotive industry. To make use of the unique benefits of data-based and knowledge-based scenario generation, [12] employs an approach that integrates both methods.

Compared to the automotive industry, there are limited measurement data sets available for rail applications due to the challenges of operating rail vehicles and the high financial commitment. Train drivers require specialized training and are not permitted to operate in the operational area for personal use. Furthermore, the rail network is highly utilized, providing limited opportunities for specific measurement runs. For this reason, we presented in a position paper our current development status of a knowledge-based approach to create scenarios for rail transport on the example of ASO [13].

Figure 1 illustrates the process of deriving appropriate test scenarios. The figure was originally derived from [13] but has been slightly modified to illustrate the distinction between the unstructured knowledge entities and the structured object database. At the initial stage of the process, we define the ATO-System, including its functional requirements. To ensure clarity in test operation, we divide the overall system at [14] into use cases, from each of which we derive a set of test scenarios. Then the ODD of the ATO-System is defined. For this purpose, we are developing a railway-specific systematic to describe the scenery, the environmental conditions, and the dynamic elements corresponding with the system. The ODD for the ASO-System is established by the prevailing state of development of the taxonomy, as delineated in the subsequent Sect. 2.2, with due consideration to the publication of [15]. The subsequent step involves creating a railway-specific dataset based on specific knowledge sources. Afterward, the scenario description is performed using the 7-Layer Shunting Model introduced in [16], which takes the dataset as an input to create a structured set of scenario objects. The main procedure and implementation of the subsequent scenario combination is presented in Chapter 3 [13].

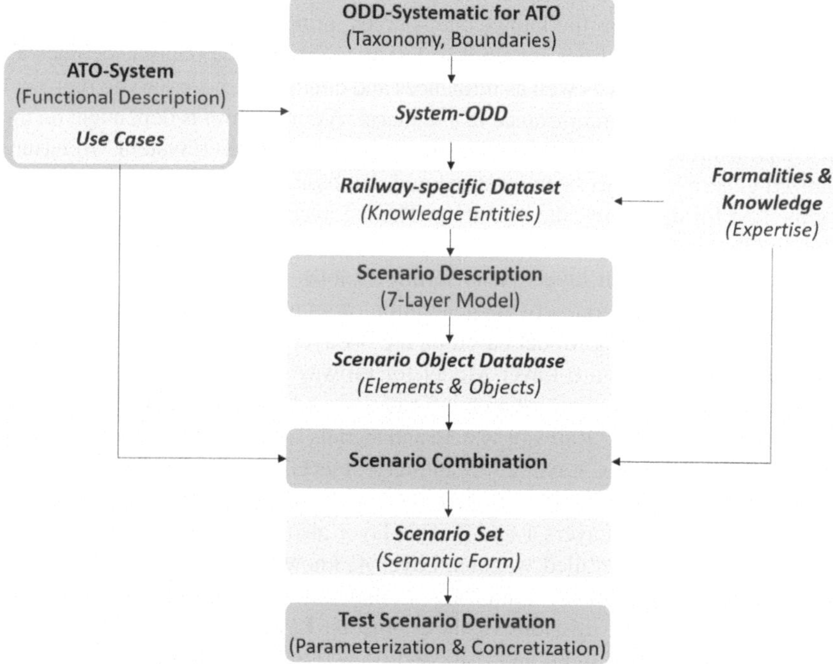

Fig. 1. Method of Scenario Generation adapted from [13].

In order to generate a railway-specific dataset and corresponding scenario object database, it is essential to have a comprehensive understanding of the application area and the tasks of the system. The ASO-System will be utilized at a German shunting yard as a GoA4 (Grade of Automation) system, and will fully replace the duties of a locomotive shunting driver. Therefore, a comprehensive knowledge base of the shunting yard's structure, procedures, processes, and tasks is necessary. In [14], we have described how to derive the basic tasks of an automated shunting locomotive as use cases through operational analysis. This is achieved using rules and guidelines, such as train service instruction [17], signal regulation [18], and railway construction and operating regulations [19], as well as corresponding technical literature [20, 21]. Additionally, the sources can be used to determine the basic structure and layout of a shunting yard. To create a complete understanding of the environment and its objects, we research publicly available data sets and draw on our own experience through system development and measurement data recording at the shunting yard. However, the amount of measurement data available is too small to allow a targeted data-based scenario derivation. Therefore, the analysis of measured data is only included as an additional source of knowledge. Statistics on accidents and operational analysis will be used to consider exceptional and potential failures occurring during regular operations. Examples of known sources are the investigation reports of the German Federal Bureau of Railway Investigation [22] and its open dataset on hazardous incidents in railway operations that have been finally investigated [23]. Another source includes expert knowledge from specialists in railroad technology and staff at the shunting yard. The ODD of the ASO-System, in combination with input from the knowledge sources, provides the basis for creating a dataset of all knowledge entities required to test the system. The dataset includes all static and dynamic elements as well as influences and conditions, necessary to represent the scenery, situation, and circumstance in a scenario. As the dataset is dependent on the System-ODD, it must be generated and customized for each ATO-System. To ensure an organized generation process and a structured database of the objects, it is useful to define a method for describing the scenarios. The 6-Layer Model [10] was introduced in the automotive industry by the Pegasus project [2] and assigns entities that can occur in a scenario to six different layers. This sorting enables a structured organization of the object data set and consequently the generation of scenarios. Additionally, we have defined the 7-Layer Shunting Model based on the 6-Layer Model in [16]. The existing model has been adapted to a 6-Layer Model for railway applications, with the addition of a seventh layer as a superordinate information and status level. The Layers are defined as follows: Layer 1, "Railway system and signals", describes the track topology and scenery of the scenarios. Layer 2, "Stationary objects", contains all not moveable objects. Layer 3, "Temporary changes of Layers 1, 2, (& 4)", prescribes unplanned and short-term changes to Layers 1 and 2. This layer also covers special situations of Layer 4 objects, such as derailed wagons. Layer 4, known as "Dynamic objects", is responsible for assigning railway vehicles and other movable objects. This layer also defines the trajectories and missions of these objects. Layer 5, "Environmental conditions", describes weather, light, and soil conditions. Layer 6, "Digital information", specifies digital information such as location signals, digital maps, or the status of railway traffic lights. Layer 7, "Shunting order", contains the information necessary for executing a shunting movement. This includes details about the locomotive's start and end points, track information like speed ranges, as well as the safely occurring objects of the other layers. Applying the 7-Layer method to the previously created dataset enables the creation of a structured database. This categorizes all information that influences the ASO-System, including statically and dynamically occurring objects, information on the area of application, derived shunting tasks and use cases, positioning and orientation options for the objects, object properties, and layer definitions. A further explication of the information and the handling of the knowledge data as well as the structure and linking of the entries in the database is provided in Sect. 3.1 [13].

2.2 Towards an Operational Design Domain for Railway Applications

The utilization of an ODD is becoming increasingly prevalent across several sectors, serving to delineate the field of application and area of use of an ADS. In order to guarantee a uniform methodology for defining an ODD for an automated system, it is recommended to adhere to a pre-established taxonomy. In publication [15], we have devised a railway-specific taxonomy for the definition of ODDs for ATO-Systems, based on the standards of the automotive industry [24, 25]. Figure 2 illustrates the fundamental structure of the ODD, comprising four principal levels: Scenery, Environmental Conditions, Dynamic Objects, and Operational Conditions [15].

The attributes of the scenery encompass all fundamental descriptions of the infrastructure and stationary objects within the operational domain of the automated system. Furthermore, this entails the delineation of particular zones, as well as the definition of the intended route, the associated structures, and potential situations that may give rise to accidents. The environmental conditions attribute encompasses a range of factors that can potentially impact the operational effectiveness of the ATO-System. These include weather-related phenomena, such as precipitation and wind, as well as particles that may impair visibility. Additionally, the attribute considers the diverse types and occurrences of illumination, along with the connectivity and communication associated with the ATO-System. The attributes of dynamic objects are those that the ATO-System is required to react to or interact with. This section describes the different road users and their respective movement behaviors. Furthermore, the ego-vehicle is also classified. The fourth overarching attribute represents the operational conditions. That top level is described as the clearest differentiation from the automotive industry counterpart. In addition to the intended use, which is divided into passenger and freight transport, a list is provided of the operational tasks of the ATO-System. Such tasks include, for instance, monitoring the entry and exit of passengers at the railway station and the maintenance of operational communication [15].

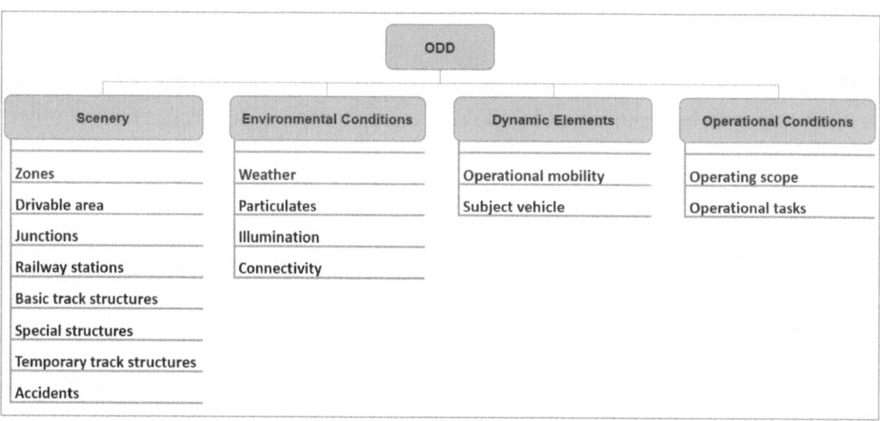

Fig. 2. ODD Taxonomy [15].

3 Successive Combinatorial Approach to Generate a Converging Set of Scenarios

A significant challenge inherent to scenario-based testing is the generation of a comprehensive set of scenarios. The term "completeness" should be employed with caution, as the intricacy of an ATO-System and the heterogeneity of the application domain make it challenging to ascertain which scenarios are essential for comprehensive system testing. Consequently, our objective is to develop a scenario set that is as convergent as possible. This is justified in connection with the structured generation process. To achieve this objective, the following chapter will initially present the structure and fundamental composition of the object database. Subsequently, an account is given of the logical combination process of scenario generation and the rules and correlations that apply. In conclusion, the concept of convergence is defined, and the methodological approach to achieving a converging scenario set is presented.

3.1 Set up a Structured Object Database

An organized database structure is helpful for combinatorics. Figure 3 illustrates the methodology for deriving the objects necessary for scenario generation and their subsequent storage within the database. The knowledge sources enumerated in [13] constitute the foundation for this approach, parallel to the use cases derived in [14] and the ODD attributes described in [15]. By defining the use cases and ODD attributes, it is possible to identify the specific knowledge sources that should be utilized. The components that may be present within a given scenario are derived from each source, and the individual terms and descriptions are grouped to form specific knowledge entities. These entities are structured following the 7-Layer model described in [16] and subsequently transferred to the scenario object database. The dataset entries are divided into two categories: "Class" and "Object". For instance, the Layer 4 class wagon can be further divided into specific objects such as flat wagon, tank wagon, container wagon, and so on. In addition, each object is defined by a set of attributes pertaining to potential spatial positioning and orientation, as well as mobility and occurrence. Furthermore, some objects are already stored as separate additional objects in typical states or constellations. For example, the class tree may be represented by the object conifer in single, group, or row object constellations.

Fig. 3. Structure Object Database Generation.

Table 1 displays the number of objects currently stored in the database for the example of an ASO. In establishing the database, an effort was made to encompass as many distinctive objects as feasible while also delineating more universally applicable objects to guarantee the lucidity of the database and the ensuing combinatorics. In the case of the class tree, for example, a distinction is made between deciduous trees and conifers, as well as three different size definitions of trees. Nevertheless, no additional subdivision into tree species is undertaken. Further research will be conducted to investigate the influence of detailed variations of individual objects, such as differences in color or specific dimensions and types, on the results of the system testing.

Table 1. Number of Objects in each Layer.

Layer 1	Layer 2	Layer 3	Layer 4	Layer 5	Layer 6	Layer 7
44	43	9	103	52	4	23

3.2 Logical Combination Process

A suitable scenario set is generated by combining objects and situations in a logical process. The aim is to generate as many realistic scenarios as possible from the objects stored in the database within the scenario combination. It is possible to change both the total number of objects and the occurrence of several identical objects in a scenario. This can be described mathematically using the stochastic field of combinatorics. To maintain clarity, we follow an ordered approach, where the combinatorics is available as a variation with repetitions. However, the procedure is complex due to the rules and relationships listed below, which results in combinatorics that are difficult to express mathematically. Therefore, we describe the linking of objects in different scenarios through the program flow of the combinatorics setup. We refer to this process as a scenario combination in our terminology and differentiate the term from the stochastic combination.

Figure 4 displays the flowchart of the prototype scenario combination program. The process structure was previously presented in [13]. However, the approach and implementation of combinatorics were still outstanding at that time. The program follows a step-by-step approach to ensure clarity and traceability of the combinatorics. Its output is a semantic scenario set corresponding to the ODD. The input variable is the database of scenario objects, specified in the previous chapter.

The combination process starts with the Scenario Initialization, which generates basic information about the scenario. By referring to a specific use case, the database objects can be pre-filtered directly. This is done to eliminate unnecessary entities from the combinatorics and increase the relevance of generated scenarios. Additional information is determined based on the use cases through Layer 7. The combinatorics consider safely occurring objects. Limits and conditions of the ego-vehicles, such as speed regulations or starting conditions, are also specified.

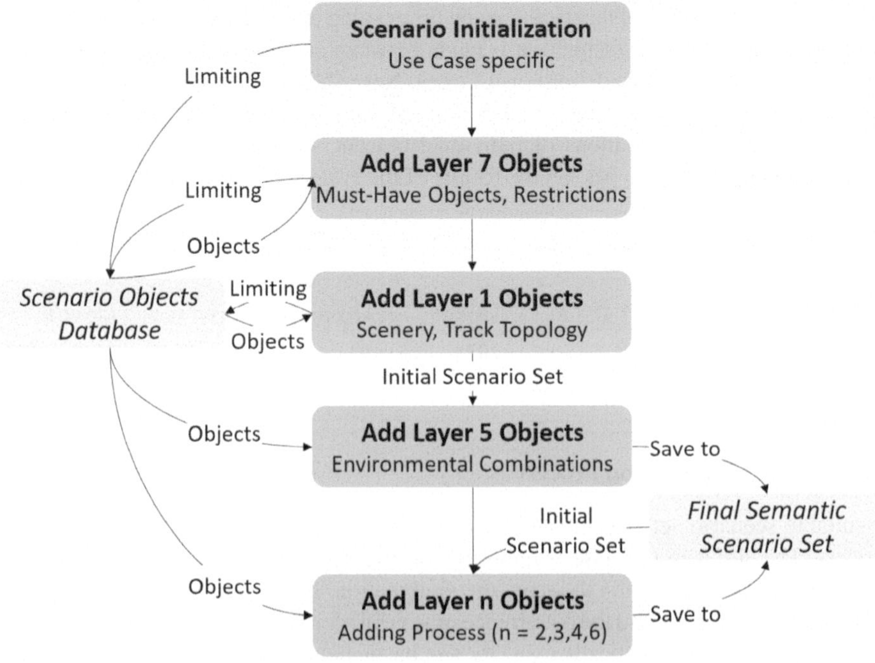

Fig. 4. Flowchart - Combination Process [13].

In the next step, the Layer 1 objects define the track topology and scenery. In a previous process, pre-defined "maps" are created to represent the resulting various constellations for use in our virtual environment [26]. This simplifies further combinatorics and enables a more straightforward automated interface for scenario construction in the simulation environment. Two approaches are possible for creating the maps. On one hand, it is possible to create generic sceneries based on Layer 1 objects and conditions. This involves defining all potential track topologies of the ego-track in conjunction with possible neighboring tracks and adding the signals and sensors required by building regulations. On the other hand, the second approach is more specific to the ASO-System, resulting in a more efficient but also system-specific generation of the maps. The analysis focuses on the system's area of application and derives an intersection of the track topologies. One benefit of this method is the ability to define realistic position coordinates for system testing. The use of localization systems is widespread in automated operations. However, both methods are restricted to mapping the ego-track with only one neighboring track on each side. This limitation is due to the focus of environmental monitoring on the clearance gauge and adjacent areas. Additionally, there is no interaction with tracks further away. Areas where multiple switches are crossed are excluded from both approaches. These areas are represented in separate maps. In cases where the ATO-System is limited, such as when it is restricted to a specific track or in the case of using a fully digital twin of the application area, unchangeable Layer 2 objects are also predefined in the map. These objects may include light poles, catenary, or constructions. Each map covers a specific area of the ASO-System's operational area, which may reduce the number of possible objects for a scenario on that map.

To create an initial scenario set, the specifications from the use cases and Layer 7 objects are combined. It is important to note that individual use cases only occur in certain areas of the shunting yard and can only be combined with specific maps. The initial scenario set serves as input for the subsequent combinatorics. The addition of further layer objects requires general and specific rules and correlations.

3.3 Rules and Correlations

Each scenario should include exactly one environmental condition to be fully defined. Therefore, the objects from Layer 5 are added to the initial scenario set in the first step. During the combination, it is important to ensure that only logical conditions are created. For instance, it is not possible to have high temperatures and snow at the same time. In the database, the objects are assigned to the classes Temperature, Precipitation, Wind regime, Humidity, Daytime, Light conditions, Source of light, and Soil conditions. The logical rules combine an object from each class, also taking into account the absence of precipitation and wind. The objects are differentiated based on the ODD defined at the beginning and the resulting dataset. It is important to note that this state of scenario generation is the most abstract and does not require any fine-grained semantic subdivision. For the precipitation class, it is recommended to divide it into the objects rain, snow, hail, sleet, and no precipitation. It is not necessary to subdivide it into heavy rain and drizzle. This can be achieved in the later stages of scenario generation. Parameter spaces are created as logical scenarios to cover the semantic variables. By adding the environmental conditions, the first final semantic scenarios are generated and saved. Using the most recent set of semantic scenarios as input, the objects from the remaining layers are added in ascending order. Newly generated scenarios are stored in the scenario set and used as supplementary initial input for the following layer. The rules for the addition of the objects are also defined with the help of the sources of knowledge.

The process for adding objects from Layers 2–4 is shown in a simplified flowchart in Fig. 5. The process has an identical basic structure across all three layers, but specific rules apply to individual layers, classes, and objects. At the beginning of each class per layer, each object is assigned a position in the scenario. Figure 6 displays the possible positions, which are divided into lateral and longitudinal distances. The boundary of the clearance profile of the ego-track is considered as the center for the lateral division of the position ranges. There can be up to five areas on each side of this central borderline. To ensure the specified track spacing, a side track must always be at least one area away from the ego-track and occupy two areas. Therefore, it cannot be at position $x = -2$ or 2. In this way, the track spacing is in accordance with the infrastructure. The fields outside right and left are considered to be the edge areas. Positions outside these areas are not taken into account as they do not affect the object detection system due to the offset. The dimensions of the longitudinal fields are determined by the underlying map. The longitudinal distance is measured from the starting point of the ego-vehicle in the scenario. The areas, namely "near", "near to middle", "middle", "middle to far" and "far", are divided into five equal parts using the route length of the map as a reference, which is mentioned with "L" in Fig. 6. When positioning objects, they can be classified as either on track or off track. However, some objects can cover both areas. Every non-moving object in addition to its position has an alignment. The alignment of an object can vary depending on its possible positioning, track-bound characteristics, and symmetry. Moving objects are assigned a trajectory, which is described in more detail in the description of the specific rules of Layer 4. It is specified that only one object should be present in each position field. Depending on the size of the object, it may occupy one or more lateral fields. To achieve a logical accumulation of objects in a small area, the object constellations listed in the previous chapter can be used as single objects (e.g. group of trees, row of trees). A row always has the length of the corresponding position field. This approach indirectly limits the maximum number of objects that can occur, thereby improving generation performance. In order to efficiently generate differentiable scenarios, it is important to consider that objects do not need to be placed in positions covered by larger objects, as this does not significantly affect the scenario. The adequacy of the current position distribution in producing a realistic scenario must be further examined using the results of the initial scenario sets. However, the position rules can be easily adjusted at a later stage.

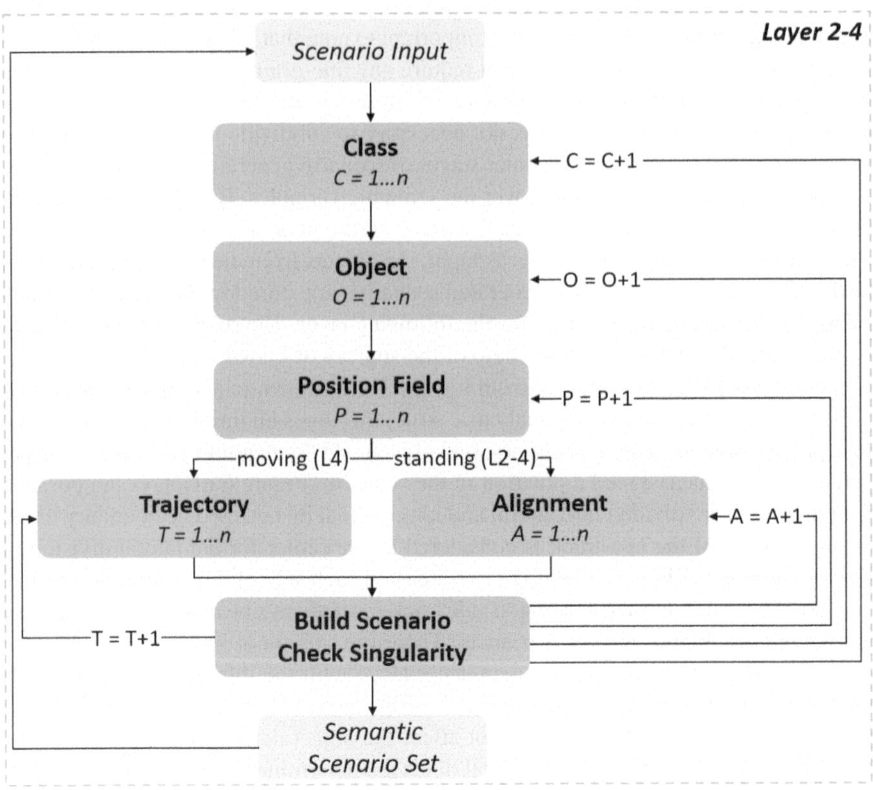

Fig. 5. Flowchart – Object Adding Process of Layer 2–4.

After adding the first object of the class to the initial scenario, its position is changed. The same process is then repeated with the next object in the class, creating a new scenario with each position and object variation. If an object can occur multiple times in a scenario, the process is repeated up to the maximum number of that object. Whenever more than one object appears in a scenario, it is always necessary to check whether a position is already occupied before adding it. Each new scenario is stored in the final semantic scenario set after creation and also serves as an initial scenario for subsequent combinations. Before saving, the prototype program checks if the scenario already exists in the set.

Additional specific rules must be observed depending on the layer, classes, or individual objects. These rules may pertain to positioning or correlation with other objects. Layer 2 comprises the group of stationary objects, which can be divided into five classes. Constructions are infrastructure objects such as buildings, bridges, and poles. Vegetation is divided into the classes of trees, bushes, and grass, with distinctions made based on size and characteristics such as deciduous or coniferous trees as well as dense or permeable undergrowth. The materials class comprises all additional stationary objects located in the area around the track at a shunting yard, such as stacks of sleepers or rails. Although these objects are not firmly anchored, they often remain in position for a long period, making them a specific object in a scenario. When adding Layer 2 classes, it should be noted that they are not placed on a track position. For larger objects, it is necessary to occupy two or more positions to ensure they are outside the clearance gauge of the track. However, individual tufts of grass can be placed on the ego-track without following this rule, representing track vegetation.

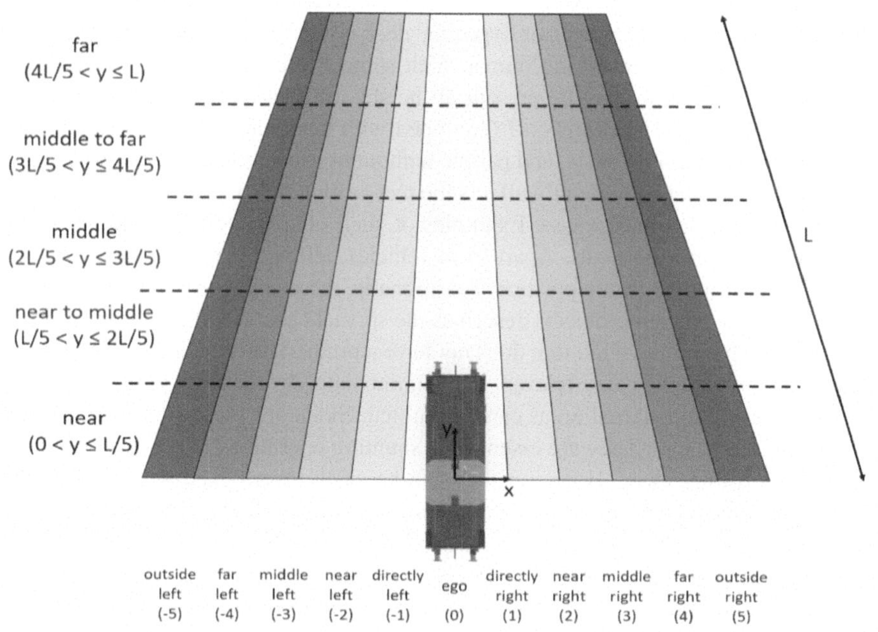

Fig. 6. Positioning Fields of Objects. "L" depends on the length of the map.

Temporary changes in Layer 3 refer to situations and objects that deviate from the standard state for a relatively short period. The layer is divided into four classes: momentary objects, emergencies, construction tracks, and track closures. Momentary objects are objects that are out of place and do not typically occur in that position or state. These include for example fallen trees, abandoned bicycles, or even misplaced cargo on a wagon on the neighboring track. Apart from the misplaced cargo, these incidents are independent in terms of their placement. Common emergencies on the track include derailed vehicles, catenary hanging down, fires, and accidents. The last-mentioned situations are location-independent, whereas track emergencies are track-fixed. Construction work in the track area can take on various forms and is also fixed to the track. If the work is located on the main track, it must be accompanied by a track closure, such as a Sh2 board.

Layer 4 comprises dynamic objects that can move within the scenery or are generally moveable. Railway vehicles are divided into three classes. Traction units include all standard powered vehicles such as locomotives of various types. Self-moving railway vehicles that are different from this, fall into the class of auxiliary vehicles, such as two-way vehicles or battery-towing vehicles. The third group comprises railway wagons of various designs, (flat wagons, container wagons, stand-in deck coach carriers, etc.), visible loads (containers, cars, logs, etc.), and constellations (single wagons, rows of wagons of various configurations). These classes are all track-fixed. The road vehicles class includes cars, trucks, small motor vehicles, and bicycles of various designs. These vehicles can only appear next to the track area unless a railway crossing is present on the map. Large emergency vehicles are an exception to the rule and can cross tracks without a level crossing in case of an emergency to reach the accident scene. Living organisms are grouped into five classes. Animals can be classified as small (e.g. bird, cat, rabbit), medium (e.g. dog, fox, wild boar), or large (e.g. deer, cow, horse). In the case of humans, there are two classes: human and human with subject. Human describes individuals or groups of people who may be present at the shunting yard. These individuals can be further divided into shunting staff (equipped with personal protective equipment), people with high-visibility vests, and people without high-visibility vests. If a person is carrying an object that significantly affects the recognition image, they will be assigned to the human with a subject class. Examples of such objects include a bicycle being pushed or a hand transport cart. Apart from vehicles, all the objects mentioned above can theoretically appear in any position. Additionally, there are two special classes. The group of strongly changing objects describes the special case of a small moving object like leaves or a bag in the wind that does not have a predictable trajectory. The objects' influence on the system is only relevant in the immediate surroundings of the ego-track, so positioning in the external areas can be omitted. Skids are also listed as a separate class for shunting yards. They are essential in shunting operations to prevent stationary wagons from rolling away. However, they can be easily overlooked when left on the track and, in severe cases, can cause the locomotive to derail. Skids are available in new, rusty and used, as well as double skids. Regarding positioning, skids are only relevant on the ego-track and have a specific placement on the rail, either on the left, right, or both sides. Additionally, wagons should not be placed in front of a skid as it renders the object meaningless for the scenario.

As additional rules, living organisms have a pose for positioning, which would have to be included in Fig. 5 as an additional loop after the alignment. Furthermore, for railway vehicles, only one wagon, row, or wagon combination is permitted on the ego-track to prevent three solo wagons from being spaced out on the track.

The rules and conditions for Layer 4 objects are the most comprehensive. It is important to distinguish between stationary objects and those that move with a trajectory. Every Layer 4 object, except for strongly moving objects, can be stationary. The positioning of stationary objects follows the same order as Layer 2 objects. An object without movement is referred to as a standing object.

When generating trajectories for moving objects, as shown in the left branch of Fig. 5, there are additional rules to follow. Each trajectory is defined by three points: start, anchor, and end. The start point corresponds to the initial position of the object and is subject to the same rules. When determining the other points, it must be ensured that no object is present at these points and that the trajectory does not intersect with an existing object. Additionally, the space requirements of larger objects must be taken into account. Road vehicles should only cross a track via a level crossing. It should be noted, however, that in certain cases, such as the presence of emergency vehicles or vehicles involved in accidents, a vehicle may be situated on or crossing the track away from a level crossing. Additionally, a movement logic must be implemented to prevent road vehicles from having to make a complete change of direction at the anchor point, which may not be feasible due to physical and technical limitations. To avoid duplication in trajectory generation, a condition is set that the anchor point cannot be the same as the start or end point, as the trajectory is also mapped in other trajectories. Each point of the trajectory is assigned an object speed, and the corresponding object acceleration is determined from the change in speed between the points. The point information is combined to determine the trajectory path and movement vector of an object in the scenario. Rail vehicles have special trajectories due to their rail-bound nature and can only move on their initial track with predefined speed patterns. When a row of wagons is on the siding, it can be used to represent a parallel hump or an incoming mainline train. An exception to this is the solo wagon, which has no trajectory and appears to be stationary. To initiate the movement of the trajectory, a trigger is defined that is activated depending on a predefined distance between the locomotive and the dynamic object.

The final stage of combinatorics involves adding Layer 6 objects, which include metadata available to the ASO-System. This includes the classes digital maps, position coordinates, signal status as well as train radio. The scenario thus contains the necessary background conditions required for the error-free operation of the system or that influence objects in the other layers.

The combination process gives rise to a considerable number of semantic scenarios. These descriptions, which are still relatively abstract, can be converted into what is known as logical scenarios through subsequent parameterization. In this instance, the set of abstract scenarios already comprises some semantic descriptions corresponding to logical parameter spaces. Consequently, these can be replaced by suitable value ranges in the parameterization step. The subsequent step in this process is the concretization of the parameters, which involves defining suitable step sizes for the parameter spaces to obtain concrete scenarios for the test execution. It is crucial to assess the extent to which notable discrepancies emerge from the coverage of the parameter spaces.

3.4 Convergence of Scenario Generation

The term convergence is employed across numerous disciplines and can be defined in a number of ways, including as a process of approaching a limit value or target. Within the context of our approach to scenario-based testing of highly automated rail vehicles, we define the convergence concept of scenario generation as a comprehensive set of scenarios that closely approximates full test case coverage and exhibits a high degree of complete coverage of the population.

The most significant challenge in scenario generation is the generation of a targeted and convergent set of scenarios based on the derived knowledge and the defined ODD. To achieve this, it is necessary to examine the criteria for integrating the knowledge and the ODD into the methodology, as well as the structured combination of knowledge entities into scenarios. The justification is integrated into the methodological generation process, enabling the convergence of the scenario set to be checked in parallel with the generation process. The rationale behind the convergence of the scenario set is based on the fulfillment of multiple convergence conditions throughout the generation process. Figure 7 provides a visual representation of the aforementioned procedure.

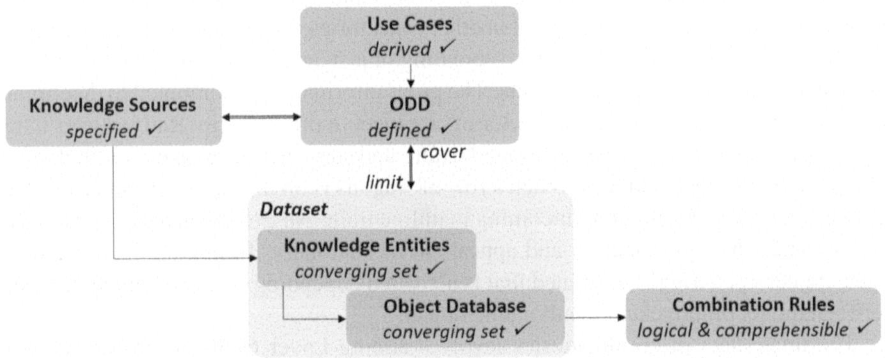

Fig. 7. Methodical Approach for a converging Scenario Set.

The initial stage of the convergence conditions entails deriving the use cases, which are based on the requirements for the ATO-System. The use cases map the system's functions and tasks, providing a comprehensive overview of its operational capabilities. This is achieved through a structured representation of the processes and a step-by-step transfer into use cases [14]. Subsequently, the ODD of the system is defined following the taxonomy developed in [15], and the attributes are determined on a use case-specific basis. The application of the taxonomy allows for the provision of a comprehensive ODD definition. It is also essential to ensure that all the requisite knowledge sources for the specific ATO-System are identified. This is achieved through a preliminary investigation of the subject areas and data sources enumerated in [13]. The knowledge entities are derived from each analyzed source in accordance with the ODD attributes and stored in a data set. Upon completion of analysis of the primary topics, the assumption is made that a convergent set of knowledge entities exists, provided that new sources do not result in a notable expansion of the data set. The structure of the 7-Layer Model facilitates the transfer of knowledge entities to the object database [16]. In accordance with the identification of the knowledge entities, the database of scenario objects also constitutes a converging set. In the final step, the rules and procedures of the combination must be explained in a logical and comprehensive manner so that the resulting set of scenarios can also be justified as converging.

In order to provide evidence of a converging scenario set, it is necessary to confirm the specification and convergence of the individual components of the process chain. Moreover, the procedure and rules of combinatorics must be presented in a manner that is both intelligible and logical. If these conditions are met, it can be assumed that the resulting set of scenarios is also convergent for the ODD that was defined at the outset.

4 Conclusion and Discussion

When implementing a driverless system, it is crucial to ensure that its reliability matches that of a human driver. Generating a scenario set that accurately represents a wide range of situations is a significant challenge. To automate the generation process, it is necessary to define the objects that may be encountered in the scenario, as well as their rules for combination and positioning. The paper focuses on the ability to map the complex field of application of the system using manageable rules and object combinations. It is noted that scenario-based testing is not yet widely used in rail transportation, and there are no comprehensive software solutions, such as OpenSCENARIO of the automotive industry. This study demonstrates that a structured process and a manageable number of defined conditions and rules can be used to generate a comprehensive scenario set for testing an ATO-System. Our research will investigate the extent to which a convergent scenario set can be proven using the defined railway-specific dataset and established combinatorial rules. We are continuously reviewing the knowledge-based dataset to identify and address any data gaps. Furthermore, we will investigate the variability of objects in terms of their positioning, size, design, and quantity. To enhance the combination program, a more detailed examination of the implementation of semantic language is necessary. It must be examined whether the purely functional programmed implementation can be further developed in terms of performance and handling using existing approaches, such as ontology.

At present, a functional prototype of a tool for the combination of scenarios is being developed. The paper demonstrates how scenarios can be generated for the example of an ASO and outlines the specific conditions and rules that must be considered. The step-by-step approach facilitates traceability in the development process. The results are significantly integrated into our research's toolchain for scenario-based testing of ATO-Systems [27]. Further investigation is required to confirm the applicability of the methodological generation approach. In particular, the convergence approach of the scenario set requires closer examination concerning the individual convergence criteria. It is important to note that the initial definitions of use cases and ODD attributes, as well as the convergence of the objects derived from the knowledge sources, are all consistent. Moreover, it should be noted that the principles of combinatorics also result in a convergent semantic scenario set. In addition, the parameterization and concretization of the abstract scenarios must be distinct defined, and demonstrated methodically throughout the generation process. Subsequently, the resulting concrete scenarios can be generated and evaluated as test cases in our virtual test environment, in conjunction with suitable evaluation criteria [26]. The results are used in an iterative process to review the method.

Acknowledgments. This work was partly accomplished within the project VAL, FKZ 5320000013, EBA Az. 8fd/003–1255#008-VAL, funded by the German Federal Ministry of Digital and Transport.

References

1. Zintel, M., Pluchet, J., Hensler, A., Bamberger, V., Baron, R., Watson, S.: 'Rail 2040', Arthur D. Little, (2023). Accessed 16 Jan 2024. https://www.adlittle.com/sa-en/insights/report/rail-2040
2. Pegasus, 'Projekt zur Etablierung von generell akzeptierten Gütekriterien, Werkzeugen und Methoden sowie Szenarien und Situationen zur Freigabe hochautomatisierter Fahrfunktionen', (2020). https://www.pegasusprojekt.de
3. Schuldt, F.: Ein Beitrag für den methodischen Test von automatisieren Fahrfunktionen mit Hilfe von virtuellen Umgebungen, Braunschweig (2017). http://publikationsserver.tu-braunschweig.de/get/64747
4. Riedmaier, S., Ponn, T., Ludwig, D., Schick, B., Diermeyer, F.: Survey on scenario-based safety assessment of automated vehicles. IEEE Access **8** (2020). https://doi.org/10.1109/ACCESS.2020.2993730
5. Cai, J., Deng, W., Guang, H., Wang, Y., Li, J., Ding, J.: A survey on data-driven scenario generation for automated vehicle testing. Machines **10**(11), 11 (2022). https://doi.org/10.3390/machines10111101
6. The MathWorks, Inc., Overview of Scenario Generation from Recorded Sensor Data. Accessed 15 Jan 2024. https://www.mathworks.com/help/driving/ug/overview-of-scenario-generation-from-recorded-sensor-data.html
7. Bagschik, G., Menzel, T., Maurer, M.: Ontology based scene creation for the development of automated vehicles (2018). https://arxiv.org/pdf/1704.01006.pdf
8. Fremont, D.J., Yue, X., Dreossi, T., Ghosh, S., Sangiovanni-Vincentelli, A., Seshia, S.A.: Scenic: Language-Based Scene Generation, Electrical Engineering and Computer Sciences University of California at Berkeley, (2018). https://www2.eecs.berkeley.edu/Pubs/TechRpts/2018/EECS-2018-8.pdf
9. Menzel, T., Bagschik, G., Isensee, L., Schomburg, A., Maurer, M.: Detaillierung einer stichwortbasierten Szenariobeschreibung für die Durchführung in der Simulation am Beispiel von Szenarien auf deutschen Autobahnen, Workshop Fahrerassistenzsysteme und automatisiertes Fahren, vol. 12 (2018). https://www.uni-das.de/
10. Scholtes, M. et al.: 6-Layer model for a structured description and categorization of urban traffic and environment. IEEE Access **9** (2021). https://doi.org/10.1109/ACCESS.2021.3072739
11. ASAM e. V., 'ASAM OpenSCENARIO® DSL'. Accessed 12 Jan 2024. https://www.asam.net/standards/detail/openscenario-dsl/

12. Hao K., et al.: 'Bridging Data-Driven and Knowledge-Driven Approaches for Safety-Critical Scenario Generation in Automated Vehicle Validation (2023). Accessed, 15 Jan 2024. http://arxiv.org/abs/2311.10937
13. Greiner-Fuchs, L., Cichon, M.: Knowledge-Based Approach to Generate Scenarios for Testing Highly Automated On-Sight Train Operations. In: Proceedings of the 10th International Conference on Vehicle Technology and Intelligent Transport Systems, pp. 394–401. Angers, Frankreich, (2024)
14. Hofmeier, T., Greiner-Fuchs, L., Schäfer, S., Cichon, M.: Task analysis of a shunting locomotive to derive use-cases for scenario based tests of ATO Functions. In: 9th Auto Test Conference, Stuttgart (2022). https://www.researchgate.net/
15. Greiner-Fuchs, L., Cichon, M.: A framework to define operational design domains for automated train operations. IEEE Access. https://doi.org/10.1109/ACCESS.2024.3495977
16. Greiner-Fuchs, L., Schäfer, S., Hofmeier, T., Cichon, M.: 7-Layer Shunting Model: Generische Szenariobeschreibung automatisierter Rangierfunktionen. In: International Rail Symposium Aachen, Aachen (2023). https://irsa.eurailpress.de/
17. DB Netz AG, 'Richtlinie 408 - Züge fahren und Rangieren: Ril408'. DB Kommunikationstechnik GmbH, Dec. 12, 2021. [Online]. Available: https://www.dbinfrago.com/web
18. DB Netz AG, 'Richtlinien 301 – Signalbuch: Ril301'. DB Kommunikationstechnik GmbH, (2020). https://www.dbinfrago.com/web
19. Eisenbahn Bau- und Betriebsordnung: EBO (1967). https://www.gesetze-im-internet.de/ebo/EBO.pdf
20. Stuhr, H., Schneider, P., Karch, S.: Schienengüterverkehr: Marktumfeld, Produktion, Technik und Innovation. Wiesbaden: Springer Fachmedien Wiesbaden (2023). https://doi.org/10.1007/978-3-658-38753-2
21. Menius, R., Matthews, V.: Bahnbau und Bahninfrastruktur: Ein Leitfaden zu bahnbezogenen Infrastrukturthemen. Wiesbaden: Springer Fachmedien Wiesbaden (20200. https://doi.org/10.1007/978-3-658-27733-8
22. BEU, Bundesstelle für Eisenbahnfalluntersuchung. Accessed 04 Jan 2024. https://www.eisenbahn-unfalluntersuchung.de/EUB/DE/Publikationen/publikationen_node.html
23. BEU, 'Bundesstelle für Eisenbahnfalluntersuchung - Open Data'. Accessed 04 Jan 2024. https://www.eisenbahn-unfalluntersuchung.de/EUB/DE/Publikationen/Open_Data/Open_Data_node.html
24. British Standards Institution (BSI), Operational design domain (ODD) taxonomy for an automated driving system (ADS). Specification. London, United Kingdom: BSI Standards Limited (2020). https://www.bsigroup.com/en-GB/
25. ISO, ISO 34503:2023(E) Road Vehicles — Test scenarios for automated driving systems — Specification for operational design domain (2023). https://www.iso.org/standard/78952.html
26. Schäfer, S., Greiner-Fuchs, L., Hofmeier, T., Koch, P., Cichon, M.: Virtual Validation Method of Automated On-Sight Driving Systems for Shunting Operations. In BOOK OF ABSTRACTS, Belgrade, Serbia: University of Belgrade – The Faculty of Transport and Traffic Engineering (2023). https://doi.org/10.37528/FTTE/9788673954677/RailBelgrade.2023.ZE
27. Greiner-Fuchs, L. Schäfer, S., Hofmeier, T., Cichon, M.: Database-supported methodical approach for the development of a toolchain for the evaluation of ATO functions using a scenario-based test methodology. In: Proceedings of the Fifth International Conference on Railway Technology: Research, Development and Maintenance, in Paper 13.4. Montpellier, France: Civil-Comp Press (2022). https://doi.org/10.4203/ccc.1.13.4

Uncertainty Representation in a SOTIF-Related Use Case with Dempster-Shafer Theory for LiDAR Sensor-Based Object Detection

Milin Patel[1] and Rolf Jung[2](✉)

[1] Institute for Driver Assistance and Connected Mobility (IFM), Benningen, Germany
milin.patel@hs-kempten.de
[2] Kempten University of Applied Sciences, Kempten, Germany
rolf.jung@hs-kempten.de

Abstract. Uncertainty in LiDAR sensor-based object detection arises from environmental variability and sensor performance limitations. Representing these uncertainties is essential for ensuring the Safety of the Intended Functionality (SOTIF), which focuses on preventing hazards in automated driving scenarios. This paper presents a systematic approach to identifying, classifying, and representing uncertainties in LiDAR-based object detection within a SOTIF-related scenario. Dempster-Shafer Theory (DST) is employed to construct a Frame of Discernment (FoD) to represent detection outcomes. Conditional Basic Probability Assignments (BPAs) are applied based on dependencies among identified uncertainty sources. Yager's Rule of Combination is used to resolve conflicting evidence from multiple sources, providing a structured framework to evaluate uncertainties' effects on detection accuracy. The study applies variance-based sensitivity analysis (VBSA) to quantify and prioritize uncertainties, detailing their specific impact on detection performance.

Keywords: Automated driving systems (ADS) · Dempster-Shafer theory · Object Detection · SOTIF-related use case · Uncertainty representation

1 Introduction

The safety of the intended functionality (SOTIF), as defined by ISO 21448 [13], focuses on addressing hazards arising from functional insufficiencies in automated driving systems (ADS), particularly those caused by incomplete specifications of the intended functionality. SOTIF emphasizes identifying and mitigating risks associated with these insufficiencies, especially in environments with diverse and unpredictable conditions where operational parameters are not well-defined.

For environmental perception in autonomous driving, ADS rely on a combination of sensors, including cameras, radar, and LiDAR, integrated with machine

F. Calise et al. (Eds.): SMARTGREENS 2024/VEHITS 2024, CCIS 2954, pp. 178–193, 2026.
https://doi.org/10.1007/978-3-032-23187-1_10

learning algorithms for object detection and classification. LiDAR sensors are specifically chosen for their capability to provide accurate 3D representations of the environment [5]. The process of 3D object detection using LiDAR data includes data acquisition, preprocessing (removing noise and irrelevant points), segmentation (grouping processed points into clusters representing potential objects), feature extraction, and classification. Lastly, tracking monitors detected objects across frames to predict their future positions [24].

However, the performance of LiDAR sensors is significantly affected by environmental conditions, which introduces uncertainty in object detection. These uncertainties arise due to factors like absorption, scattering, and refraction of LiDAR beams, which affect detection range and data quality. Consequently, machine learning models must adapt to handle these uncertainties effectively [17].

Uncertainty can be categorized into two types: aleatoric and epistemic. Aleatoric uncertainty arises from inherent environmental variability, while epistemic uncertainty stems from incomplete knowledge or limitations in the system's model [7,10]. To represent and manage these uncertainties, this paper employs dempster-shafer theory (DST) [21], a mathematical framework that combines evidence from multiple sources, particularly in scenarios with incomplete or conflicting information [20].

DST is selected for this research due to its flexibility in representing uncertainty without requiring prior probabilities, which can be difficult to determine or justify [8,23]. Unlike Bayesian methods, which rely on potentially biased prior distributions, DST integrates evidence from multiple sources without enforcing a single probabilistic outcome, making it particularly effective in complex systems where data may be unreliable or contradictory [22]. Additionally, DST allows for the representation of both uncertainty and ignorance, which is important when evidence is insufficient to fully support any hypothesis [8]. Compared to bayesian probability, fuzzy logic, and possibility theory, DST offers an adaptable approach to uncertainty representation [8,25].

Despite its computational challenges and difficulties in managing high-conflict evidence, DST's method for combining diverse sources of information enables a nuanced representation of uncertainty, justifying its application in this paper for ensuring the reliability of ADS [22,23,25].

Extended Evidential Networks (EEN), introduced in [2], are used to model and represent aleatoric, epistemic, and ontological uncertainties. The EEN framework integrates plausibility functions from DST into traditional Bayesian networks, capturing these uncertainties. This approach is applied in a SOTIF context through a case study on a perception function in highly automated driving vehicles, highlighting its role in identifying areas for model refinement to improve safety analysis. This work differs by applying DST to LiDAR-based object detection and focusing on developing DST-informed mitigation strategies, particularly through sensitivity analysis.

This paper extends previous research [16], which evaluated the adaptability and performance of deep learning (DL)-based 3D object detection methods using LiDAR data in a SOTIF-related scenario. Building on this foundation, the current work applies DST to specifically address and manage uncertainties in LiDAR-based object detection within the same context. This extension shifts the focus from performance evaluation to a detailed analysis of uncertainty representation, with the objective of developing targeted mitigation strategies informed by DST.

1.1 Major Contribution

The main contributions of this paper are summarized as follows:

(i) Presentation of a systematic approach for identifying, classifying, and representing uncertainties in a SOTIF-related scenario involving LiDAR-based object detection.
(ii) Application of DST to represent uncertainties through a case study on a SOTIF-related scenario involving LiDAR-based object detection.

1.2 Research Questions

This paper aims to address the following research questions:

RQ1. How can Dempster-Shafer Theory (DST) be applied to represent and manage uncertainties in LiDAR-based object detection within a SOTIF-related Use Case?
RQ2. How does DST facilitate the quantification and prioritization of identified uncertainties in LiDAR-based object detection, and how do these prioritized uncertainties specifically affect detection accuracy within the defined SOTIF-related scenario?

1.3 Structure of the Paper

Following the introduction, this paper is structured as follows. Section 2 presents the methodology for identifying and representing uncertainty in LiDAR-based object detection within a SOTIF-related context. Section 3 demonstrates the application of this methodology to a SOTIF-related use case, including sensitivity analysis and mitigation strategy development. Finally, Sect. 4 summarizes the findings and proposes directions for future research.

2 Proposed Method for Representing Uncertainty in SOTIF-Related Use Case

This chapter outlines a methodology for identifying and representing uncertainty in LiDAR-based object detection within a SOTIF-related Use Case. The workflow, illustrated in Fig. 1, includes defining the Use Case, categorizing sources of uncertainty, and applying DST to represent these uncertainties. The workflow follows a parallel approach, where defining uncertainty states and mapping dependencies occur simultaneously, ensuring all influencing factors are considered together.

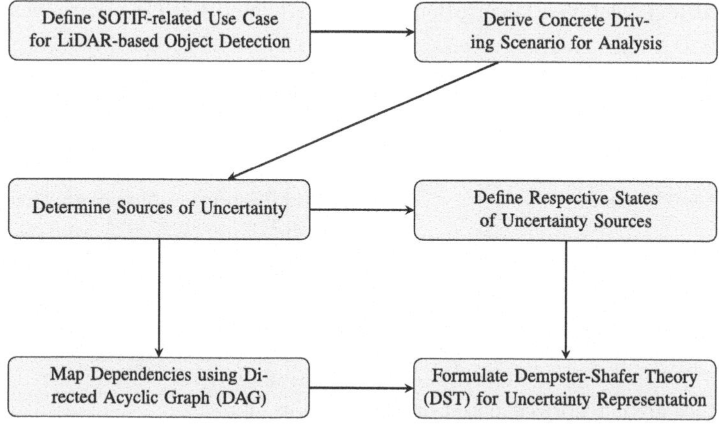

Fig. 1. Workflow for representing uncertainty in a SOTIF-related Use Case.

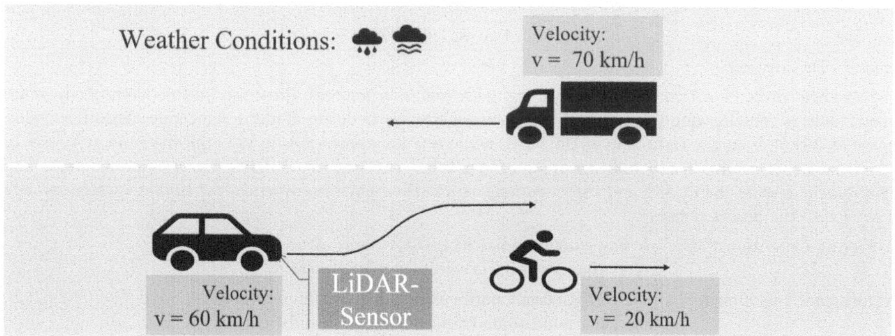

Fig. 2. SOTIF-related Use Case: Ego-Vehicle interacting with a cyclist and oncoming truck in adverse weather.

2.1 Description of SOTIF-Use Case and Scenario

This subchapter describes the SOTIF-related Use Case and the derived scenario, which involves a LiDAR-equipped vehicle navigating a two-lane country road under adverse weather conditions. Figure 2 depicts the scenario, where the Ego-Vehicle must avoid a cyclist while managing oncoming traffic and challenging weather conditions.

The key variables defining the Use Case, including road type, weather conditions, and road users, are detailed in Table 1.

To systematically represent SOTIF-related aspects, Table 2 outlines how the scenario is derived from the defined Use Case, focusing on triggering conditions, performance insufficiencies, and potential hazardous behaviors.

Table 1. Detailed Description of SOTIF-Related Use Case Variables.

Operational Design Domain (ODD) Taxonomy	
Permanent-Regional Variable *	– Roadway Type → Traffic way - *Two-way, Divided* – Roadway Surface and Features Type → Lane Type - *Single Lane, Asphalt*
Permanent-Local Variable *	– Road Geometry → Alignment - *Straight* – Lane Type - *Narrow Lane*
Compounding Event or Condition Scenario Variable *	– Weather → Particulate Matter → *Fog* – Weather → Precipitation - *Rain* – Light Conditions → Ambient Light - *Daylight*
Non-typical Event and Condition Scenario Variable *	– Roadway Users → Non-vehicle Permitted on Roadway - *Bicyclist*

The variables are categorized based on the study in [3].

Table 2. Systematic Description of SOTIF-Related Use Case and Derived Scenario.

Use Case	Operating on a two-way country road
Scenario Description	
The scenario involves a two-lane country road with one lane for each direction and no dedicated cyclist lane. The Ego-Vehicle, equipped with a LiDAR sensor, travels at 60 km/h in the right lane. Ahead, a cyclist moves at 20 km/h on the right side of the road, while a truck approaches in the opposite lane at 70 km/h. Adverse weather conditions, including rain and fog patches, challenge the LiDAR sensor's performance. The Ego-Vehicle detects the cyclist and the oncoming truck, then plans to overtake the cyclist by temporarily moving into the adjacent lane	
Triggering Condition (TC)	– Fog causing noise in LiDAR point cloud data – Wet road surface increasing braking distance
Performance Insufficiency	– LiDAR sensor performance degrades in adverse weather conditions (rain and fog) – Insufficient training data for the deep learning model to handle foggy or rainy conditions
Potential Hazardous Behavior	– Incorrect estimation of the cyclist's position, leading to a potential collision – Inaccurate perception of the oncoming truck, leading to a potential head-on collision

2.2 Sources of Uncertainty in SOTIF-Related Use Case for LiDAR Sensor-Based Object Detection

This subchapter identifies and categorizes the sources of uncertainty in LiDAR-based object detection, distinguishing between aleatoric and epistemic uncertainties, as shown in Table 3. Aleatoric uncertainties arise from environmental factors, including rain intensity, fog density, and road surface conditions, which directly impact the performance of the LiDAR sensor. Epistemic uncertainties result from system limitations, encompassing the sensor's performance under specific conditions, the presence of noise in the data, and the adequacy of the DL model's training, which influence the accuracy of object detection and classification.

Table 3. Categorization of Sources of Uncertainty in LiDAR-Based Object Detection.

Uncertainty Source	Category	Interdependencies
Rain Intensity	Aleatoric	Variability in rain intensity affects road wetness, surface reflectivity, and LiDAR signal scattering
Fog Density	Aleatoric	Changes in fog density cause LiDAR signal scattering and noise in data
Wet Road Conditions	Aleatoric	Moisture levels on the road, influenced by rain and fog, affect reflection variability and surface characteristics
LiDAR Sensor Performance	Aleatoric & Epistemic	Performance is influenced by environmental factors (aleatoric) and sensor limitations (epistemic)
Noise in LiDAR Data	Aleatoric	Environmental factors like rain and fog introduce noise into LiDAR data, reducing accuracy
Scattering of LiDAR Signals	Aleatoric	Surface type, fog, and rain cause scattering, reducing signal clarity
Reflection Variability	Aleatoric	Reflection variability arises from wet road conditions and surface type characteristics
Object Proximity	Aleatoric	Variability in detecting objects based on distance and speed relative to the sensor
Surface Type	Aleatoric	Different surface characteristics (absorption, transmission, reflection) impact how LiDAR signals behave
Deep Learning Model Training Quality	Epistemic	The diversity and quality of training data impact model generalization and accuracy
3D Object Detection Accuracy	Epistemic	Uncertainty arises from sensor data limitations and model inaccuracies in detecting objects

The sources of uncertainty listed in this table are adapted from SOTIF scenario variables [3], and LiDAR sensor model and 3D object detection deep learning model parameters as described in [9] and [18].

2.3 Representing Dependencies Between Uncertainty Sources

A directed acyclic graph (DAG), shown in Fig. 3, is used to map the dependencies between various sources of uncertainty in LiDAR-based object detection. This representation demonstrates how environmental and system factors interact to influence detection accuracy. Each node in the DAG corresponds to a specific source of uncertainty, while the edges indicate the conditional relationships between these sources, showing how they collectively impact the system's overall performance and decision-making processes [12].

As depicted in Fig. 3, the dependencies show that rain intensity and fog density directly affect wet road conditions, which subsequently influence both

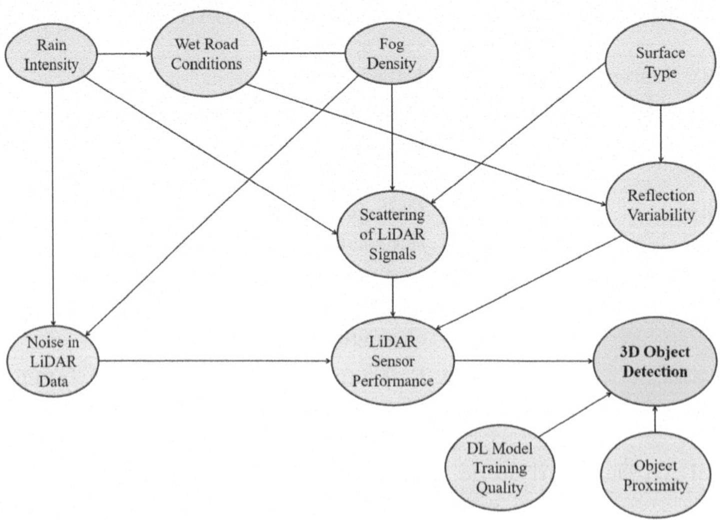

Fig. 3. DAG representing dependencies among uncertainty sources in a SOTIF-related Use Case for LiDAR-based object detection.

reflection variability and LiDAR sensor performance. Surface type also affects the scattering of LiDAR signals and reflection variability. These factors collectively influence LiDAR sensor performance, directly affecting the accuracy of 3D object detection. Additionally, DL model training quality and object proximity impact object detection performance, determining the system's ability to accurately identify and classify objects within the environment.

The identified uncertainties are classified into distinct states, as summarized in Table 4. These states represent the specific levels or conditions under which each source of uncertainty may occur. In the following chapter, these uncertainties will be analyzed using DST by assigning conditional Basic Probability Assignments (BPAs) to each source, according to its respective state.

Table 4. State Categories of Uncertainty Sources.

State Category	Uncertainty Sources
Low, Medium, High	Rain Intensity, Fog Density, Noise in LiDAR Data, Scattering of LiDAR Signals, Reflection Variability
Dry, Moist, Saturated	Wet Road Conditions
Good, Moderate, Poor	LiDAR Sensor Performance, Deep Learning Model Training Quality
Close, Medium, Far	Object Proximity
Absorption, Transmission, Reflection	Surface Type

2.4 Formulating Dempster-Shafer Theory

In this study, DST is applied to represent and manage uncertainty in LiDAR-based object detection. The main components of DST include the Frame of Discernment (FoD), BPA, and the belief (Bel) and plausibility (Pl) functions. These components work together to provide a structured framework for uncertainty representation [4,19].

Frame of Discernment (FoD). The FoD, denoted as Θ, represents the set of all possible outcomes or hypotheses within the system. Each element θ_i corresponds to a potential outcome of the LiDAR-based object detection process, and the FoD is defined as:

$$\Theta = \{\theta_1, \theta_2, \theta_3, \ldots, \theta_n\} \tag{1}$$

Basic Probability Assignment (BPA). The BPA, $m(A)$, assigns a measure of belief to each subset $A \subseteq \Theta$, indicating the degree of evidence that supports A. The BPA must satisfy:

$$m(\emptyset) = 0 \quad \text{and} \quad \sum_{A \subseteq \Theta} m(A) = 1 \tag{2}$$

In this study, BPAs are derived from simulation data, capturing both aleatory and epistemic uncertainties.

Belief and Plausibility Functions. The belief function, $Bel(A)$, and the plausibility function, $Pl(A)$, provide lower and upper bounds, respectively, for the probability of A. The belief function is defined as:

$$Bel(A) = \sum_{B \subseteq A} m(B) \tag{3}$$

This represents the minimum belief committed to A based on the available evidence. The plausibility function is defined as:

$$Pl(A) = \sum_{B \cap A \neq \emptyset} m(B) \tag{4}$$

which accounts for all evidence that does not contradict A. The interval $[Bel(A), Pl(A)]$ represents the range within which the true probability of A lies, accommodating both certainty and uncertainty [14].

Dempster's Rule of Combination. Dempster's rule is used to combine evidence from multiple sources. The combined BPA for any subset $C \subseteq \Theta$, denoted as $m_{12}(C)$, is calculated as:

$$m_{12}(C) = \frac{1}{1-K} \sum_{A \cap B = C} m_1(A) \times m_2(B) \tag{5}$$

where K is the conflict coefficient, quantifying the degree of conflict between evidence sources:

$$K = \sum_{A \cap B = \emptyset} m_1(A) \times m_2(B) \quad (6)$$

Dempster's rule ensures that conflicting evidence is appropriately weighted, with $m_{12}(C)$ representing the combined belief in C based on both sources [1].

Yager's Modified Rule of Combination. In cases of significant conflict between evidence sources, Yager's modification of Dempster's rule is applied. This approach redistributes conflicting belief to the universal set Θ, with the modified belief assigned to Θ as:

$$q(\Theta) = m_1(\Theta) \times m_2(\Theta) + \sum_{A \cap B = \emptyset} m_1(A) \times m_2(B) \quad (7)$$

This method retains and addresses conflicting information without normalization, making it particularly suitable for complex systems like LiDAR-based object detection, where multiple forms of evidence must be reconciled [20]. In this study, Yager's rule is employed to manage the high levels of conflict present in the evidence sources.

3 Method Application on SOTIF-Related Use Case

This chapter applies DST to a SOTIF-related Use Case in LiDAR-based object detection. The workflow in Fig. 4 outlines the process of defining the FoD, categorizing uncertainty sources based on their impact on detection accuracy, performing a variance-based sensitivity analysis, and suggesting mitigation measures for the most significant uncertainties. The FoD defines possible detection outcomes, and BPAs assign probabilities based on uncertainty sources. Both inputs are necessary for the combination process, enabling conflict resolution through Yager's Rule.

This parallel structure allows the combination of evidence to consider both the hypotheses and their assigned probabilities simultaneously, enabling conflict resolution through Yager's Rule.

3.1 Defining the Frame of Discernment (FoD)

The Frame of Discernment (FoD) for this Use Case includes four possible outcomes relevant to LiDAR-based object detection:

- θ_1: Detection of a Cyclist
- θ_2: Detection of a Truck
- θ_3: No Detection, but object present (False Negative)
- θ_4: Incorrect Detection, but no object present (False Positive)

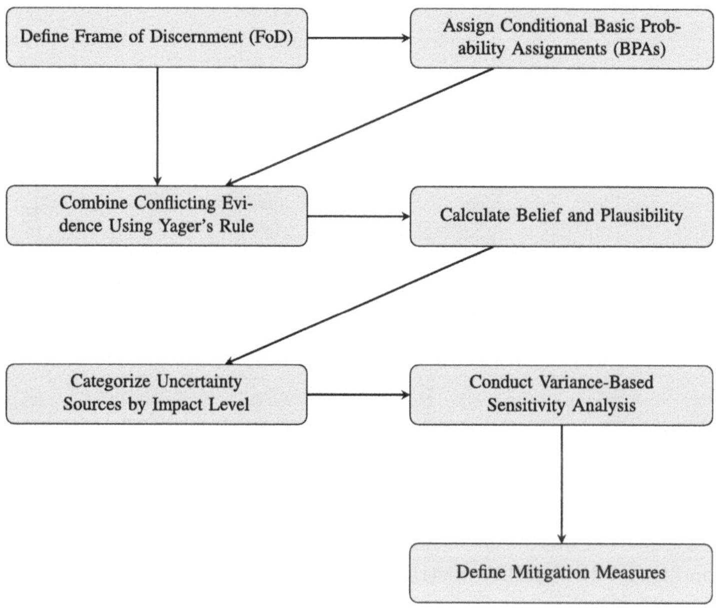

Fig. 4. Workflow for applying DST in a SOTIF-related Use Case.

These outcomes, represented as $\Theta = \{\theta_1, \theta_2, \theta_3, \theta_4\}$, form the basis for analyzing how uncertainties impact the performance of the LiDAR-based object detection system. A false negative refers to a missed detection when an object is actually present, while a false positive refers to an incorrect detection when no object is present.

3.2 Assigning Conditional Basic Probability Assignments (BPAs)

Conditional BPAs are assigned based on the dependencies among various sources of uncertainty, as illustrated in Fig. 5. The uncertainty sources, denoted as $S = \{S_1, S_2, \ldots, S_n\}$ (Table 3), have corresponding states X_s as shown in Table 4. For each detection outcome $\Theta = \{\theta_1, \theta_2, \theta_3, \theta_4\}$, conditional BPAs $m(x)$ are generated based on the dependencies of each source state $x \in X_s$ and are normalized to ensure that $\sum_{A \subseteq \Theta} m(A) = 1$.

Figure 5 presents selected uncertainty sources to provide a focused evaluation, as including all uncertainties would lead to repetitive information without adding new insights. The results highlight the conditional dependencies between uncertainties, revealing how environmental conditions influence object detection outcomes.

Rain intensity leads to a significant increase in False Positives as intensity rises, reflecting reduced sensor performance in adverse weather such as heavy rain. In contrast, fog density shows stable false positive probabilities across states but greater variability in detecting cyclists and trucks, indicating reduced sen-

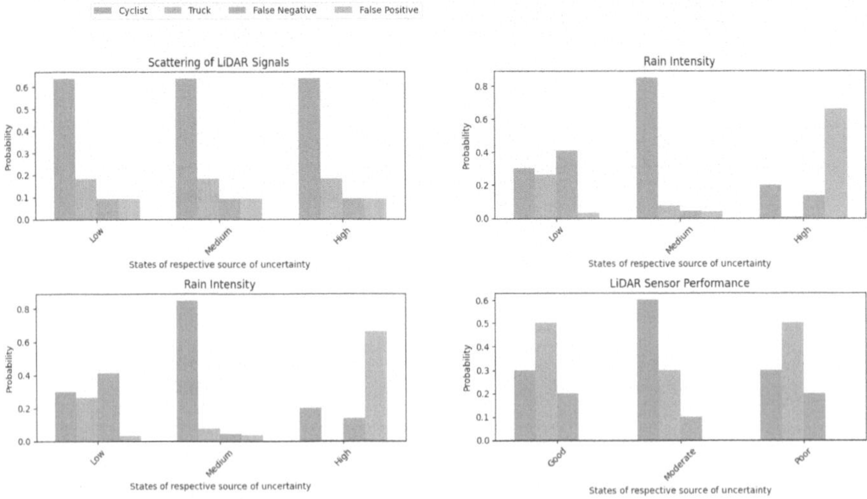

Fig. 5. Conditional Probability distributions for detection outcomes across various sources of uncertainty.

sor reliability under foggy conditions. Similarly, scattering of LiDAR signals correlates with increased False Negatives at higher scattering levels, suggesting compromised detection accuracy for objects like cyclists and trucks when environmental factors distort the signal.

3.3 Combining BPAs Using Yager's Rule of Combination and Calculating Belief and Plausibility

Yager's Rule of Combination was applied to integrate BPAs from different sources of uncertainty, particularly when evidence is conflicting. Conflicting evidence occurs when different sources provide varying levels of belief in certain outcomes, making it challenging to combine them directly without bias. Yager's rule redistributes the conflicting mass to the universal set Θ, ensuring that no single outcome is disproportionately influenced by conflicting evidence.

Figure 6 demonstrates how different uncertainty sources affect the belief and plausibility values for each detection outcome. A higher plausibility value compared to belief indicates that the outcome is possible across a broader range of scenarios, although with less certainty.

For cyclist detection, reflection variability and rain intensity show higher plausibility values compared to belief, suggesting the system detects cyclists under specific conditions but with reduced confidence in accuracy. For truck detection, reflection variability and LiDAR sensor performance play a significant role in reducing detection confidence under adverse conditions. While similar patterns are observed in other detection outcomes, only cyclist and truck detections are shown here to avoid redundant information.

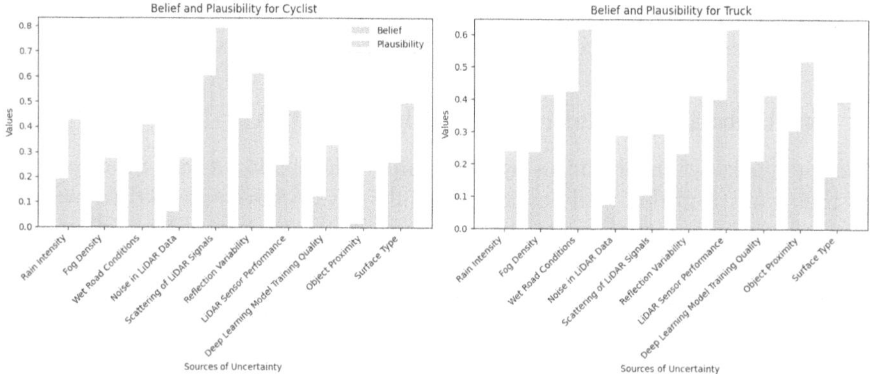

Fig. 6. *Bel* and *Pl* for detection outcomes across various sources of uncertainty.

3.4 Impact Levels of Uncertainty Sources

Uncertainty sources were categorized by calculating the difference between their plausibility and belief values, represented as $U(A) = Pl(A) - Bel(A)$ for each subset $A \subseteq \Theta$. This difference quantifies the uncertainty associated with each source. The uncertainty levels were classified into three categories: Low, Moderate, and High, based on thresholds derived from the distribution of uncertainty values.

The classification thresholds were set using the 25th and 75th percentiles of the maximum uncertainty values across all sources, corresponding to $\tau_1 = 0.2$ and $\tau_2 = 0.5$. Sources with $U(A) < \tau_1$ were categorized as Low Impact, those with $\tau_1 \leq U(A) < \tau_2$ as Moderate Impact, and those with $U(A) \geq \tau_2$ as High Impact. These thresholds effectively segment the uncertainty distribution, as shown in Table 5.

Table 5. Impact Levels of Uncertainty Sources on Detection Variability.

Impact Level	Sources of Uncertainty
High Impact	Rain Intensity, LiDAR Sensor Performance, Surface Type
Moderate Impact	Wet Road Conditions, Noise in LiDAR Data, Deep Learning Model Training Quality, Object Proximity
Low Impact	Fog Density, Scattering of LiDAR Signals, Reflection Variability

The impact levels in Table 5 reflect the overall effect of each uncertainty source on detection performance, while Table 4 lists the specific states (e.g.,

Low, Medium, High) under which these uncertainties occur. The states serve as inputs to determine their contribution to the overall impact levels.

3.5 Variance-Based Sensitivity Analysis (VBSA)

After categorizing uncertainties by their impact levels, it was essential to quantify their contributions to detection variability. VBSA was applied to evaluate how variations in input uncertainties influence overall detection performance, particularly in systems with interdependent factors [15].

The analysis focuses on uncertainty sources to assess their impact on detection accuracy under different environmental conditions. VBSA systematically allocates the total variance in performance across these uncertainty sources, providing insights into how each source interacts with others [6]. This method identifies the sources with the most significant impact on performance variability [11], which is essential for managing uncertainty and improving system reliability.

$$\mathrm{Var}_{Bel}(S_i) = \mathrm{Var}(Bel(S_i)), \quad \mathrm{Var}_{Pl}(S_i) = \mathrm{Var}(Pl(S_i)) \tag{8}$$

The variance for each uncertainty source S_i is calculated to determine how belief and plausibility values fluctuate under different conditions. Comparing these variances helps identify which sources contribute most to system variability.

As shown in Fig. 7, the VBSA results shows that scattering of LiDAR signals and rain intensity generate the highest variance in detection performance, particularly under challenging environmental conditions. Wet road conditions and LiDAR sensor performance also contribute significantly to performance variability.

3.6 Mitigation Measures to Address Key Uncertainties

Based on the findings from VBSA, mitigation measures are suggested to address uncertainties that significantly impact the performance of the LiDAR-based object detection system. The recommendations focus on reducing detection variability and enhancing system robustness across different operational environments:

(a) Develop adaptive algorithms for LiDAR-based object detection to adjust to varying weather conditions, including rain intensity and fog density, improving detection accuracy in challenging environments.
(b) Apply noise reduction techniques to minimize the impact of environmental interference on LiDAR data, enhancing detection performance in adverse conditions.
(c) Expand training datasets with simulated data from extreme weather conditions to improve the model's generalization and maintain accuracy across different real-world scenarios.

These measures directly address the most significant uncertainties identified through the DST framework and VBSA.

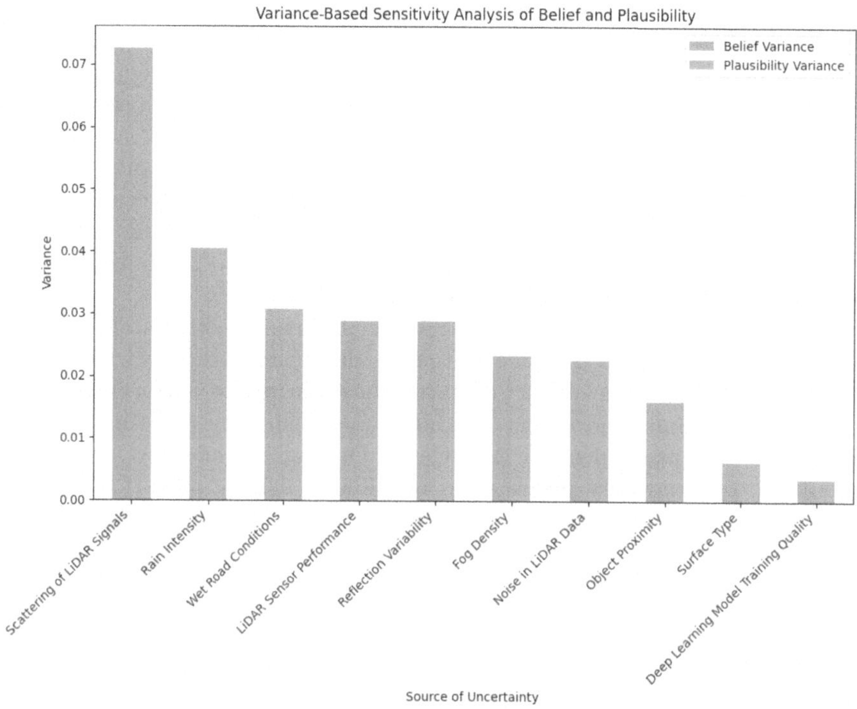

Fig. 7. Variance-Based sensitivity analysis of *Bel* and *Pl*.

4 Conclusion and Future Research Directions

This paper investigates the application of Dempster-Shafer Theory (DST) to address uncertainties in LiDAR-based object detection within a SOTIF-related Use Case. To answer the first research question (Subsect. 1.2), the study defines a SOTIF-related Use Case (Subsect. 2.1), identifies relevant sources of uncertainty (Table 3), and applies DST to model these uncertainties. The Frame of Discernment (FoD) models detection outcomes, and BPAs are calculated based on the available evidence (Subsect. 2.4). Yager's Rule of Combination is used to resolve conflicting information from different sources (Subsect. 3.3), providing a structured and objective representation of uncertainty.

To address the second research question (Subsect. 1.2), the study quantifies and prioritizes uncertainties based on their impact on detection performance. Using belief and plausibility functions, the uncertainties are categorized by their influence on detection accuracy (Subsect. 2.3). The VBSA further quantifies the contribution of each uncertainty source (Subsect. 3.5), with environmental factors such as rain intensity, surface type, and LiDAR sensor performance having the most significant effect on detection variability (Fig. 7).

Mitigation measures are proposed to address the identified uncertainties, focusing on improving LiDAR sensor performance under adverse weather conditions and refining training datasets to include extreme weather scenarios. These recommendations, discussed in Subsect. 3.6, aim to improve system reliability by addressing critical environmental and sensor limitations.

Several limitations are acknowledged in this study. First, the subjectivity in assigning BPAs may introduce bias. Second, the static analysis does not capture temporal dynamics, which are crucial for real-time decision-making in dynamic environments. Additionally, the conclusions are sensitive to the initial assumptions and the choice of combination rules in DST.

Future research could extend this static analysis into a dynamic framework, tracking uncertainty propagation over time as the vehicle interacts with its environment. Modeling the evolution of uncertainties in sensor performance, environmental conditions, and object proximity would improve real-time decision-making and risk assessment in Automated Driving Systems (ADS). Further exploration of uncertainty propagation in different driving scenarios and integrating DST with temporal models, such as Hidden Markov Models (HMMs) or Bayesian Networks, could reveal additional insights into system behavior. Simulation-based studies could also validate these uncertainty models by comparing their predictions with real-world data, leading to more effective uncertainty management techniques.

Acknowledgements. This research was funded by the Institute for Driver Assistance and Connected Mobility (IFM) at Kempten University of Applied Sciences. The IFM specializes in the development and validation of driver assistance systems and connected mobility, focusing on functional safety, cybersecurity, and testing methodologies. I extend my gratitude to my team at IFM for their valuable support and contributions in the areas of functional safety and cybersecurity.

References

1. Dempster, A.P.: Upper and lower probabilities induced by a multivalued mapping. Ann. Math. Stat. **38**(2), 325–339 (1967). https://doi.org/10.1214/aoms/1177698950
2. Adee, A., Munk, P., Gansch, R., Liggesmeyer, P.: Uncertainty representation with extended evidential networks for modeling safety of the intended functionality (sotif) (2020)
3. Becker, C., Brewer, J.C., Yount, L., et al.: Safety of the intended functionality of lane-centering and lane-changing maneuvers of a generic level 3 highway chauffeur system (2020)
4. Campos, F., Cavalcante, S.: An extended approach for dempster-shafer theory. In: Proceedings Fifth IEEE Workshop on Mobile Computing Systems and Applications, pp. 338–344 (2003)
5. Cao, L., He, Y., Luo, Y., Chen, J.: Layered sotif analysis and 3σ-criterion-based adaptive ekf for lidar-based multi-sensor fusion localization system on foggy days. Remote Sens. **15**(12) (2023). https://doi.org/10.3390/rs15123047. https://www.mdpi.com/2072-4292/15/12/3047

6. Shahsavani, D., Grimvall, A.: Variance-based sensitivity analysis of model outputs using surrogate models. Environ. Model. Softw. **26**(6), 723–730 (2011)
7. Der Kiureghian, A., Ditlevsen, O.: Aleatory or epistemic? Does it matter? Struct. Saf. **31**(2), 105–112 (2009)
8. Dezert, J., Wang, P., Tchamova, A.: On the validity of dempster-shafer theory. In: 2012 15th International Conference on Information Fusion, pp. 655–660 (2012)
9. Dosovitskiy, A., Ros, G., Codevilla, F., Lopez, A., Koltun, V.: Carla: an open urban driving simulator. In: Conference on Robot Learning, pp. 1–16 (2017)
10. Gruber, C., Schenk, P.O., Schierholz, M., Kreuter, F., Kauermann, G.: Sources of uncertainty in machine learning–a statisticians' view. arXiv preprint arXiv:2305.16703 (2023)
11. Hall, J.W.: Uncertainty-based sensitivity indices for imprecise probability distributions. Reliabil. Eng. Syst. Saf. **91**(10), 1443–1451 (2006)
12. Hewawasam, R., Premaratne, K.: Dependency based reasoning in a dempster-shafer theoretic framework. In: 2007 10th International Conference on Information Fusion, pp. 1–8 (2007). https://doi.org/10.1109/ICIF.2007.4408135
13. ISO 21448:2022: Road vehicles – safety of the intended functionality (2022). https://www.iso.org/standard/77490.html
14. Klir, G., Yuan, B.: Fuzzy Sets and Fuzzy Logic, vol. 4. Prentice hall, New Jersey (1995)
15. Liu, X., Wei, P., Rashki, M., Fu, J.: A probabilistic simulation method for sensitivity analysis of input epistemic uncertainties on failure probability. Struct. Multidiscip. Optim. **67**(1), 3 (2024)
16. Patel, M., Jung, R.: Simulation-based performance evaluation of 3d object detection methods with deep learning for a lidar point cloud dataset in a sotif-related use case, 2184-495X (2024). https://doi.org/10.5220/0012707300003702
17. Peng, T., Kim, B.: Improving accuracy of pseudo-lidar for 3d object detection by accurate depth estimation. In: 2023 IEEE 6th International Conference on Knowledge Innovation and Invention (ICKII), pp. 440–443 (2023). https://doi.org/10.1109/ICKII58656.2023.10332716
18. Prince, S.J.D.: Understanding Deep Learning. MIT press, Cambridge (2023)
19. Rakowsky, U.K.: Fundamentals of the dempster-shafer theory and its applications to system safety and reliability modelling. J. Polish Saf. Reliabil. Assoc. **2** (2007)
20. Sentz, K., Ferson, S.: Combination of evidence in dempster-shafer theory (2002)
21. Shafer, G.: A Mathematical Theory of Evidence, vol. 42. Princeton University Press, Princeton (1976)
22. Wang, P.: A defect in dempster-shafer theory. In: Lopez de Mantaras, R., Poole, D. (eds.) Uncertainty in Artificial Intelligence, pp. 560–566. Morgan Kaufmann, San Francisco (1994). https://doi.org/10.1016/B978-1-55860-332-5.50076-6. https://www.sciencedirect.com/science/article/pii/B9781558603325500766
23. Wilson, N.: The assumptions behind dempster's rule. In: Uncertainty in Artificial Intelligence, pp. 527–534 (1993)
24. Wu, Y., Wang, Y., Zhang, S., Ogai, H.: Deep 3d object detection networks using lidar data: a review. IEEE Sens. J. **21**(2), 1152–1171 (2021). https://doi.org/10.1109/JSEN.2020.3020626
25. Zio, E., Pedroni, N.: Literature review of methods for representing uncertainty (2013)

A Heuristic Approach to Optimal Meeting Points in Multi-modal Ride-Sharing Networks

Julien Baudru[1,2(✉)] and Hugues Bersini[1,2]

[1] IRIDIA, Université Libre de Bruxelles (ULB), Brussels, Belgium
julien.baudru@ulb.be
[2] FARI, AI for the Common Good Institute, Brussels, Belgium

Abstract. This paper addresses the challenge of determining an equitable meeting point for carpooling participants, ensuring that both walkers and drivers have equivalent travel times. The proposed solution automatically generates a fair meeting point in real time. The paper first reviews the current state of the art in this domain, then provides a formal problem definition. We present both an exact solution and a heuristic algorithm, which includes an efficient technique for pruning a multi-modal road network. The two methods are then compared in terms of execution time and solution quality. Additionally, we explore the impact of various algorithmic parameters on performance. Finally, both algorithms were tested under extreme conditions on the entire road network of Belgium to assess their scalability and robustness. The paper concludes by outlining potential directions for future research.

Keywords: Ride-sharing · Car-pooling · Sustainable mobility · Smart transportation · Multi-modal networks · Road networks

1 Introduction

Over the last decades, the use of private vehicles has exploded, leading to an increase in traffic congestion, pollution, and accidents. Various solutions already exist, such as public transport, however, since not all cities have a well-developed public transport network, ride-sharing seems to be the most viable alternative for users in terms of economy, ecology, and comfort [23]. Car-pooling can be described as a shared transport system in which users take a common path and therefore vehicle to reach their different, or common, destinations. This transport system is based on the shared use of private vehicles. Another definition provided by [12] is given in Text 1.

Private cars are utilized by various households or organizations in either a centralized (one large, open group) or decentralized system (several small, closed groups). The vehicle is owned by one member of the carpool group or can be jointly owned by several group members.

Text 1. Definition of ride-sharing.

F. Calise et al. (Eds.): SMARTGREENS 2024/VEHITS 2024, CCIS 2954, pp. 194–216, 2026.
https://doi.org/10.1007/978-3-032-23187-1_11

However, the primary aim of existing car-pooling solutions is to be profitable, either for the companies offering this services for the private drivers like BlaBlaCar or Lyft. This raises the question of fair car-pooling. In the particular context of universities, solving this challenge becomes important not only for the reasons listed above but also because according to [15] around 78% of students travel alone by car. In addition, according to [9], the propensity to practice peer-to-peer car-pooling is higher among younger people. Given that this research is ultimately intended to be offered as an application to students at the Université Libre de Bruxelles (ULB), the aforementioned arguments strongly support the usefulness and potential of our work. In the literature, main focus of studies on carpooling concerns the matching of users, in this field a distinction is commonly made between two categories of car-pooling problems. The first, known as the Daily Car Pooling Problem (DCPP), aims to assign pedestrians to drivers and define the paths they will take, while minimizing total travel costs and respecting the constraints of time and seats available in the car. The DCPP problem is known as NP-hard since this is a particular case of the Vehicle Routing Problem (VPR) which has been proved NP-hard by [18]. The second, known as the Long Term Car Pooling Problem (LTCPP), aims to create pools of users, knowing that some users may be drivers one day and pedestrians another, while maximizing the size of these pools, minimizing the distance covered by the drivers and respecting the same constraints as for the DCPP. In addition, the Car-Pooling Problem (CPP) usually falls into three types: (1) The many-to-one problem, which requires moving from multiple origins to a single destination, like the to-work problem; (2) The one-to-many problem, which involves moving from one origin to multiple destinations, like the return-from-work problem and; (3) The many-to-many problem, which involves moving from multiple origins to multiple destinations, like the dial-a-ride problem. It is important to indicates that the dial-a-ride problem differs from the CPP on the vehicle ownership. In dial-a-ride, the driver serves the passengers full-time, whereas, in CPP, the vehicle belongs to the participants, who can either act as drivers or passengers.

However, as [8] point out, in the majority of car-pooling systems proposed today, DCPP or LTCPP, users have to explicitly specify the pickup and drop locations. The solution proposed in this article solves this problem by automatically generating a meeting point that is fair to all users in real time. This problem can be formulated as follows: *Given a walker and a driver, what are their respective shortest paths to reach a meeting point in such a way that each user has equivalent travel times to reach the common destination?* The meeting point M is described as the rendezvous point between a driving user and a walking user. Note that the problem described could be extended to several users of each type. The dropping point D, on the other hand, is defined as the point where the driver drops a walking user in order for both to continue their journeys to their respective destinations. If we consider a simpler case where the dropping D and destination points are identical, the problem can be seen as a special case of the many-to-one problem in car-pooling and this problem can be called the search for the optimal meeting point (OMP). However, the OMP problem usually deals with distance, in these pages we'll be looking at a variant that focuses on travel time. The Fig. 1 illustrates the described problem. Here, we consider the case with identical dropping and destination points, and where we have only two users, a driver and a walker and we assume that both users start their journeys simultaneously.

This paper builds upon and extends our previous work [2], where we initially proposed a heuristic algorithm for optimal meeting point determination in ride-sharing scenarios. In this extended version, we provide a more comprehensive analysis and evaluate its performance on larger, more complex road networks.

In the remainder of this article, we present the state of the art in the field, then describe the problem formally, followed by a detailed explanation of the exact solution and our heuristic algorithm, which includes a simple technique for pruning a multi-modal road network. Next, we compare the two methods in terms of execution time and solution quality, and study the influence of various parameters on different aspects of our algorithm. Additionally, we test both algorithms under extreme conditions on the entire road network of Belgium to evaluate their robustness at scale. Finally, we present future avenues of research.

2 Similar Works

In this section, we look into research on car-pooling, optimal meeting points (OMP), and road networks. This summary of the current state of research contextualizes our study within the existing literature, highlighting the connections and distinctions between our research and these crucial topics in transportation and urban planning.

2.1 Ride-Sharing

Concerning the particular context of shared cars between members of a university, which is also the ultimate practical objective of our research, in [4] the authors propose a system called *PoliUniPool* in which optimal groups of users within the various universities of Milan are created using a guided Monte Carlo simulation. However, this system cannot provide real-time results and requires prior offline calculation. In addition, in [13] the authors propose an algorithm called Karlsruhe Rapid Ridesharing (KaRRi) for scheduling a fleet of shared vehicles. The advantage of this solution is that it allows the insertion of new passengers on existing paths. This algorithm is based on the idea of the LOUD system proposed by [5] using the bucket contraction hierarchies (BCH) technique for road networks avoiding a large number of calls to the Dijkstra algorithm. However, unlike our work, the latter does not take into account the characteristics of the road networks associated with the different modes of transport. In addition, KaRRi has the particularity of being able to handle numerous pickup and dropping points. Finally, the [13] have shown that it is possible to reduce trip time and vehicle operating time by extending ride-sharing with walking. To our knowledge, [13] are among the few to address the multi-modal aspect of the road network in the context of ride-sharing but we can also cite the related work of [16] and [20].

2.2 Optimal Meeting Point (OMP)

In [11], the authors model the problem of finding the optimal meeting point for two users having their own source and destination points where they need to meet before going to their destinations. They define a minimum path pair (MPP) query, which consists of two pairs of source and destination and a user-specified weight α to balance the two different needs. The parameter α reflects the need to go to the optimal meeting point ($\alpha \geq 2$) or to go directly to the destination by the shortest path ($\alpha = 0$). The weight α describes the requirement of meeting. The larger α is, the stronger the demand will be. Thanks to the α parameter, the authors introduce the notion of certainty concerning the meeting point, as in some cases the meeting is not possible or beneficial for any user. Finally, they proposed an efficient algorithm based on a point-to-point shortest path and two fast approximate algorithms with approximation bounds. This point-to-point algorithm surpassed the two-phase convex-hull-based pruning algorithm HullWindow (HW2) proposed by [22] to compute the OMP. In [14], the authors proposed two novel parameterized solutions based on Dynamic Programming (DP) to solve the problem of optimal multi-meeting points in the context of ride-sharing for a group of users.

2.3 Road Networks

In [21], the authors define three types of proximity relations that induce location constraints to model continuous spatio-temporal queries among sets of moving objects in road networks. These distance computations are the *max-pairwise-distance*, the *min-sum-distance*, and the *min-max-distance*, some of them will be discussed later in the Sect. 6.1. The authors proposed a novel moving object indexing technique that achieves good performances on real-world data thanks to a partitioning scheme for road networks. In [19], the authors compare four state-of-the-art techniques to find the shortest path in the context of road networks, these techniques are: Spatially Induced Linkage Cognizance (SILC), Path-Coherent Pairs Decomposition (PCPD), Contraction Hierarchies (CH), and Transit Node Routing (TNR). They conclude that CH was the preferable choice when both space efficiency and time efficiency are major concerns. Additionally, [1] introduces the concept of Highway Dimension, demonstrating that real-world road networks have a hierarchical structure that allows for exact shortest-path computations in logarithmic time. While previous methods lacked efficiency in constructing the necessary shortcut hierarchies, [6] propose a novel algorithm that efficiently computes these hierarchies and supports updates in time and space $O(V \log(U + |V|))$.

3 Problem Formulation

Before presenting the proposed algorithm, we first formalize the problem in a simplified manner. To recall, we focus on a case with two users, a pedestrian and a driver, sharing the same destination point. In this configuration, we want to find the meeting point that minimizes the travel time for both users.

3.1 Optimal Meeting Point (OMP)

We define two directed weighted graphs, $G_w = \{V, E\}$ the walking graph and $G_d = \{V, E\}$ the driving graph representing the road networks for each user u, an example is given in Fig. 1. Let a be the starting point of the walking user u_w, b the starting point of the driving user u_d and d the shared destination point of u_w and u_d. Then, we define the combined directed weighted graph $G = \{V, E\}$ with $V = \{v_1, v_2, ..., v_n / v_i \in (G_w \cap G_d) \cup (a, b)\}$, i.e. the set of road intersections common to G_w and G_d with the starting points of the two users. The edges of $G = \{V, E\}$ are defined as $E = \{arc(i, j)/i \in V, j \in V\}$, i.e. the set of roads between these intersections. An example of such a graph is given in Fig. 2. Practical details of the combine network creation are given in Sect. 5.1.

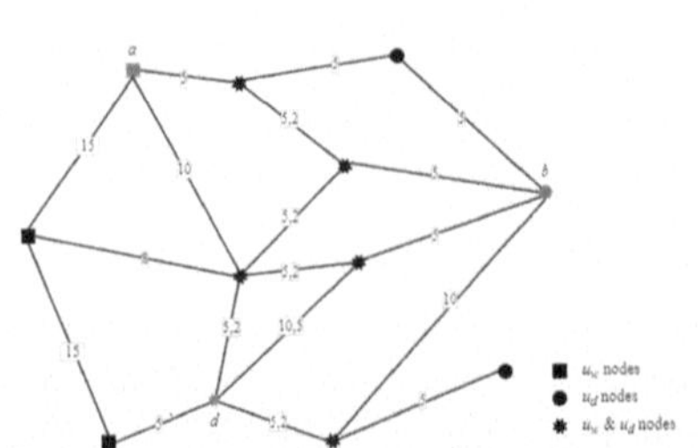

Fig. 1. G_w & G_d networks [2].

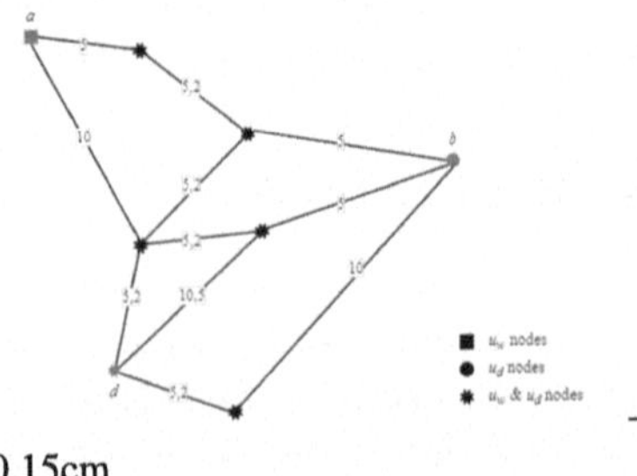

0.15cm

Fig. 2. G network [2].

For each $arc(i, j)$, a non-negative travel cost $\delta_{i,j}$ is associated, it corresponds to the distance of the road between intersections i and j, each $arc(i, j)$ also have a travel speed $\sigma^u_{i,j}$ depending on the user u. We denote by $p_u(i, j)$ the subset of V containing the sequence of nodes $\{v_1, v_2, ..., v_n\}$ from the arcs included in the path of user u to travel from the source i to the destination j. We denoted by $t^u_{i,j}$ the travel time for user u to complete path $p_u(i, j)$, this value is given by the Eq. 1.

$$t^u_{i,j} = \sum_{v,v' \in p_u(i,j)} \left(\frac{\delta_{v,v'}}{\sigma^u_{v,v'}} \right) \tag{1}$$

Objective Functions. Based on these definitions, we can establish several objective functions. The two popular ways to define the OMP are the *min-max* and the *min-sub*. For the *min-max*, a first approach involves choosing m in such a way as to minimize the travel time of both user like in the Eq. 2.

$$f = \min_{m} \left[max \left(t^{u_w}_{a,m} + t^{u_d}_{m,d} \, , \, t^{u_d}_{b,m} + t^{u_d}_{m,d} \right) \right] \tag{2}$$

Given that the travel time from the meeting point m to the common destination d is the same for both car-poolers, Eq. 2 can be rewritten as Eq. 3.

$$f = \min_{m} \left[max \left(t^{u_w}_{a,m} \, , \, t^{u_d}_{b,m} \right) \right] \tag{3}$$

A second approach involves choosing m in such a way that it minimizes the travel time for each user while ignoring the common path for the walker u_w like in the Eq. 4.

$$f = \min_{m} \left[max \left(t^{u_w}_{a,m} \, , \, t^{u_d}_{b,m} + t^{u_d}_{m,d} \right) \right] \tag{4}$$

For the *min-sub*, a variant approach involves choosing m in such a way that it minimizes the difference between the travel times to the meeting point m for each user, i.e. their travel times must be as close as possible. The waiting time $t_{wait} = \left| t^{u_w}_{a,m} - t^{u_d}_{b,m} \right|$ at the meeting point m is minimized by the Eq. 5.

$$f = \min_{m} \left| t^{u_w}_{a,m} - t^{u_d}_{b,m} \right| \tag{5}$$

3.2 Alternative Formulations

Minimum Steiner Tree (MST). The described problem can also be seen as a variant of the minimum Steiner tree (MST) problem. For a set of nodes $W = \{v_1, v_2, ..., v_n\}$, a subset of V, the Steiner tree is a tree denoted S which spans all the nodes in W. In the present case, W contains at least the source nodes and the common destination node, such that $W = \{a, b, d, ..., v_n\}$ and the meeting point m will be one of the v_i nodes in S. The travel time of S is given by the Eq. 6.

$$t^u_S = \sum_{v,v' \in S} \left(\frac{\delta_{v,v'}}{\sigma^u_{v,v'}} \right) \tag{6}$$

The minimum Steiner tree is the Steiner tree with the minimum travel time $t^u_{i,j}$ for each user u is denoted by $S*$. The MST is the S that minimizes the Eq. 7.

$$f = \min_{S} t^u_S \tag{7}$$

Minimum Path Pair (MPP). Another way of formulating this problem is to think in terms of the minimum path pair (MPP). The objective is to find the path pair that minimizes a given function for two pairs of source and destination, namely, (v^1_s, v^1_t) and (v^2_s, v^2_t), with a parameter α. There are 3 costs: (1) The cost of the path of p^1 from v^1_s to v^1_t; (2) The cost of the path of p^2 from v^2_s to v^2_t and;

(3) the cost between the two such paths p^1 and p^2. Let $w(p)$ be the cost of a path p, and the distance between two paths, $p1$ and $p2$, be $\delta(p^1, p^2)$. The MPP is the pair of path to minimize the Eq. 8.

$$f = \min_{p^1,p^2} w(p^1) + w(p^2) + \delta(p^1, p^2) \tag{8}$$

The path distance of a path p, $w(p)$, is defined as the sum of weights of its constituent edges like in the Eq. 9.

$$w(p) = \sum_{v,v' \in P} w(v, v') \tag{9}$$

And the distance between the two paths p^1 and p^2, $\delta(p^1, p^2)$, is the shortest distance between a pair of nodes, v_i^1 and v_j^2, this value is given by the Eq. 10.

$$\delta(p^1, p^2) = \min_{v_i^1 \in p^1, v_j^2 \in p^2} \delta(v_i^1, v_j^2) \tag{10}$$

4 Exact Solution

In this section, we present two variants of the algorithm for finding the exact OMP and the paths that allow each user to reach their destination. We compare the complexities of both algorithms and detail their operations.

To solve the problem of defining the rendezvous point exactly, the OMP, one naive solution is to compute the shortest path for each of the possible configurations. Algorithm 1 describes such a procedure. For each node $v \in G$, v is taken as a potential candidate to be m, the meeting point, the shortest path is calculated using Dijkstra between a and v, between b and v and between v and d. We then calculate the travel times of the various shortest paths using the appropriate objective Function 3, 4 or 5. And if the result obtained is better than the last best, we keep v as the current m and stop the value of the best result. Then, we repeat this operation on the entire network.

Algorithm 1. OMP - Naive exact solution algorithm.

1: $v_{best} \leftarrow None$
2: $t_{best} \leftarrow \infty$
3: **for** $v \in G$ **do**
4: $\quad t_{a,v}^{u_w} \leftarrow dijkstra(a, v)$
5: $\quad t_{b,v}^{u_d} \leftarrow dijkstra(b, v)$
6: $\quad t_{v,d}^{u_d} \leftarrow dijkstra(v, d)$
7: $\quad t_{max} \leftarrow f(t_{a,v}^{u_w}, t_{b,v}^{u_d}, t_{v,d}^{u_d})$
8: $\quad$ **if** $t_{max} < t_{best}$ **then**
9: $\quad\quad t_{best} \leftarrow t_{max}$
10: $\quad\quad v_{best} \leftarrow v$
11: $m \leftarrow v_{best}$

Let V be the number of nodes in G. The Dijkstra's algorithm can run in nearly linear time [7], here Dijkstra has a time complexity in $O_D(V\ logV)$. The Eq. 11 gives the total worst-case complexity for Algorithm 1.

$$O_{total} = 3 * O_D(V\ logV) * V \tag{11}$$

A less naive version for finding the OMP consists of computing and storing all the shortest paths beforehand, and therefore all the travel times, to each of the intersections in the network from the two starting points of the users. Next, the objective function is evaluated on the basis of the calculated values as before. This version is given by the Algorithm 2 and greatly reduces the number of Dijkstra operations performed. The Eq. 12 gives the total worst-case complexity for Algorithm 2.

$$O_{total} = 3 * O_D(V\ logV) \tag{12}$$

Figures 3 and 4 show practical examples of results obtained with the Algorithm 2. In red, is the path taken by the driver u_d, in blue is the path taken by the pedestrian u_w, and in green is the path traveled together, i.e. the actual ride-sharing.

5 Our Contribution

In this section, we present the proposed heuristic version of the optimal algorithm presented in Sect. 4 and detail the methods used to achieve faster execution.

Algorithm 2. OMP - Optimal exact solution algorithm.

```
1: v_best ← None
2: t_best ← ∞
3: t_a^{u_w} ← dijkstraLabel(a)
4: t_b^{u_d} ← dijkstraLabel(b)
5: t_d^{u_d} ← dijkstraLabel(d)
6: for t_{a,b,d} ∈ [t_a^{u_w}, t_b^{u_d}, t_d^{u_d}] do
7:     t_max ← f(t_{a,v}^{u_w}, t_{b,v}^{u_d}, t_{v,d}^{u_d})
8:     if t_max < t_best then
9:         t_best ← t_max
10:        v_best ← v
11: m ← v_best
```

5.1 Multi-modal Pruning

To reduce the search space, we can take advantage of the multi-modal aspect of the problem. We can make the assumption that the meeting point must be accessible to both users u_w and u_d. Thus we can remove all road intersections v_i that are not common to both users, i.e. keeping only the nodes

Fig. 3. Example of a solution N°1 [2]. (Color figure online)

Fig. 4. Example of a solution N°2 [2]. (Color figure online)

Fig. 5. Nodes pruned to obtain $G = G_w - (G_w \cap G_d)$ graph [2]. (Color figure online)

Fig. 6. Nodes pruned to obtain $G = G_d - (G_w \cap G_d)$ graph [2].

$V = \{v_1, v_2, ..., v_n / v_i \in (G_w \cap G_d)$. An examples of deleted nodes are given in red, in Fig. 5 we show the nodes unreachable by car in the pedestrian network G_w and in Fig. 6 we show the nodes unreachable by walk in the car network G_d.

Since $|G_d - (G_w \cap G_d)| < |G_w - (G_w \cap G_d)|$ there are less nodes to delete, then the deleting process is faster.

For the resulting graph G for the study case of Brussels, compared with the G_w graph, this technique achieves an average reduction of 4.18% in the number of nodes and 4.65% in the number of edges. However, compared with G_d, this technique reduces the number of nodes by 1.092% and increases the number of edges by 1.032%. Since fewer road intersections are accessible by car, it is preferable in terms of execution time to prune the driving graph G_d rather than the walking graph G_w. The advantage of this technique is that the more different modal networks are integrated, such as the network of public transport stops, the more efficient the pruning will be. Indeed, the number of intersections common to all networks decreases with the number of transport modes taken into account.

5.2 Heuristic Algorithm

The main idea behind the Algorithm 3 is to reduce the search space of the OMP. To achieve this, we apply the following pre-processing: (1) First, we take the node located at the $\frac{1}{k}$ of the way along the shortest path between the two users a and b on the side of the walker, we name this intermediate node x. (2) We take the node located at the $\frac{1}{k}$ of the way along the shortest path between this node x and the destination d on the side of node x, and name this node y. (3) By using the $getNodesAtNSteps(N, y)$ function, we retrieve all nodes that are within N steps from the node y, Fig. 7 shows how this function works for values of N ranging from 0 to 3. (4) Finally, we give this set of nodes to the exact Algorithm 2, which searches for the OMP in this set rather than in the entire graph. Figure 8 shows a graphical representation of the selection of x and y nodes.

Algorithm 3. OMP - Heuristic algorithm.

1: $SP_{a,b} \leftarrow dijkstra(a, b)$
2: $x = SP_{a,b}[: len(SP_{a,b})//k]$
3: $SP_{x,d} \leftarrow dijkstra(v, d)$
4: $y = SP_{x,d}[: len(SP_{x,d})//k]$
5: $neighbors \leftarrow getNodesAtNSteps(N, y)$
6: $m \leftarrow Algorithm2(neighbors, a, b, d)$

Let $M = |neighbors|$, V be the number of nodes in G and a Dijkstra algorithm with a time complexity in $O_D(V\ logV)$. The Eq. 13 gives the total worst-case complexity for the Algorithm 3.

$$O_{total} = [2 * O_D(V\ logV)] + [3 * O_D(M\ logM)] \quad (13)$$

Since $M < V$ and only two Dijkstra calls are made on the entire graph, in the best case we can improve execution time for large graphs.

The k value should be chosen to be closest to the weakest (or slowest) user, i.e. the pedestrian. This has the effect of reducing the search space in the zone for which both users have an equivalent travel time. We call this value the $Xratio$ on the shortest path between the two users and the $Mratio$ for that on the shortest path between x and the destination. In the example of the Fig. 8, we have $\frac{1}{k} = Xratio = Mratio = \frac{1}{4}$. Different values of k and N have been tested in Sect. 6.3 to assess their correctness regarding the exact algorithm.

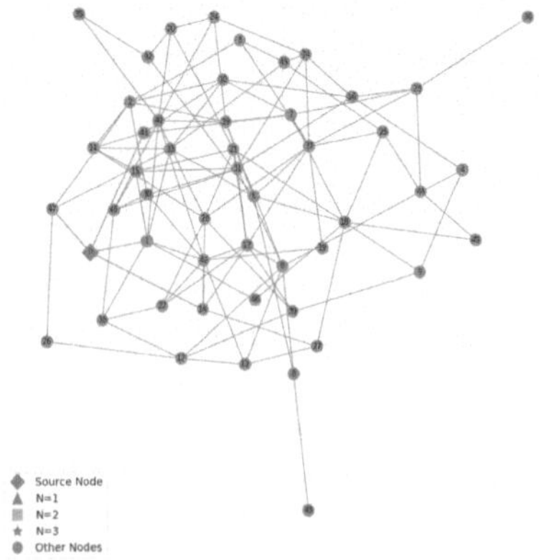

(a) $getNodesAtNSteps(N, y)$ with $N = 0$

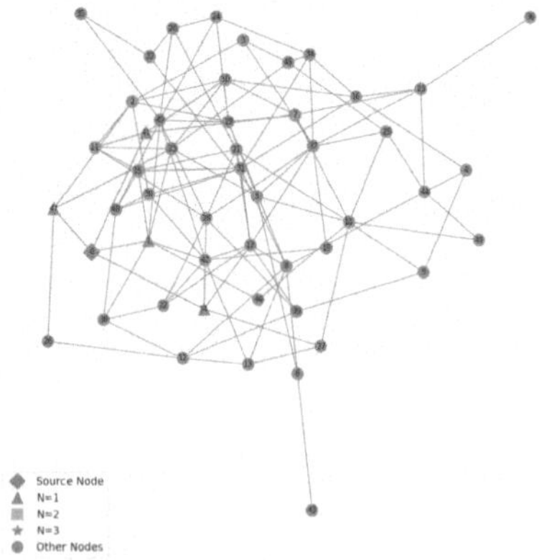

(b) $getNodesAtNSteps(N, y)$ with $N = 1$

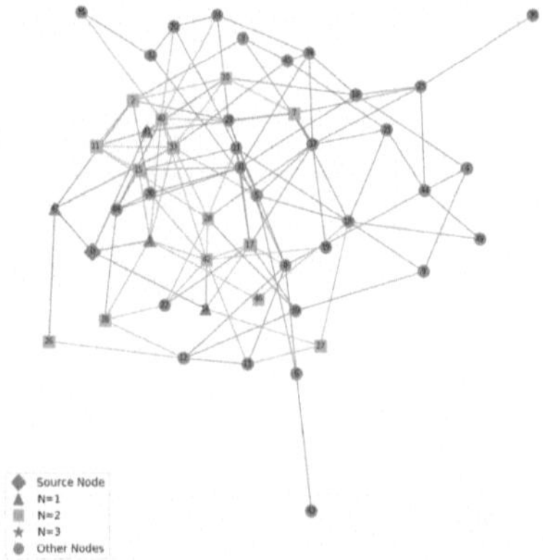

(c) $getNodesAtNSteps(N, y)$ with $N = 2$

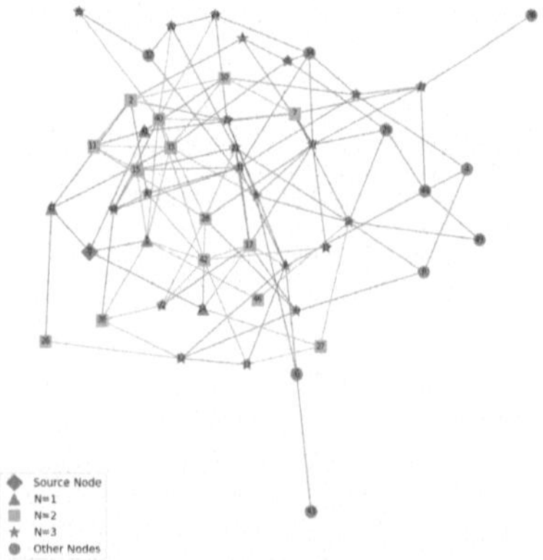

(d) $getNodesAtNSteps(N, y)$ with $N = 3$

Fig. 7. $getNodesAtNSteps$ for $N = [0, 1, 2, 3]$.

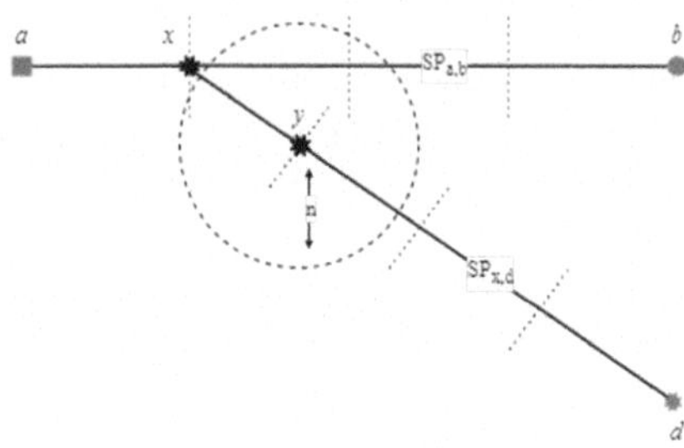

Fig. 8. Selection of the nodes x and y for pre-processing of the heuristic algorithm [2].

6 Results

In this section, the various results obtained are presented. All experiments were carried out on a Windows 11 machine equipped with an 8-core AMD Rizen 7 5800X processor with a frequency of 3.80 GHz and 32 GB of RAM. For the sake of quick prototyping, and despite its high resource requirements, the various algorithms have been written in Python 3.10.11. In the current version of the code, graphs are stored in the form of a dictionary of dictionaries via the NetworkX library [10]. For each experiment, we choose the starting point a for the walker and b for the driver randomly in G and we select a common destination point d randomly in G as well.

Table 1 shows a set of small cities in Belgium. These data were used to quickly test the results obtained by the different algorithms. Table 2 shows the properties of the different larger road networks which are also evaluated in this section.

Table 1. Dataset of small graphs from Belgium [2].

G	Nodes	Edges	Max deg	Avg. deg
LOM (Lommel, Belgium)	1716	4173	8	4.86
MEC (Mechelen, Belgium)	1954	4393	8	4.50
MOU (Mouscron, Belgium)	1957	4389	8	4.49
LEV (Leuven, Belgium)	2390	5296	9	4.43
TOU (Tournai, Belgium)	2770	6407	9	4.63
MON (Mons, Belgium)	3002	6620	10	4.41

Table 2. Dataset of large graphs [2].

G	Nodes	Edges	Max deg	Avg. deg
BRU (Brussels, Belgium)	3040	6961	10	4.57
BAR (Barcelona, Spain)	8870	16518	9	3.72
PAR (Paris, France)	9602	18523	10	3.86
BER (Berlin, Germany)	28003	73031	12	5.22
ROM (Rome, Italy)	43168	89595	10	4.15
NY (New York, USA)	55335	139652	11	5.05

6.1 Objective Function Evaluation

In this section, we compare the effects of the different objective functions proposed in Sect. 3.1 on the results given by the exact solution. For each objective

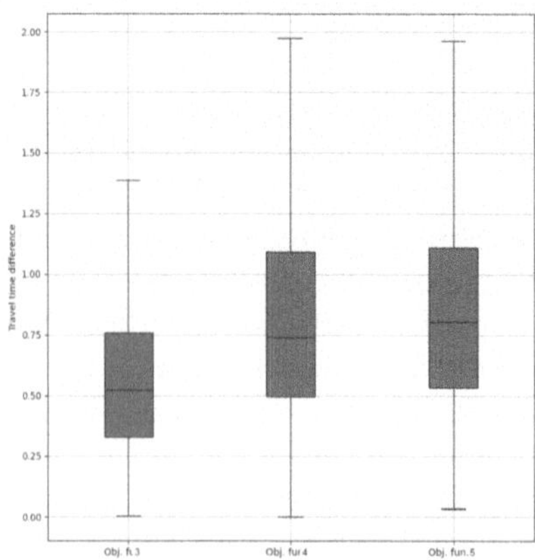

Fig. 9. Difference in travel time between driver and walker to joint the meeting point for each the objective functions on Dataset 1.

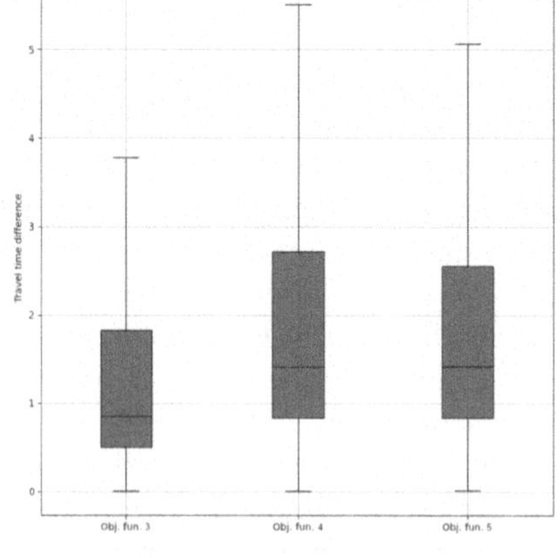

Fig. 10. Difference in travel time between driver and walker to joint the meeting point for each the objective functions on Dataset 2.

function, we compare the total travel time for the passenger with the one of the driver. As in [13], we have assumed 4.5km/h for the travel speed of the walker (passenger), and we take the maximum speed allowed on the roads for the travel speed of the driver.

Figures 9 and 10 show the difference in travel time between the two users to reach the OMP over 100 random iterations on the different road networks. These figures show that for the objective Function 3, the average difference between the travel times of the two users is smaller than in the case of the objective Functions 4 and 5.

Figures 11 and 12 show the difference between the travel time of the shortest path from the source to the destination and the travel time of the path passing through the OMP, i.e. carpooling, to join the destination. For both figures, the time differences are separate for each user and compute over 100 random iterations on the different real road networks. In Figs. 11 and 12, the negative values indicate that the travel time by ride-sharing is shorter than the direct path, and inversely for the positive values. For three objective functions, on average, the application of a ride-sharing path is largely beneficial in terms of pedestrian travel time $t^{u_w}_{a,d}$ compared with the time he takes to cover the direct shortest path to the destination. We note that on average ride-sharing represents a loss of time for the car user $t^{u_d}_{b,d}$ compared with the direct shortest path to the destination, this is due to a detour to the OMP. However, in practice, this difference should be limited since it is rare for cars to be able to travel at the maximum speed allowed on the roads, due to traffic jams in big cities, in addition to regular stops at red traffic lights and others.

In the remainder of this article, the objective Function 3 has been chosen by default for the heuristic and the exact algorithm, as it is the one that gives

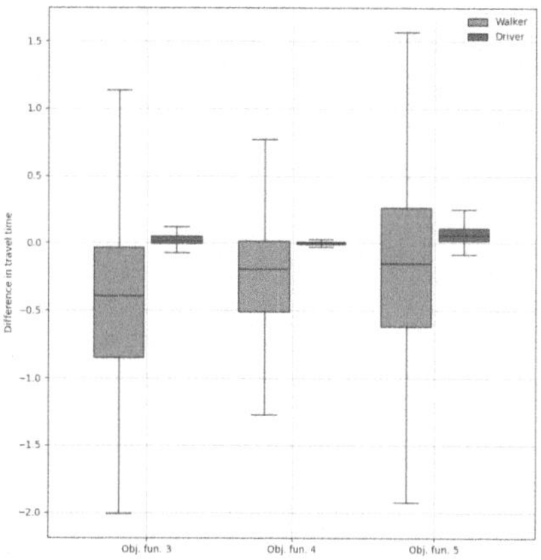

Fig. 11. Difference in travel time between shortest path and for and ride-sharing path for each the objective functions on Dataset 1.

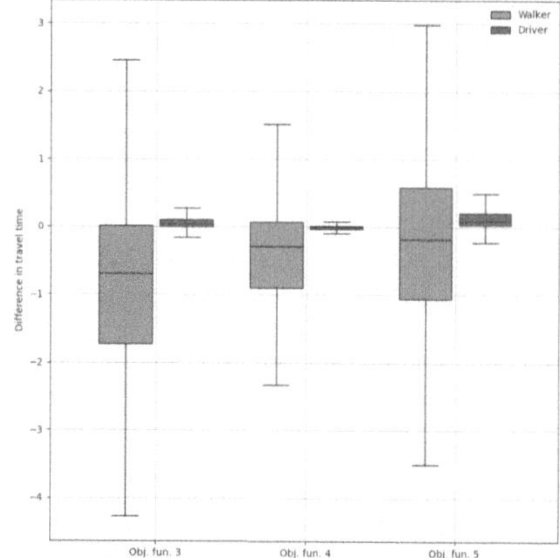

Fig. 12. Difference in travel time between shortest path and for and ride-sharing path for each the objective functions on Dataset 2.

the smallest average difference in travel time between both users involved in ride-sharing, i.e. the fairest. Also, this objective function allows pedestrians to save the most time compared with their initial journey. Thus, we extend the definition of the optimal meeting point (OMP) to the meeting point for which the travel times of users are fair.

6.2 Run Time

In this section, we compare the execution time of the variants of the heuristic Algorithm 3 with the exact solution over 100 random iterations on the different real road networks.

Table 3 gives the average execution time depending on N for each graph in Dataset 1. We note that on small graphs of ≈ 2500 nodes, only the version of the heuristic algorithm with $N = 20$, or less, speeds up the time needed to find the OMP.

Table 4 gives the average execution time depending on N for each graph in Dataset 2. We note that the algorithm heuristic becomes quicker than the exact algorithm for graphs with a number of nodes $|G| >\approx 10000$ and values of $N \leq 50$.

For both datasets, we observe that the execution time of the heuristic algorithm depends directly on the value of N chosen. Also, for each experiment, all execution times are below 1 s on average, showing that the algorithm can indeed be used in real time. Finally, we can see that the smaller the value of N, the shorter the execution time, but a low value of N also has downside effects, as we show in Sect. 6.3 (Figs. 13 and 14).

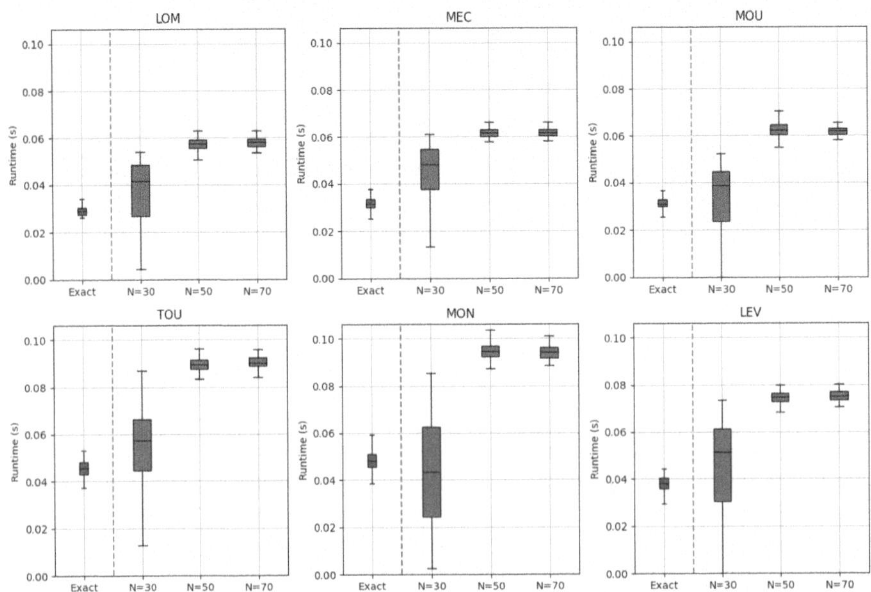

Fig. 13. Average run time (seconds) on Dataset 1 for $N = 30$, $N = 50$ and $N = 70$.

Table 3. Run time (seconds) on Dataset 1 depending on N value [2].

G	N = 20	N = 30	N = 40	N = 50	N = 60	N = 70	Exact
LOM	0.0214	0.0388	0.0518	0.057	0.0567	0.0587	**0.0209**
MEC	**0.019**	0.0443	0.0608	0.0601	0.0601	0.0645	0.0231
MOU	**0.0161**	0.0387	0.0561	0.0593	0.0626	0.0605	0.0221
LEV	**0.0257**	0.0533	0.0713	0.0757	0.0775	0.0755	0.0282
TOU	**0.0199**	0.0562	0.0818	0.0859	0.0901	0.0922	0.033
MON	**0.0181**	0.0537	0.0829	0.0923	0.0968	0.0987	0.0347
Total	**0.02**	0.0475	0.0674	0.0717	0.0739	0,075	0.027

Table 4. Run time (seconds) on Dataset 2 depending on N value [2].

G	N = 30	N = 40	N = 50	N = 60	N = 70	N = 100	Exact
BRU	0.0696	0.0954	0.1006	0.1003	0.1018	0.1012	**0.0356**
BAR	**0.06**	0.1296	0.1759	0.2197	0.2717	0.2799	0.0987
PAR	**0.0547**	0.1181	0.1905	0.2506	0.2932	0.3028	0.1144
BER	**0.1122**	**0.2603**	**0.4199**	0.6353	0.7869	1.1125	0.4738
ROM	**0.0948**	**0.2758**	**0.5337**	0.8632	1.2001	1.5273	0.6365
NY	**0.1839**	**0.5296**	**0.9135**	1.3986	1.8006	2.1712	0.9224
Total	**0.0958**	**0.2348**	0.389	0.7248	0.7423	0.9158	0.3802

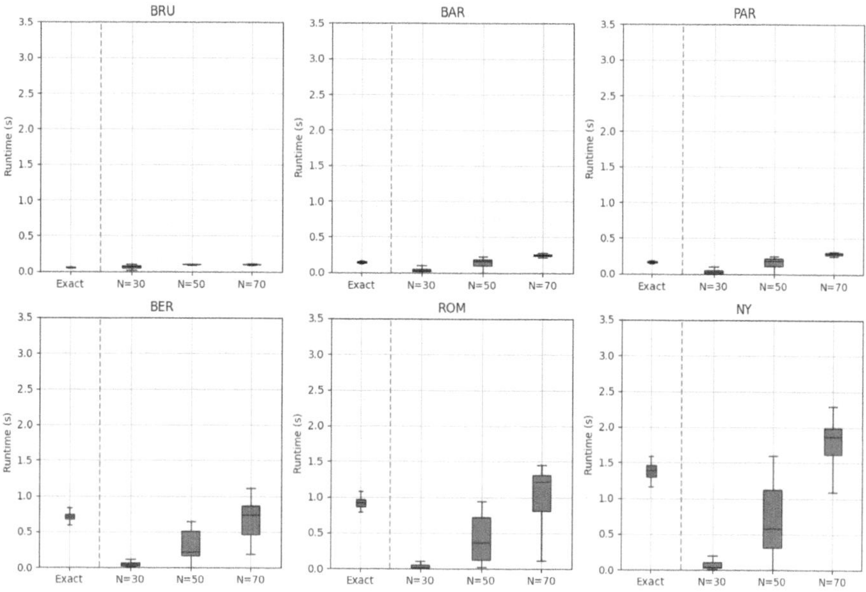

Fig. 14. Average run time (seconds) on Dataset 2 for $N = 30$, $N = 50$ and $N = 70$.

6.3 Solution Correctness and Quality

In this section, we compare the results of the exact algorithm with the results obtained by the heuristic algorithm.

The approximation error $\bar{\epsilon}_N$ is calculated by taking the difference between the length of the shortest path SP to the candidate point m for the OMP found by the proposed algorithm and the length of the shortest path to the exact OMP em over k random iterations for the parameter N. Equation 14 formulates the error used in the remainder of this section.

$$\bar{\epsilon}_N = \frac{1}{k} \sum_{i=1}^{k} \left| lenght(SP_{a,m}^{(i)}) - lenght(SP_{a,em}^{(i)}) \right| \tag{14}$$

In other words, the error $\bar{\epsilon}_N$ gives the average difference in number of road intersections between the solution found by the heuristic algorithm and the solution found by the exact algorithm. This error can therefore reach values superior to 1. Note that other measures such as the difference in travel time or distance can also be considered.

Effect *Xratio* and *Mratio* on Solution Quality. In order to evaluate which values of $Xratio$ and $Mratio$ produce the best quality solutions for the heuristic algorithm, we tested ratio values k in $[2, 4, 8, 12, 16, 32, 64]$ with $Xratio =$

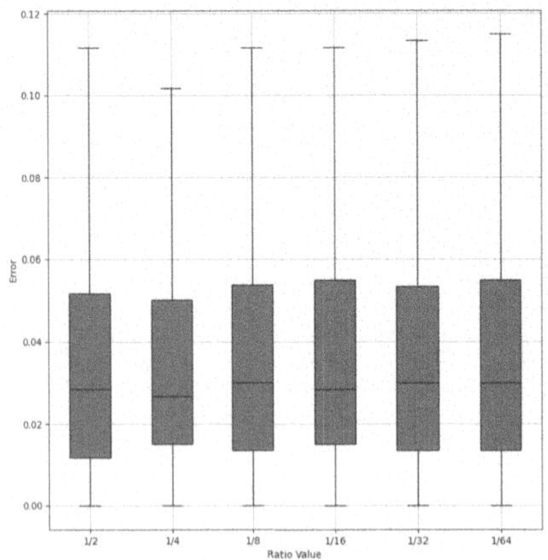

Fig. 15. Average error of approximation on Dataset 1 for $Xratio = Mratio = [\frac{1}{2}, \frac{1}{4}, \frac{1}{8}, \frac{1}{16}, \frac{1}{32}, \frac{1}{64}]$.

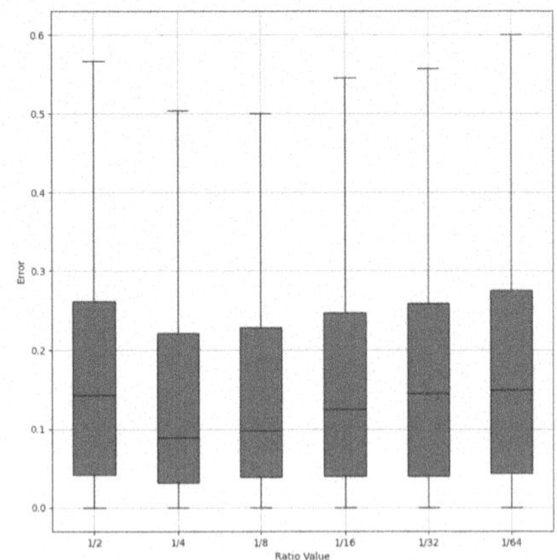

Fig. 16. Average error of approximation on Dataset 2 for $Xratio = Mratio = [\frac{1}{2}, \frac{1}{4}, \frac{1}{8}, \frac{1}{16}, \frac{1}{32}, \frac{1}{64}]$.

$Mratio$ over 100 random iterations on the real road networks. Figure 15 shows the average number of incorrect solutions found by the heuristic algorithm with $N = 50$ for the Dataset 1 and Fig. 16 shows the results for the Dataset 2 with the same values for N and k.

For both Datasets, 1 and 2, $k = 4$ is the value for which the error is minimized. We note that on average the number of errors is higher for Dataset 2, this is due to the value of N chosen for this experiment, more details are given in Sect. 6.3. Thus, it seems that $Xratio = Mratio = \frac{1}{4}$ is the optimal value for the both datasets tested. In addition, the value chosen for $Xratio = Mratio$ has no effect on the execution time of the algorithm.

Effect of N on Solution Quality. Figure 17 shows the average error obtained by variants of the algorithm heuristic compared to the exact algorithm over 100 random iterations on the Dataset 1 with $Xratio = Mratio = \frac{1}{4}$. Figure 18 shows the average error obtained by variants of the algorithm heuristic compared to the exact algorithm over 100 random iterations on the Dataset 2 with $Xratio = Mratio = \frac{1}{4}$.

Thanks to the Table 5, we note that with $N \geq 40$ and over the heuristic Algorithm 3 manages to find the same solution as the exact Algorithm 2 for the small graph Dataset 1 in at least 94% of the cases, but this is at the expense of execution time.

Thanks to the Table 6, we note that with $N \geq 100$ and over the heuristic Algorithm 3 manages to find the same solution as the exact Algorithm 2 for the large graph Dataset 2 in at least 97% of the cases, but this is also at the expense of execution time.

For both datasets, the quality of the heuristic algorithm solutions depends directly on the value of N chosen, the approximation error increases as N

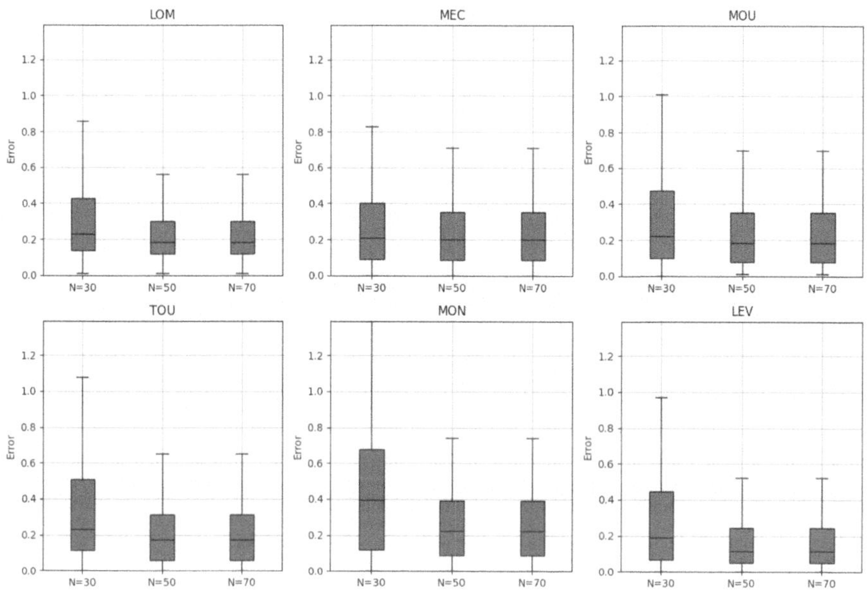

Fig. 17. Average error of approximation on Dataset 1 for $N = 30$, $N = 50$ and $N = 70$.

Table 5. Percent of correct solutions depending on N value for Dataset 1 [2].

Network	N = 20	N = 30	N = 40	N = 50	N = 60	N = 70
LOM	0.52	0.82	0.95	0.99	1	1
MEC	0.51	0.9	0.99	0.99	1	1
MOU	0.39	0.71	0.9	0.98	0.98	0.98
LEV	0.46	0.77	0.91	0.97	0.97	0.97
TOU	0.38	0.83	0.97	0.98	0.98	0.98
MON	0.24	0.66	0.97	0.98	0.98	0.98
Total	0.416	0.782	**0.948**	**0.982**	**0.985**	**0.985**

Table 6. Percent of correct solutions depending on N value for Dataset 2 [2].

Network	N = 30	N = 40	N = 50	N = 60	N = 70	N = 100
BRU	0.83	0.96	0.97	0.97	0.97	0.97
BAR	0.33	0.66	0.81	0.91	0.93	0.94
PAR	0.27	0.54	0.79	0.9	0.92	0.95
BER	0.15	0.28	0.51	0.63	0.74	0.97
ROM	0.02	0.2	0.41	0.63	0.82	1
NY	0.1	0.31	0.5	0.76	0.88	0.98
Total	0.283	0.492	0.665	0.8	0.876	**0.968**

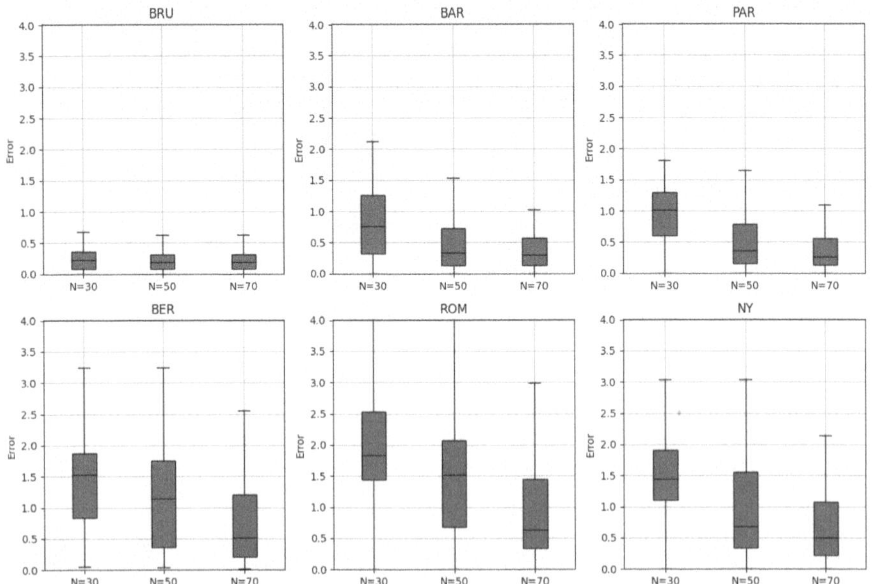

Fig. 18. Average error of approximation on Dataset 2 for $N = 30$, $N = 50$ and $N = 70$.

decreases. Indeed, the more we extend the search area, the more likely we are to find the OMP within it. It can also be seen that the larger the network studied, the higher the value of N must be chosen to achieve a high percentage of correct solutions.

Trade-Off Between Solution Quality and Runtime. The optimal value of N is the one for which the algorithm is balanced between the execution time t_N and the error $\bar{\epsilon}_N$. Thus, the optimal of N, N_{opt}, should satisfies the Eq. 15.

$$N_{opt} = \min_{N} Cost(N) \tag{15}$$

The $Cost$ function of the heuristic algorithm is defined by the Eq. 16 where w is a weight parameter that allows to adjust the balance between quality $1 - \epsilon_N$ and runtime.

$$Cost(N) = w \times (1 - \bar{\epsilon}_N) - (1 - w) \times t_N \tag{16}$$

Thanks to Tables 3 and 5, we note that for smaller networks there is no advantage in using our algorithm instead of the exact solution as our algorithm is slower in the majority of cases studied. However, thanks to the Tables 4 and 6 and according to the Eq. 15 and 16 with $w = 0.5$, for large networks, we found that $N_{opt} = 50$ is the perfect compromise between speed and quality among the tested datasets and values of N.

6.4 Performances Under Extreme Conditions

We conducted the same experiments as those described in Sects. 6.2 and 6.3 on the entire road network of Belgium. This network has 7.13 times more nodes and 6.72 times more edges than the largest previously tested network, namely New York. Details concerning the road network are given in Table 7. The objective of this final experiment is to evaluate the proposed algorithm under extreme conditions.

Table 7. Belgium road network.

G	Nodes	Edges	Max deg	Avg. deg
BEL (Belgium)	395045	938624	14	4.75

From Fig. 19, we observe that even for large values of N, our algorithm successfully identifies the fair meeting point in a shorter time compared to the exact algorithm. We can conclude that the reduction in running time compare to the exact algorithm becomes even more significant as the network size $|G|$ increases. However, in this specific case, a real-time application of the heuristic algorithm is only feasible for values of $N \leq 50$.

Figure 20 shows that the average error, measured by the number of intersections, ranges between 1 and 3.5 for all tested value of N. Based on previous results, we can conclude that as the network size increases, the approximation error also grows for a given N value.

These two experiments conducted under extreme conditions allow us to conclude that the proposed algorithm maintains its properties, even when faced with larger-scale constraints.

7 Future Works and Materials

In future research, we would like to extend the scope of this study by including more users and other modes of transport, to better reflect real-world carpooling conditions. It would be essential to remove the requirement for users to start their journeys simultaneously because this constraint is not realistic in practice. As done for example by [17] or [3], we would like to take potential waiting times of the passenger into account. Also, it would be interesting to solve this problem from the point of view of MST or MPP and compare the results with the current version using OMP. Finally, we would like to experiment with the impact of $Xratio \neq Mratio$ on solution quality, as well as more efficient programming language or data structures for the graphs.

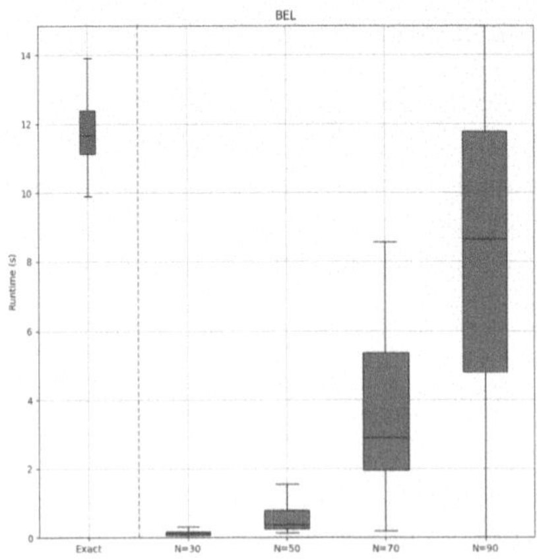

Fig. 19. Average run time (seconds) on Network 7 for $N = 30$, $N = 50$, $N = 70$ and $N = 90$.

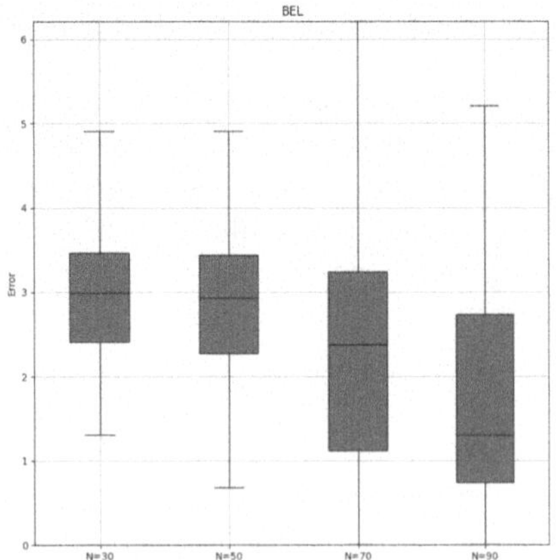

Fig. 20. Average error of approximation on Network 7 for $N = 30$, $N = 50$, $N = 70$ and $N = 90$.

In order to enable repeatability of the results is available in open access, you can send an email to julien.baudru@ulb.be to obtain access to the GitHub repository.

8 Conclusion

We have proposed a heuristic algorithm that reduces the search space through pruning, leveraging the multi-modal nature of carpooling and an approximation of the optimal meeting point (OMP) location. Our results show that, unlike the exact solution, the execution time of the heuristic algorithm is almost unaffected by the size of the road network. In the best case for large networks dataset, the algorithm finds the OMP 5.01 times faster than the exact solution, with an average relative error of approximately 1.5 road intersections. Even for small values of N, our algorithm consistently produces solutions that differ by at most 2 road intersections, on average, from the exact solution. We have also demonstrated that the algorithm is particularly effective for large-scale road networks with node counts exceeding 10,000. Additionally, our solution is applicable in real time for small values of $N < 50$ in road networks comprising approximately 400,000 nodes and 940,000 edges, the Belgium road network. In conclusion, the proposed algorithm efficiently approximates the OMP by minimizing travel time differences between users while providing optimal paths for them to meet and continue to their shared destination.

Acknowledgements. This project was supported by the FARI - AI for the Common Good Institute (ULB-VUB), financed by the European Union, with the support of the Brussels Capital Region (Innoviris and Paradigm). Thanks to Brice Petit and Lluc Bono Rosselló from IRIDIA for their feedback and suggestions.

References

1. Abraham, I., Delling, D., Fiat, A., Goldberg, A.V., Werneck, R.F.: Highway dimension and provably efficient shortest path algorithms. J. ACM **63**(5) (2016). https://doi.org/10.1145/2985473
2. Baudru, J., Bersini, H.: Heuristic optimal meeting point algorithm for car-sharing in large multimodal road networks. In: Proceedings of the 10th International Conference on Vehicle Technology and Intelligent Transport Systems - Volume 1: VEHITS, pp. 427–436. INSTICC, SciTePress (2024). https://doi.org/10.5220/0012719100003702
3. Bilali, A., Dandl, F., Fastenrath, U., Bogenberger, K.: An analytical model for on-demand ride sharing to evaluate the impact of reservation, detour and maximum waiting time, pp. 1715–1720 (2019). https://doi.org/10.1109/ITSC.2019.8917280
4. Bruglieri, M., Ciccarelli, D., Colorni, A., Luè, A.: Poliunipool: a carpooling system for universities. Procedia - Soc. Behav. Sci. **20**, 558–567 (2011). https://doi.org/10.1016/j.sbspro.2011.08.062. https://www.sciencedirect.com/science/article/pii/S187704281101442X, the State of the Art in the European Quantitative Oriented Transportation and Logistics Research – 14th Euro Working Group on Transportation & 26th Mini Euro Conference & 1st European Scientific Conference on Air Transport
5. Buchhold, V., Sanders, P., Wagner, D.: Fast, Exact and Scalable Dynamic Ridesharing, pp. 98–112 (2021). https://doi.org/10.1137/1.9781611976472.8
6. Collette, S., Iacono, J.: Distances and shortest paths on graphs of bounded highway dimension: simple, fast, dynamic, pp. 2657–2678. https://doi.org/10.1137/1.9781611977912.95
7. Dijkstra, E.: A note on two problems in connexion with graphs. Numerische Mathematik **1**, 269–271 (1959). http://eudml.org/doc/131436
8. Gedam, C., Sahare, M., Sachdeo, R., Kulkarni, N.: Smart transportation based car pooling system. In: E3S Web Conference, vol. 170, p. 03004 (2020). https://doi.org/10.1051/e3sconf/202017003004
9. Gärling, T., Gärling, A., Johansson, A.: Household choices of car-use reduction measures. Transp. Res. Part A: Policy Pract. **34**(5), 309–320 (2000)
10. Hagberg, A., Swart, P., S Chult, D.: Exploring network structure, dynamics, and function using networkx. Technical report, Los Alamos National Lab. (LANL), Los Alamos, NM (United States) (2008)
11. Huang, W., Zhang, Y., Shang, Z., Yu, J.X.: To meet or not to meet: finding the shortest paths in road networks. IEEE Trans. Knowl. Data Eng. **30**(4), 772–785 (2018). https://doi.org/10.1109/TKDE.2017.2777851
12. Rodenbach, J., Seeuws, B., Matthijs, J.: Impact report, car-sharing in Belgium in 2022 (2022). https://www.autodelen.net/wp-content/uploads/2023/03/Impact-report-Car-sharing-in-Belgium-in-2022.pdf
13. Laupichler, M., Sanders, P.: Fast many-to-many routing for ridesharing with multiple pickup and dropoff locations (2023)
14. Li, R.H., Qin, L., Yu, J.X., Mao, R.: Optimal multi-meeting-point route search. IEEE Trans. Knowl. Data Eng. **28**(3), 770–784 (2016). https://doi.org/10.1109/TKDE.2015.2492554
15. Luè, A., Colorni, A.: A software tool for commute carpooling: a case study on university students in Milan. Int. J. Serv. Sci. **2** (2009). https://doi.org/10.1504/IJSSCI.2009.026540

16. Masoud, N., Jayakrishnan, R.: A real-time algorithm to solve the peer-to-peer ride-matching problem in a flexible ridesharing system. Transp. Res. Part B: Methodol. **106**, 218–236 (2017)
17. Psaraftis, H.N.: A dynamic programming solution to the single vehicle many-to-many immediate request dial-a-ride problem. Transp. Sci. **14**(2), 130–154 (1980). http://www.jstor.org/stable/25767975
18. Toth, P., Vigo, D., Toth, P., Vigo, D.: Vehicle Routing: Problems, Methods, and Applications, 2nd edn. (2014)
19. Wu, L., Xiao, X., Deng, D., Cong, G., Zhu, A.D., Zhou, S.: Shortest path and distance queries on road networks: an experimental evaluation. CoRR abs/1201.6564 (2012). http://arxiv.org/abs/1201.6564
20. Wu, T., Xu, M.: Modeling and optimization for carsharing services: a literature review. Multimodal Transp. **1**(3), 100028 (2022)
21. Xu, Z., Jacobsen, H., et al.: Processing proximity relations in road networks, pp. 243–254 (2010). https://doi.org/10.1145/1807167.1807196
22. Yan, D., Zhao, Z., Ng, W.: Efficient algorithms for finding optimal meeting point on road networks. Proc. VLDB Endow. **4**(11), 968–979 (2011). https://doi.org/10.14778/3402707.3402734
23. Yu, B., et al.: Environmental benefits from ridesharing: a case of Beijing. Appl. Energy **191**, 141–152 (2017)

Enhancing Trajectories from Collective Perception Messages for Performance Measurements at Signalized Intersections

Michael Klöppel-Gersdorf(✉), Adrien Bellanger, Ina Partzsch, and Thomas Otto

Fraunhofer IVI Institute for Transportation and Infrastructure Systems, Dresden, Germany
{michael.kloeppel-gersdorf,adrien.bellanger,ina.partzsch, thomas.otto}@ivi.fraunhofer.de

Abstract. While Vehicle-to-Everything (V2X) messages from connected vehicles can act as reliable data sources in real-time road infrastructure monitoring, their low penetration rates cannot guarantee a continuous monitoring in practice. Here, Collective Perception (CP), especially from infrastructure units, can help to bridge the gap. Unfortunately, objects detected by infrastructure are inherently more noisy and, often, a complete trajectory over an intersection cannot be obtained. To overcome this problem, we present an approach to augment trajectories collected by CP with data gathered from connected vehicles, thereby allowing a continuous monitoring.

Keywords: Vehicle-to-everything communication · ITS-G5 · Intersections · Intersection monitoring · Trajectory prediction

1 Introduction

With the ever increasing traffic and limited resources for new traffic infrastructure, the need to optimize existing road networks arises. The first step in this optimization is to detect bottle necks by continuously monitoring the infrastructure. While this can be done with already existing or additional new sensors, these cover only points in space (e.g., induction loops), rely on optimal visual circumstances (e.g., cameras) or add considerable costs for equipment as well as operation (e.g., radar and lidar sensors).

One approach to overcome these obstacles is to use already existing data transmitted by connected vehicles and infrastructure, thereby reducing the costs and also allowing an ad-hoc installation without integration in already existing systems. In the following, the special case of signalized intersections will be considered, although the approach can easily be extended to other traffic elements. In general, there exists a wide variety of performance parameters for signalized intersections [12], one of which is Level of Service (LoS) [1,15]. Retrieving traffic information from connected vehicles is not a new idea, as this was already proposed to determine arrival rates [17] or queue lengths [7], which are also metrics connected with quality of service at an intersection. In a previous paper, LoS determination from Cooperative Awareness Message (CAM) or

F. Calise et al. (Eds.): SMARTGREENS 2024/VEHITS 2024, CCIS 2954, pp. 217–227, 2026.
https://doi.org/10.1007/978-3-032-23187-1_12

Basic Safety Message (BSM) was already considered [11]. While this is feasible in theory, today's low penetration of connected vehicles currently does not allow a continuous monitoring. To overcome these shortcomings, Collective Perception (CP) can be used. The main idea of Collective Perception Message (CPM) is to transmit information about objects perceived by vehicle or infrastructure to increase safety [13]. In this way, not only connected vehicles can be detected but also other traffic participants in sensor range. As of now, no commercially available vehicle transmits such information, therefore the focus is on infrastructure elements and especially connected and sensing intersections. Such intersections are available in several European cities as part of the C-Roads project and other research projects, where they are used to implement the Vulnerable Road User (VRU) protection use case. As the protection of VRUs has a high importance (e.g., there is an increase in bicycle incidents in Germany [14]), the appearance of even more such systems is likely.

As the goal of connected and sensing infrastructure is currently based on VRU protection, there are several issues which have to be tackled to make the obtained data also available for monitoring tasks. These issues include partial trajectories (i.e., the object could not be tracked across the whole intersection), occlusion (i.e., sensors cannot perceive the whole intersection area) as well as sensor specific issues (e.g., it is very difficult to obtain 3D-positions from single camera images or the camera is only calibrated for certain areas).

In this paper, we propose an approach that leverages the high reliability of CAM-based trajectories to enhance and complete the potentially corrupted CPM-based trajectories, thereby providing a comprehensive real-time picture of movements at an urban intersection. The approach will be demonstrated at an existing signalized and connected intersection in the city of Dresden, Germany. This paper is an extension of a previously published paper [10].

The paper is organized as follows: In the next section, our approach will be introduced, followed by results from a real intersection in Sect. 3. The paper is concluded in Sect. 4.

2 Approach

In this section, the proposed approach is discussed in detail, starting with the data sources (V2X messages), followed by the description of the clustering algorithm for CAM and, finally, by describing how the clusters can be used to augment partial trajectories from CPM.

2.1 Data Sources

For the proposed approach we rely on the European V2X messages CAM, CPM, and Map Extended Message (MAPEM).

For the clustering step (see below), CAMs [3] transmitted by commercial vehicles are used, as these are rather accurate (The connected vehicles on the road today typically report a position error of approx. 3 m). At the time of writing, about 0.5% of all vehicles at the test side use V2X technology based on ETSI ITS-G5. From all information available in Cooperative Awareness Message (CAM) (e.g., dynamic state but also status of turn indicators) only the position information and the station id is used. Using these two data points a trajectory can be obtained. Although the station id changes every 60 s for privacy reasons, this does not overly influence the collection of data. While it would be possible to stitch together trajectories after a change of id, at least at the low penetration rates present today, the standard discourages from doing so. As such, trajectories with changing ids are discarded.

Due to the low penetration of connected vehicles, objects sensed by infrastructure can be used as a replacement data source. Such sensed objects can be communicated using the CPM [6], which was specified by ETSI in 2023. It can be used to relay object information in a local coordinate system centered at the sensing entity. Similar to CAMs, CPM contains a position and object id per detected object which allow to obtain trajectories for every detected object. The CPM contains also a category to be able to differentiate VRUs from vehicles. Even if the size of the message is limited, the object inclusions rules proposed by ETSI [6] assure that all objects are sending at least once per second, and changes with a big influence on the object trajectory should be send as soon as possible. A visualization of CPM objects can be found in Fig. 1.

Last, the MAPEM [5] is used to extract information about the intersection layout, especially the lane layout and the associated driving maneuvers (straight, left, right, u-turn). While this annotation is optional in the standard, it is mandated by regulations (e.g., the European Handbook for MAPEM and SPATEM creation[1]). The MAPEM content of an example intersection can also be found in Fig. 1. Additionally, the dynamic traffic light state obtained from the Signal, Phase and Timing Extended Message (SPATEM) [5] is also shown. Actually, the SPATEM could provide further information on the intersection (e.g., allowing to detect red light violations), but was not considered as a data source in this study.

2.2 Trajectory Clustering

In this section, the methodology for clustering trajectories is described. Here, a trajectory is considered to be a sequence of two dimensional coordinates, i.e.,

$$T = (\boldsymbol{x}_0, \ldots, \boldsymbol{x}_n) . \tag{1}$$

Since we are not interested in the dynamical behavior of the traffic participants, any temporal information is dropped from the trajectories. In clustering, a set of complete (i.e., crossing the whole intersection) trajectories

$$\{T_1, \ldots, T_m\} \tag{2}$$

is used.

For trajectory clustering we rely on the work described in [10], which proposed a clustering and prediction approach based on the works of Bannerjee et al. [2] and Wu et

[1] https://www.c-roads.eu/platform/about/news/News/entry/show/release-20-of-c-roads-harmonised-c-its-specifications.html, visited on 2024-09-05.

al. [16]. The main idea is using a hierarchical clustering scheme, where in the first step the net movement vector of the trajectories, defined by

$$\boldsymbol{m}(T) = \boldsymbol{x}_n - \boldsymbol{x}_0, \tag{3}$$

is compared to predefined principal vectors $p_0, \ldots, p_k$, describing the straight motion over the intersection. More clearly, the cosine given by

$$\cos(\angle(\boldsymbol{m}(T), \boldsymbol{p}_i)) = \frac{\langle \boldsymbol{m}(T), \boldsymbol{p}_i \rangle}{\|\boldsymbol{m}(T)\| \|\boldsymbol{p}_i\|}, i = 0, \ldots, k, \tag{4}$$

where $\langle \cdot, \cdot \rangle$ denotes the scalar product, is used to separate straight movements from turns and also to derive the general direction of motion. In the original paper [10], these principal vectors were determined manually. In the current approach, these vectors are generated directly from the geometry given in the MAPEM. Using such information allows the approach to easily scale to any connected intersection.

After this first step, movements are already separated in straight movements and turning movements. Still, traffic on multi-lane streets are still in one cluster. In addition, turning movements need to be separated, as, e.g., a turn from west to north actually has a similar net vector of movement $\boldsymbol{m}(T)$ as a turn from south to east.

In a next step, the turning movements and the streams along the two-lane streets need to be separated. Let the length of a trajectory T be defined as

$$length(T) = \sum_{i=1}^{n} \|\boldsymbol{x}_i - \boldsymbol{x}_{i-1}\|. \tag{5}$$

Then, similar to [16], the distance between two trajectories can defined as

$$dist(T_1, T_2) = \frac{area(T_1, T_2)}{length(T_1) + length(T_2)}, \tag{6}$$

where the $area(\cdot, \cdot)$ is defined by the area of the polygon generated by the two trajectories, i.e., if $T_1 = (\boldsymbol{x}_0^1, \ldots, \boldsymbol{x}_{n_1}^1)$ and $T_2 = (\boldsymbol{x}_0^2, \ldots, \boldsymbol{x}_{n_2}^2)$, the area of the polygon $(\boldsymbol{x}_0^1, \ldots, \boldsymbol{x}_{n_1}^1, \boldsymbol{x}_{n_2}^2, \ldots, \boldsymbol{x}_0^2)$. Note that the coordinates of the second trajectory are reversed here. This area can be computed by geometric packages like Shapely in Python [8].

For turning movements, usually two clusters need to be separated. This can be done by choosing one trajectory randomly and, for all trajectories in the cluster $T_1, \ldots, T_l$, calculating the distance to the reference trajectory is computed. Trajectories following a similar movement will show only minimal distance in comparison to movements on the other side of the intersection. Both clusters can then easily be separated using a simple threshold for distance.

Separating the two-lane traffic uses a four-step procedure. Starting with a randomly chosen reference trajectory T_1, the distances to all other trajectories in this cluster are computed. In the first step, a trajectory T^{b_1} is computed as

$$T^{b_1} = \arg \max_{T = T_2, \ldots, T_m} dist(T_1, T). \tag{7}$$

In the second step, the trajectory T^{b_2} is computed as

$$T^{b_2} = \arg \max_{T=T_1,\dots,T_m} dist(T^{b_1}, T). \tag{8}$$

As a third step, the distance of all trajectories to T^{b_1} and T^{b_2} are calculated. Finally, the trajectories are clustered depending on whether they are closer to T^{b_1} or T^{b_2}.

The last step of the clustering algorithm consists of determining reference trajectories for all clusters, which is computed as the central element of a cluster. The approach used is similar to the procedure used for separating two-lane traffic. Again, a trajectory T^{b_1} is determined as above. Next, the distance $dist(T^{b_1}, \cdot)$ is determined for all trajectories inside the cluster. The reference trajectory is then chosen as the trajectory with median distance to T^{b_1}. This results in a set of reference trajectories $\{R_1, \dots, R_s\}$, where s is the number of different driving relations at the signalized intersection.

2.3 Collective Perception Message (CPM) Trajectory Completion

Similarly to [10], the calculated trajectory clusters can be used to enhance and complete partial trajectories from CPM. For a partial trajectory P, candidate clusters are determined as

$$\{R \in \{R_1, \dots, R_s\} : weighteddist(P, R) < d_t\} \tag{9}$$

where d_t is a distance threshold and $weighteddist(\cdot, \cdot)$ is defined as follows:

$$ADE(T_1, T_2) = n^{-1} \sum_{i=0}^{n} algebraicdist(\boldsymbol{x}_i^1, T_2), \tag{10}$$

$$FDE(T_1, T_2) = algebraicdist(\boldsymbol{x}_n^1, T_2), \tag{11}$$

where $algebraicdist(\cdot, \cdot))$ is the algebraic distance of the point in the first argument to the line string in the second argument. Then

$$weighteddist(T_1, T_2) = \alpha ADE(T_1, T_2) + (1 - \alpha) FDE(T_1, T_2),$$

for a given $0 \leq \alpha \leq 1$.

In a second step, the partial trajectory will be compared against all trajectories in the candidate clusters, again using $weighteddist$. As prediction, the historical trajectory with overall the least distance is returned.

3 Evaluation and Discussion

3.1 Intersection

The proposed approach is evaluated using a real intersection in the Dresden testbed in Germany. The intersection is a public intersection, connecting Bergstrasse, Mommsenstrasse and Haeckelstrasse (compare Fig. 1 left hand side). Nearby, on top of a building of the Technical University Dresden, one Flir Dual Aid camera is installed, allowing the monitoring of the whole intersection (see Fig. 1 left hand side). Video processing is similar to the Fraunhofer Smart Intersection [9], although here only one camera is available, making it difficult to calculate accurate 3D positions of objects.

Fig. 1. Overview over the test side. The left hand image shows an air view, with the MAPEM information as overlay. Also seen are the detected objects as white boxes. The red X marks the location of the camera surveilling the intersection. Right hand side shows an example image from the camera (not synchronized to the first image). Some of the lanes are clearly occluded. Correspondingly, objects are also missing on the left hand side. (Color figure online)

3.2 Trajectory Clusters

Using a Road-Side Unit (RSU) at the intersection, 1761 trajectories from CAM were collected over a time frame of six weeks. These were clustered using the introduced approach. Results from the first and second stage of clustering can be found in Fig. 2. The distribution of trajectories on the different driving is shown in Table 1. It is clearly seen that the clusters are unbalanced. This especially concerns the east-west and west-east relation. Clustering the data took less than 2 s with unoptimized Python code on an office notebook with an Intel i7-10850H and 32 GB of RAM.

Table 1. Distribution of trajectories in the different clusters. Cluster names indicate geographical direction.

Relation	ns-1	ns-2	we	es	en	se	ne	u-turn
#Trajectories in CAMs	348	494	1	3	9	2	9	4
#Trajectories in CPMs	14741	8485	54	309	416	140	512	62
Relation	sn-1	sn-2	ew	nw	sw	wn	ws	
#Trajectories in CAMs	381	441	1	28	21	12	7	
#Trajectories in CPMs	13723	18250	20	1026	434	718	92	

3.3 Enhancing CPM Trajectories

We collected 88 h of CPM trajectories between the 4th of July and 26th of August, 2024 at several times of the day. This data contains 59655 trajectories of which 39975

Fig. 2. Trajectory clusters after first step (left hand side) and second step (right hand side) of the hierarchical clustering scheme.

(or about two third) are incomplete. Many of these trajectories are incomplete due to occlusion (see Fig. 3) and artifacts in object detection. Still, compared to the number of trajectories obtained via CAM, this is a much more comprehensive data set. Using the proposed approach, all except 125 trajectories could be augmented. Of these 125 trajectories (as shown in Fig. 3 on the right hand side) some (especially along the west-south driving direction) could possibly be augmented if there were more trajectories available in the CAM data set, while others are clearly an artifact from video processing. Augmenting the nearly forty thousand trajectories took 6342 s, or about 0.15 s each. This is again using unoptimized Python code.

Table 2. Overview over the number of reference trajectories determined by the proposed approach.

# of reference trajectories matched	0	1	2	3	4	5	6	7
# of trajectories	125	5339	17854	8999	5059	2387	186	26

3.4 Discussion

Using the proposed approach, it was possible to augment nearly all partial trajectories given by CPM. The missing trajectories form 0.2% of all detected trajectories and can be mainly explained by sensing artifacts. But even if it was possible to match a trajectory, it cannot always be assured that this coincides with the actual trajectory. To further analyze this, the number of candidate reference trajectories generated by the approach were evaluated. The results can be found in Table 2. Over half of all trajectories generate

Fig. 3. CPM trajectories (left hand side). Green trajectories are complete, while the red ones are only partial. There is a clear spot behind the trees (compare also Fig. 1) were no trajectories could be tracked. Right hand side shows the 25 trajectories, which could not be augmented by the proposed approach. (Color figure online)

one or two candidates. Here, the two reference candidates are mainly a result of the two-lane approaches, where every cluster can be relatively close to the partial trajectory. If there are more than two candidates, the trajectories are mostly located in the middle of the intersection or is the trajectories are very short, which causes more initial matches. While it is not possible to check all 16657 trajectories with more than two matches, at least the 26 trajectories with seven matches were checked and no abnormalities were found. These trajectories and their augmentation are shown in Fig. 4. Given the huge amount of overall trajectories we assume that the influence of falsely augmented trajectories is negligible, at least from the performance measurement point of view. The same does not hold true, if CPMs are actually used for safety purposes, rendering the proposed approach currently unusable for this application.

At the moment, analysis is done off-line, but generally the proposed algorithm could also work on-line, even when using the unoptimized Python version.

Looking at the comparison in Table 1 it also becomes apparent, the there is a large difference between the distributions of driving relations in data gathered from CAM and CPM. This indicates that relying on CAM alone might lead to difficulties in monitoring.

4 Conclusions and Outlook

In this paper an approach to augment partial trajectories available from CPM was proposed. Using data of a real intersection, it was shown that nearly all partial trajectories could be completed, thereby allowing to conduct monitoring tasks.

While the results are overall satisfying, the approach heavily relies on data received from commercially available vehicles. This can limit the feasibility of the approach, as some clusters may be underrepresented in the initial data. This challenge can at least partly be overcome by collecting more sample data. Furthermore, we anticipate that the proportion of V2X-equipped vehicles will increase, enhancing the availability of reference trajectories in the near future. This expectation is based on Euro NCAP's plans to incorporate communication into vehicle assessments[2], likely boosting technology penetration rates.

The imbalance in cluster sizes also influences the overall computation time. This is due to the fact that in the second stage of the algorithm there is a comparison with all trajectories in the cluster, which means up to 500 comparisons for the largest cluster. To reduce the load, spectral clustering could be used in a third stage, identifying different characteristics within one cluster and using only the representatives for the sub-clusters for comparison.

Fig. 4. CPM trajectories with seven reference trajectories generated by the proposed approach. No obvious false augmentation is visible.

In the current work, only the movement of vehicles is augmented. Especially at urban intersections, VRU also play an important role. Although there is a V2X message to track these traffic participants directly (the VRU Awareness Message (VAM) [4]), currently no public data is available. Therefore, the current approach is not usable for a lack of comparison data.

[2] Compare https://cdn.euroncap.com/media/74468/euro-ncap-roadmap-vision-2030.pdf, page 6.

This paper's measurements are based on 802.11p as the transmission technology, the approach can be easily generalized to other technologies like C-V2X, since ETSI message formats such as CAM and SPATEM are technology agnostic.

Acknowledgments. This research is financially supported by the German Federal Ministry for Economic Affairs and Climate Action (BMWK) under grant number FKZ 19A22009F (VALISENS). We would like to thank Hsi Chen for carrying out some of the analysis steps, Rutuja Mohekar for collecting sample CPM data and Joerg Holfeld for providing some of the visualizations.

Disclosure of Interests. The authors have no competing interests to declare that are relevant to the content of this article.

References

1. Handbuch für die Bemessung von Straßenverkehrsanlagen, Teil S - Stadtstraßen. Standard, Forschungsgesellschaft für Straßen- und Verkehrswesen (2015)
2. Banerjee, T., Huang, X., Chen, K., Rangarajan, A., Ranka, S.: Clustering object trajectories for intersection traffic analysis [clustering object trajectories for intersection traffic analysis]. In: Proceedings of the 6th International Conference on Vehicle Technology and Intelligent Transport Systems - VEHITS (2020). https://doi.org/10.5220/0009422500980105. https://par.nsf.gov/biblio/10332852
3. ETSI EN 302 637-2 V1.4.1 (2019-04) Intelligent Transport Systems (ITS); Vehicular Communications; Basic Set of Applications; Part 2: Specification of Cooperative Awareness Basic Service. Standard, ETSI (2019)
4. ETSI TS 103 300-3 V2.1.1 (2020-11) Intelligent Transport Systems (ITS); Vulnerable Road Users (VRU) awareness; Part 3: Specification of VRU awareness basic service; Release 2. Standard, ETSI (2020)
5. ETSI TS 103 301 V1.3.1 (2020-02) Intelligent Transport Systems (ITS); Vehicular Communications; Basic Set of Applications; Facilities layer protocols and communication requirements for infrastructure services. Standard, ETSI (2020)
6. ETSI TS 103 324 V2.1.1 (2023-06) Intelligent Transport Systems (ITS); Vehicular Communications; Basic Set of Applications; Collective Perception Service; Release 2. Standard, ETSI (2023)
7. Gao, K., Han, F., Dong, P., Xiong, N., Du, R.: Connected vehicle as a mobile sensor for real time queue length at signalized intersections. Sensors **19**(9) (2019). https://doi.org/10.3390/s19092059. https://www.mdpi.com/1424-8220/19/9/2059
8. Gillies, S., et al.: Shapely: manipulation and analysis of geometric objects (2007). https://github.com/Toblerity/Shapely
9. Klöppel-Gersdorf, M., Trauzettel, F., Koslowski, K., Peter, M., Otto, T.: The fraunhofer CCIT smart intersection. In: 2021 IEEE International Intelligent Transportation Systems Conference (ITSC), pp. 1797–1802. IEEE (2021)
10. Klöppel-Gersdorf, M., Otto, T.: Using v2x-information for trajectory prediction at urban intersections. In: Vinel, A.V., Berns, K., Ploeg, J., Gusikhin, O. (eds.) VEHITS, pp. 473–479. SCITEPRESS (2024). http://dblp.uni-trier.de/db/conf/vehits/vehits2024.html#Kloppel-Gersdorf24
11. Klöppel-Gersdorf, M., Partzsch, I., Chen, H., Otto, T.: Real-time level of service for signalized urban intersections based on vehicle-to-everything communication. In: Nathanail, E.G., et al. (eds.) Climate Crisis and Resilient Transportation Systems. Springer, Cham (forthcoming)

12. Nevers, B., et al.: Performance-Based Management of Traffic Signals. No. Project 03-122 (2020)
13. Schiegg, F.A., Llatser, I., Bischoff, D., Volk, G.: Collective perception: a safety perspective. Sensors **21**(1) (2021). https://doi.org/10.3390/s21010159. https://www.mdpi.com/1424-8220/21/1/159
14. Statistisches Bundesamt (Destatis): Verkehr Verkehrsunfälle 2021. Statistisches Bundesamt (Destatis), 2022 (2022)
15. Transportation Research Board: Highway capacity manual. Standard, National Research Council (2000)
16. Wu, A., Banerjee, T., Rangarajan, A., Ranka, S.: Trajectory prediction via learning motion cluster patterns in curvilinear coordinates. In: 2021 IEEE International Intelligent Transportation Systems Conference (ITSC), pp. 2200–2207 (2021). https://doi.org/10.1109/ITSC48978.2021.9564800
17. Yang, L., Wang, Y., Yao, Z.: A new vehicle arrival prediction model for adaptive signal control in a connected vehicle environment. IEEE Access **8**, 112104–112112 (2020). https://doi.org/10.1109/ACCESS.2020.3002943

POMDP-Based Trajectory Planning for On-Ramp Highway Merging

Adam Kollarčík[1,2(✉)] and Zdeněk Hanzálek[2]

[1] Department of Control Engineering, Faculty of Electrical Engineering, Czech Technical University in Prague, Prague, Czech Republic

[2] Czech Institute of Informatics, Robotics and Cybernetics, Czech Technical University in Prague, Prague, Czech Republic

{adam.kollarcik,zdenek.hanzalek}@cvut.cz

Abstract. This paper addresses the trajectory planning problem for automated vehicle on-ramp highway merging. To tackle this challenge, we extend our previous work on trajectory planning at unsignalized intersections using Partially Observable Markov Decision Processes (POMDPs). The method utilizes the Adaptive Belief Tree (ABT) algorithm, an approximate sampling-based approach to solve POMDPs efficiently. We outline the POMDP formulation process, beginning with discretizing the highway topology to reduce problem complexity. Additionally, we describe the dynamics and measurement models used to predict future states and establish the relationship between available noisy measurements and predictions. Building on our previous work, the dynamics model is expanded to account for lateral movements necessary for lane changes during the merging process. We also define the reward function, which serves as the primary mechanism for specifying the desired behavior of the automated vehicle, combining multiple goals such as avoiding collisions or maintaining appropriate velocity. Our simulation results, conducted on three scenarios based on real-life traffic data from German highways, demonstrate the method's ability to generate safe, collision-free, and efficient merging trajectories. This work shows the versatility of this POMDP-based approach in tackling various automated driving problems.

Keywords: On-ramp highway merging · Trajectory planning · POMDP

1 Introduction

Highway on-ramp merging is a challenging maneuver for automated vehicles. The ego vehicle must smoothly and safely transition from an on-ramp to the main highway while interacting with other vehicles. The complexity of this task is increased by the need to balance multiple objectives, such as avoiding collisions, maintaining appropriate speed, and completing the merge within the length of the merging lane.

F. Calise et al. (Eds.): SMARTGREENS 2024/VEHITS 2024, CCIS 2954, pp. 228–244, 2026.
https://doi.org/10.1007/978-3-032-23187-1_13

This paper addresses the highway on-ramp merging problem using an approach based on Partially Observable Markov Decision Processes (POMDPs). POMDPs provide a robust framework for planning and decision-making in scenarios involving uncertainty and incomplete information. As a result, this approach is well-suited to handle the unpredictable behavior of other drivers and the inherent noise in sensor data.

Building on our previous work [8] in automated intersection crossings, we extend the application of POMDPs to the highway merging scenario. This involves enhancing the vehicle dynamics model to account for the lateral movements required to perform a lane change. The simulation results, based on real-world traffic data, demonstrate the effectiveness of the proposed method in producing safe and efficient merging maneuvers.

2 Related Work

Planning approaches for automated vehicles can be divided into three main categories: rule-based, reactive, and interactive methods [3,5]. Rule-based and reactive methods do not account for the interconnected behavior of drivers, which is crucial for ensuring safety in automated driving [17]. As a result, these methods are inadequate for handling complex scenarios such as unsignalized intersection crossings or on-ramp highway merging.

Interactive methods, which can be further categorized into centralized or decentralized, offer a more sophisticated approach by considering the interactions between vehicles [3]. Centralized methods typically rely on communication between vehicles (*Vehicle-to-Vehicle*, V2V), between vehicles and infrastructure (*Vehicle-to-Infrastructure*, V2I), or a combination of both (*Vehicle-to-Everything*, V2X), to develop a unified global strategy or an informed local strategy [3,19]. While these approaches show promise when most vehicles are equipped for such communication, this is unlikely to be the case in the near future [11]. Therefore, decentralized methods are going to be essential in the coming years. These decentralized approaches can be further divided into three main groups: game theory-based, probabilistic, and data-driven methods [17].

In recent years, the on-ramp highway merging problem has been studied thoroughly for the so-called *connected and autonomous vehicles* (CAVs), capable of real-time communication [22], fitting into the centralized category. Other approaches, such as [12], use game theory techniques to determine the intentions of other drivers and then use model predictive control (MPC) to generate appropriate trajectories. In [21], the authors provide an in-depth analysis of other highway merging methods, and they present a so-called *reference model*, a benchmark model used for verifying automated vehicle technologies. Their reference model utilizes a Monte Carlo tree search and, again, MPC to perform the merge. Additionally, various reinforcement learning methods have been proposed to tackle this problem [2,18].

This paper extends our previous work [8], in which we implemented and evaluated a probabilistic method based on Partially Observable Markov Decision Processes (POMDPs) for collision-free trajectory planning at unsignalized intersections. Originally introduced in [5], this method has been extended to various scenarios, such as roundabout navigation [1] and merging in congested traffic [6]. Additionally, several enhancements have been proposed, including the consideration of occlusions caused by both static and dynamic objects [4] and improvements in behavior prediction using dynamic Bayesian networks [16]. However, to our knowledge, this method has not yet been applied to highway on-ramp merging, as explored in this paper.

3 Methodology

To formulate the on-ramp highway merging problem as a POMDP, we begin by providing a formal problem definition. Next, we briefly describe POMDPs and the solver utilized in our approach. Following this, we explain the topology discretization, which reduces the complexity of the problem. Then, we provide a detailed explanation of the models employed for vehicle dynamics and observations and the associated reward function, which encourages collision-free and efficient merging maneuvers.

3.1 Formal Problem Definition

We seek to determine a collision-free trajectory for an ego vehicle during a highway on-ramp merging scenario, where the vehicle must accelerate to achieve a safe velocity before changing lanes to enter a highway. We assume that the topology of the highway is known beforehand and that the position $\boldsymbol{p}_i = [x_i,\ y_i]^\top$, velocity $\boldsymbol{v}_i = [v_{x,i},\ v_{y,i}]^\top$, unit heading vector $\boldsymbol{\theta}_i$, width W_i, and length L_i measurements of all n relevant other (non-ego) vehicles $i \in \{1, \ldots, n\}$ are available at every sample time k. Our additional assumptions are that (i) non-ego vehicles maintain their lanes, and (ii) that the ego vehicle's state information is known perfectly.

The trajectory of the ego vehicle is defined by a sequence of control inputs: the longitudinal acceleration a_0^k of the ego vehicle (denoted with the zero subscript) and the difference $\Delta\theta^k$ between the ego vehicle's heading and the current lane direction. The trajectory is deemed collision-free if, at every time step $k \geq 0$, there is no overlap between the bounding rectangles defined by the ego vehicle's position $\boldsymbol{p}_0^k$, heading vector $\boldsymbol{\theta}_0^k$, width W_0, and length L_0, and the corresponding parameters $\boldsymbol{p}_i^k$, $\boldsymbol{\theta}_i^k$, W_i, L_i of each non-ego vehicle i.

3.2 POMDPs

Partially Observable Markov Decision Processes provide a framework for decision-making and planning under uncertainty [9]. A POMDP is defined by the tuple $\langle S, A, O, T, Z, R, \gamma \rangle$, where S is the set of states, A is a set of actions, O is the set of observations, T is a set of conditional transition probabilities between states, Z is a set of conditional observation probabilities, R is the reward function, and $\gamma \in (0,\ 1]$ is the discount factor. The probabilities of transition from state $s \in S$ to state $s' \in S$ with action $a \in A$ are given by $T(s'|a, s)$. Similarly, the probability of observation $o \in O$ in state $s \in S$ with action $a \in A$ is $Z(o|a, s)$.

Due to partial observability, where observations are the only source of information, the knowledge of the current state might be represented by a probability distribution over the set of states, known as *belief* $b \in B$, where B is the *belief space.* The belief is updated based on the previous belief b, observation $o \in O$, and action $a \in A$, as follows:

$$b'(s') \propto Z(o \mid a, s') \sum_{s \in S} T(s' \mid a, s) b(s), \tag{1}$$

where $b(s)$ denotes the probability of being in state s under the belief b.

The objective of a POMDP planner is to find a policy $\pi : B \rightarrow A$, that maximizes the expected sum of discounted rewards referred to as the *value function* V:

$$V = \mathbb{E}\left[\sum_{k=0}^{\infty} \gamma^k R(\boldsymbol{s}_k, a_k) \,\middle|\, b, \pi\right]. \tag{2}$$

To obtain such policy, we use the sampling-based solver *TAPIR* [7], which implements the *Adaptive Belief Tree* algorithm (ABT). This sampling approach does not require us to compute transition or observation probabilities explicitly. Instead, we model the discrete-time stochastic system with difference equations, as detailed in Sects. 3.5 and 3.6.

3.3 Adaptive Belief Tree Algorithm

The Adaptive Belief Tree algorithm [10] is an online and anytime algorithm that employs Monte Carlo tree search to find approximate solutions for POMDPs. A belief tree $\mathcal{T}$ is constructed by sampling an initial belief with n_{par} particles, which are then propagated by actions according to the transition (dynamics) and observation (measurement) models. At each step, the particles are also assigned a reward $r = R(s, a)$, generating sequences of N quadruples (s, a, o, r) representing state trajectories, where N is the depth parameter of the belief tree. Those trajectories, referred to as *episodes*, are also assigned a heuristically computed expected reward for all future states until a terminal state is reached.

Once the tree is constructed, the policy is selected to maximize the average reward of all episodes $h \in H(b, a)$ that include the action-belief pair (b, a) at depth l:

$$\pi(b) = \arg\max_{a \in \mathcal{T}(b)} \frac{1}{|H(b, a)|} \sum_{h \in H(b,a)} \left(\sum_{i=l}^{N} \gamma^{i-l} r_i \right), \tag{3}$$

The average reward is also used to select the actions for particle propagation. Initially, actions not yet selected for the current belief are chosen uniformly at random. When there are no unused actions left, the *upper confidence bound* (UCB) is employed to address the exploration-exploitation trade-off:

$$a_{\text{sel}} = \underset{a \in A}{\arg\max} \left[\frac{1}{|H(b,a)|} \sum_{h \in H(b,a)} \left(\sum_{i=l}^{N} \gamma^{i-l} r_i \right) + c \sqrt{\frac{\log \sum_a |H(b,a)|}{|H(b,a)|}} \right], \quad (4)$$

where c is the tuning parameter for the UCB.

After applying the action $\pi(b_0)$ and obtaining new measurements, the belief is updated. Also, the corresponding branches of the belief tree are reused, with the current belief becoming the new root of the tree. This process is repeated until the goal (terminal state) is reached. To avoid particle depletion, new particles are generated if needed to maintain the n_{par} particles.

3.4 Topology Discretization

Following our original paper's approach, the highway is discretized into a set of m lanes as illustrated in Fig. 1. Each lane is assigned a unique integer identifier $\mu \in \{1, \ldots, m\}$ allowing us to reduce the state description of non-ego vehicles to a triplet of values $\boldsymbol{s}_i = [p_i\,,\ v_i\,,\ \mu_i]^\top$, where μ_i is the lane the i-th vehicle is using, p_i is the position along that lane, and v_i is its longitudinal velocity. To allow the ego vehicle to move in the lateral direction, we must extend its state description $\boldsymbol{s}_0 = [p_0\,,\ d_0\,,\ v_0\,,\ \mu_0]^\top$ by a signed distance d_0 from the lane μ_0 (see Fig. 2), where the sign determines left (positive) or right (negative) direction with respect to the orientation of the lane.

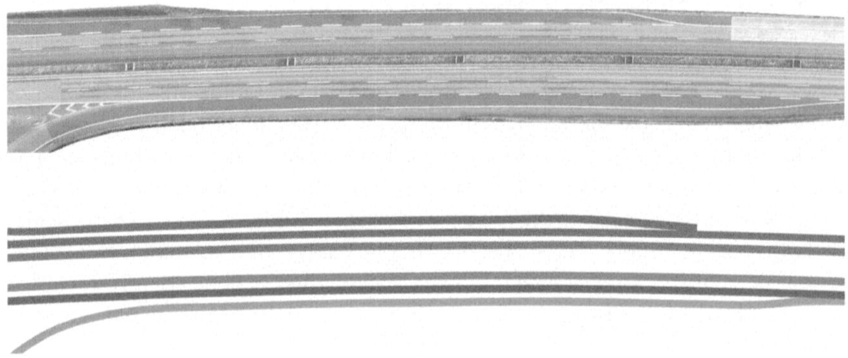

Fig. 1. Picture of a highway [14] (up) and discrete set of corresponding lanes (down).

The lanes are extracted using the *lanelet2* [15] map from the ExiD [14] dataset in the OSM XML format. Each lane is stored as two cubic splines with additional information such as length, width, and neighbor lane relations at each lane segment. As a result, we obtain mapping from the lane position to the global coordinates $\phi_\mu(p) : p \to \mathbb{R}^2$, and mapping to the unit heading $\psi_\mu(p) : p \to \boldsymbol{y} \in \mathbb{R}^2 : \|\boldsymbol{y}\| = 1$. We employ a projection search algorithm from global coordinates to lane position $\epsilon_\mu(\boldsymbol{p}) : \boldsymbol{p} \to \mathbb{R}$ to determine the nearest point on the lane.

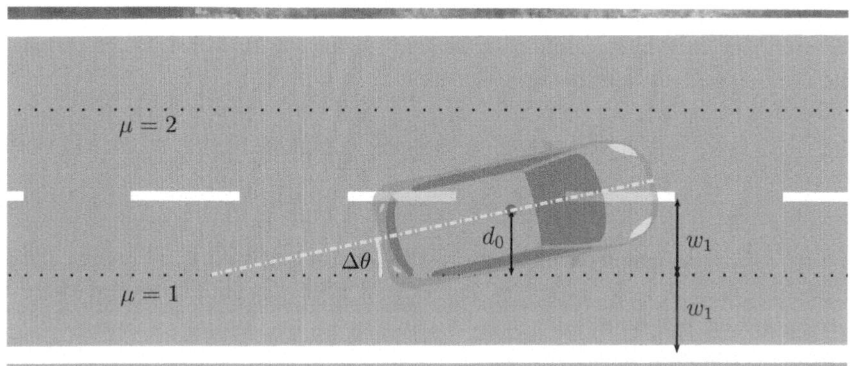

Fig. 2. A diagram of a lane change illustrating certain parameters and states.

The global position of the ego vehicle can be computed by combining those mappings:

$$\boldsymbol{p} = \boldsymbol{\lambda}_\mu(p, d) = \boldsymbol{\phi}_\mu(p) + d \begin{bmatrix} 0 & -1 \\ 1 & -0 \end{bmatrix} \boldsymbol{\psi}_\mu(p), \tag{5}$$

where the matrix multiplication of the heading vector generates a perpendicular vector to the path at the position p. The signed distance from a lane at a global position $\boldsymbol{p}$ can be computed similarly as well:

$$d = d_\mu(\boldsymbol{p}) = \boldsymbol{\psi}_\mu(p)^\top \begin{bmatrix} 0 & -1 \\ 1 & -0 \end{bmatrix} \boldsymbol{p} - \boldsymbol{\phi}_\mu(\epsilon_\mu(\boldsymbol{p})). \tag{6}$$

3.5 Dynamics Model

In this section, we present our dynamics model that approximates how the states of the vehicles evolve over time. For the non-ego vehicles, we use a simple single-mass model that effectively describes their movement along the predefined lanes based on their acceleration or deceleration. The mathematical description is as follows:

$$p_i^{k+1} = p_i^k + v_i^k \Delta t + \frac{1}{2} a_i \Delta t^2 + \nu_1, \quad i \in \{1, \dots, n\}, \tag{7}$$

$$v_i^{k+1} = v_i^k + a_i \Delta t + \nu_2, \quad i \in \{1, \dots, n\}, \tag{8}$$

$$\mu_i^{k+1} = \mu_i^k, \quad i \in \{1, \dots, n\}, \tag{9}$$

where the Δt is the time between subsequent samples k and $k+1$. The Gaussian noise variables $[\nu_1, \nu_2]^\top \sim \mathcal{N}(\mathbf{0}, \boldsymbol{Q})$ with zero mean and covariance $\boldsymbol{Q}$ represent inaccuracies in the model.

For the ego vehicle, we utilize a discretized Frenet frame point model [13], allowing for the lateral movement necessary to perform a lane change. First, we define auxiliary variables $\hat{p}_0$ and $\hat{d}_0$ representing the position and signed distance in the next step if no lane change occurred:

$$\hat{p}_0 = p_0^k + \frac{v_0^k \cos(\Delta\theta^k)}{1 - d_0^k \kappa_{\mu_0}(p_0^k)} \Delta t, \tag{10}$$

$$\hat{d}_0 = d_0^k + v_0^k \sin(\Delta\theta^k) \Delta t, \tag{11}$$

where $\kappa_{\mu_0}(p_0^k)$ is the signed curvature of the lane at position p_0^k. Then we check whether the vehicle exceeds the width $w_{\mu_0^k}$ of the lane μ_0^k. If so, and there is a corresponding neighbor lane, a lane change occurs, and state variables are changed accordingly:

$$p_0^{k+1} = \begin{cases} \epsilon_{\mu_{\text{left}}}(\boldsymbol{\lambda}_{\mu_0^k}(\hat{p}_0, \hat{d}_0)) & \text{if } -\hat{d}_0 > w_{\mu_0^k}(\hat{p}_0) \text{ and } \mu_0^k \text{ has left at } \hat{p}_0, \\ \epsilon_{\mu_{\text{right}}}(\boldsymbol{\lambda}_{\mu_0^k}(\hat{p}_0, \hat{d}_0)) & \text{if } -\hat{d}_0 > w_{\mu_0^k}(\hat{p}_0) \text{ and } \mu_0^k \text{ has right at } \hat{p}_0, \\ \hat{p}_0 & \text{otherwise,} \end{cases} \tag{12}$$

$$d_0^{k+1} = \begin{cases} d_{\mu_{\text{left}}}(\boldsymbol{\lambda}_{\mu_0^k}(\hat{p}_0, \hat{d}_0)) & \text{if } -\hat{d}_0 > w_{\mu_0^k}(\hat{p}_0) \text{ and } \mu_0^k \text{ has left at } \hat{p}_0, \\ d_{\mu_{\text{right}}}(\boldsymbol{\lambda}_{\mu_0^k}(\hat{p}_0, \hat{d}_0)) & \text{if } -\hat{d}_0 > w_{\mu_0^k}(\hat{p}_0) \text{ and } \mu_0^k \text{ has right at } \hat{p}_0, \\ \hat{d}_0 & \text{otherwise,} \end{cases} \tag{13}$$

$$v_0^{k+1} = v_0^k + a_0 \Delta t, \tag{14}$$

$$\mu_0^{k+1} = \begin{cases} \mu_{\text{left}} & \text{if } -\hat{d}_0 > w_{\mu_0^k}(\hat{p}_0) \text{ and } \mu_0^k \text{ has left at } \hat{p}_0, \\ \mu_{\text{right}} & \text{if } -\hat{d}_0 > w_{\mu_0^k}(\hat{p}_0) \text{ and } \mu_0^k \text{ has right at } \hat{p}_0, \\ \mu_0 & \text{otherwise.} \end{cases} \tag{15}$$

Furthermore, we need to predict the accelerations for the non-ego vehicles. For the sake of simplicity, we follow our previous approach and employ the so-called intelligent driver model (IDM) [20]:

$$a_i^k = a_{\max} \left[1 - \left(\frac{v_i^k}{v_{\text{des}} + \omega_1} \right)^\delta - \left(\frac{d^*(v_i^k, v_{\text{lead}})}{d_{\text{lead}}} \right)^2 \right] + \omega_2, \quad i \in \{1, \dots, n\} \tag{16}$$

$$d^*(v_i^k, v_{\text{lead}}) = d_{\min} + v_i^k \tau + \frac{v_i^k (v_i^k - v_{\text{lead}})}{2\sqrt{a_{\max} |a_{\min}|}}, \quad i \in \{1, \dots, n\} \tag{17}$$

where $a_{\max}$ is the maximal acceleration, $a_{\min}$ is the minimal acceleration (maximal deceleration), v_{des} is the desired velocity, $d_{\min}$ is the minimal distance, τ is the time headway, δ is the acceleration exponent, v_{lead} is the velocity of the leading (approached) vehicle, and $[\omega_1, \omega_2]^\top \sim \mathcal{N}(\mathbf{0}, \boldsymbol{\Sigma})$ is Gussian noise with variance $\boldsymbol{\Sigma}$ accounting for model inaccuracy and variance in desired velocity values for different drivers. The acceleration a_0 of the ego vehicle and heading angle deviation $\Delta\theta$ are obtained from the POMDP policy (3).

3.6 Observation Model

The observation model describes the accuracy of our measurements and how these measurements relate to the states we defined in the previous sections. This is used to generate the particles and to ensure that our current belief of the state corresponds to the obtained measurements.

Let $\boldsymbol{z}_i^k$ denote the observation vector of the i-th vehicle at time step k. These observations are acquired through spline mappings, as detailed in Sect. 3.4:

$$\boldsymbol{z}_i^k = \begin{bmatrix} \boldsymbol{\phi}_{\mu_i^k}(p_i^k) \\ v_i^k \boldsymbol{\psi}_{\mu_i^k}(p_i^k) \\ \boldsymbol{\psi}_{\mu_i^k}(p_i^k) \end{bmatrix} + \boldsymbol{\zeta}, \qquad i \in \{1, \dots, n\}, \tag{18}$$

where $\boldsymbol{\zeta} \sim \mathcal{N}(\boldsymbol{0}, \boldsymbol{R})$ represents Gaussian observation noise with zero mean and covariance matrix $\boldsymbol{R}$, encapsulating the measurement inaccuracy together with the error caused by projecting a two-dimensional position on a curve.

Furthermore, we need to estimate the lanes μ_i^k the vehicles are driving in. In contrast to the planning for unsignalized intersections, highway's topology is simpler having no overlapping segments. This makes the distance from the lane center a good indicator of whether a vehicle is in a particular lane. Nevertheless, additional information, such as vehicle orientation, can also be utilized, as the added complexity is negligible. Thus, we compute the probability of being in a lane for each vehicle based on likelihoods f_1 and f_2 of these two features shown in Fig. 3:

$$f_1(i, \mu) = e^{-\left(\frac{D_i^k(\mu)}{w_\mu}\right)^4}, \tag{19}$$

$$f_2(i, \mu) = e^{3\left(\alpha_i^k(\mu) - 1\right)}, \tag{20}$$

where $D_i^k(\mu) = \|\boldsymbol{p}_i^k - \boldsymbol{\phi}_\mu(\epsilon_\mu(\boldsymbol{p}_i^k))\|$ is the distance from the closest point on the lane with width $w_\mu = w_\mu(\epsilon_\mu(\boldsymbol{p}_i^k))$, and $\alpha_i^k(\mu) = \boldsymbol{\theta}_i^k \cdot \boldsymbol{\psi}_\mu(\epsilon_\mu(\boldsymbol{p}_i^k))$ is the dot product of the path heading and the measured heading of a vehicle. The resulting probability distribution is a combination of these likelihoods:

$$P(i, \mu) = \frac{f_1(i, \mu) f_2(i, \mu)}{\sum_{j=1}^{m} f_1(i, j) f_2(i, j)}. \tag{21}$$

3.7 Reward Function and Heuristics

In this section, we describe the reward function and the heuristic used to evaluate the future rewards of newly discovered nodes in the belief tree, as mentioned in Sect. 3.3. The reward function is the primary mechanism for specifying the desired behavior of the ego vehicle, making its formulation critical for achieving our objectives. In conjunction with this, the heuristic is designed to estimate future rewards, guiding the exploration process towards the most promising nodes within the belief tree, thus enhancing the efficiency of the UCB algorithm.

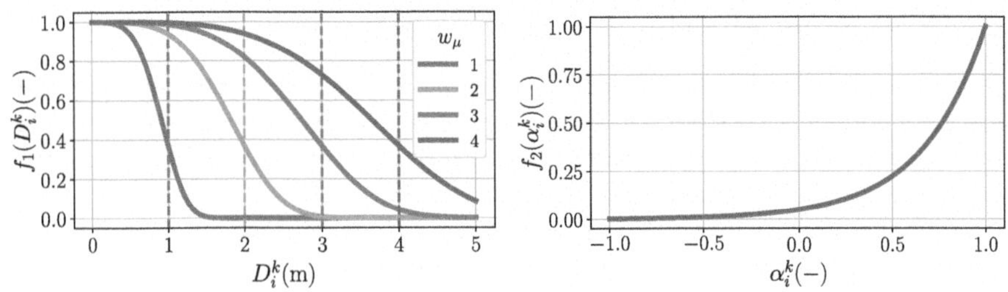

Fig. 3. Likelihood functions of features f_1(left), and f_2(right).

The reward at each time step r^k, is composed of five terms, each evaluating a specific requirement. These terms are r_{vel} for velocity, r_{input} for control inputs, r_{change} for a lane change, r_{crash} for collisions, and a direct quadratic component penalizing deviations from the path's centerline with coefficient $R_{\text{center}} \geq 0$:

$$r^k = r_{\text{vel}}(\boldsymbol{s}_0^k) + r_{\text{input}}(a_0^k, \Delta\theta^k) + r_{\text{crash}}(\boldsymbol{s}^k) + r_{\text{change}}(\boldsymbol{s}^k) - R_{\text{center}}\left(d_0^k\right)^2 . \quad (22)$$

The velocity reward ensures that the ego vehicle follows the desired velocity profile. It is determined by the deviation from the reference velocity $\Delta v = v_{\text{des}} - v_0^k$:

$$r_{\text{vel}}(v_0^k) = \begin{cases} -R_{\text{vel}}\Delta v & \text{if } \Delta v \geq 1\,, \\ -R_{\text{vel}}\Delta v^2 & \text{otherwise,} \end{cases} \quad (23)$$

where R_{vel} is a positive weight.

The input reward function penalizes high acceleration and steering inputs, promoting a smoother ride and increased comfort. It is computed using quadratic penalty function, weighted by $R_{\text{acc}} \geq 0$ for acceleration and $R_{\text{steer}} \geq 0$ for steering:

$$r_{\text{acc}}(a_0^k, \Delta\theta^k) = -R_{\text{acc}}\left(a_0^k\right)^2 - R_{\text{steer}}\left(\Delta\theta^k\right)^2 . \quad (24)$$

The collision avoidance component is designed to prevent crashes and to keep the vehicle within the highway boundaries. A negative reward $-R_{\text{crash}}$ is assigned when a collision is detected or if the bounds are exceeded. Otherwise, it is set to zero:

$$r_{\text{crash}}(\boldsymbol{s}^k) = \begin{cases} -R_{\text{crash}} & \begin{array}{l}\text{if collision detected, or} \\ \text{if bounds exceeded,}\end{array} \\ 0 & \text{otherwise.} \end{cases} \quad (25)$$

Collision detection relies on the overlap of vehicle bounding rectangles, as explained in Sect. 3.1. The bounds of the highway are exceeded if

$$\pm\left[d_0 + W_0 \cos(\Delta\theta) + L_0 \sin(\Delta\theta)\right] > w_{\mu_0}, \quad (26)$$

while the current lane μ_0 has no left or right neighbor lane.

Finally, the lane change reward r_{change} enforces the vehicle to change the line to join the highway. A constant penalty $-R_{\text{cst}}$ is applied every time step k the vehicle is not in the desired lane. An additional penalty is imposed based on the remaining time $t_{\text{left}} = (l_{\mu_0} - p_0^k)/v_0^k$ and the remaining distance until the end of the merging lane of length l_{μ_0}. Last, the square distance to the desired lane $d_{\text{des}} = d_{\mu_{\text{des}}}(\boldsymbol{\lambda}_{\mu_0^k}(p_0^k, d_0^k))$ is also penalized to attract the ego vehicle to the desired lane:

$$r_{\text{change}}(\boldsymbol{s}_0^k) = \begin{cases} -R_{\text{cst}} - R_{\text{end}}\left(\frac{1}{t_{\text{left}}} + \frac{p_0^k}{l_{\mu_0}}\right) - R_{\text{dist}}(d_{\text{des}})^2 & \text{if } \mu_0^k \neq \mu_{\text{des}}, \\ 0 & \text{otherwise.} \end{cases} \tag{27}$$

For the heuristic h estimating the future reward for state $\boldsymbol{s}$, we employed a simple estimation of the minimal time required to reach the desired lane μ_{desired} combined with the crash penalty:

$$h(\boldsymbol{s}^k) = -R_h \left| \frac{d_{\mu_{\text{desired}}}}{v_0^k \sin(\Delta\theta_{\text{max}})} \right| + r_{\text{crash}}(\boldsymbol{s}^k). \tag{28}$$

This should guide the UCB algorithm towards states close to the desired lane while avoiding crashes.

4 Results

Having formulated the problem of on-ramp highway merging as a POMDP, we now present the results, which demonstrate the planning capabilities our method. We ran multiple simulations using three scenarios of three different highway entries from the ExiD dataset [14], which contains over sixteen hours of aerial footage of real-life traffic at highway entries and exits in Germany. In our simulations, we replaced the merging vehicle from the data with our ego vehicle, allowing to reuse the recorded reactions of the other cars as an approximation of interactions with our ego vehicle.

Our simulation software was primarily implemented in C++ using the TAPIR toolbox and ROS1. The simulations were conducted on a laptop with an Intel i5-11500H CPU and showed real-time capable runtimes under our parameter settings. However, it should be noted that the precise real-time performance was not our primary focus and requires further investigation. The parameter values used in our simulations are listed in Table 1.

Table 1. Parameter values for on-ramp highway merging.

	Description	Value
A	action set	$\{-1, -0.5, 0, 0.5, 1\}$ m s$^{-2}\times$ $\{-2, -1, -0.5, 0, 0.5, 1, 2\}$ deg
Δt	time step length	1 sec
c	UCB parameter	200000
N	ABT depth	10
n_{ep}	ABT number of episodes	10000
n_{par}	ABT number of particles	1000
γ	discount factor	1
$\boldsymbol{Q}$	dynamics covariance	$\boldsymbol{0}$
$\boldsymbol{\Sigma}$	IDM covariance	diag$(9, 0.04)$
v_{des}	desired velocity	27.8 m s $^{-1}$
$a_{\max}$	IDM maximal acceleration	1 m s $^{-2}$
$a_{\min}$	IDM minimal acceleration	-1 m s $^{-2}$
τ	IDM time headway	1.5 s
δ	IDM acceleration exponent	4
$d_{\min}$	IDM minimal distance	1 m
$\boldsymbol{R}$	observation covariance	diag$(0.01, 0.01, 0)$
R_{center}	centerline reward coef.	500
R_{acc}	acceleration reward coef.	100
R_{steer}	steering reward coef.	$10 \cdot (180/\pi)^2$
R_{vel}	velocity reward coef.	100
R_{crash}	crash reward coef.	1000000
R_{cst}	wrong lane constant reward coef.	1000
R_{end}	wrong lane end reward coef.	10000
R_{dist}	wrong lane distance reward coef.	500
R_{h}	heuristics coef.	100

4.1 Simulations

We conducted 30 simulations for each scenario to evaluate the performance of the ego vehicle under varying traffic conditions. Each scenario is illustrated with a time-lapse figure showing the superimposed trajectories of all 30 simulations. We also present velocity and control input graphs to provide further information.

In the first scenario, the ego vehicle initiates a merge onto the highway at a speed of 18 m/s, with three other vehicles present in the target lane. Across all 30 simulations, the ego vehicle successfully changed lanes within 4 s, as seen in the time-lapse in Fig. 4. Although the trailing vehicle appears to get too close post-merge, that is just a consequence of using pre-recorded data. In reality, the trailing vehicle would have had sufficient time to react and slow down; however, because the replaced vehicle in the data was farther away, this adjustment did not occur. As depicted in Fig. 5, the ego vehicle accelerated uniformly at approximately 0.5 m/s^2 throughout the maneuver.

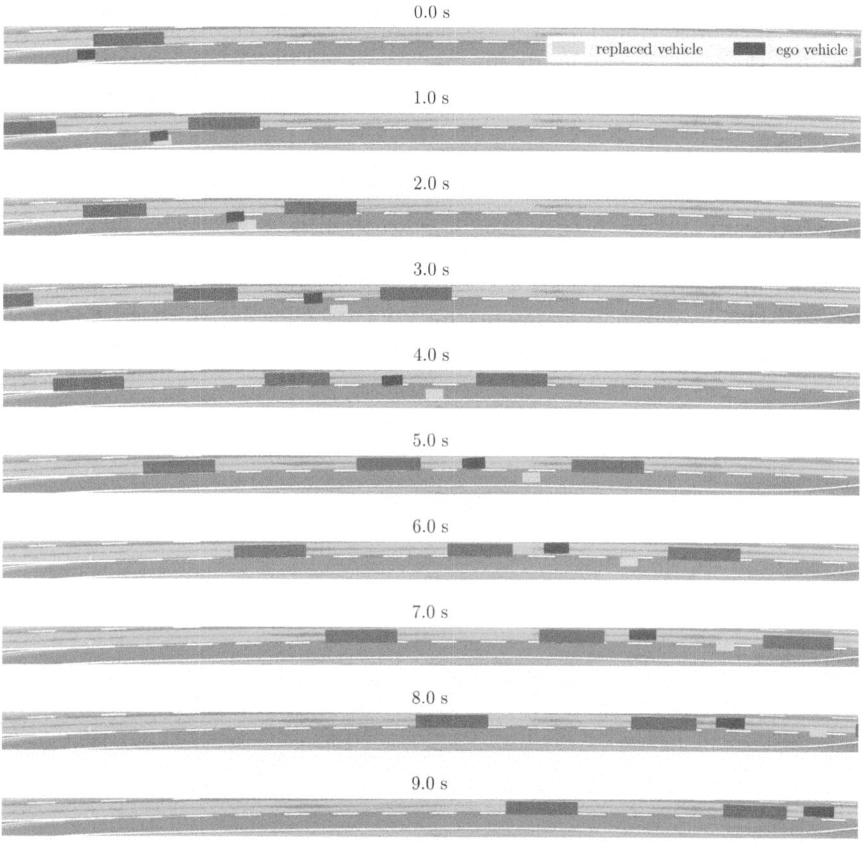

Fig. 4. Time-lapse of the 30 simulations for Scenario 1. Simulated ego vehicles are represented as semi-transparent blue rectangles, non-ego vehicles are shown as red rectangles. The cyan rectangle shows how a real vehicle we replaced with our ego vehicle performed the merge. (Color figure online)

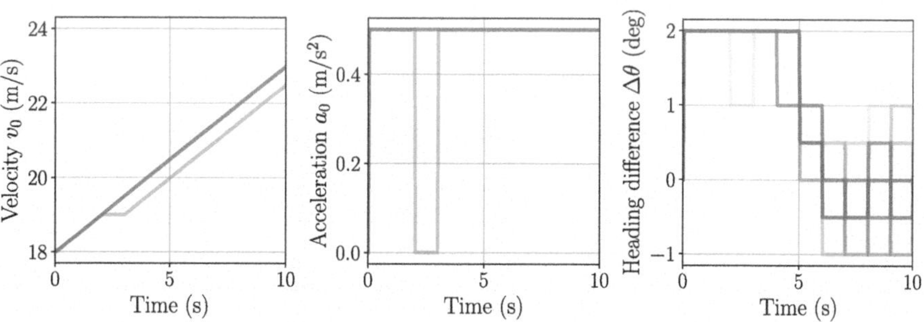

Fig. 5. Velocity and input values of 30 simulations for Scenario 1. The opacity of each line segment represents the total number of simulations sharing the values.

In the second scenario, the ego vehicle starts merging at a higher speed, around 22 m/s. The time-lapse in Fig. 6 shows that the ego vehicle successfully completed the lane change in all 30 simulations within approximately 8 s. This time, the ego vehicle closely mimicked the behavior of the original car. As illustrated in Fig. 7, the ego vehicle exhibited gradual acceleration during the merge.

In the third scenario, the ego vehicle starts at an initial speed of 20.5 m/s. Unlike the previous scenarios, the ego vehicle does not accelerate during the maneuver, as it would not have been feasible to achieve a velocity high enough to merge in front of the adjacent vehicle before the end of the merge lane. The time-lapse in Fig. 8 and the velocity/acceleration graphs in Fig. 9 confirm this behavior. The ego vehicle maintains its velocity, allowing the faster adjacent vehicle to pass, and completes the merge successfully in all simulations within 8 s.

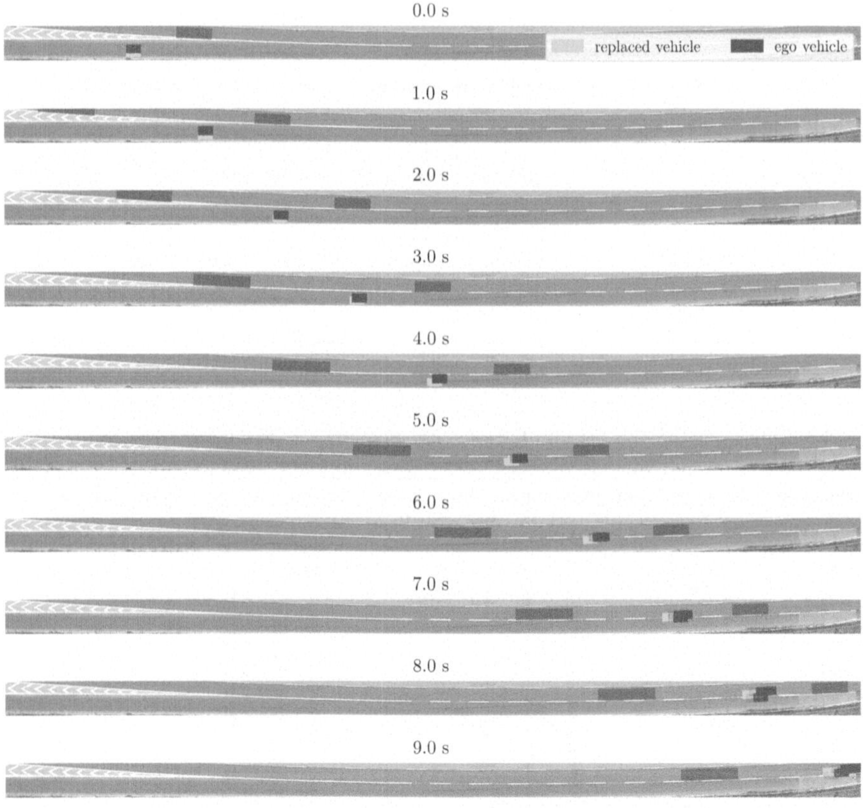

Fig. 6. Time-lapse of the 30 simulations for Scenario 2. Simulated ego vehicles are represented as semi-transparent blue rectangles, non-ego vehicles are shown as red rectangles. The cyan rectangle shows how a real vehicle we replaced with our ego vehicle performed the merge. (Color figure online)

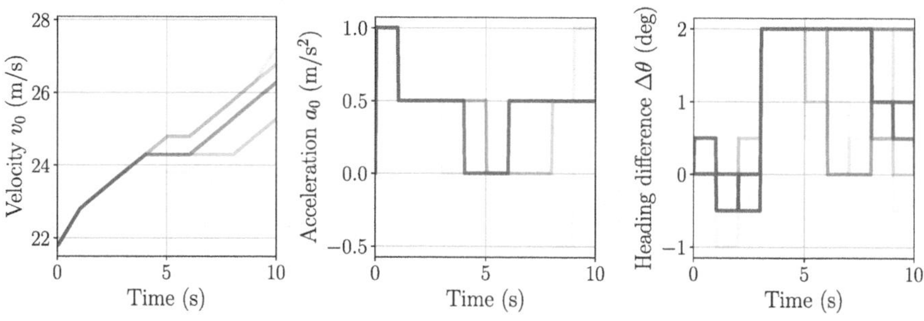

Fig. 7. Velocity and input values of 30 simulations for Scenario 2. The opacity of each line segment represents the total number of simulations sharing the values.

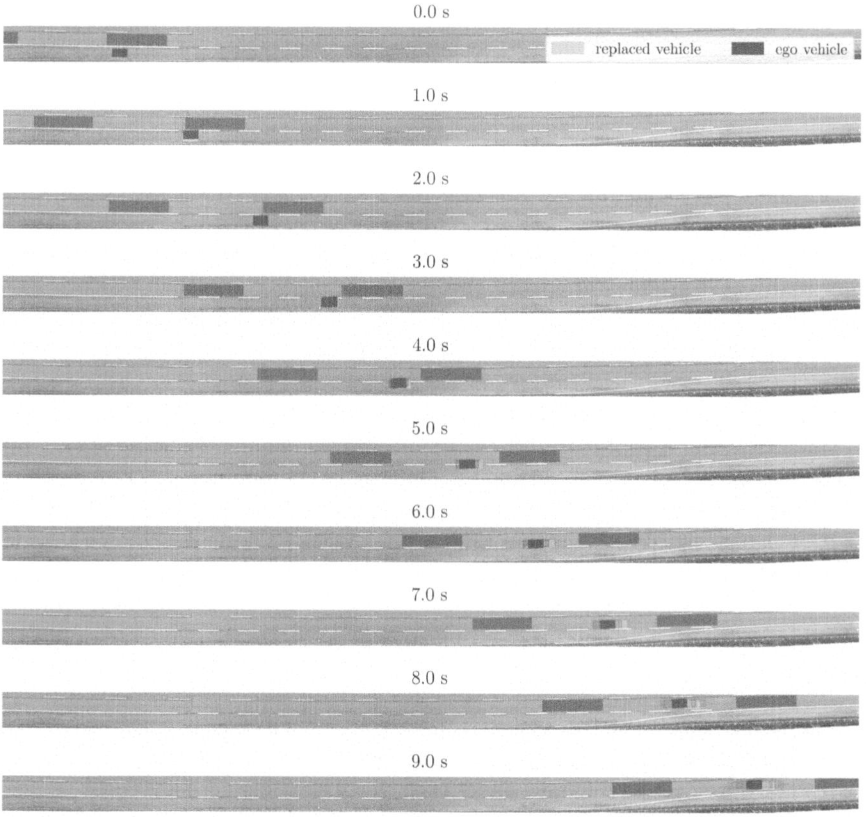

Fig. 8. Time-lapse of the 30 simulations for Scenario 3. Simulated ego vehicles are represented as semi-transparent blue rectangles, non-ego vehicles are shown as red rectangles. The cyan rectangle shows how a real vehicle we replaced with our ego vehicle performed the merge. (Color figure online)

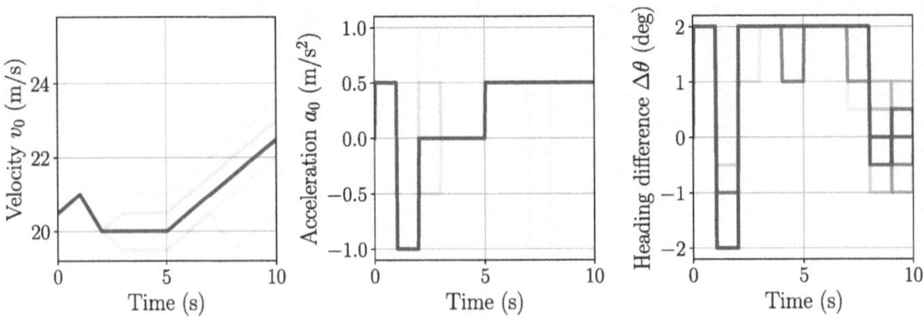

Fig. 9. Velocity and input values of 30 simulations for Scenario 3. The opacity of each line segment represents the total number of simulations sharing the values.

5 Conclusion

This paper presents an extension of our previous work on POMDP-based trajectory planning [8] by adapting the method to the problem of highway on-ramp merging. We demonstrated how this problem can be effectively modeled as a POMDP, integrating vehicle dynamics, measurements, and probabilistic decision-making to handle the uncertainties and interactions present in real-world highway scenarios.

Our simulation results, based on three distinct highway merging scenarios using real-world traffic data from the ExiD dataset, show that the proposed method consistently generates safe and efficient merging maneuvers. The approach successfully handles varying traffic conditions, including different vehicle speeds.

This work highlights the effectiveness and versatility of POMDP-based planning in addressing complex challenges in automated driving. Looking ahead, further investigation into the real-time capabilities of the method will be crucial for real-world deployment. Additionally, future work will focus on scenarios where assertive driving is critical, such as interactions with other drivers in dense traffic during rush hours. While the POMDP framework is well-suited for these challenges, modeling such interactions and moving beyond offline data evaluation to more interactive testing will be essential to capture these dynamic environments fully.

Acknowledgments. This work was co-funded by the European Union under the project ROBOPROX (reg. no. CZ.02.01.0100/22_0080004590) and by the Technology Agency of the Czech Republic under the project Certicar CK03000033.

References

1. Bey, H., Sackmann, M., Lange, A., Thielecke, J.: POMDP Planning at Roundabouts. In: 2021 IEEE IV Workshops, pp. 264–271 (2021). https://doi.org/10.1109/IVWorkshops54471.2021.9669232
2. Bouton, M., Nakhaei, A., Fujimura, K., Kochenderfer, M.J.: Cooperation-aware reinforcement learning for merging in dense traffic. In: 2019 IEEE Intelligent Transportation Systems Conference (ITSC), pp. 3441–3447 (2019). https://doi.org/10.1109/ITSC.2019.8916924
3. Eskandarian, A., Wu, C., Sun, C.: Research advances and challenges of autonomous and connected ground vehicles. IEEE Trans. Intell. Transp. Syst. **22**(2), 683–711 (2021). https://doi.org/10.1109/TITS.2019.2958352
4. Hubmann, C., et al.: A POMDP maneuver planner for occlusions in urban scenarios. In: 2019 IEEE IV, pp. 2172–2179 (2019). https://doi.org/10.1109/IVS.2019.8814179
5. Hubmann, C., Schulz, J., Becker, M., Althoff, D., Stiller, C.: Automated driving in uncertain environments: planning with interaction and uncertain maneuver prediction. IEEE Trans. Intell. Veh. **3**(1), 5–17 (2018). https://doi.org/10.1109/TIV.2017.2788208
6. Hubmann, C., Schulz, J., Xu, G., Althoff, D., Stiller, C.: A belief state planner for interactive merge maneuvers in congested traffic. In: 2018 21st International Conference on Intelligent Transportation Systems (ITSC), pp. 1617–1624 (2018). https://doi.org/10.1109/ITSC.2018.8569729
7. Klimenko, D., Song, J., Kurniawati, H.: TAPIR: A software toolkit for approximating and adapting POMDP solutions online. In: IEEE ICRA (2014)
8. Kollarčík, A., Hanzálek, Z.: Parameter adjustments in POMDP-Based trajectory planning for unsignalized intersections. In: Proceedings of the 10th International Conference on Vehicle Technology and Intelligent Transport Systems - VEHITS, pp. 522–529 (2024). https://doi.org/10.5220/0012742400003702
9. Kurniawati, H.: Partially observable Markov decision processes and robotics. Annu. Rev. Control Robot. Auton. Syst. **5**(1), 253–277 (2022). https://doi.org/10.1146/annurev-control-042920-092451
10. Kurniawati, H., Yadav, V.: An online POMDP solver for uncertainty planning in dynamic environment. In: Inaba, M., Corke, P. (eds.) Robotics Research: The 16th International Symposium ISRR, pp. 611–629. Springer Tracts in Advanced Robotics, Springer International Publishing, Cham (2016). https://doi.org/10.1007/978-3-319-28872-7_35
11. Litman, T.: Autonomous Vehicle Implementation Predictions: Implications for Transport Planning (2023)
12. Liu, K., Li, N., Tseng, H.E., Kolmanovsky, I., Girard, A.: Interaction-aware trajectory prediction and planning for autonomous vehicles in forced merge scenarios. IEEE Trans. Intell. Transp. Syst. **24**(1), 474–488 (2023). https://doi.org/10.1109/TITS.2022.3216792
13. Micaelli, A., Samson, C.: Trajectory tracking for unicycle-type and two-steering-wheels mobile robots. Research Report RR-2097, INRIA (1993). https://inria.hal.science/inria-00074575
14. Moers, T., Vater, L., Krajewski, R., Bock, J., Zlocki, A., Eckstein, L.: The exid dataset: a real-world trajectory dataset of highly interactive highway scenarios in Germany. In: 2022 IEEE Intelligent Vehicles Symposium (IV), pp. 958–964 (2022). https://doi.org/10.1109/IV51971.2022.9827305

15. Poggenhans, F., et al.: Lanelet2: a high-definition map framework for the future of automated driving. In: 2018 IEEE ITSC, pp. 1672–1679 (2018). https://doi.org/10.1109/ITSC.2018.8569929
16. Schulz, J., Hubmann, C., Morin, N., Löchner, J., Burschka, D.: Learning interaction-aware probabilistic driver behavior models from urban scenarios. In: 2019 IEEE IV, pp. 1326–1333 (2019). https://doi.org/10.1109/IVS.2019.8814080
17. Schwarting, W., Alonso-Mora, J., Rus, D.: Planning and decision-making for autonomous vehicles. Annu. Rev. Control Robot. Auton. Syst. **1**(1), 187–210 (2018). https://doi.org/10.1146/annurev-control-060117-105157
18. Toghi, B., Valiente, R., Sadigh, D., Pedarsani, R., Fallah, Y.P.: Cooperative autonomous vehicles that sympathize with human drivers. In: 2021 IEEE/RSJ International Conference on Intelligent Robots and Systems (IROS), pp. 4517–4524 (2021). https://doi.org/10.1109/IROS51168.2021.9636151
19. Tong, W., Hussain, A., Bo, W.X., Maharjan, S.: Artificial intelligence for vehicle-to-everything: a survey. IEEE Access **7**, 10823–10843 (2019). https://doi.org/10.1109/ACCESS.2019.2891073
20. Treiber, M., Hennecke, A., Helbing, D.: Congested traffic states in empirical observations and microscopic simulations. Phys. Rev. E **62**(2), 1805–1824 (2000). https://doi.org/10.1103/PhysRevE.62.1805
21. Wang, C., Guo, F., Zhao, S., Zhu, Z., Zhang, Y.: Safety assessment for autonomous vehicles: a reference driver model for highway merging scenarios. Accident Anal. Prevention **206**, 107710 https://doi.org/10.1016/j.aap.2024.107710, https://www.sciencedirect.com/science/article/pii/S0001457524002550 (2024)
22. Zhu, J., Easa, S., Gao, K.: Merging control strategies of connected and autonomous vehicles at freeway on-ramps: a comprehensive review. J. Intell. Connected Veh. **5**(2), 99–111 (2022). https://doi.org/10.1108/JICV-02-2022-0005

Model Predictive Control of CACC with Disturbance Estimation

Anas Abulehia(✉), Reza Dariani, and Julian Schindler

German Aerospace Center (DLR), Institut für Verkehrssystemtechnik, Lilienthalplatz 7, 38108 Braunschweig, Germany
{a.abulehia,reza.dariani,julian.schindler}@dlr.de

Abstract. To tackle traffic congestion and improve fuel efficiency, we propose a Cooperative Adaptive Cruise Control (CACC) system using Model Predictive Control (MPC). This system maintains optimal vehicle spacing in a string of vehicles, reducing stop-and-go traffic and fuel consumption. Unlike human drivers, the CACC system can significantly decrease inter-vehicle distances, enhancing traffic flow and reducing aerodynamic drag. Our approach integrates disturbance estimation and intent sharing via Lagrangian interpolation, resulting in improved state tracking and reduced computational demands.

Keywords: Cooperative adaptive cruise control (CACC) · Model predictive control · Intent sharing · Disturbance estimation · Connected and automated vehicles

1 Introduction

Mobility is essential to human life, influencing everything from daily commutes to visits to far-off destinations. It's a fundamental aspect of our existence. In 2012, the global average distance traveled per person was 7,000 mi per year. The Vast majority of this travel was done using vehicles such as cars, taxis, buses, and other similar forms of transportation. Assistive Driving System such as Cruise Control and Adaptive cruise control aimed to easy and enhance the driving they also have a potential on Macroscopic level in both safety efficiency and traffic flow improvements [9].

Assistive driving systems have evolved significantly over the last 30 years. Cruise Control where the vehicle is able to maintain a set speed independently the an additional advancement occurred. The Adaptive cruise control is able to main speed and keep minimum distance to the leading vehicle. Both Systems do not exhibit any form of communication.

Cooperative adaptive cruise control (CACC) [12] is an extension of ACC that utilizes communication most of the times to other vehicle(s).

This paper focuses on the Vehicle-to-Vehicle (V2V) Cooperative Adaptive Cruise Control (CACC) system. The first section of this paper discusses the components of the CACC system, which include the vehicle system, intent sharing,

F. Calise et al. (Eds.): SMARTGREENS 2024/VEHITS 2024, CCIS 2954, pp. 245–257, 2026.
https://doi.org/10.1007/978-3-032-23187-1_14

disturbance estimation, and the control system. This is followed by the simulation scenario and evaluation. Finally, the paper concludes with a discussion of the findings.

2 Problem Statement

In this section, we introduce the components of the CACC system, including vehicle dynamics, the CACC system design, disturbance estimation, and the integration of the intent-sharing concept.

2.1 Vehicle Dynamics

Focusing on the longitudinal dynamics of the ego vehicle i. The vehicles are modeled as double integrator however, in our work we use more detailed model. The longitudinal dynamics is described as

$$F_{net} = F_{trac} - F_{areo} - F_{roll} - F_{grade} \tag{1}$$

substituting each term with its value, dividing the equation by the vehicle mass m , we get

$$a = u - \frac{1}{2m}\rho C_d A v^2 - C_r g - mgsin(\theta) \tag{2}$$

The Eq. 2 shows the nonlinearity of the acceleration due to the drag and rolling resistance. The vehicle state-space representation with u as the input signal is shown in the Eq. 3. We also observed in [4] that introducing additional system state to compensate for the error make the system more likely to oscillate and impacting the following vehicles. Therefore we refrain from having any relative states in the ego vehicle dynamics.

$$\begin{bmatrix} \dot{q}_i(t) \\ \dot{v}_i(t) \end{bmatrix} = \begin{bmatrix} 0 & 1 \\ 0 & 0 \end{bmatrix} \begin{bmatrix} q_i(t) \\ v_i(t) \end{bmatrix} + \begin{bmatrix} 0 \\ 1 \end{bmatrix} \text{u(t)} + \begin{bmatrix} 0 & 0 & 0 \\ -1 & -1 & -1 \end{bmatrix} \begin{bmatrix} \frac{1}{2m}\rho C_d A(v_i(t))^2 \\ C_r g \\ gsin(\theta) \end{bmatrix} \tag{3}$$

The nonlinear state space representation is used as the system for state closed loop response of the system. Discrete time system is necessary for any computational control algorithm. Using euler method with discretization sample dt

$$\begin{bmatrix} q_i(k+1) \\ v_i(k+1) \end{bmatrix} = \begin{bmatrix} 1 & dt \\ 0 & 1 \end{bmatrix} \begin{bmatrix} q_i(k) \\ v_i(k) \end{bmatrix} + \begin{bmatrix} 0 \\ dt \end{bmatrix} \text{u(k)} + \begin{bmatrix} 0 & 0 & 0 \\ -dt & -dt & -dt \end{bmatrix} \begin{bmatrix} \frac{1}{2m}\rho C_d A(v_i(k))^2 \\ C_r g \\ gsin(\theta) \end{bmatrix} \tag{4}$$

2.2 CACC System

We approach the CACC system in a slightly different way. Typically, the dynamics equations describe the error dynamics between two vehicles with integration [13]. In our work, we compute the desired states, such as q_i and v_i, and the control algorithm determines the acceleration input u that drives the system toward these desired states (first-order controller). The headway policy equation defines the desired displacement h_i^* for a vehicle i. It is formulated as the sum of a safe distance d_0 and the product of the time headway t_i and the vehicle velocity v_i. It is known that such a policy helps ease the conditions for string stability [14].

$$h_i^*(t) = d_0 + t_i v_i(t), \tag{5}$$

This formulation can be rewritten in terms of the vehicle i displacement q_i:

$$q_i^*(t) = q_{i-1} - (d_0 + t_i v_i). \tag{6}$$

To ensure consistency in the system, the desired velocity state v_i^* should match v_{i-1}. With this, we establish a reference for all system states (Figs.1, 2 and 4).

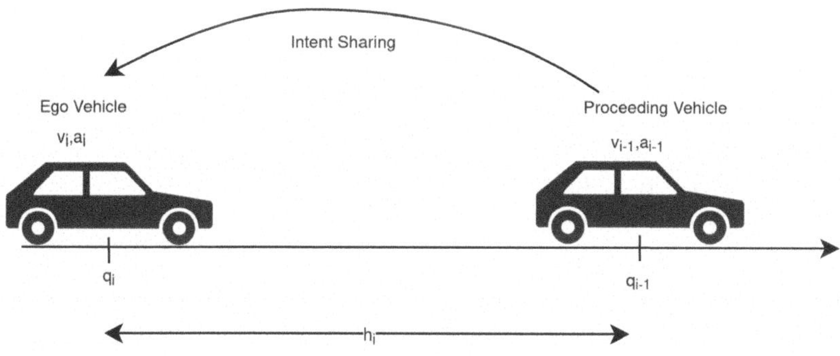

Fig. 1. Diagram of the vehicles.

2.3 Intent Sharing

Intent sharing is a cooperative driving automation technology in which nearby vehicles share information such as state and intent (planned vehicle trajectory). Several studies have demonstrated the benefits of intent sharing [2] [1]. The intent sharing message contains the vehicle's trajectory in addition to status information. According to [5], the optimal duration for the future trajectory is 3.5 s, we use a longer horizon of 5 s. The intent sharing message is assumed to be deterministic.

Discrete-time intent sharing requires $(n + 1) \times N$ data points to be transmitted. On the receiver side, interpolation is needed due to transmission delays and time alignment with the receiver. Instead of discrete values for intent sharing of the vehicle trajectory, we use an interpolated Lagrange function for the states of the preceding vehicle. This approach requires an interpolation algorithm (see Algorithm 1) to be executed on the transmitter side. The transmitted data are the interpolation coefficients and the time interval of validity. The size of the packet to be sent is $n \times N+2$. This leads to a reduction of the required bandwidth by nearly N points. Any computation on the receiver side due to communication delays or different sampling times used in each vehicle is eliminated. where n is the size of the state vector to be transmitted and N the number of samples to be transmitted.

Algorithm 1. Lagrange Interpolation.

Require: A set of points $(q_0, v_0), (q_1, v_1), \ldots, (q_N, v_N)$
Ensure: The Lagrange interpolating polynomial $L(x)$
  Initialize ${}^{q}L(q) \leftarrow 0$, ${}^{v}L(v) \leftarrow 0$
  for $k = 0$ to N **do**
    Initialize ${}^{q}L_k(q) \leftarrow 1$
    Initialize ${}^{v}L_k(v) \leftarrow 1$
    for $j = 0$ to N **do**
      if $j \neq k$ **then**
        ${}^{q}L_k(q) \leftarrow^{v} L_k(v) \times \frac{(q-q_j)}{(q_k-q_j)}$
        ${}^{q}L_k(v) \leftarrow^{q} L_k(v) \times \frac{(v-v_j)}{(v_k-v_j)}$
      end if
    end for
    ${}^{q}L(q) \leftarrow^{q} L(q) + q_k \times^{q} L_k(q)$
    ${}^{v}L(v) \leftarrow^{v} L(v) + v_k \times^{v} L_k(v)$
  end for
  return ${}^{q}L(q),^{v} L(v)$

2.4 Disturbance Estimation

The vehicle longitudinal dynamics are nonlinear, as shown in Eq. 4. We can treat the system as nonlinear and design a nonlinear controller, or alternatively, we can use a disturbance estimation algorithm based on a Kalman filter. This algorithm estimates the total disturbance acting on the system, which is then fed into the linear control algorithm. The Kalman filter is a model-based estimation technique. The model used in the estimation algorithm is different from the vehicle dynamics model and is referred to as the Internal Model. In the Internal Model, all forces acting on the vehicle are lumped into a variable d. The discrete state-space model of the disturbance estimation model is shown in Eq. 9. Figure 3 illustrates the Kalman filter algorithm; note that we have dropped the subscript i. The algorithm includes a prediction step and an update step. [6] explains the Kalman filter algorithm and its derivation.

$$\begin{aligned}\mathbf{x}[k+1] &= \mathbf{\Phi}\mathbf{x}[k] + \mathbf{\Gamma}\mathbf{u}[k] + \mathbf{w}[k],\\ \mathbf{y}[k] &= \mathbf{C}\mathbf{x}[k] + \mathbf{n}[k],\end{aligned} \tag{7}$$

where

$$\begin{aligned}\text{system state:} \quad & \mathbf{x}_k \in \mathbb{R}^n\\ \text{initial state:} \quad & \mathbf{x}_0 \in \mathbb{R}^n \sim \mathcal{N}\left(\check{\mathbf{x}}_0, \check{\mathbf{P}}_0\right)\\ \text{input:} \quad & \mathbf{u}_k \in \mathbb{R}^n\\ \text{process noise:} \quad & \mathbf{w}_k \in \mathbb{R}^n \sim \mathcal{N}\left(\mathbf{0}, \mathbf{Q}_k\right)\\ \text{measurement:} \quad & \mathbf{y}_k \in \mathbb{R}^m\\ \text{measurement noise:} \quad & \mathbf{n}_k \in \mathbb{R}^m \sim \mathcal{N}\left(\mathbf{0}, \mathbf{R}_k\right)\end{aligned} \tag{8}$$

$$\begin{bmatrix} v_i[k+1] \\ d_i[k+1] \end{bmatrix} = \begin{bmatrix} 1 & -dt \\ 0 & 1 \end{bmatrix} \begin{bmatrix} v_i[k] \\ d_i[k] \end{bmatrix} + \begin{bmatrix} dt \\ 0 \end{bmatrix} u_i[k] \tag{9}$$

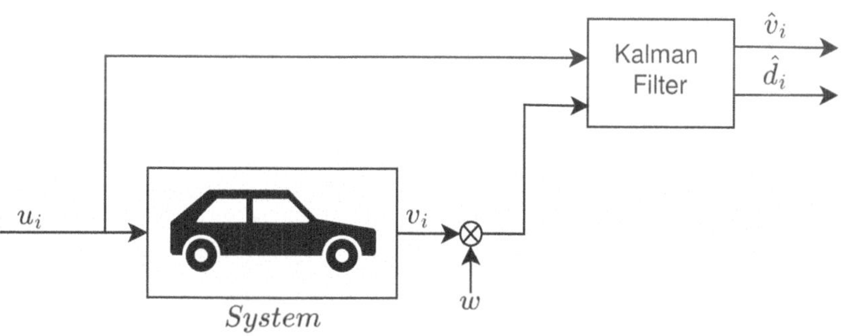

Fig. 2. Diagram of Ego Vehicle with the Estimator.

2.5 String Stability

String stability is an important aspect of any CACC (Cooperative Adaptive Cruise Control) or platoon system. It is a property of a system that contains multiple components, such as vehicles in our case. The term "string stability" refers to the ability of a system to attenuate any disturbances within a string of vehicles. It is known that if string stability is not satisfied, the traffic flow will be jeopardized. Although the concept seems simple, mathematically it is not straightforward. The literature contains many definitions of string stability. S. Feng et al. [7] presented a survey of string stability definitions. It is also noted that the definition used in the literature often depends on the problem formulation. For instance, when the problem formulation is in the time domain,

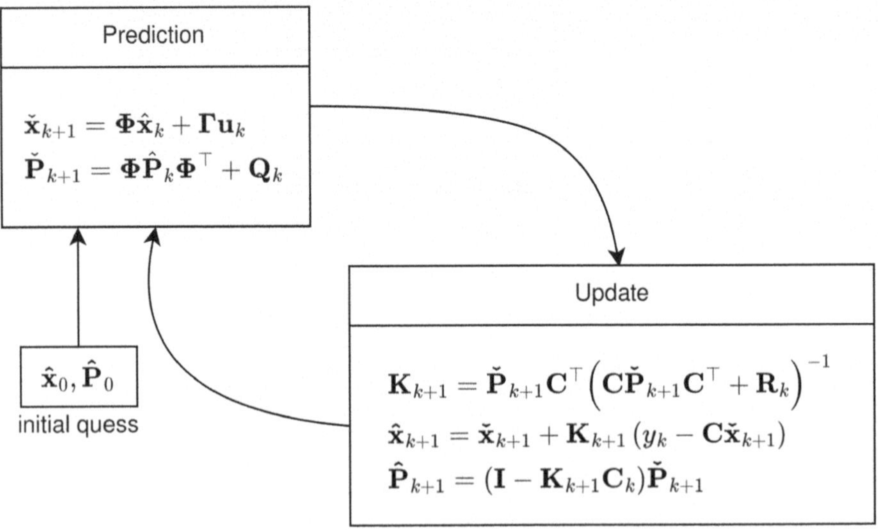

Fig. 3. Diagram of Kalman Filter Algorithm.

frequency-domain definitions are not suitable. In this work, we use the definition from [8]:

Definition 1. ***String Stability:*** *A vehicle platoon is string stable if, for a step change in the velocity of the lead vehicle* $v_1(t)$ *at time* $t = 0$*, there exist constant scalars* $\gamma_i \in (0, 1)$ *for* $i = 2, \ldots, V$ *such that:*

$$\max_{t \geq 0} |a_{i+1}(t)| \leq \gamma \max_{t \geq 0} |a_i(t)| \quad \text{for} i = 2, \ldots, V - 1. \tag{10}$$

String stability is seen as a way of ensuring that following vehicles behave similarly to the lead vehicle. However, each vehicle has its own dynamics. The definition can be relaxed by considering a short period of time H instead of identical time points. The modified string stability condition is given by:

$$|a_i(t)| \leq \gamma \max_{\tau \in [t-H, t]} |a_{i-1}(\tau)| \tag{11}$$

3 Methodology

The control algorithm runs independently on each vehicle. As a baseline, we use a Linear Quadratic Regulator (LQR), while our proposed approach focuses on a Model Predictive Controller (MPC). Any shared parameters between the two are fixed to compare their responses. The system of equations in 3, without external disturbance, is known as the double integrator system and is well studied in [10] and several controllers were presented. The definition of the reference signal $\bar{x}_i$ is shown in Eq. 12:

$$\bar{x}_i(t) = \begin{bmatrix} \bar{q}_i(t) \\ \bar{v}_i(t) \end{bmatrix} = \begin{bmatrix} q_{i-1}(t) - d_0 - t_i v_i \\ v_{i-1}(t) \end{bmatrix} \tag{12}$$

We aim to use a first-order controller because, in our previous work [4], we observed that a higher-order controller is harder to tune, especially when focusing on string stability.

3.1 Baseline

[checked] The baseline algorithm is the Linear Quadratic Regulator (LQR). The linear quadratic control problem is an optimal control problem where the control law is a full state feedback to the system. In this work, we assume the states of the vehicle, q_i and v_i, are true and fully observable. The problem is mathematically formulated by minimizing the cost function $\boldsymbol{J}$ in Eq. 13, where $\boldsymbol{Q}$ and $\boldsymbol{R}$ are the state cost matrix and control input cost matrix, respectively. Both are symmetric, positive semi-definite matrices.

$$\min_{u(t)_i} \int_0^\infty \left\{ (x_i(t) - \bar{x}_i(t))^\top \mathbf{Q} (x_i(t) - \bar{x}_i(t)) + u_i(t)^\top \mathbf{R} u_i(t) \right\} dt \tag{13}$$

subject to

$$\dot{x}_i(t) = A x_i(t) + B u_i(t) \tag{14}$$

$$x_i(0) = x_0 \tag{15}$$

This problem has a closed-form solution using Pontryagin's Minimum Principle [11]. The solution leads to the optimal control signal $u(t)$, with the subscript i indicating the signal associated with vehicle i:

$$u_i(t) = -\boldsymbol{K} x_i(t) \tag{16}$$

We set $\boldsymbol{Q}$ and $\boldsymbol{R}$ to be identity matrices of size n and m, respectively.

3.2 Receding Horizon

[checked]Model Predictive Control (MPC) formulates the control problem as an optimization problem. The MPC algorithm predicts the future states of a system over a specified time window, called the prediction horizon. This prediction is based on a mathematical model. Using the current states of the system, along with the predicted future states, system inputs, and constraints, a quadratic cost function is constructed. This transforms the control problem into a quadratic programming problem.

$$J = \sum_{j=0}^{N-1} \left[(x_i[k+j] - \bar{x}_i[k+j])^\top \boldsymbol{Q} (x_i[k+j] - \bar{x}_i[k+j]) + (u_i[k+j])^\top \boldsymbol{R} (u_i[k+j]) \right] \tag{17}$$

subject to

$$x_i[k+1] = A_d x_i[k] + B_d u_i[k] \tag{18}$$

$$x_i[k] \in \mathcal{X} \tag{19}$$

$$u_i[k] \in \mathcal{U} \tag{20}$$

The string stability conditions could also be formulated as constraints; however, formulating these constraints is very sensitive because it might lead to a non-solvable quadratic programming (QP) problem for the numerical solver. We have incorporated the disturbance into the system in the algorithm to compensate for any deviations caused by unmodeled elements, such as drag, roll, and grade forces, in the problem formulation (see Eq. 17).

The diagram in the figure shows the complete system. It includes an input signal generator for determining the desired state over a 5-second horizon, a model-based optimization component for solving the control signal $u_i[k]$, and a vehicle reacting to the input signal. Lastly, there is an estimation component responsible for determining the lumped disturbance acting on the vehicle, which is then fed back into the predictive controller to compensate for it at the current time instance.

4 Simulation Setup

In this section, we outline the simulation setup used to evaluate the performance of our proposed control algorithms. The simulation environment is designed to replicate realistic driving conditions and vehicle dynamics. One key component of our simulation is the velocity profile of the leading vehicle, which serves as a reference for the following vehicles in the control algorithm.

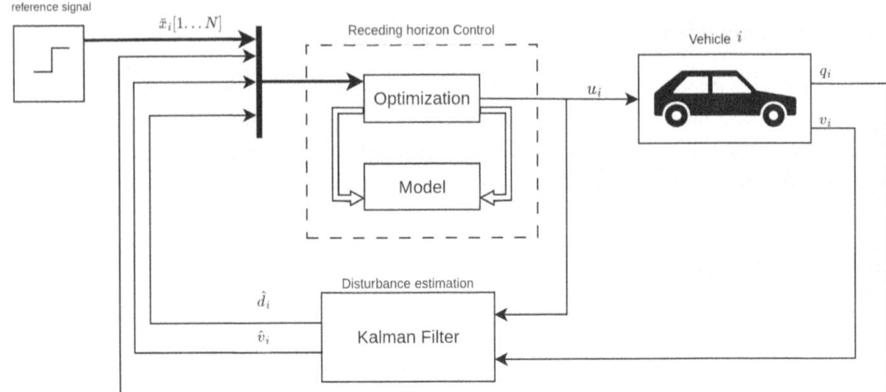

Fig. 4. Diagram of Receding Horizon Approach with disturbance estimation.

As depicted in Fig. 5, the velocity profile of the leading vehicle consists of three distinct phases: an initial acceleration phase to a constant cruising speed, followed by a further acceleration to a peak velocity, and finally a deceleration back to a stop. This profile is used to test the responsiveness and adaptability of the control algorithms under various driving conditions and transitions between different speed levels. The profile is a reference signal created and does not include any vehicle dynamics of the leading vehicle. It is more challenging for the follower controller to deal with this profile than with real vehicle velocity profile.

The simulation incorporates various scenarios, and disturbances (e.g., drag, roll, and grade forces). Performance metrics, such as string stability, root mean squared error, and response to disturbances, are used to assess the system's effectiveness. The following subsections provide a detailed description of each aspect of the simulation setup, including how the control algorithms manage the changes in the leading vehicle's velocity profile(Table 1 and 2).

Table 1. Nominal Vehicle Parameters.

Parameter	Value	Description
m	1500 kg	Vehicle mass
ρ	$1.225\,\text{kg/m}^3$	Air density
c_d	0.3	Drag coefficient
A	$2.2\,\text{m}^2$	Cross-sectional area of the vehicle
c_r	0.01	Rolling resistance coefficient
g	$9.81\,\text{m/s}^2$	Gravitational acceleration
α	0.0	Slope angle (assumed flat ground)

5 Results

In this section, we present the results of our simulations designed to evaluate the performance of the proposed Model Predictive Control (MPC) algorithm in a cooperative adaptive cruise control (CACC) system. We compare the results with a baseline Linear Quadratic Regulator (LQR) approach to highlight the improvements in string stability , and responsiveness to disturbances.

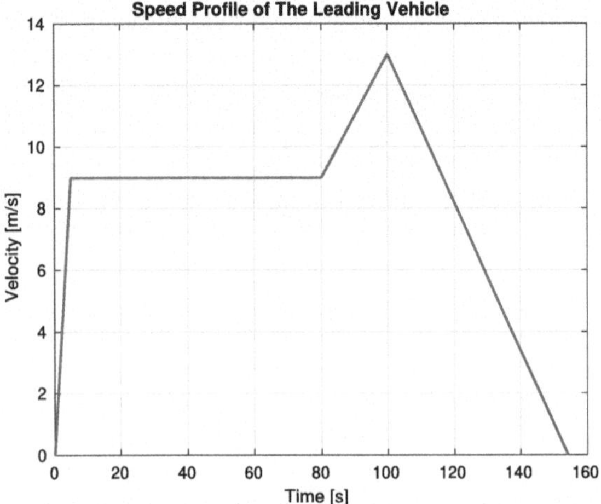

Fig. 5. Speed profile of the Leading vehicle used in the simulation.

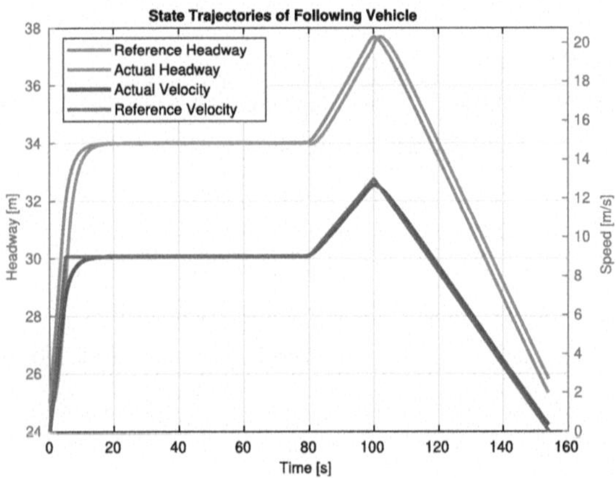

Fig. 6. State Trajectory of the Following Vehicle with MPC.

5.1 Reference Deviation

We conducted simulations under reference velocity shown in 5. The performance metrics are RMS and Infinity norm. The results of the MPC and the baseline are shown in Figs. 6 and 7. It is worth mentioning that using MPC without intent sharing led to identical behavior to the LQR controller. In other words, if no prior information about the input is known using MPC has less significant advantage.

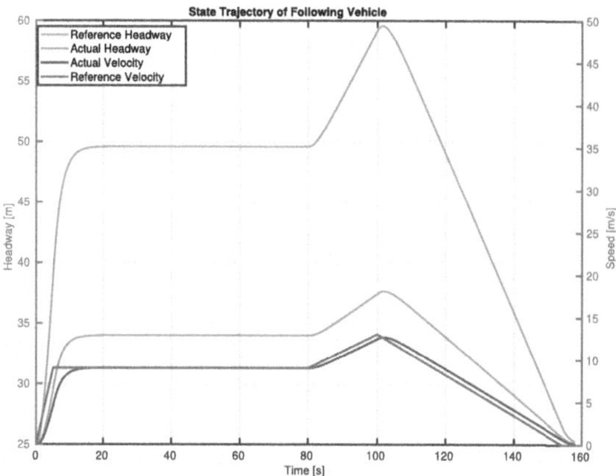

Fig. 7. State Trajectory of the Following Vehicle with the Baseline Controller.

Table 2. Infinity Norm and RMS Norm of Each State for Baseline and MPC Controllers.

State	Controller	Infinity Norm ($\|\cdot\|_\infty$)	RMS Norm (RMS)
q (Position)	Baseline (LQR)	$21.947[m]$	$14[m]$
q (Position)	MPC	$3.2729[m]$	$0.62127[m]$
v (Velocity)	Baseline (LQR)	$4.4908[m/s]$	$0.81537[m/s]$
v (Velocity)	MPC	$2.0682[m/s]$	$0.39851[m/s]$

5.2 String Stability

The proposed Model Predictive Control (MPC) algorithm maintains better spacing between vehicles compared to the Linear Quadratic Regulator (LQR) baseline, especially in variable-speed scenarios. Although our controller was not explicitly designed to consider string stability, we analyze the system's response in this section from a string stability perspective. Figure 8 shows the accelerations of both the leader and the follower. The regions where string stability is violated are highlighted in yellow. The parameters used in the string stability definitions are $\gamma = 1$ and $H = 1$ [s].

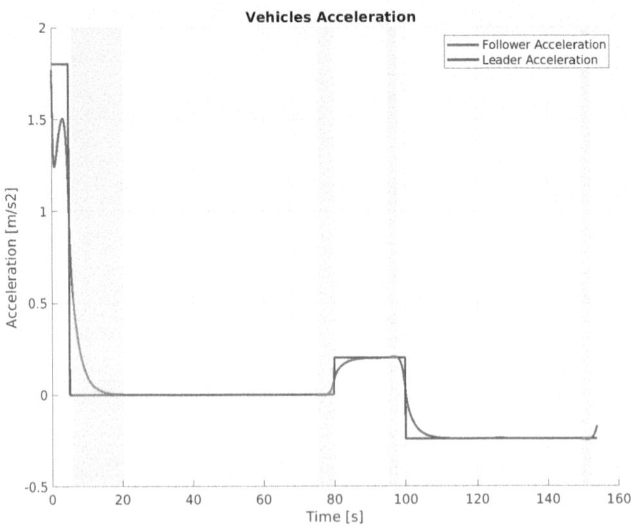

Fig. 8. Acceleration profiles of the leader and follower vehicles over time. The shaded region indicates where the follower's acceleration violates the condition Eq. 10, signifying a violation of string stability.

6 Conclusion

In conclusion, the Model Predictive Control (MPC) algorithm successfully tracks the state references, whereas the Linear Quadratic Regulator (LQR) fails to do so. The inclusion of disturbance estimation significantly enhances the reference state tracking. Additionally, intent sharing makes the MPC approach highly effective. We were able to derive a first-order controller for the Cooperative Adaptive Cruise Control (CACC) system, and using Lagrangian interpolation reduces the required bandwidth and simplifies the computations on the receiver side. Overall, our system—comprising MPC, estimation, and intent sharing via Lagrangian interpolation—proves to be a robust and efficient solution.

Future Work. While the current system shows promising results, future work will focus on explicitly addressing string stability. Incorporating string stability into the controller design will be essential for improving safety and performance, particularly in vehicle platooning scenarios.

References

1. Ahmadreza, M., Sergei, A. S., Hongsheng, L.: Benefits of intent sharing in cooperative platooning, Published In: 2024 IEEE Vehicular Networking Conference (VNC)
2. Wang, H. M., Avedisov, S.S., Altintas, O., Orosz, G.: Multi-vehicle conflict management with status and intent sharing, Published In: 2022 IEEE Intelligent Vehicles Symposium (IV), pp. 04–09, IEEE

3. Wang, H.M., Avedisov, S. S., Molnár, T. G., Hamdi, A.S., Onur, A., Gábor, O.: Conflict analysis for cooperative maneuvering with status and intent sharing via V2X communication, IEEE Trans. Intell. Veh
4. Abulehia, A., Dariani, R., Schindler, J.: Optimal velocity model based CACC controller for urban scenarios VEHITS, pp. 327–335 (2024)
5. Kanipakam, L., Sakr, A.H., Avedisov, S.S., Moradipari, A.: Cooperative adaptive cruise control based on intent sharing messages and reinforcement learning. In: 2024 IEEE Vehicular Networking Conference (VNC), pp. 188–194, IEEE (2024)
6. Rhudy, M.B., Salguero, R. A., Holappa, K.: A kalman filtering tutorial for undergraduate students. Int. J. Comput. Sci. Eng. Surv. (2017). Academy and Industry Research Collaboration Center https://doi.org/10.5121/ijcses.2017.8101
7. Feng, S., et al.: 1367–5788. Pergamon (2019). https://doi.org/10.1016/j.arcontrol.2019.03.001
8. Kianfar, R., et al.: Design and experimental validation of a cooperative driving system in the grand cooperative driving challenge. IEEE Trans. Intell. Trans. Syst. **13**(3), 2012, IEEE
9. Shladover, S. E., Nowakowski, C., Lu, X., Ferlis, R.:Cooperative adaptive cruise control: definitions and operating concepts, Transp. Res. Rec., 2489, SAGE Publications Inc. https://doi.org/10.3141/2489-17
10. Rao, V. G., Bernstein, D. S.: Naive control of the double integrator. IEEE Control Syst. Mag, **21**(5), 86–97, 2001, IEEE. https://doi.org/10.1109/37.954521
11. , Pontryagin, Lev Semenovich, Mathematical Theory of Optimal Processes, The Mathematical Theory of Optimal Processes. Translated by D.E. Brown. By L.S. Pontryagin, V.G. Boltyansky, R.V. Gamkrelidze and E.F. Mishchenko.,: Oxford. England, UK, Oxford (1964)
12. Milanés, V., Shladover, S.E., Spring, J., Nowakowski, C., Kawazoe, H., Nakamura, M.: Cooperative Adaptive Cruise Control in Real Traffic Situations. IEEE Trans. Intell. Transp. Syst. https://doi.org/10.1109/TITS.2013.2278494
13. Naus, Gerrit J. L., Vugts, René P. A., Ploeg, J., van de M., Marinus J. G., Steinbuch, M.: String-Stable CACC design and experimental validation: a frequency-domain approach, IEEE Trans. Veh. Technol. https://doi.org/10.1109/TVT.2010.2076320
14. Barooah, P., Hespanha, J. P.: Error amplification and disturbance propagation in vehicle strings with decentralized linear control In: Proceedings of the 44th IEEE Conference on Decision and Control, and the European Control Conference, CDC-ECC '05. https://doi.org/10.1109/CDC.2005.1582948

Boosting VRU Awareness: Bounding Box Strategies for V2X Clustering

Leonardo Barbosa da Silva[1(✉)], Silas Correia Lobo[2], Evelio Martín García Fernández[1], and Christian Facchi[2]

[1] Department of Electrical Engineering, Universidade Federal do Paraná, Curitiba, Brazil
{leonardobarbosa,evelio}@ufpr.br

[2] CARISSMA (C-ECOS), Technische Hochschule Ingolstadt, Ingolstadt, Germany
SilasCorreia.Lobo@carissma.eu, Christian.Facchi@thi.de

Abstract. On Vehicle-to-Everything networking, *Vulnerable Road User* (VRU) is the name attributed to traffic members that are at a higher safety risk in mobility systems, such as pedestrians, cyclists and road workers. VRUs transmit *VRU Awareness Messages* (VAMs) to actively broadcast their position and kinematics to other traffic members and road infrastructure. Through the exchange of VAMs, the VRU Basic Service contains a clustering functionality that groups VRUs with similar behavior to prevent channel congestion in crowded traffic scenarios. A cluster leader is responsible for transmitting VAMs that describe the group, generating a bounding box geometric shape that describes the space occupied by its members. The current VAM standard however, does not provide strategies to produce these shapes and does not elaborate on methods to evaluate shapes. This work offers algorithms to construct these geometries and discusses metrics to compare the generated bounding box types. Simulation results show that each shape type can be useful in distinct use cases. It also shows that changes must be done in the currently proposed standard operation message triggering, as the results indicate that channel occupation was not mitigated by the functionality.

Keywords: Vulnerable road users · VRU clustering · Cluster bounding boxes · V2X communication · Vulnerable road user awareness message · VRU basic service

1 Introduction

In transportation systems, the *Vulnerable Road Users* (VRUs) concept is used to describe the group composed of pedestrians, cyclists, road workers, etc. A report from the *European Road Safety Observatory* (ERSO) shows that in 2021 nearly half of the traffic accidents fatalities in the European Union were VRUs, with pedestrians corresponding to one out of every five deaths [4]. This indicates that this set of individuals really are at a higher risk in mobility scenarios, and thus new solutions are needed to ensure their protection.

The *Vehicle-to-Everything* (V2X) protocols aim to provide additional safety to road users by improving awareness through the use of wireless messages. There are two

F. Calise et al. (Eds.): SMARTGREENS 2024/VEHITS 2024, CCIS 2954, pp. 258–284, 2026.
https://doi.org/10.1007/978-3-032-23187-1_15

main technologies at the forefront of the state of the art: the *Cellular-V2X* (C-V2X) that originates from the *Long-Term Evolution* (LTE) standard, and the WiFi-based V2X approaches, derived from the IEEE 802.11p standard. Both alternatives allocate the 5.9 GHz frequency band [12].

Through the definition of the *Intelligent Transport Systems* (ITS) concept, the *European Telecommunications Institute* (ETSI) proposed the WiFi-based ITS-G5 standard [6]. The ITS-G5 services are categorized by the *CAR 2 CAR Communication Consortium* (C2C-CC) based on a deployment roadmap, with the Day 3+ release proposing active broadcast of V2X messages by VRUs [2].

With the VRU active advertisement functionality in mind, ETSI published the 103 300 series of reports and specifications that propose a *VRU Awareness Message* (VAM) [9–11]. VAMs are the basis for the *VRU Basic Service* (VBS), which describes operations, message generation rules, and transmission trigger conditions. The generation time depends on channel occupation through the use of the *Decentralized Congestion Control* (DCC) mechanism [8]. The VBS have many potential applications, such as collision avoidance, additional protection on driver's blind spots, and intersection management [3].

In traffic scenarios crowded with VRUs, the implementation of the VBS could result in plenty of VAMs with similar data elements being sent. This can then lead to unnecessary increase in channel congestion and additional processing workload to the ITS stations in the local network [11]. As a countermeasure, the VBS offers an optional *clustering* functionality, through which VRUs with similar position and kinematics are treated as a single entity represented by a leader node that broadcasts VAMs in the name of the whole group. To advertise the set of members, the leader must include a data field in its VAM that represents the area occupied by the cluster participants. These objects can assume three different geometrical shapes: *circle*, *rectangle*, or *polygon*. However, ETSI 103 300 does not offer strategies on how to produce these constructs, nor does it discuss each option's impact on the VBS's performance.

Solutions to implementation gaps in clustering on the VBS are offered in this work, offering a set of algorithms to generate the bounding box shapes. The *Cluster Map* data object introduced in is used to construct the list of cluster compatible VRUs, necessary for the formation and maintenance of cluster shapes. Testing the proposed strategies is a simulated traffic scenario implemented in the open-source framework *Artery*[1] [20]. The impact of each bounding box shape on the VBS uses metrics such as VRUs per bounding box area, increment to message size, number of VAMs sent, total cluster operations, and Channel Busy Ratio.

This work enhances and extends [1] by evaluating a new set of simulation results, with a duration of 30 s instead of 15 s. Longer simulations led to new conclusions, insights and more parameters to be discussed. The bounding box shape generation strategies proposed in [1] are once again used, as well as the Cluster Map data structure and the Cluster Density metric.

The remainder of this chapter is structured as follows: Sect. 2 presents an overview of the VBS and its gaps. Section 3 proposes VRU cluster bounding box formation strategies and Sect. 4 defines metrics to compare the shapes generated from these methods.

[1] http://artery.v2x-research.eu/.

Section 5 describes the tools used to simulate the service, and Sect. 6 discusses the obtained results. Section 7 concludes this work and suggests future steps.

2 VRU Basic Service

On the VBS, transmission of a VAM are triggered due to elapsed time or a change in either kinematics or position above a predefined threshold. The interval between consecutive message generation ranges from a minimum of 100 ms up to 5 s. VAMs contain the mandatory containers: ITS Protocol Data Unit (PDU) Header, Basic Container, and High Frequency Container. These are contained in every message and broadcast each device's Station ID, message generation time, VRU profile, position, and kinematics. These messages also contain among its optional containers the Cluster Information Container (CIC) and the Cluster Operation Container (COC), handled by a *cluster management* function in the facilities layer [11]. The manager uses a set of parameters determined in the VBS to decide when it is necessary to perform cluster formation, joining, leaving, and breaking up operations. Key values that are relevant to this study are defined by ETSI 103 300 and given in Table 1.

Table 1. Cluster parameter values from [11].

	Parameter name	Meaning	Value
Cluster Decision	numCreateCluster	Minimum amount of nodes to form a cluster	3 to 5 VRUs
	minClusterSize	Minimum cluster size (only used at cluster creation)	1 VRU
	maxClusterSize	Maximum cluster size	20 VRUs
	maxClusterDistance	Maximum distance between VRU and edge of the cluster	3 to 5 m
	maxClusterVelocityDifference	Maximum velocity difference within the cluster	5%
Cluster Membership	timeClusterJoinNotification	Standalone VRU emits a warning of a join operation for this duration	3 s
	timeClusterJoinSuccess	Standalone VRU waits this duration for leader to confirm its addition to the cluster	0.5 s
	timeClusterBreakupWarning	Leader VRU emits a warning of a break up operation for this duration	3 s
	timeClusterContinuity	Passive VRU waits this duration for a new VAM from the Leader before considering that the connection is lost	2 s
	timeClusterLeaveNotification	Passive VRU emits a warning of a leave operation for this duration	1 s

2.1 VBS Clustering Operations

In the regular VBS operation a VRU operates *standalone*, periodically broadcasting VAMs with the mandatory containers (Fig. 1). Meanwhile, it also monitors received V2X messages, parsing them and updating its *Local Dynamic Map* (LDM) with the detected objects from the awareness notifications [7]. If enabled, *cluster management* will constantly check for opportunities to create a cluster or join a pre-existing one.

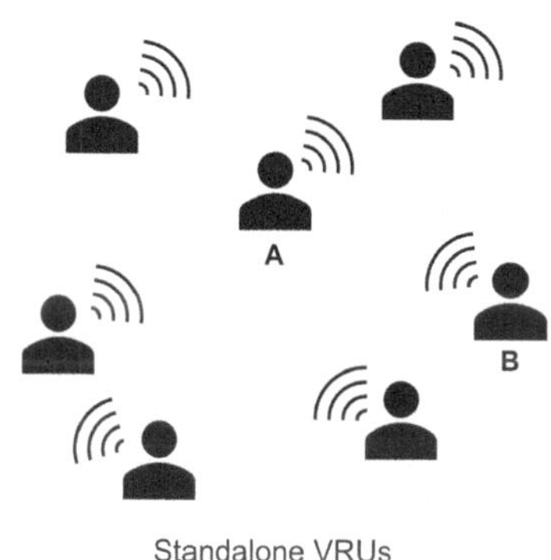

Fig. 1. Standalone VRUs in a network.

Based on ETSI 103 300, cluster creation on a VBS is triggered when a minimum of *numCreateCluster* (default: 3) *standalone* VRUs with ITS capabilities are at a limit distance of *maxClusterDistance* (default: 5 m), heading in a similar direction and with similar speed, with a difference smaller than *maxClusterVelocityDifference* (default: 5%). This ETSI specification does not detail much about the process of leader selection beyond this point, and as such, this work presumes that the first device that detects this condition adopts the role of cluster leader. The leader then creates a bounding box containing only itself and starts transmitting cluster VAMs as done by VRU A in Fig. 2.

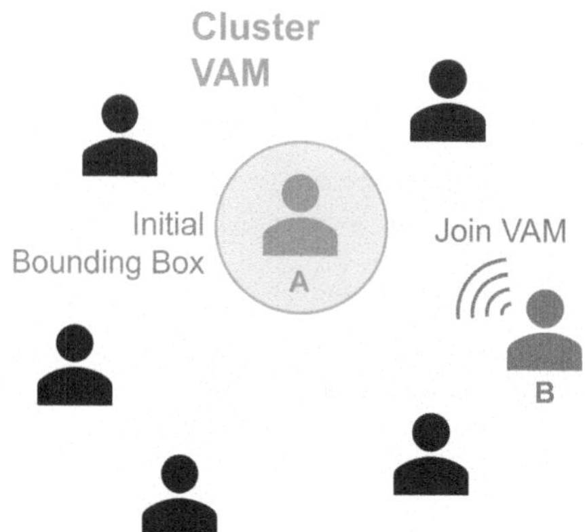

Fig. 2. Initial bounding box formation and join VAMs.

As also shown in Fig. 2, *standalone* VRUs in the vicinity that receive a compatible cluster VAM, send a join VAM for 3 s by including the COC with the *ClusterJoinInfo* data field, specifying the target cluster's ID and the duration for which the VRU will continue sending standalone VAMs. A VRU can only join clusters with cardinality below *maxClusterSize* (default: 20) VRUs [11].

After receiving join messages, the leader updates the bounding box to fit the new members, and send new cluster VAMs. VRUs that sent join notifications will then parse the cluster VAMs and check if they are included in the new bounding box. After successfully joining, the VRU assumes a *passive* role, ceasing VAM transmission but monitoring leader messages to ensure that speed difference and distance are still suitable (Fig. 3).

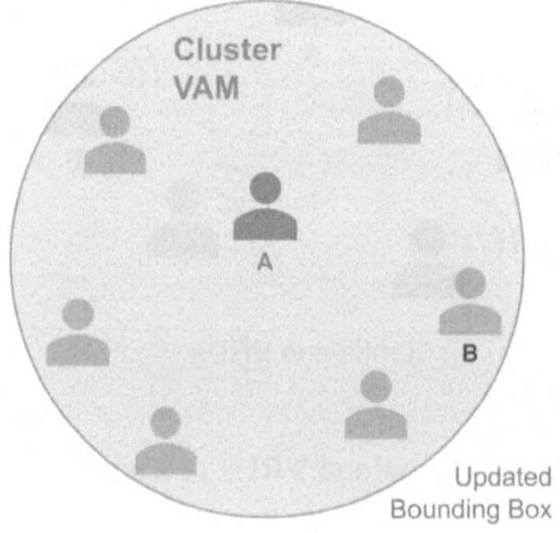

Fig. 3. Cluster in maintenance mode, with members as *passive* VRUs.

The exchange of messages between a VRU cluster leader (VRU A) and a standalone turned cluster member (VRU B) during a cluster formation event are shown in Fig. 4.

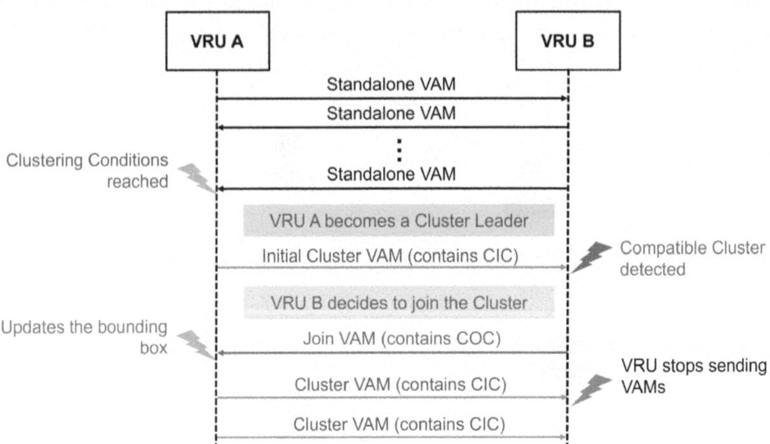

Fig. 4. Message diagram between two VRUs during a cluster creation event.

A member can decide to leave a cluster when its kinematics and/or position are incompatible with the group, when no VAM has been received from the leader within 2 s, or due to a cluster break-up notification from the leader. The leave VAM, just like the the join message, also includes a COC, containing the target cluster's ID and stating the reason for the operation on its *ClusterLeaveInfo* data field.

During a cluster's lifespan, the leader sends VAMs containing a CIC that describes a geometry encapsulating every member. This shape, named bounding box, can be one of three possible types: circle, rectangle, or polygon, each taking a varying amount of parameters as shown in Fig. 5. The circle has a center point (*C.a*) and radius (*C.b*). The rectangle includes a center point (*R.a*), half-length (*R.b*), half-width (*R.c*), and orientation (*R.d*). The polygon consists of a sequential list of all the offset points (*P.a.1*, ..., *P.a.n*) that form its vertices, without an explicit upper bound.

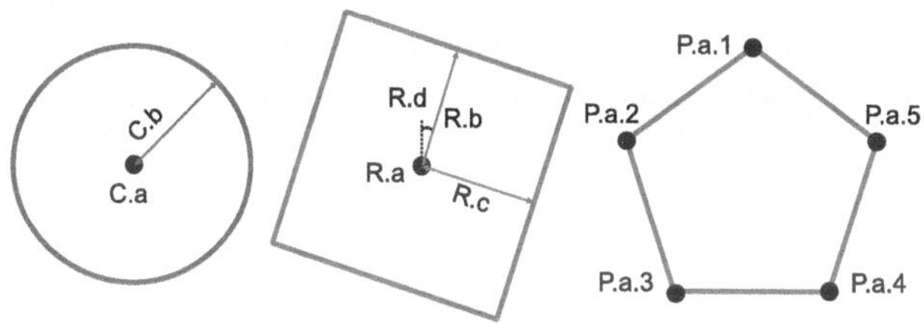

Fig. 5. Parameters used to describe a Bounding Box shape in the CIC [1].

The leader listens for operation VAMs addressed to its ID, adjusting the cluster shape and cardinality according to valid join and leave messages. If it determines that a cluster should be dispersed, the leader sends a VAM containing a COC with the *clusterBreakupInfo* data field. This message includes a breakup reason and a time at which the leader will stop transmitting cluster VAMs.

2.2 Functional Gaps of the VBS

As the current ETSI 103 300 VBS standard development is ongoing, it has functional gaps hindering complete implementation of the clustering functionalities. This subsection describes the enhancements suggested in other publications [1, 15] which were incorporated in this study.

The first issue is related to the (*T_GenVamMax*) parameter. This value controls the largest possible time interval between consecutive message generations from a VRU using the VBS, meaning that in highly congested scenarios, a node may transmit consecutive VAMs spaced by 5 s as per ETSI 103 300. This value is incompatible with the operation of a VRU as a *cluster leader*, which would trigger "leader-lost" leave operations from its members due to them not receiving cluster VAMs from the leader in an interval of *timeClusterContinuity* (default: 2 s). To prevent this, if a VRU has the role of a cluster leader, its *T_GenVamMax* value is changed to 2 s to match the timeout from cluster continuity.

Currently, the VBS does not offer conditions for a cluster creation to timeout. This means that a leader could get stuck in the initial stages of a cluster creation by waiting indefinitely for other VRUs to send join notifications if a number of a least *numCreateCluster* VRUs is never reached. Since the broadcast of a cluster VAM demands more processing than a *standalone* message, it makes no sense to keep a VRU in this state for long periods. Thus, a "Cluster creation failed" event is suggested to be triggered when a leader does not receive sufficient valid joins in the span of *timeLeaderWaiting* (default: 2 s).

The initial bounding box, as required by the VBS, must contain only the cluster leader. The service description however, does not offer a methodology to build this initial shape. It is then proposed that this shape should always be a circle with a radius of half the distance to the closest compatible VRU. A circle is chosen due to it requiring the smallest amount of data elements to be generated, while also only requiring information about the leader's position and one more compatible VRU. The selected radius calculation guarantees that this parameter is adaptable to the list of potential members, while ensuring a non-negative area that covers only the leader.

A buffer distance

$$d_{Bf} = v_{VRU} \cdot t_{VAM}, \tag{1}$$

is calculated using the highest VRU velocity within the cluster members (v_{VRU}) and the VAM assembly time (t_{VAM}). This value is added to the edge of all shapes, increasing the bounding box area. This functionality improves robustness of these geometries against delays and position errors, which could result in uncertainty if a node is covered by a bounding box when they are located at shape's edge.

Furthermore, the VBS does not currently offer a manner for a cluster leader to breakup a cluster due to insufficient members. This can be an issue when recalculating a bounding box when, after a series of member quitting a cluster, its cardinality falls below the default *numCreateCluster* value of 3 VRUs. In this situation, the generation of rectangular or polygonal shapes would be impossible. This study suggests that a cluster should dissolve whenever a leader identifies that the cardinality is below *numCreateCluster* for the duration of a timeout *timeLeaderWaiting*. This parameter provides some time for join requests to be received and processed by the leader while also matching the suggested timeout for the initial formation of the cluster.

2.3 Related Works

At the moment, research on the VRU Basic Service often focuses on scenarios containing only *standalone* VRUs, for instance, discussing how VAMs enhance VRU detection time and evaluating the use of the VBS alongside Collective Perception Messages (CPMs) [16]. Other works focus on the VAM generation, suggesting that the triggering conditions of these messages should take into account other factors, such as the profile of the VRUs [19], or proposing an adaptive context-aware message transmission scheme based on position and kinematics [27].

Regarding VRU Clustering on the context of the VBS, Rupp and Wischhof demonstrate that this feature reduces the numbers of VAMs sent in a traffic scenario, with high cardinality amounts providing the most significant benefit. The study, however, also shows that clustering increases the position error when compared to standalone nodes. Furthermore, an alaysis of the parameter *maxClusterVelocityDifference* shows that the default value of 5% is not effective, suggesting an increase of this value to 25% [21].

Simulation results obtained by Lobo et al. compare the VBS performance on a traffic scenario with and without clustering enabled. They indicate that clustering reduces the Channel Busy Ratio parameter, which ensures that the DCC function of the service operates further from its channel occupation, preventing the formation of queues and message drops. Thus, message latency and Packet Error Rate are also reduced [15].

At the moment, few research related to the geometrical shaping of the VRU clusters has been conducted. This topic is particularly challenging because the ETSI 103 300 standard defines the bounding box shapes that the VBS should offer but does not elaborate on how to produce these geometries. Furthermore, even when accounting for other wireless network technologies that support clustering, bounding box shaping is a unique problem to VRU clustering, as most applications do not need to worry about the shape their list of members produces. For instance, *Wireless Sensor Networks* and *Radio Frequency Identification* systems deal with the clustering various devices based on their position [13,22]. Both these technologies, however, deal with devices meant to remain static most of the time. Thus not concerning themselves with the kinematics or shape formed by the set of objects, treating clusters as amorphous point clouds.

In the domain of collision detection simulations, a variety of computational geometry strategies are applied to simplify one or more complex geometries into simpler-to-process *Bounding Volumes* (BV). The BVs can take the form of geometries such as circles, rectangles, and polygons, used for ray-tracing and hitbox detection in physics simulators, computer animations, and video games [5]. Furthermore, research in *Light Detection and Ranging* (LiDAR) also implement BV strategies, using them to take a set of detected points in a 3D space and convert it into a perceived object. For example, BVs using LiDAR data are used in autonomous driving for object detection [24], assessment of object orientation [14], and collision detection [25].

The present study uses the algorithms presented by Barbosa da Silva et al. that suggests clustering creation and maintenance strategies, as well as implements computational geometry techniques to construct the bounding boxes prescribed in the ETSI 103 300 technical specifications, introducing the Cluster Density comparison metric to evaluate the performance of the shape types, and discussing briefly potential situations in which each geometry can offer the most benefits [1]. At a similar moment, Xhoxhi et al. also presented a set of metrics to compare the different shape types for VRU Clustering in the context of VAMs and CPMs, introducing the Cluster Accuracy (CA) and Comprehensive Area Density Information (CADI) metrics. Also offering an algorithm that selects the most appropriate shape based on the CADI score [26].

3 Bounding Box Generation

To evaluate the effects of the different bounding box shape types on the clustering of VRUs on the VBS, previous implementations of the ETSI 103 300 [11] standard on the *Artery* V2X simulation were extended. In [16], the VAM containers and the message transmission triggers were developed for *standalone* VRUs, providing the basis for the VBS in the simulation framework. Continuing the VBS development, [15] implements the VRU cluster management functionality and polygonal bounding box generation. The cluster manager is a class present in every ITS-Station that contains the VBS and is responsible for: storing the VRU's role, parsing the CIC and COC contained in VAMs, generating bounding boxes, and monitoring the LDM for conditions to trigger the cluster creation, join, leave, and breakup events.

This section includes algorithms to manage the cluster creation and maintenance. As part of the maintenance of a cluster, this work uses the strategies from [1] to generate the three cluster bounding box shapes described in ETSI 103 300, implementing strategies based on computational geometry to form these structures. These strategies are supported by the *Cluster Map* data structure, that stores data from cluster-compatible VRUs, providing a *standalone* VRU with means to determine if it should create a cluster while also providing the *cluster leader* with data regarding its members.

3.1 Cluster Map Concept

This study uses the *Cluster Map* (CM) concept introduced in [1] as a tool to support the cluster management functionality of the VBS. The CM stores position, kinematics, and station Id of cluster-compatible VRUs perceived through the LDM. The purpose of the CM, as illustrated in Fig. 6, is to offer a data structure that is simpler to iterate during the VBS functional pipeline, supporting the operations of cluster creation and management. A CM is instantiated in every VRU assigned with a *standalone* or *cluster leader* role.

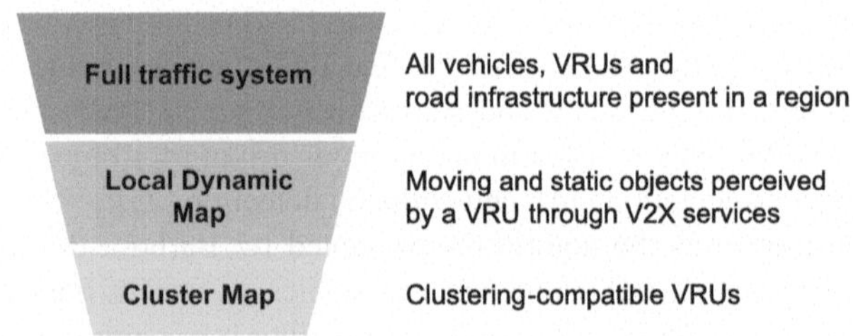

Fig. 6. Funneling of perceived traffic nodes in a region. Cluster Map acts as a specialized LDM [1].

Initially, the CM stores a list of cluster-compatible VRUs perceived in the LDM, with a *standalone* VRU using this structure to evaluate if it is able to create a new cluster and assume the leader role. At this instant, the CM is used to estimate the cardinality of the cluster-to-be and calculate the radius of the initial bounding box. The potential cardinality is determined by adding the amount of VRUs contained on the CM, plus the leader. After successful cluster creation, a new CM is used to track the cluster member nodes and is only updated by the leader through valid join and leave VAMs from compatible nodes. This ensures proper cluster management by the leader who must validate the received operations and keep track of the members' positions, enabling it to properly update the bounding box. The CM is the primary data source for the proposed bounding box generation strategies, being used to produce a point cloud that indicates the position of the set of VRUs to be clustered.

3.2 Initial Bounding Box

The first iteration of a cluster must contain only the leader in its bounding box, also meaning that the cardinality must always be of one (*minClusterSize*) at the start [11]. The operation begins with the *standalone* VRU that decided to create a cluster, called ego VRU, generating an empty *initial Cluster Map* (iCM). Next, it iterates the LDM, searching for all the perceived VRUs (P) and determining compatibility with itself (E). The first parameter evaluated for this decision is the Euclidean distance

$$d = \sqrt{(x_E - x_P)^2 + (y_E - y_P)^2}, \tag{2}$$

between the positions of each perceived VRU (x_P, y_P) and the ego VRU (x_E, y_E). Since elevation differences are irrelevant to this study, 2D coordinates suffice. If the distance (d) is less than 5 m, E and P are compatible. The second parameter, speed difference (v_{diff}), is given by

$$v_{diff} = \left| \frac{v_E - v_P}{v_E} \right| \cdot 100\%, \tag{3}$$

the ratio of the absolute values for the speed of both ego (v_E) and perceived (v_P) VRUs, with a maximum compatible difference of 5%. If P has both d and v_{diff} within the acceptable limits, the VRU's is included the iCM. While iterating through these candidates, ego must keep record of the smallest valid distance (d_{min}) among all the euclidian distances calculated from the iCM, using it later as a parameter to generate the initial cluster bounding box.

After evaluating all the perceived VRUs, ego verifies the amount of nodes stored in the iCM. If it contains at least two VRUs, a cluster creation is possible, since the potential cluster can reach the minimum cardinality of three (*numCreateCluster*). Next, the ego VRU switches roles and becomes a leader, starting the cluster-creation cycle. Algorithm 1 describes this decision workflow.

Algorithm 1. Cluster creation decision workflow [1].

```
   Data: Ego VRU's status and LDM
   Result: Cluster Creation Decision
 1 initialization;
 2 while VRU's role is standalone do
 3 |   update LDM;
 4 |   check LDM for compatible VRUs;
 5 |   generate iCM with compatible VRUs;
 6 |   if iCM size ≥ 2 then
 7 |   |   set VRU's role as cluster leader;
 8 |   |   produce initial cluster bounding box;
 9 |   |   generate random cluster ID;
10 |   |   include CIC in VAM;
11 |   |   send initial cluster VAM;
12 |   else
13 |   |   send standalone VAM;
14 |   end
15 end
```

To ensure that the first iteration of a cluster only contains the leader, the initial shape shall always be a circle. As per ETSI 103 300, this geometry is given by a node center point (*C.a*) and a radius (*C.b*). The first element is a tuple of x and y offset distances in centimeters between the *cluster leader* and the actual center of the proposed bounding box. In this case, the bounding box is centered on ego's position, resulting in a node center point of (0,0). The radius is obtained by dividing d_{min} in half, placing the edge of the circle between the leader and the closest compatible VRU contained in the iCM, ensuring that only the leader is contained in the shape.

The leader adds *C.a* and *C.b* to the CIC of the cluster VAM, starting to broadcast the clustering opportunity shortly after. The transmission of the initial shape continues until the cluster creation cycle is concluded by having at least *numCreateCluster* members added through received join VAMs, or is terminated due to an elapsed time above the proposed *timeLeaderWaiting* timeout threshold.

After generating the initial bounding box, the cluster manager discards the iCM, and creates an empty *maintenance Cluster Map* (mCM) to contain the data objects of actual cluster members. The main difference between these CMs is that the iCM contains a list of all the LDM-perceived VRUs that are cluster-compatible, acting as a list of potential members. The mCM on the other hand, stores only valid member VRUs that have actively sent join VAMs to the leader that have been parsed and validated by the cluster manager tool.

When the mCM has sufficient members (*numCreateCluster*) added through valid join VAMs, the leader stops sending the initial cluster VAM and enters a maintenance mode. In this state, the VAMs are constructed with a CIC describing a bounding box and cardinality based on its cluster participants, being constructed and sent every generation time (*T_GenVam*). The manager continues in the maintenance mode until a breakup occurs due to insufficient cardinality or other reasons listed in the ETSI 103 300 technical specification [11]. The cluster maintenance cycle executed by the leader is shown in Algorithm 2.

Algorithm 2. Cluster maintenance by the leader [1].

```
   Data: mCM and received VAMs
   Result: Updated cluster
 1 initialization;
 2 while VRU Role is leader do
 3 |   parse received VAMs;
 4 |   if VAM's COC contains cluster ID then
 5 |   |   if Operation is Join then
 6 |   |   |   add new VRU to mCM;
 7 |   |   |   update bounding box;
 8 |   |   else if Operation is Leave then
 9 |   |   |   remove VRU from mCM;
10 |   |   |   if mCM size < 3 for over 2 s then
11 |   |   |   |   trigger breakup Operation;
12 |   |   |   |   include COC to VAM;
13 |   |   |   |   set VRU's role as standalone;
14 |   |   |   else
15 |   |   |   |   update bounding box;
16 |   |   |   end
17 |   |   end
18 |   end
19 |   include CIC to VAM;
20 |   send cluster VAM;
21 end
```

The *update bounding box* steps on lines 7 and 15 of Algorithm 2 vary depending on the chosen shape type. Subsects. 3.3, 3.4, and 3.5 describe the strategies employed to generate each geometry type. Using the cluster members positions from the mCM, these methods generate a bounding box enclosing the point cloud of participants and provides the cluster management tool with the data elements that must be added to the CIC.

The *Axis Aligned Bounding Box* (AABB) algorithm aids the formation of the circle and rectangular geometries. This strategy, of time complexity $\mathcal{O}(n)$, uses the coordinates of the VRUs in the mCM point cloud to determine the lowest-leftmost (*min*) and the highest-rightmost VRUs (*max*). These points describe the minimum non-rotated rectangular that envelops all the mCM nodes [5].

3.3 Circular Bounding Box

A circular bounding box on the VBS requires two data elements: the node center point *C.a* and the radius *C.b*. The most straightforward strategy to determine the shape's center would be to take the average Cartesian coordinates of the points. However, this approach may result in a radius twice as large as necessary when the points are not uniformly distributed. To avoid this issue, another method to determine the center of a point cloud is to first create an AABB around it and consider the center of the resulting envelope as the center of this set of points [5]. For the circle radius, it is only necessary to determine the distance d_{max} between the furthest VRU of the mCM and the AABB center. The creation of this box follows Algorithm 3 which has a time complexity of $\mathcal{O}(n)$.

Algorithm 3. Circular Bounding Box formation [1].

```
   Data: mCM
   Result: Circle CIC data elements
 1 initialization;
 2 calculate AABB from mCM;
 3 obtain min and max from AABB;
 4 get center C from min and max;
   // Get largest distance to center
 5 for each VRU object in mCM do
 6 |  get current VRU position P;
 7 |  get distance d_cp between C and P;
 8 |  if d_cp > d_max then
 9 |  |  d_max ← d_cp;
10 |  end
11 end
12 obtain leader position P_leader;
13 C.a ← offset between P_leader and C;
14 C.b ← d_max;
15 return C.a and C.b;
```

3.4 Rectangular Bounding Box

A rectangular bounding box is described in the CIC by a node center point *R.a*, half-length *R.b*, half-width *R.c*, and orientation *R.d*. Since this rectangle must also take orientation into account, it cannot simply be a AABB. Thus, the proposed strategy is to iterate the point cloud from the mCM at different rotations and generate an AABB each time, calculating the resulting area on each step and selecting the envelope with the smallest area, calling it (AAABB_{min}). To obtain the half-length and half-width, the (*min*, *max*) pair from AAABB_{min} are used by comparing the *x* and *y* coordinates as in Algorithm 4. This method has time complexity $\mathcal{O}(n)$.

Algorithm 4. Rectangular Bounding Box formation [1].

```
Data: mCM
Result: Rectangle CIC data elements
1  initialization;
2  create a point cloud from mCM;
   // Get smallest rotated cloud area
3  for θ within (0, 2π) do
4  |   rotate cloud θ counterclockwise;
5  |   calculate AABB from rotated cloud;
6  |   calculate area A from AABB;
7  |   if A < A_min then
8  |   |   A_min ← A;
9  |   |   AABB_min ← current AABB;
10 |   |   θ_min ← current θ;
11 |   end
12 |   increment 0.1 to θ;
13 end
14 get min and max from AABB_min;
15 R.a ← center from min and max;
16 R.b ← (max.x − min.x) * 0.5;
17 R.c ← (max.y − min.y) * 0.5;
18 R.d ← θ_min;
19 return R.a, R.b, R.c, and R.d;
```

3.5 Polygon Bounding Box

In the VBS a polygon bounding box is described by a list of offsets from one vertex to the next. In the approach of this study, all the VRUs contained in the mCM are vertex-candidates to form the geometry, resulting in a max number of 20 (*maxClusterSize*) total offsets. It is important to note that a method to select the vertices is necessary, as a simple ordered list with all mCM points could lead to holes and spikes in the bounding box. To avoid these imperfections in a polygon, the shape must be convex, meaning that all the interior angles must be under 180°. To ensure convex polygon generation, a Convex Hull algorithm that implements the Graham Scan is used [23].

This approach uses the VRUs' positions from the mCM, first searching for the single lowest vertical position or the leftmost if multiple points share the y-lowest position, calling it VRU_{low}. It then sorts the point cloud based on the polar coordinates related to VRU_{low}, iterating the resulting list starting at this reference point. At every loop iteration, selecting triplets of consecutive points, with the central point as a vertex candidate. Two segments are created with a triplet, with the first formed by drawing a straight line from the leftmost and the central point. The second segment is generated with another straight line from the central to the rightmost point. It then evaluates through a cross product if the two segments formed between the candidate and the neighbor points generate a left (counterclockwise) turn, meaning it has an interior angle under 180°.

If true, a new pair of segments is formed by shifting the three selected points one unit down the list. If the internal angle is above the threshold, the vertex-candidate generates a right turn or is collinear to its neighbors and the point should be removed from the list. In this case, the selection is backtracked in one position, using a previously approved vertex and checking if, with the new right neighbor point, it still produces a left turn [23]. The scan, presented in Algorithm 5, ends when the list of potential vertices is exhausted, containing only left turns and with the last segment reaching the start point. The selection of VRU_{low} has time complexity $\mathcal{O}(n)$, while the scan is $\mathcal{O}(n \log n)$.

Algorithm 5. Polygonal Bounding Box formation [1].

```
   Data: mCM
   Result: Polygon CIC data elements
 1 initialization;
 2 get point list from mCM;
 3 iterate list and get VRU_low;
   // Produce the convex hull
 4 sort list by polar coordinates to VRU_low;
 5 list starts and ends at VRU_low;
 6 while right of vertex not VRU_low do
 7     get vertex candidate C;
 8     get left L and right R adjacent points;
 9     CL ← (x_L − x_C, y_L − y_C);
10     CR ← (x_R − x_C, y_R − y_C);
11     P ← CL × CR;
12     if P > 0 then
13         keep candidate in the list;
14         get next candidate;
15     else
16         remove candidate from the list;
17         move to previous vertex;
18     end
19 end
20 get the list of n ∈ N vertices;
21 calculate the offset of consecutive vertices;
22 each offset is assigned to a P.a.n;
23 return all P.a.n offsets;
```

Resulting bounding boxes obtained by using the strategies from Algorithms 3, 4, and 5 for the same set of four VRUS is shown in Fig. 7. Here it is shown that all methods are capable of constructing shapes covering all the points while occupying the smallest possible area. However, it is noticeable that the circle generates a larger bounding box for the same point cloud, while the rectangle and polygon produce a more well-fitted perimeter.

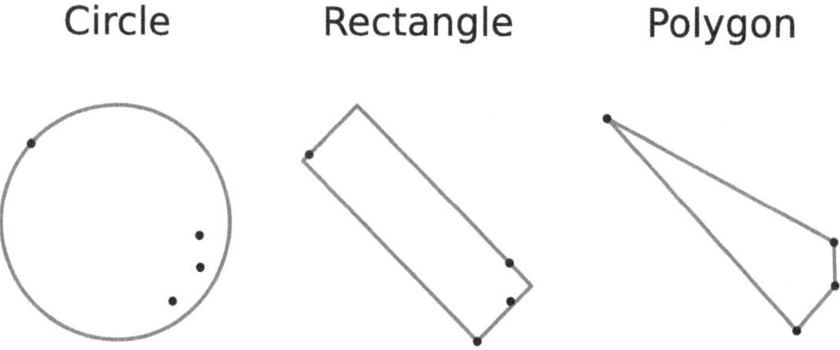

Fig. 7. Bounding boxes for the same set of points [1].

4 Metrics Definition

Since cluster VAMs do not disclose the exact position of their members within a bounding box, the complete geometries must be treated by other road users as solid objects. And thus, touching any part of the shape should be intrepreted as a collision and must be avoided at all costs in order to ensure VRU safety. This means that other road users that encounter a cluster bounding box should brake or move around them to avoid a crash. As such, it is crucial to refrain from generating a shape much bigger than what is needed to cover all participants, as large boxes might block traffic on segments of sidewalks or streets. Another potential issue of excessive size is the overlap of nearby cluster geometries, which could confuse a VRU about which cluster to join and a vehicle about how to avoid the clusters properly. To compare how good each shape type is at representing its members without occupying an excessive area, the cluster density

$$D = \frac{cluster\ cardinality}{bounding\ box\ area} \tag{4}$$

introduced in [1] is used. It is calculated from the ratio of the cardinality of a cluster per its area in VRUs/m^2. The higher the density, the better a shape type is at representing a set of VRUs without contributing to the blockage of pathways and risk of bounding box overlap.

Moreover, evaluating the average number of clusters and the number of operations triggered is relevant to observe their influence on the message size and on the amount of VAMs sent. Both of these are associated with Quality of Service, since both more VAMs being transmitted and larger increments to the VAMs can lead to an increase on the occupation of the wireless channel. The metric *Channel Busy Ratio* (CBR) defined as

$$CBR = \frac{T_{Busy}}{T_{CBR}}, \tag{5}$$

where T_{Busy} is the time a single channel is busy with transmissions, and T_{CBR} is the interval standardized by the ITS-G5 (normally 100 ms) to calculate this ratio. The CBR is used in V2X services to determine how occupied a channel is. One of its main uses is in the DCC [8] mechanism, responsible for queueing and dropping messages to reduce the congestion when the CBR reaches the threshold of 0.65.

5 Simulation Environment

To test the presented shaping strategies and compare the geometries using the metrics defined in Sect. 3, the V2X simulation framework Artery is used to connect the traffic and network simulators used for this study, while also providing the middleware and facilities necessary for the ITS-G5 stack.

5.1 Traffic Scenario

Simulation of Urban MObility (*SUMO*)[2] [18] handles the traffic simulation, generating the trips of pedestrians and vehicles on a given map. Aiming to create a traffic scenario resembling a real-world application, a crowded pedestrian crossing from Ingolstadt (Germany) provided by InTAS [17] was used. It occupies an area of roughly 5,082 m^2 and contains a pair of two-way streets, one with 5 lanes, and one with 6 as shown in Fig. 8. A set of 3,042 pedestrians and 70 vehicles are injected at random times and positions in the simulation. The steady increase in active actors in the simulated area produces various clustering opportunities and operation triggers, also causing a rise in channel occupation over time. The simulation spans 30 s, processed in steps of 0.10 s each.

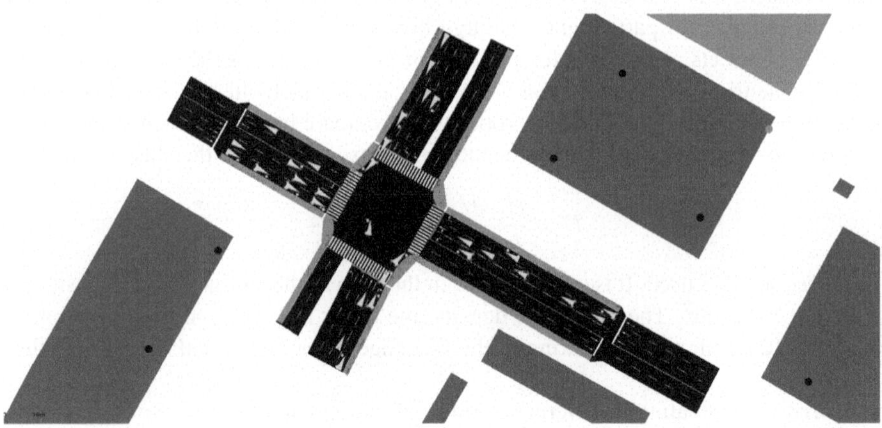

Fig. 8. InTAS-based Artery V2X simulation scenario.

5.2 Network Simulator

OMNeT++[3] is a discrete-event network simulator, with sequential simulation steps. This fact makes it possible to synchronize *OMNeT++* and *SUMO* events, establishing a

[2] https://eclipse.dev/sumo/.

[3] https://omnetpp.org.

bidirectional flow of data and commands between the two tools, using *TraCI*[4]. Support for the Access Layers (PHY and MAC) of the ITS-G5 V2X protocol are provided by *INET*[5].

5.3 V2X Framework

Regarding the ITS-G5 stack, the messaging protocol *Vanetza*[6] manages the GeoNetworking and DCC features. The V2X simulator *Artery* [20] handles the Application layer, with the services deployed and managed in each node through middleware modules. This VBS implementation builds upon the work from [15], who first introduced VRU clustering to *Artery*. These simulations extend [1], that initially proposed these shaping strategies, through longer simulations and the acquisition of resulting parameters.

The simulation runs for 30 s, with a 10 s warm-up to register the results of the system after the CBR has grown up to the DCC threshold and with clusters already formed. The triggering of events on *OMNeT++* does not occur at the exact instant in every run, having an innate probabilistic behavior. Results originate from the average of simulations using six different seeds.

In every simulation, all present VRUs have the clustering function enabled and will actively look for opportunities to interact with existing clusters or create new ones. To enable an unbiased analysis of the impact of each shape on the VBS, this work considers only one shape type per simulation run. This means that in this current work different bounding box types do not coexist. Table 2 contains the configuration parameters of the simulation stack.

Table 2. Simulation parameters.

Parameter	Value
Total simulated area	5,082 m^2
Total simulation time	30.00 s
Simulation step	0.100 s
Warm-up time	10.00 s
Seeds	[0, 23, 42, 1337, 0815, 4711]
Traffic model	InTAS
Total pedestrians	3,042
Total vehicles	70
Min. cluster size	3 VRUs
Max. Cluster Size	20 VRUs
Cluster Distance	5 m
Speed Difference	5%

[4] https://sumo.dlr.de/docs/TraCI.html.
[5] https://inet.omnetpp.org.
[6] https://www.vanetza.org.

6 Results

The VBS containing clustering functionalities and the proposed shaping strategies was deployed on the developed InTAS-based traffic scenario. Simulations using the stack from Sect. 5 were executed for the three distinct bounding box types, and also without clustering enabled, using six random seeds for each configuration. This setup resulted in twenty-four simulations, with the following results being the average values obtained from each iteration. The parameters measured are the ones proposed in Sect. 3.

When observing the area occupied by each shape (Fig. 9a), it can be observed that circles not only present the highest median, but also the biggest interquartile range, suggesting a larger variation in the recorded area values. This can be associated with the fact that circles can only adjust their radius to fit new members, leading to quadratic increases to the area. On the other hand, rectangles and polygons have similar minimum values and medians. Rectangles however, have a larger interquartile range and maximum value. The difference between rectangles and polygons can be attributed to the second having more possible vertices, resulting in a more tight-fitting bounding box shape. It is also relevant to mention that the maximum value of the polygon has a similar value to the minimum of the circle, highlighting how polygons are capable of covering member nodes while occupying less area.

Evaluating the cardinality for each shape type through Fig. 9b, it can be pointed out that circles and rectangles oscillate on a range of 7 to 9 VRUs, while the polygon ranges from roughly 6.5 to 8.5 VRUs. Considering that clusters can have cardinalities ranging from 3 to 20 VRUs, the difference between the shape types indicate that in average the geometries cover a similar amount of VRUs per cluster. However, the upper outliers in the circles and rectangles also show that with these shapes, cluster with higher cardinalities were generated, with more occurrences with circles. This could mean that these shapes, while not as tight-fitting as the polygon, are capable of encompassing more VRUs.

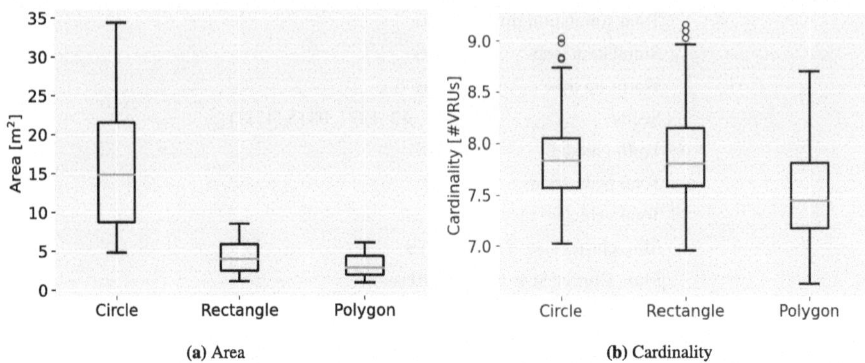

(a) Area (b) Cardinality

Fig. 9. Average cluster area and cardinality.

It can be observed in Fig. 10 that circular bounding boxes offer the lowest cluster density values. This behavior suggests that this shape type needs to occupy larger areas to cover the participating nodes of a cluster. The polygon presents the highest density overall, reaching more than five times the amount of VRUs per squared meter as the circle at 12.4 s. The rectangle is the second best, presenting similar values at roughly 11.5 and 13.5 s. These results indicate that both the rectangle and the polygon have better fitness to the original point cloud when compared to the circle since there is less area occupied without necessity. These high-density values are also associated with the limitations of pedestrian simulations in SUMO since it is unrealistic for twelve VRUs to occupy the same squared meter. However, the results should still be interpreted as an upper bound of the service, illustrating the higher clustering potential of rectangles and polygons.

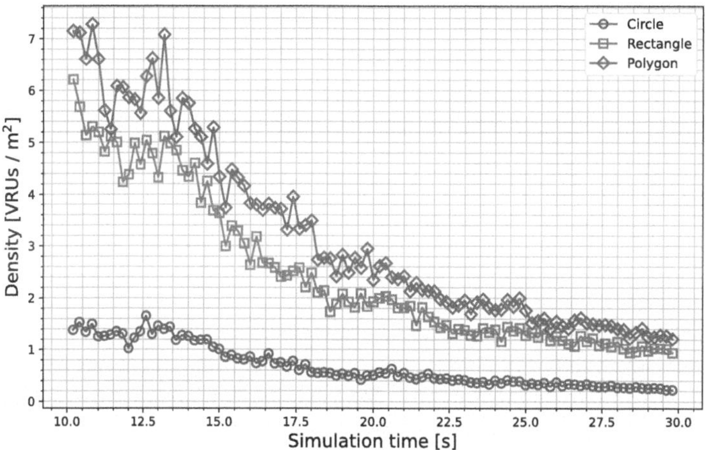

Fig. 10. Cluster density for each shape.

Moreover, the rectangles and polygons also present more spikes in the curves, as shown in Fig. 10. A possible cause is that the shapes are more susceptible to sudden cardinality changes as the VRUs join and leave clusters due to the bounding box being tighter-fitted around the point cloud. After 12.4 s, there is a noticeable decline in the densities for the three shape types, which can be associated with the VRUs drifting apart due to them taking different routes, resulting in a more sparse point cloud.

Regarding the average message size, Fig. 11 shows that the standalone scenario, in which no clustering is involved, offers the lowest increment to the message, at a constant 34 bytes. The second lowest is the circular bounding boxes, offering an average of about 36.85 bytes, confirming the assumption that this type yields the smallest increment to the CIC out of the shape types. Polygons result in the largest VAM sizes among the geometries and the highest difference between minimum and maximum reached values, respectively, 37.35 up to nearly 40 bytes. This gap could be associated with polygons being the only shape type that changes the amount of data elements included in the message depending on each cluster. As the average cluster cardinality grows due to more VRUs entering the crossing, the number of data elements needed also increases.

Once again, rectangles are an intermediate option, with an average message size larger than circles but smaller than polygons, standing approximately at 37.05 bytes.

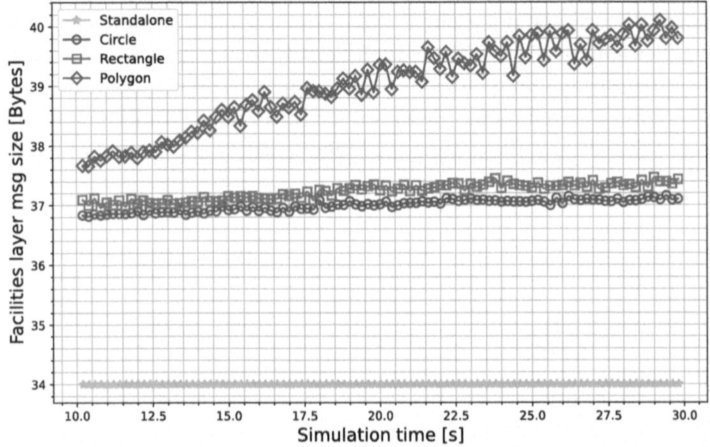

Fig. 11. Average facilities layer message size increment for each shape and standalone baseline.

When observing the number of active clusters in a simulation, Fig. 12 indicates that as time passes, the number of clusters present in the crossing increases similarly for all shape types. This increase helps explain the rising trend in average message size, with varying results based on the increment that each geometry type adds to the CIC.

Evaluation of these parameters highlights an interesting aspect of the clustering of VRUs on the VBS. The circular bounding boxes offer the smallest message increment and, therefore, are suited for applications in which channel efficiency is desired, with the drawback that the generated shape has low density. These characteristics mean that when using circular bounding boxes, it is hard to determine the position of the VRUs within the cluster.

Polygons exhibit larger average message sizes, which escalate along with cardinality. However, they offer increased cluster density, indicating a better-fitted resulting geometry. This accuracy improves safety as it is easier for other road users to avoid colliding with the member VRUs described by a polygon. Thus, this shape type is advantageous in less crowded scenarios where message sizes and channel occupation are less critical.

Rectangles offer a compromise between circles and polygons, with the second-best density and message size. New metrics can prove fundamental for this line of study, as further research into the impact of rectangles on the VBS is necessary to determine use cases in which this shape type can be beneficial. Some parameters to evaluate in the future are the position error among the members, average cluster lifetime, and rate of VRUs clustered versus non-clustered.

When the average number of cluster creation, join, leave, breakup, and regular cluster maintenance events are taken into account, it can be noted that the shape choice

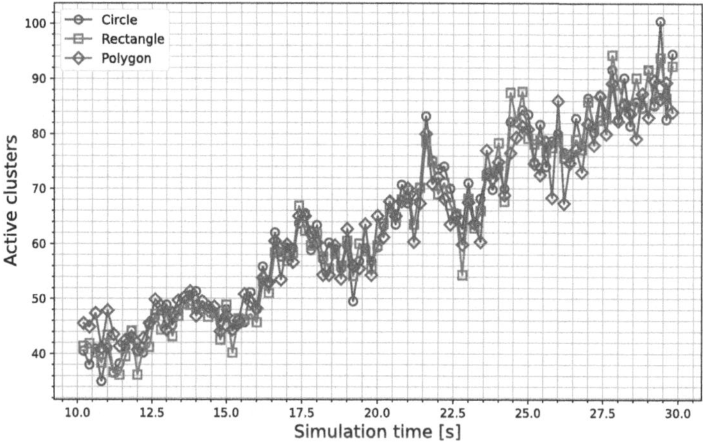

Fig. 12. Average number of active clusters for each shape.

also affects the clustering dynamics. For instance, Table 3 demonstrates that more creation and breakup operations occurred with polygon shapes, then rectangles and lastly circles. This can be related to the cluster area offered by each shape type, since larger areas lead to passive VRUs being covered for longer by a geometry before route differences lead to new cluster creations due to the VRUs stepping out of a bounding box. On the other hand, circles present more maintenance VAMs, while rectangles are second, and polygons have the least amount. This is because circles offer the least amount of creation and breakups, suggesting that cluster of that shape are maintained for longer. This results are also consistent with the amount of active clusters observed in Fig. 12, as the polygons present slightly less simultaneous clusters as the other shapes.

Rectangles exhibit more join and leave occurrences, which fits the assumptions related to the spikes from Fig. 10, that the tight-fitting nature of this shape leads to more VRUs entering and leaving a cluster coverage despite the use of the padding distance [15]. This issue is also probably due to the constraints that this shape type presents when covering a point cloud due to its limited number of vertices.

Table 3. Total amount of cluster events per shape type.

Event	Circle	Rectangle	Polygon
Creation	697.83	671.00	731.00
Join	42,115.00	42,423.67	41,885.67
Leave	41,308.67	41,623.50	41,153.00
Breakup	449.00	430.67	466.83
Maintenance	7,349.67	7,252.00	7,182.00

Another important observation from the sum of the transmitted operation VAMs from Table 3 is that the amount of events triggered during the recorded 20 s of simulation is very large. In Fig. 13, the amount of VAMs sent in a standalone scenario are compared to the total VAMs sent for each geometry type. As expected, the simulations with only standalone VRUs is the one with most VAMs sent. However, all the three shape types presented a similar curve, with more than 60 thousand VAMs sent. This indicates that despite the cardinalities of the cluster being in the range of 7 to 9 VRUS, the amount of transmitted messages has not been greatly reduced.

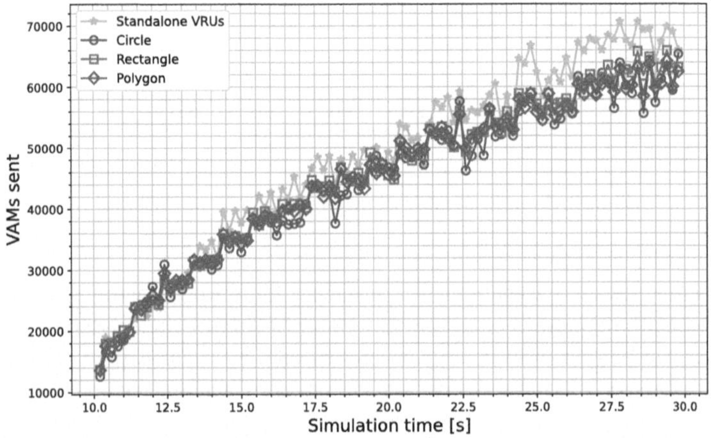

Fig. 13. Average number of VAMs sent for each shape and for the standalone baseline.

The contribution of the operation VAMs to this result is even more apparent when tallying only the VAMs from standalone VRUs and the maintenance VAMs from leaders. Figure 14 makes it clear that the largest amount of VAMs sent with clustering enabled is due to the cluster operations. This indicates that in order for VRU clustering to actually reduce effectively the number of messages transmitted in a network, the conditions for triggering operations has to be changed.

Furthermore, due to this issue, the assessment of the CBR for the VBS when using each of the shape types is inconclusive, since all geometries suffer from the large amount of VAMs sent in the simulated scenario, in a manner that the CBR is constrained to values close to the DCC threshold of 0.65 as seen in Fig. 15.

This means that in order to properly discuss in depth the Quality of Service provided by the different shape types, functional changes to the current ETSI VBS are in order. This result is very interesting, as it shows that the current technical specification requires more testing and development to be truly applicable. Changes such as different timings for the join and leave notifications, or the use of other values of distance and velocity difference could influence the amount of operations triggered. These analyses are outside the scope of this work, since present focus is on testing the methodologies to form the shapes, however they can prove to be very valuable future work in the realm of VRU Clustering.

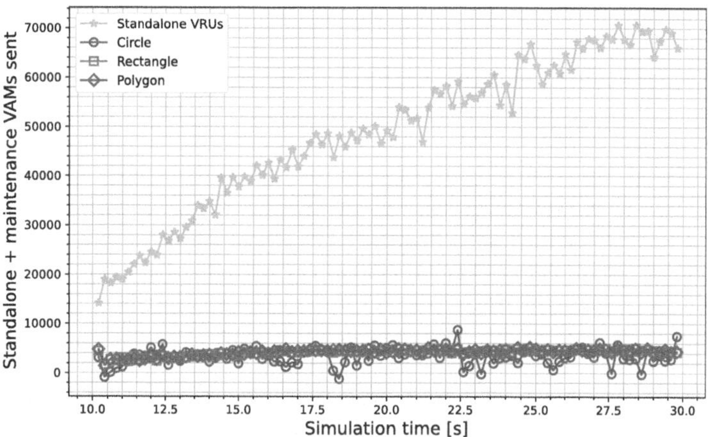

Fig. 14. Average number of VAMs sent for each shape and for the standalone baseline (excluding operations).

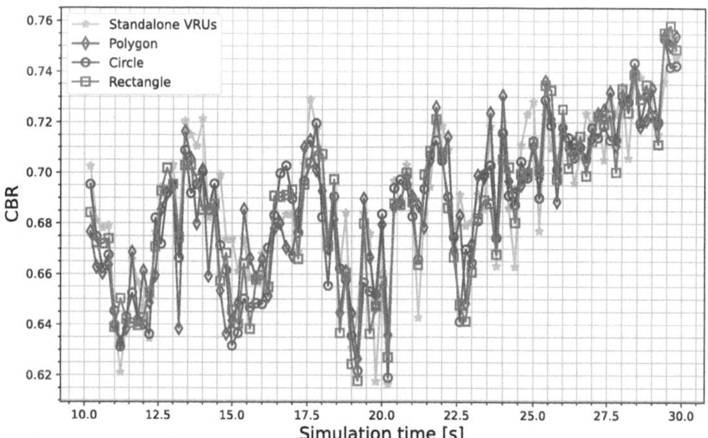

Fig. 15. Channel Busy Ratio for each shape and for the standalone scenario.

Moreover, simulating different traffic scenarios could confirm if different bounding box types are more suited for particular use cases. This confirmation could lead, for example, to the definition and standardization of parameters to implement each of the shape-generation strategies proposed in this study. Another topic to be explored is the overlap of bounding boxes, evaluating how many times this occurs and for how long these situations persist. Long and frequent overlaps could indicate a shape as inadequate for a use case since it could pose a safety or operational issue due to the region of uncertainty generated by two clusters occupying the same area.

7 Conclusion

This work contribution to the VRU Basic Service by proposing shape formation strategies for all the cluster bounding box types determined by ETSI TS 103 300. The developed methods, use the *Cluster Map* data structure and adopt computational geometry strategies to build these bounding boxes. Summarizing these methods are Algorithms 3, 4, and 5. Cluster area, cardinality, density, and also the average message size increment are selected to evaluate how each bounding box shape performs in a crowded traffic scenario. In this study, cluster density measures how well a shape type contains all its member VRUs. A higher density indicates that a cluster is capable of occupying less space to protect its participants. Average increment to the message is used to compare which shapes offer the largest increment to the VAM.

The *Cluster Map*, bounding box strategies, and metrics were then implemented in the *Artery* V2X simulation framework, with the use of a traffic scenario based on the InTAS model simulated through SUMO. In order to provide many opportunities to form clusters, the modeled simulation contains several pedestrians and vehicles circulating in a single crossing, and interact with each other. Twenty-four simulations were executed, encompassing the three shape types and a standalone control scenario, each with six different seeds.

Simulation results show that circular bounding boxes produce larger cluster areas and lower cluster density. The amount of cluster creations and breakups point to cluster with longer lifetimes. The shape is indicated for a use case that prioritizes smaller messages over spatial efficiency or shape representation accuracy. This is adequate for busy wireless channel scenarios, so reducing congestion is the priority. Polygons are recommended for the opposite scenarios, where the service can afford to send slightly larger messages with the benefit of representing the VRUs contained in the cluster with more detailed bounding box. Rectangles offer moderate cluster density and message size. Identifying use cases where rectangular bounding boxes are best suited poses a considerable opportunity for future work.

As future steps for this research, it is fundamental to improve strategies for the triggering of the cluster operations, as the current manner that ETSI 103 300 suggests its implementation defeats the purpose of clustering, as it results in nearly the same amount of messages as the standalone scenario. Some possible approaches are: the adjustment of the timings of the message operation notifications, so that these messages are sent less frequently; the implementation of cooldowns, so that a VRU that recently left a cluster waits some time before attempting to join a new cluster; or the use of the measurement of the CBR already done by the DCC mechanism to assess if the channel is available enough to send an operation VAM.

Acknowledgments. The authors would like to acknowledge and thank the Bayerisches Staatsministerium für Wirtschaft, Landesentwicklung und Energie for partially funding this work through the "RealFutuRe" project (DIK-2105-0051//DIK0281/02).

References

1. Barbosa da Silva, L., Lobo, S., Martín García Fernández, E., Facchi, C.: What is the right bounding box of a VRU cluster in v2x communication? How to form a good shape? (2024). https://doi.org/10.5220/0012699100003702
2. CAR 2 CAR Communication Consortium: Guidance for day 2 and beyond roadmap. Technical report, CAR 2 CAR Communication Consortium (2019). https://www.car-2-car.org/fileadmin/documents/General_Documents/C2CCC_WP_2072_RoadmapDay2AndBeyond.pdf
3. CAR 2 CAR Communication Consortium: Use Cases (2023). https://www.car-2-car.org/fileadmin/documents/General_Documents/C2CCC_UC_2097_UseCases_V1.0.pdf. Retrieved from http://tinyurl.com/c2ccc-UseCases
4. Decae, R.: Annual statistical report on road safety in the EU 2022. Technical report, European Road Safety Observatory, Brussels (2023). https://road-safety.transport.ec.europa.eu/statistics-and-analysis/statistics-and-analysis-archive/annual-accident-report-archive_en
5. Ericson, C.: Real-Time Collision Detection. CRC Press Inc., USA (2004)
6. European Telecommunications Standards Institute: Intelligent Transport Systems (ITS); Communications Architecture. Tech. rep., ETSI, Sophia Antipolis (2010). https://www.etsi.org/deliver/etsi_en/302600_302699/302665/01.01.01_60/en_302665v010101p.pdf
7. European Telecommunications Standards Institute: ETSI EN 302 895, Intelligent Transport Systems (ITS); Vehicular Communications; Basic Set of Applications; Local Dynamic Map (LDM), V1.1.1 (2014). https://www.etsi.org/deliver/etsi_en/302800_302899/302895/01.01.01_60/en_302895v010101p.pdf
8. European Telecommunications Standards Institute: Intelligent Transport Systems (ITS); Decentralized Congestion Control Mechanisms for Intelligent Transport Systems operating in the 5 GHz range; Access layer part. Technical report, ETSI, Sophia Antipolis (2018). https://www.etsi.org/deliver/etsi_ts/102600_102699/102687/01.02.01_60/ts_102687v010201p.pdf
9. European Telecommunications Standards Institute: Intelligent Transport Systems (ITS); Vulnerable Road Users (VRU) awareness; Part 1: Use Cases definition; Release 2. Technical report, ETSI, Sophia Antipolis (2021). https://www.etsi.org/deliver/etsi_tr/103300_103399/10330001/02.02.01_60/tr_10330001v020201p.pdf
10. European Telecommunications Standards Institute: Intelligent Transport Systems (ITS); Vulnerable Road Users (VRU) awareness; Part 2: Functional Architecture and Requirements definition; Release 2. Technical report, ETSI, Sophia Antipolis (2021). https://www.etsi.org/deliver/etsi_ts/103300_103399/10330002/02.02.01_60/ts_10330002v020201p.pdf
11. European Telecommunications Standards Institute: Intelligent Transport Systems (ITS); Vulnerable Road Users (VRU) awareness; Part 3: Specification of VRU awareness basic service; Release 2. Technical report, ETSI, Sophia Antipolis (2021). https://www.etsi.org/deliver/etsi_ts/103300_103399/10330003/02.01.02_60/ts_10330003v020102p.pdf
12. Festag, A.: Standards for vehicular communication from IEEE 802.11p to 5G. e & i Elektrotechnik und Informationstechnik **132**(7), 409–416 (2015). https://doi.org/10.1007/s00502-015-0343-0
13. Gomes, E.L., Fonseca, M., Lazzaretti, A.E., Munaretto, A., Guerber, C.: Clustering and hierarchical classification for high-precision RFID indoor location systems. IEEE Sens. J. **22**(6), 5141–5149 (2022). https://doi.org/10.1109/JSEN.2021.3103043
14. Liu, Y., Liu, B., Zhang, H.: Estimation of 2D bounding box orientation with convex-hull points - a quantitative evaluation on accuracy and efficiency. In: 2020 IEEE Intelligent Vehicles Symposium (IV), pp. 945–950. IEEE (2020). https://doi.org/10.1109/IV47402.2020.9304788

15. Lobo, S., Da Silva, L.B., Facchi, C.: To cluster or not to cluster: a VRU clustering based on v2x communication. In: 2023 IEEE 26th International Conference on Intelligent Transportation Systems (ITSC), pp. 2218–2225 (2023). https://doi.org/10.1109/ITSC57777.2023.10422659
16. Lobo, S., Festag, A., Facchi, C.: Enhancing the safety of vulnerable road users: messaging protocols for V2X communication. In: 2022 IEEE 96th Vehicular Technology Conference (VTC2022-Fall), pp. 1–7 (2022). https://doi.org/10.1109/VTC2022-Fall57202.2022.10012775
17. Lobo, S., Neumeier, S., Fernández, E., Facchi, C.: InTAS - The Ingolstadt traffic scenario for SUMO. In: SUMO Conference Proceedings, pp. 73–92 (2020). https://doi.org/10.52825/scp.v1i.102
18. Lopez, P.A., et al.: Microscopic traffic simulation using SUMO. In: 2018 21st International Conference on Intelligent Transportation Systems (ITSC), pp. 2575–2582. IEEE (2018). https://doi.org/10.1109/ITSC.2018.8569938
19. Lusvarghi, L., Grazia, C.A., Klapez, M., Casoni, M., Merani, M.L.: Awareness messages by vulnerable road users and vehicles: field tests via LTE-V2X. In: IEEE Trans. Intell. Veh. 1–15 (2023). https://doi.org/10.1109/TIV.2023.3280744
20. Riebl, R., Günther, H.J., Facchi, C., Wolf, L.: Artery: extending veins for VANET applications. In: 2015 International Conference on Models and Technologies for Intelligent Transportation Systems (MT-ITS), pp. 450–456 (2015). https://doi.org/10.1109/MTITS.2015.7223293
21. Rupp, M., Wischhof, L.: Evaluation of the effectiveness of vulnerable road user clustering in C-V2X systems. In: 2023 IEEE International Conference on Omni-layer Intelligent Systems (COINS), pp. 1–5. IEEE (2023). https://doi.org/10.1109/COINS57856.2023.10189204
22. Shahraki, A., Taherkordi, A., Haugen, Ø., Eliassen, F.: Clustering objectives in wireless sensor networks: a survey and research direction analysis. Comput. Netw. **180**, 107376 (2020). https://doi.org/10.1016/j.comnet.2020.107376
23. Shamos, M.I.: Computational geometry, Ph.D. thesis, Yale University (1978)
24. Priya, M.V., Pankaj, D.S.: 3DYOLO: real-time 3D object detection in 3D point clouds for autonomous driving. In: 2021 IEEE International India Geoscience and Remote Sensing Symposium (InGARSS), pp. 41–44. IEEE (2021). https://doi.org/10.1109/InGARSS51564.2021.9791912
25. Wang, Z., et al.: Research on lidar point cloud segmentation and collision detection algorithm. In: 2019 6th International Conference on Information Science and Control Engineering (ICISCE), pp. 475–479. IEEE (2019). https://doi.org/10.1109/ICISCE48695.2019.00101
26. Xhoxhi, E., Wolff, V.A., Li, Y., Schiegg, F.A.: Vulnerable road user clustering for collective perception messages: efficient representation through geometric shapes. In: 2024 IEEE Vehicular Networking Conference (VNC), pp. 351–356 (2024). https://doi.org/10.1109/VNC61989.2024.10575972
27. Zoghlami, C., Kacimi, R., Dhaou, R.: Dynamics of cooperative and vulnerable awareness messages in V2X safety applications. In: 2022 International Wireless Communications and Mobile Computing (IWCMC), pp. 853–858. IEEE (2022). https://doi.org/10.1109/IWCMC55113.2022.9824685

Author Index

F. Calise et al. (Eds.): SMARTGREENS 2024/VEHITS 2024, CCIS 2954, pp. 285–286, 2026.
https://doi.org/10.1007/978-3-032-23187-1

The manufacturer's authorised representative in the EU is Springer Nature Customer Service Centre GmbH, Europaplatz 3, 69115 Heidelberg, Germany. If you have any concerns regarding our products, please contact ProductSafety@springernature.com

Printed and bound by CPI Group (UK) Ltd, Croydon, CR0 4YY
07/07/2026
02160917-0008